THE LAST YEARS
OF THE
TEUTONIC
KNIGHTS

LITHUANIA, POLAND AND
THE TEUTONIC ORDER

WILLIAM URBAN

Greenhill Books

The Last Years of the Teutonic Knights
First published in 2019 by
Greenhill Books,
c/o Pen & Sword Books Ltd,
47 Church Street, Barnsley,
S. Yorkshire, S70 2AS

www.greenhillbooks.com
contact@greenhillbooks.com

ISBN: 978–1–78438–357–2

CIP data records for this title are available from the British Library

Designed and typeset by Donald Sommerville

Printed and bound in the UK by TJ International Ltd, Padstow

Typeset in 10.5/13.1 pt Minion Pro

Contents

Plates & Maps

Plates

Charles IV (1316–78), king of Bohemia and Holy Roman emperor, by an unknown artist, 1371. (Wikimedia Commons/National Gallery, Prague)

Jagiełło, by the Polish-Lithuanian painter Konstanty Aleksandrowicz. (Wikimedia Commons/Wisielec.97)

The Emperor Sigismund, by Albrecht Dürer. (Wikimedia Commons/Germanisches Nationalmuseum, Nuremberg)

Vytautas the Great in a seventeenth-century painting. (Wikimedia Commons/Vilnius Picture Gallery/Mareczko)

The battle of Nicopolis (1396) by a French miniaturist. (Wikimedia Commons/Bibliothèque nationale de France)

Prisoners at the battle of Nicopolis in an illustration for Froissart's *Chronicles*. (Wikimedia Commons/Bibliothèque nationale de France)

The city walls of Visby. (Wikimedia Commons/En-cas-de-soleil)

Königsberg in the 1600s, strongly fortified for protection from the numerous wars of that era. (Wikimedia Commons)

Jan Matejko's painting of the battle of Tannenberg. (Wikimedia Commons/National Museum, Warsaw)

Jadwiga, daughter of Jagiełło, by a German painter of the school of Mair von Landshut. (Wikimedia Commons/Burg Trausnitz, Landshut/www.culture.pl)

Sophia Jagiellon, daughter of Casimir IV, by an unknown fifteenth-century painter. (Wikimedia Commons)

Marienburg castle from the Nogat River. (Wikimedia Commons/Gregy)

The island castle at Trakai. (Wikimedia Commons/Leon Petrosyan)

The Old Town Hall of Thorn. (Wikimedia Commons/Piotr Kożurno)

Friedrich of Hohenzollern entering Constance, from *Richtenthal's Chronicle*. (Wikimedia Commons/Rosgartenmuseum, Constance)

The great beast brought from Lithuania, from *Richtenthal's Chronicle*. (Wikimedia Commons/Rosgartenmuseum, Constance)

Meeting of the Council of Constance. (Wikimedia Commons/
  Rosgartenmuseum, Constance)
Sigismund I of Poland, by the anonymous painter 'PF'.
  (Wikimedia Commons/Royal Castle Museum, Warsaw)
St Casimir of Poland by Daniel Schultz the Younger.
  (Wikimedia Commons/St Casimir Church, Cracow/BurgererSF)
Martin Truchseß von Wetzhausen. (Wikimedia Commons/
  National Library, Austria)
Duke Albrecht of Brandenburg-Ansbach, by Lucas Cranach the
  Elder. (Wikimedia Commons/Herzog Anton Ulrich Museum,
  Brunswick/Cranach Digital Archive)
Coats of arms of the grandmasters of the Teutonic Order. (Wikimedia
  Commons/ Stiftsbibliothek, St Gallen/www.e-codices.unifr.ch)

Maps

Preface

This volume is an adaptation of *Tannenberg and After*, which was published in 1999 (with a revised edition in 2002) by the Lithuanian Research and Studies Center in Chicago. I have fond memories of working with Jonas Rackauskas, Bob Vitas and the other members of the staff. We took no pay for the project, being more interested in bringing the complicated and fascinating story of the Baltic Crusades to the public than in any money we could get from a limited print run. I thank the LRSC for ceding to me its share of the copyright and wishing this publication success.

I also want to thank the Lithuanian government for its support of my books, translating several into Lithuanian, including *Tannenberg and After* in 2004 as *Žalgiris ir kas po jo*. Those also sold out quickly. Then there is Michael Leventhal and his father, at Greenhill Books, for printing the one-volume history that has been so well received. *The Teutonic Knights* has been translated into Polish, Lithuanian, Hungarian, Swedish, Italian, Portuguese and Russian.

There are so many to thank, and so many are now deceased. My dissertation adviser at the University of Texas, Archie Lewis, who taught me to think broadly and write boldly. Monmouth College, where I taught for half a century, for allowing me to teach over fifty different classes, thereby further broadening my education; and for the frequent sabbaticals that allowed me to do research in the pre-Web era. The Fulbright Commission, for joining with the German–American Club in Hamburg in 1964, to provide a very fruitful year in Germany; then in 1975 awarding me a senior research grant to work at the Johann Gottfried Herder Institut in Marburg/Lahn, Germany. The Deutscher Akademische Austauschdienst (DAAD) for the grants that stretched my slender sabbatical pay enough that I could take my family to Marburg/Lahn three times for research. Pope John Paul II for inviting me to speak at the conference on the 600th anniversary of the Christianisation of Lithuania, and his organisers Monsignor Maccaroni and Raffaele Farina. Friedrich Benninghoven, the director of the Geheimes Staatsarchivs Preussischer Kulturbesitz, for repeatedly encouraging me to keep working. Udo Arnold, the recipient of many well-deserved honours, for widening my interest to include more Polish history. Sven Ekdahl, for personal friendship as well as contributing so much to the scholarship of this era. The United States Military Academy, where I spent a month in 1985 enlarging my understanding of military history. The National Endowment for the Humanities for selecting me for three Summer Seminar programmes. The *Journal of Baltic Studies* – which I edited for five years – for including me in programmes in the Baltic States in the early nineties. The organisers of the Grunwald Conference in 2010, where I met again the foremost scholars of the history of this era. And my wife, Jackie, who accompanied me for many months in Germany, Italy, Yugoslavia and the Czech Republic; Germans knew that she was an *Ausländer* because her German was accent-free and too perfect grammatically. And our three children who made life abroad even more enjoyable.

Lastly, I must thank John Freed, professor emeritus of Illinois State University, for his many suggestions for improvements in the text.

When I began work on the Teutonic Order, there were few scholars outside Germany and Poland publishing in the field. Happily, those scholars – especially those in the Baltische Historische Kommission and the Historische Kommission für ost- und westpreussische Landes-forschung – welcomed me into their ranks, even though my books have been aimed at a more popular audience.

I hope that my narrative will describe the events in a manner that can satisfy a wide range of contemporary scholarly opinion; at the least I hope that readers will neither be harmed nor bored.

William L. Urban,
Lee L. Morgan Professor of
History and International Studies
(retired), Monmouth College,
Illinois, USA

A Note on Names

There is nothing more frustrating in the study of Central and Eastern Europe than deciding what names to use. Any choice will offend someone.

After much internal debate and outside advice, I decided to use first names that English-speaking readers are familiar with or can at least pronounce. But there are limits: Heinrich does not become Henry. For German names I have dropped the 'von' in favour of 'of'. This is a more complex problem than one might imagine. I opted for simplicity.

For places, I similarly use well-known names, but show other modern forms at their first appearance: Cracow (Kraków). For unfamiliar locations I use the names common at the time, but indicate the modern names in the same way: Marienburg (Malbork).

I worked for a very wise college president, DeBow Freed, who said, 'Always leave something in every proposal for people to correct. That way you can control the criticism.' Nomenclature works for that.

Pronunciation is always a problem. But since we live in an era of sophisticated cell phones, my suggestion is to consult Wikipedia.

Monetary values are even harder to calculate. Then, as now, inflation, devaluation, and the changing worth of gold versus silver affected prices significantly over the years. In addition, each of the many states sought to gain an advantage over its competitors by manipulating the coinage. In general, one mark equalled sixteen Bohemian silver *Gulden* or Lübeck *Schillings*. Those produced five dozen *Groschen* or 720 *Pfennige*; a florin or ducat was worth twelve *Groschen* and a *Schilling* of the Teutonic Order was worth twelve *Pfennig* and a *Halbschroter* was worth sixteen *Pfennig*. In short, it is complicated to calculate the value of any coin at a particular date; and it was no easier for most people at the time.

The relative purchasing power is also hard to calculate given the accumulated inflation of the centuries, the different markets for consumer goods, weather, war and the ease of transportation.

Sources: my original research was in Germany (Johann-Gottfried-Herder-Institut) and in major American research libraries (Chicago, Madison, Champaign-Urbana), reading deeply in the original sources and the secondary literature. More recently, I have used interlibrary loan and books I was sent to review. I don't enjoy conferences, but I've had profitable conversations at them, usually around a lively table with beers in hand.

I chose to avoid footnotes both in order to save space and to make general readers more comfortable. Specialists can inquire where I got information, though many specialists will already know. Hardly a week goes by that some student does not contact me with a question. So far I've been able to reply quickly and often at length. I try to be as generous as specialists have been to me in the past and my friends in the present.

Introduction

The birth of nations can be a difficult and painful process, the delivery assisted by great men and women who fight off foreign foes, overcome rivals, and replace ineffective customs and institutions with ones that meet the needs of the time. Those individuals were often complex figures. They often made choices other than what future generations would have preferred.

Any mention of the Teutonic Knights (the German Order of Holy Mary) will bring forth stereotypes and misconceptions. It restricted entry to the knightly membership to rich, healthy, more or less noble young men of German birth. Its members were servants of the Holy Roman Empire and the Papacy. Its most common name – der Deutsche Orden (the German Order) – reflects the hospital order founded at the siege of Acre of 1189–91 after the existing military orders refused medical care to German crusaders; the pope later added military service to its duties. Awkwardly, the national restriction made it easy for modern propagandists to argue that there was a connection between the medieval religious order and Nazi programmes designed to achieve racial purity. Hitler, however, hated nobles and Catholics, and he mistrusted generals. Consequently, he abolished the Teutonic Order as soon as he occupied Austria.

Nobles everywhere did consider themselves superior to members of the middle class and the peasantry. But the classes of German fighting men were more complex than in France and England. The number of true nobles was small; for them the Teutonic Knights provided an impressive but affordable induction into knighthood while having a safe and comfortable crusading experience. The majority of German men-at-arms belonged to the *Ministeriale* class that supplemented its income from hereditary estates by serving as tax-collectors and managers; it would be a mistake to equate this class of lower nobility with the knights of France, and even less with those of England, but they were all ambitious to rise in status and wealth. Those who entered the military order achieved social respectability and an assured livelihood.

Their veneration of the Virgin Mary was conventional but deeply felt. Eric Christiansen has correctly noted that the order's chroniclers often portrayed her as a war goddess, while the lacerated body of Christ symbolised the sufferings of Christendom at the hands of pagans. Soldier-saints were also popular, especially St George, with the dragon representing militant paganism.

The two states associated with the Teutonic Order (Prussia and Livonia) were well organised, but they were still based on feudal institutions, staffed and overseen by individuals raised in feudal environments. While feudalism was a collection of customs and laws that gave stability to government and upper-class society, these were not the same everywhere. Poland and Prussia cannot be fully understood by reference to French and British models, while feudalism did not exist in Lithuania at all.

Nor was it known among the Tatars, that semi-nomadic Turkish-speaking tribal people who lived in the Crimea and along the Don and Volga rivers. The rivalries among their khans assured that few died of old age; their ferocity in battle and their cruelty to enemies was legendary.

The knights of the military order were cruel and cynical too. That was a part of the upper-class mindset of the era, and was not fully offset by religious piety and the demands of chivalry. The knights, priests and serving brethren of the order – and the handful of nuns as well – were part of a complex religious world.

Chivalry was important. It was even spreading into east-central Europe at the time, but the interest in crusading in Poland and Hungary had always been attached to royal endeavours. Knights from western Europe were more attracted to the fantastic chivalric ceremonies of the Teutonic Order than to the massacre of pagan villagers in Lithuania. Just looking at the pictures in Stephen Turnbull's *Crusader Castles of the Teutonic Knights* will help understand why contemporaries were so impressed.

The medieval world was changing rapidly by 1350, and the days of the military orders were numbered. The greatest military order, the Templars, had been destroyed by the king of France; the next greatest, the Hospitallers, was defending its possessions in the Mediterranean in ways hardly to be distinguished from piracy. The kings of Castile, Aragon and Portugal were using their military orders to assist campaigns that eventually reconquered lands lost to Islam centuries earlier. Similarly, crusades against the Turks in the Balkans were led by secular rulers.

This is where the crusades in the Baltic are so different. The defeat of paganism, not Islam, was their goal. To a certain extent Poles were protected from Lithuanians by great swamps and forests, and somewhat sheltered from Tatars by the vastness of the steppe. In contrast, the inhabitants of Prussia were safeguarded from pagan Lithuanians only by a few hundred Teutonic Knights who provided professional leadership to perhaps 10,000 armed men called from their fields and workshops; and a dense forested wilderness of swamps and lakes.

Observers believed that the Teutonic Order was close to victory over paganism in the 1370s – the Lithuanians were reeling from repeated defeats, so that it seemed it would be only a matter of time before some prince decided to accept a Roman Catholic baptism. That would not mean that the crusade was finished, because apostasy (throwing off the faith) was common, and because the Lithuanian princes were masters of diplomacy and propaganda – Lithuanian rulers had often promised to undergo baptism, then changed their minds or become victims of pagan palace coups.

Even after the conversion of the Lithuanians in 1386, there were few churches and even fewer priests. Clerics willing to go to Lithuania must have resembled German priests in rural Prussia and Livonia: half-educated or less; barely able to speak the language; depressed by loneliness and failure; and wandering off to the cities, sometimes not even leaving a vicar to carry out the most rudimentary duties. Their notorious drunkenness and quarrelsomeness, however, usually ended with no injuries worse than bruises since they were not trained in the use of arms.

Training converts was difficult. Few former pagans saw any attraction in a life of poverty. Some of the prominent nobles known as boyars were already Orthodox and shared their Ruśian subjects' suspicions that the new religion contained unsettling and dangerous innovations such as papal authority and clerical celibacy.

The Teutonic Knights long had an ally in the Polish dukes of Masovia, whose lands abutted Prussia and Lithuania. The wilderness between their lands had been a neutral zone for hunting. Now both Germans and Poles were beginning to settle those dark swamps and forests, but most of the peasants and knightly administrators were Polish because after the Black Death most poor Germans found opportunities at home and, therefore, were reluctant to move to distant, dangerous frontiers.

Livonia presented a similar problem. The Livonian Order was a semi-autonomous branch of the Teutonic Knights, staffed by knights and priests who spoke Low German. It ruled over native tribes in the countryside and German burghers in the cities, but long had an adversarial relationship with the city of Riga and its archbishop. The greater danger, however, came from the Russian Orthodox warriors of Novgorod, Pskov, Smolensk and Polotsk; those cities were so closely aligned with Lithuanian princes that any dispute could become a great war. The Livonian Order cooperated with the grandmaster in his wars with Lithuania as much as communications permitted. That is why the campaigns against Samogitia were so important: conquest of that region would allow messengers and armies to travel back and forth throughout the year rather than waiting until the sea appeared safe enough to sail on. Storms generally kept all vessels in harbour through the long winters.

Warfare was changing. Cannon, though still primitive, had already demonstrated their effectiveness in sieges. Though not yet light enough to be wheeled around a battlefield, when properly positioned or mounted on wagons, culverins, matchlocks and handguns could be devastatingly employed against masses of men and horses. For these reasons, most commanders preferred to fight defensive battles. This was especially true when there was a considerable disparity in numbers, and the Teutonic Knights were usually outnumbered, because the Lithuanians could bring reinforcements from Ruś (premodern Russia) when they had adequate warning.

The Teutonic Knights had technological advantages over their enemies (the latest armour, missile weapons, engineering), but their greatest assets were their constant training for war, an iron discipline, a willingness to die that secular knights and pagan warriors could not afford to share, and confidence in their comrades.

It would be incorrect to suggest that the members of the Teutonic Order did nothing but fight. The moments of war were less common than one might imagine. Nor did they just sit around, drink and talk of war, as their enemies claimed. They lived in fortified convents, where they ate simple meals while listening to priests read religious texts and the history of their order. In addition to a daily round of religious services and participating in the seasonal fasts and celebrations, they had many duties to perform, not the least of which was the supervision of the castles, governing their subjects and training the militias. But life was not dull – they exercised, cared for their horses, hunted, played board games and conversed. Their behaviour and piety impressed every visitor.

To judge by the number of autumn fairs, Prussian commerce was expanding by 1400. Foreign trade was largely an exchange of bulk shipments of grain and beer for Flemish cloth and iron, Russian furs and honey for Scandinavian and (later) English wool, and local wood and amber for the products of western artisans, fish and salt. However, competitors were bypassing the traditional Hanseatic League middlemen with such success that Danzig (Gdańsk), the military order's most dependable supplier and purchaser of goods, was suffering. High tolls in the Danish Sound, English pirates and Flemish regulations presented diplomatic problems to the grandmaster. One possible solution was to open new markets such as Scotland; another was to put pressure on the competitors' royal patrons.

No one even considered opening Prussia and Livonia to free trade – the margin of economic survival was too slender to take risks, and everyone everywhere believed that regulation of production and sales was necessary for social and political stability. This was a *corporate era* and the grandmasters provided good examples of beneficent government looking out for the interests of both the elite and the general citizenry. It represented what all members of society – from pope to peasant – believed in during this time.

Other ideas accepted without question were serfdom, the genetic superiority of nobles, the inevitability of famines and plagues, and the reality of visions and miracles. Superstition was rife: pagans followed the flight of birds, Christians the wandering of the stars. Crusaders fought for their faith, angered that pagans were selling Poles, Germans, Prussians and Livonians into slavery, but they made captured pagans into serfs or even sold them into slavery.

The slave trade ran from the Baltic region across Ruś to the Black Sea, where Tatars sold captives to middlemen for transport to Byzantium, Italy and the Middle East; with the expansion of the Ottoman Empire, the slave trade would become even more important.

The *Drang nach Osten*, the German 'Push to the East', had lost much of its force after the ravages of the Black Death. Germans who had immigrated to Poland earlier were being absorbed into the majority population; in contrast, the Germans who had been settled in Prussia were beginning to absorb the native peoples; in fact, the Teutonic Order passed laws which encouraged everyone to help the Prussians master the German language.

It would be a mistake to confuse this with nineteenth-century Germanisation or twentieth-century racism. The Teutonic Order was concerned mainly about religious orthodoxy and taxes. Since paganism seemed tied to the Prussian language, it could be rooted out only when the Prussians spoke German. In addition, Germans worked their fields communally in a three-field system (grain, beans, and fallow land) and paid higher taxes, so it was expected that when the Prussians adopted German habits, they would abandon their less productive individual farms worked on a two-field system (grain and fallow land), their small wooden ploughs, and begin to produce grain for the export market; then they could pay higher taxes.

In short, in an era when religious affiliation was closely connected to ethnic identification, it was a matter of concern to the Teutonic Order that immigration from Germany had dwindled to a trickle, making it more difficult to complete the conversion of the Prussians and to establish settlements in the border wilderness.

The balance of power in Europe was seemingly slipping to the south. Germany no longer provided sufficient glue to hold the Holy Roman Empire together; and while Germans could persuade themselves that the problem lay in the personality of the emperor, there was a general fear of a strong ruler. This apprehension was shared by the three archbishops and four secular rulers who elected the Holy Roman emperor, and by the Polish knights and prelates about their own hereditary monarchs, and by the Hungarians and Italians; everywhere regions, clans and families strove to rise while pushing down their competitors. Meanwhile, the one truly powerful ruler in Europe, the Turkish sultan, was demonstrating what a unified state could achieve.

Brutal warfare, cruel fate and monumental incompetence had destroyed optimism about the future. While we can see these struggles as the birth pangs of new national states, contemporaries could only fret that their monarchs were both too weak to protect the state against attack, and too strong to be trusted not to abuse their powers.

There was a strong suggestion in the Polish claims for regional hegemony that the only effective state was a secular monarchy, hence that the Teutonic Order had no justification for existence beyond helping secular and clerical rulers in times of crisis. While the Teutonic Knights argued that militant paganism was still a danger, victory seemed so near that some observers began to look for some new task that their military order could take up safely and honourably.

In short, east-central Europe was reaching one of those interesting moments that could be called 'turning points'. Sometimes the potential for change fails to become reality. But sometimes it restructures the balance of power, the distribution of wealth, the way men and women think about their world and the potential for yet further change. Historians designate the immediate past and the future of such moments as distinct eras. They often see great battles as the turning point, when in reality those often prove only that the decisive moment had already passed.

The challenge facing the Teutonic Knights was how to survive in a changing world.

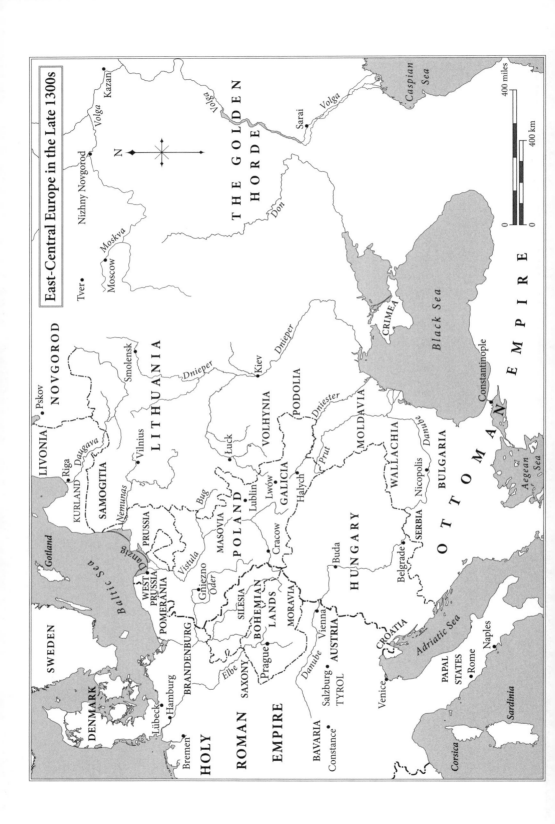

East-Central Europe in the Late 1300s

SWEDEN

DENMARK

Bremen

Lübeck

Hamburg

HOLY

ROMAN

EMPIRE

BAVARIA

Constance

Baltic Sea

Gotland

BRANDENBURG

SAXONY

Elbe

Prague

BOHEMIAN

LANDS

SILESIA

MORAVIA

Oder

Gniezno

WEST

PRUSSIA

POMERANIA

Danzig

Vistula

PRUSSIA

KURLAND

Riga

Daugava

LIVONIA

Nemunas

SAMOGITIA

Vilnius

LITHUANIA

Bug

MASOVIA

POLAND

Lublin

Cracow

Łuck

Lwów

GALICIA

Halych

VOLHYNIA

Dniester

PODOLIA

Dnieper

Kiev

Dnieper

Smolensk

Pskov

NOVGOROD

Tver

Moscow

Moskva

Nizhny Novgorod

Kazan

Volga

Volga

THE GOLDEN

HORDE

Don

Sarai

Volga

Caspian

Sea

CRIMEA

Black Sea

Constantinople

OTTOMAN EMPIRE

BULGARIA

Nicopolis

Danube

SERBIA

Belgrade

WALLACHIA

MOLDAVIA

Prut

HUNGARY

Buda

Vienna

AUSTRIA

Salzburg

TYROL

Danube

CROATIA

Venice

Adriatic Sea

PAPAL

STATES

Rome

Naples

Corsica

Sardinia

Aegean

Sea

N

400 miles

400 km

0

0

Chapter 1

The Balance of Forces in Central Europe

The Teutonic Knights in the Fourteenth Century

As the year 1350 approached, the Black Death had just struck, killing a third or more of the population of Europe; Germany and France were in such turmoil that few knights could leave home to go on crusade in Prussia. Moreover, the Lithuanian pagans were on the offensive, striking into Prussia and Poland. Even more dangerously, Tatars of the Golden Horde were crossing the steppe to attack Russia, Poland, Moldavia, and even Bulgaria and Serbia. Meanwhile, the Ottoman Turks were advancing in the Balkans against the weakened Christian kingdoms there. A working Tatar–Turkish alliance had been formed by Uzbeg (Khan Öz Beg, 1282–1341), the Tatar khan who suppressed the Buddhist and shamanist traditions in favour of Islam. He loosened the ties to the Mongol dynasty ruling China and strengthened his hold on the princes in Ruś. He made his state rich from tribute and the sale of slaves.

This was the moment that the military order found its paladin, Winrich of Kniprode, the inspiring figure who would lead the Teutonic Knights to their greatest victories. During the years that Winrich governed as grandmaster, 1351–82, his military order grew in power and prestige. However, there were in fact three *Landmeister* at the head of the Teutonic Order: the grandmaster in Prussia, the Livonian master, and the German master. Their state was well organised – the senior officers being responsible for specific regions, their immediate subordinates commanding impressive castles, and other officers supervising native tribes and ecclesiastical properties. Careful record-keeping and regular inspections assured honesty and frugality.

The officer assigned to live with or near the native Prussians was called an advocate (*Vogt*). He trained the militia, saw that it had proper uniforms and weapons, and probably spoke the local language well. Advocates for larger regions were essentially governors.

The native Prussians had been reconciled to their loss of independence, partly because they retained their free status and individual farmsteads, partly because conversion to Christianity meant little except giving up polygamy and cremation, and because they had suffered from Lithuanian raids intended to force them back into paganism; the taxes and tithe were unwelcome, but they recovered some of that cost by serving as light cavalry in the armies of the Teutonic Knights.

The Teutonic Knights saw two ways that the crusade in Prussia could end victoriously. One was the total defeat of the pagans, with Lithuanians accepting their leadership for further crusades; another was that one of the pagan dukes would lead his people to baptism and then govern as a Christian monarch – that had happened before, in the thirteenth century. In fact, few nations accepted Christianity as the result of missionaries' daring ministry alone. Conversion was a complex matter that also involved war, trade, dynastic marriages and culture; Christians also knew how to drain swamps, build windmills and collect taxes – formerly pagan rulers appreciated these skills.

A Glorious Era in Poland and Hungary

East-central Europe in the mid-1300s was dominated by two dynasties, the Angevins and the Luxemburgs, both of which had acquired power there though marriage. The head of the first family was Louis the Great of Hungary (1326–82). Well-educated, he spoke French, German and Latin, was conventionally pious, was experienced in war and diplomacy, and moderate in his habits. He became king of Poland in 1370 because his mother was the sister of the last king of the Piast dynasty, Casimir the Great (1310–70).

The head of the Luxemburgs was Charles IV (Karel, Karl, 1316–78), king of Bohemia and Holy Roman emperor. He spoke Latin, German, French and Italian; and he learned the language of his people, Czech. He was a warrior, politician, and patron of artists and architects – one still finds his name everywhere in his capital, Prague. He wrote an auto-biography and was a famous lawmaker, most notably persuading the electors of the Holy Roman Empire to endorse the Golden Bull of 1356, thereby establishing a procedure for electing emperors that eliminated papal interference.

The courts of these rulers were famous for their lavish encouragement of the arts, chivalric entertainment and intellectual life. Prague (Praha) and Buda (on the right bank of the Danube River with the castle and royal residence) were filled with foreign visitors, commercial activity and the unending construction of new churches and palaces; Cracow (Kraków) was rather shabby by comparison, but growing. All three cities were populated largely by Germans and Jews, but that was of little importance, because the native peoples preferred traditional rural life to crowded and disease-ridden cities where their agricultural skills were nearly worthless. Nobles, too, preferred life in the country.

Louis and Charles governed personally, deciding even small matters in formal hearings that must have seemed interminable, and they moved constantly about their realms – partly so that no one community would be overburdened by feeding and housing the courtiers and staff, partly to see for themselves how the country was being governed in their names, and partly from boredom; they tired of hunting in the same forests day after day. The daily business of government was seldom exciting. They had to deal with self-important nobles and clergymen, alternately flattering, placating and bullying them; they occasionally met representatives of the small middle class, but expected the lower classes to pay taxes quietly and perform unremunerated services. The royal household was filled with petty jealousies, outsized ambitions, quarrels over status, and sexual intrigues. The monarch was expected to resolve them all. This was a difficult task, because everywhere local concerns outranked national ones. Governing was a long negotiation with contending parties whose ancient feuds and current ambitions were only occasionally outweighed by the common interest in curbing royal authority.

By comparison, the Teutonic Order in Prussia was visited mainly to see its magnificent army in action and to enjoy lavish banquets in primeval woods, within hearing of the angry howls of dangerous pagans. Squires from France, England and Germany hoped to be dubbed knights there, and everyone expected to bring home stories that would entertain peers for years. Other than the banquets for guests, court life in Prussia was dull. Its sister state in Livonia was even less exciting. Both survived because of the careful management of their resources, not because the lands were rich – both lands were too far north, too filled with forests and swamps, and the native peoples lacked the skills necessary to prosper in the cities visited by Hanseatic merchants. The bureaucracy, supervised personally by the grandmaster and a small group of officers, made the slender resources of Prussia turn a profit. Meanwhile, rich estates in the Holy Roman Empire helped support crusaders on their overland travel through Poland to Prussia or the sea voyage to Livonia.

This made the lands of the military order sufficiently rich to attract the attention of neighbouring monarchs, but defeating the proud army of the Teutonic Knights and taking their well-built castles would be too expensive and time-consuming. Moreover, if any ruler had proposed it, his nobles and clergymen would have objected.

But circumstances were slowly changing, and 'the German Order' (as contemporaries referred to the Teutonic Knights) could do little to slow developments that they could not yet perceive as threatening.

Louis the Great of Hungary and Poland

When Louis became king of Hungary in 1342, his uncle, Casimir the Great, asked for his aid in wars against Lithuania and the Tatar khan over possession of Halych (Halicz) and Volhynia; in return, the Polish king promised to name Louis as his heir. There was a territorial aspect to the agreement – Louis would allow Casimir to occupy the eastern lands they conquered, then inherit them, with the understanding that if Casimir had a male heir, he would pay Louis for the territory. Louis thought little about it – in that era promises were lightly made and easily forgotten, and he had business in Naples (to revenge the murder of his younger brother by his wife) and on his southern frontier (where another brother died falling off his horse). But this promise was kept.

Few expected Casimir to fail at producing a legitimate son – he already had several children by mistresses – but all five of his legitimate children were daughters. Moreover, his marital history was irregular: his beloved Lithuanian first wife died, then he locked the unpleasant second spouse in a distant castle and married his mistress, whom he divorced on the basis of a falsified papal dispensation, then remarried. On Casimir's death in a hunting accident, his crown went to Louis. The union of the two kingdoms was purely personal – the nobles and clergy jealously guarded their prerogatives so that no king could become a tyrant. Louis nevertheless extended his united realm eastward and to the south, onto the steppes (modern Ukraine), into Moldavia and Wallachia (modern Romania), and down the Adriatic coast (modern Croatia). This was possible partly because he could use both Polish and Hungarian resources for every project, partly because when involved in any activity that benefited only one kingdom, he did not have to fear the other intervening.

His expansion of the frontier towards the Black Sea won the approval of the Papacy, making this reaction against Tatar attacks into a quasi-crusade. As Paul Knoll observed, it was the origin of a popular claim that Poland was the shield of Christendom against eastern paganism and Islam. But it was a difficult policy to sustain, and soon this territory came under Hungarian control, then after 1370 morphed into a new state – Moldavia – where politics were unstable and volatile.

Poland was lightly populated, and it had not been long since its provinces were essentially independent, the crown being held by the eldest member of the Piast dynasty, not its strongest. As the *Oxford History of Poland–Lithuania* notes, Poland was an unstable monarchy before Casimir came to the throne. Then Louis was a foreigner with foreign interests who disliked the weather in Poland and never bothered to learn the language. His wife, the famously handsome Elizabeth (1339–87), was a Bosnian, with roots even farther away, and for seventeen years their marriage was childless.

Hungary was ethnically divided – Magyars (Hungarians), Slovaks, Croats, Germans, Romanians, Vlachs. Moreover, it spread across a great plain with flooding rivers and swamps, ringed by mountains that impeded trade and travel, and with one great river, the Danube, that could not be navigated to the Black Sea because of the rapids called the Iron Gates. In this kingdom, too, Louis was widely viewed as a foreigner who paid too much attention to foreign enterprises.

These enterprises included taking the Dalmatian coast from Venice, with Genoese assistance, and forcing Venice to capitulate to his demands for easy access to Italy (and hence to Naples, which he still regarded as his ancestral home); it also included siding with Genoa and Byzantium in the Black Sea against Venice. Proposals for new crusades abounded, together with numerous minor campaigns, but Christian disunity prevented much from being achieved.

Late in life Louis still had neither son nor prospects of having one, and his health was visibly declining from a disfiguring skin disease – both leprosy and syphilis have been suggested. No longer having the energy or desire to prevent the dissolution of his united realm, he watched fearfully as events unfolded. In geopolitical terms, a division of the realm made little sense – Poland could not deal effectively with pagan Lithuanians to the east, Tatars to the south-east, or the Teutonic Order to the north; Hungary would have to fight alone against the Turks along the Lower Danube. However, self-interest disguised as national feelings almost always trumps logic. It was not as though Louis had done much for Poland. His main interest had been hunting; when he made war it was mostly for the benefit of Hungary, and even for distant Naples; the Turks were becoming a threat, but almost nobody wanted to see it.

As Norman Davies noted in *God's Playground*, Louis had introduced many Hungarian customs into Poland during his short reign, and none were to be rescinded when he died. By abdicating power to the nobility, he was setting Poland on the course that would continue for centuries – a weak monarchy, a rebellious nobility and an independent church. This showed itself in the negotiations over the future of the realm.

Under the circumstances, the best that King Louis could do in his last days was to secure the Polish succession for his eldest surviving daughter, Maria (1371–95), and Hungary for the younger, Jadwiga (Hedwig, 1373/4–99). He engaged Maria to Sigismund of Luxemburg (1368–1437), the second son of Charles IV and a great-grandson of Casimir the Great; for Jadwiga he made an arrangement with Wilhelm (*c.* 1370–1406), the young Habsburg prince of Styria in what is today Austria – she was four at the time.

The two marriages seemed to make good geographic sense. Sigismund's Brandenburg territory was close to Poland, and surely everyone could see the advantages of combining Styria, Hungary and Croatia to oppose aggression by the Turks or Venice. However, Sigismund was dependent on help from his brother, the king of Bohemia, and Wilhelm could not get much aid from his father, because he was involved in a losing war with his Swiss subjects. Moreover, both Poles and Hungarians were reluctant to have any German ruler – and while they recognised the validity of hereditary claims, they believed that the nation (the people, the community of nobles and commoners) was even more important. In short, the crown was superior to its wearer, and the people decided who should wear it.

Charles IV of Luxemburg

Charles had been lucky in every respect. First of all, as Holy Roman emperor and king of Bohemia, he had been immensely rich and powerful. Unlike his neighbours, who were preoccupied by fears that a succession crisis would lead to civil war, he had three sons. He promised Bohemia to the eldest son, by his first marriage (Wenceslaus), Brandenburg to the next (Sigismund), by his second marriage, and held the third (Johann) in reserve, giving him the strategic northern territory of Görlitz that included a part of the Neumark. Secondly, Charles was better able to tap into the patriotic instincts of his German subjects by the reforms he made in the Holy Roman Empire, by limiting the opportunities for popes to interfere in the electoral process, and by giving lip service to national institutions such as the German Order.

His brother was given Moravia, the beautiful rolling country between Silesia, Little Poland and Lower Austria. He passed it on to his son Jobst (1354–1411), a now forgotten figure who had become powerful by marrying the daughter of a Piast prince who had been one of Louis the Great's closest associates – Ladislas Opole (Władysław Opolczyk, 1332–1401).

Once Charles became emperor, he did not continue his youthful participation in the military order's crusades against Lithuanian pagans, but he encouraged others to do so. Perhaps he would have been more active if he had possessed even greater financial resources, but Charles was too cautious a manager to waste anything; this ability to discern priorities among possibilities may have been the secret to his political successes.

When Charles IV died in 1378, Wenceslaus was elected first king of Bohemia, then Holy Roman emperor. In 1381 he sent Sigismund to Cracow to learn Polish and to become acquainted with the land and its people, anticipating that he would become king of Poland as had two previous Bohemian monarchs; he gave him Neumark to facilitate communication between Brandenburg and Poland.

The Teutonic Order in Prussia

Through these years the Teutonic Order was greatly assisted by these rulers in their crusades against Samogitia and Lithuania, crusades which appeared to be leading to the conversion of those pagan societies. But that story has already been well told by numerous scholars. Our narrative commences with the rise of three monarchs whose long lives intertwined with the history of the military order in the years of its greatness and its long decline.

Sigismund

Few of the plans for the succession in Poland and Hungary worked as hoped. Right from the beginning, Sigismund was arrogant and greedy. These characteristics, which one might expect of a fourteen-year-old, became habits that would bedevil the politics of east-central Europe for more than five decades. Even so, he might have got away with it if he had shown real skill at dissimulation, but there was a child-like quality to Sigismund even when he was an aged and very jaded monarch. When the Polish nobles asked the child-candidate for Maria's hand to promise that he would reside in Poland if his wife became their monarch, he refused. If he did that, he would lose all hope of adding the Hungarian crown to his wife's inheritance, thereby maintaining the union of the two kingdoms. He might also have given some indications that he was hoping to succeed his half-brother Wenceslaus as king of Bohemia, because Wenceslaus was already showing signs of his alcoholism and poor judgement. Once he passed on, Sigismund was likely to become Holy Roman emperor. But Sigismund had a tendency to speak before he thought. Sometimes he did not even think *after* he spoke, so that he could repair the damage.

Neither the Poles nor the Hungarians were enthusiastic about becoming a minor partner in a great empire. Though their lands were important in their own right, everyone understood that the centre of European population and wealth was the Holy Roman Empire, and therefore they feared that Sigismund would give that region, especially Germany and Bohemia, undue attention. Sigismund does not seem to have made significant efforts to calm Polish and Hungarian fears that their interests would be neglected. But, then, he was only fourteen.

On the positive side, Sigismund possessed remarkable energy. He was even somewhat manic, always on the move, always looking for new diversions. In the realms of politics and sex Sigismund never seemed to flag. He dreamed boldly and put into words magnificent visions. A master of many languages, he rarely needed an interpreter, and he unfailingly charmed his audience, whether assemblies of nobles, gatherings of clergy, other monarchs in private meetings, or women looking for adventure.

The Poles were already tired of being the afterthought in their monarchs' plans, but that was nothing compared to what Sigismund might do. Already in 1376 they had forced the first of three regents to resign – Louis's mother, Elisabeth (1305–80), the sister of Casimir the Great, after the Polish garrison in Cracow had killed 160 of her Hungarian guards in a riot. The Poles then rejected the succession plans, arguing that Sigismund was a German and that Maria was a name which should be reserved for the Mother of God; they renounced their oaths to Sigismund and Maria, and began looking for somebody more suitable as a monarch; unfortunately for their plans, the Silesian Piasts were too intimidated by Sigismund's strength to offer themselves as candidates, and so were the Piast dukes of Masovia.

This led the youthful Sigismund and his advisers to believe that they could wear any opposition down. Hostility to foreigners was nothing new in Poland or anywhere else; indeed, the last Bohemian king who had dared to wear the Polish crown had been assassinated. Even at this early age Sigismund exhibited a willingness to use terror against enemies, a rashness that later became a trademark. Perhaps this trait encouraged rebel garrisons in Silesia and Little Poland to hold out, thereby endangering his lines of communication to Brandenburg, Bohemia and Hungary.

The only beneficiaries of continued conflict would be the mercenaries who were enriching themselves from countrysides which had long been spared war. When it became apparent that Maria could not even hold on to Hungary unless she agreed to live there, she faced losing both kingdoms. The solution was for the two sisters to exchange crowns, giving Poland to the younger, Jadwiga, who had been living in Hungary with her mother, and Maria becoming queen of Hungary. In 1384, when the Polish nobles and clergy agreed to accept Jadwiga, her mother, Elizabeth, allowed the ten-year-old girl to proceed to Cracow. Elizabeth remained in Hungary to help her elder daughter.

Maria and her mother had not expected a friendly reception, but they were still stunned to learn that the Hungarian nobles wanted to marry her to Duke Louis of Orleans (1372–1407), the son of Charles V of France, who had a vague claim on the throne that would have been unimportant in less confusing times. This was a stratagem clearly designed to weaken royal authority. Sigismund arrived only in the nick of time to marry the heiress himself, becoming thereby not king, but regent (a technicality he worked around later). The queen mother's opposition to Sigismund's plans consisted mainly of righteous indignation, but she managed to insist that Maria was too young for sex. As it happened, Maria clearly disliked what she saw in her husband.

It wasn't physical – Sigismund was an athlete and his mother was famous for her ability to bend horseshoes; nor was it a lack of education – he could speak German, French, Italian and Latin. But Sigismund made no secret of his intention to seek the company of other women until their marriage was consummated and probably afterwards (indeed, he became a sexual athlete). This was not something that an eleven-year-old girl could understand, or that pious clergy and laymen could overlook.

As soon as Sigismund left to fetch an army from Bohemia, Maria and her mother were pressed by the nobles to swear fealty to a newly arrived relative from Naples with a claim to the throne, Charles of Durazzo (1345–86), whose navy would be useful in the struggle with Venice over control of the Adriatic coast. Charles 'the Little' (as his enemies called him) had already murdered one queen and was clearly not above doing away with a couple more, but Elizabeth was one stab swifter than he. However, when Elizabeth was taken prisoner by vengeful adherents of Charles's party, her supporters were executed and their heads placed on public display in Naples.

Sigismund arrived with an army in the winter of 1386/7 to rescue his bride, but he had to watch helplessly as the captors strangled Elizabeth and hung her body from a window. Maria was a horrified witness too; and she was told that she would be next unless the siege was lifted. Sigismund, understanding that the garrison was composed of desperate men who could not be overawed by the forces at his disposal, left to raise a larger army. This was not easy: to pay the mercenaries, Sigismund had to sell Brandenburg to his cousin, Jobst of Moravia, and Wenceslaus sold Luxemburg to Jobst. This time, when Wenceslaus and Sigismund brought their armies into Hungary, they succeeded in crowning Sigismund, liberating Maria, then restoring order. Sigismund executed some of the kidnappers with the sword, others he sent into exile.

Sigismund came to an arrangement with prominent clergy and nobles, who agreed to accept him as king in return for his allowing them to take for themselves royal estates and prerogatives. He was young yet, and did not know how to deal with proud nobles and clergymen, much less how to reclaim royal lands and offices. He still faced a serious challenge from the king of Naples, the Turkish sultan on his southern frontier, and his own wife's awareness that the crown belonged to her family, not his. In addition there was disorder in Bosnia. But there was more to Sigismund than a brute relying on brute force. He was learning that more could be achieved by negotiation, by dividing his enemies, and by making sweet promises, than by direct action taken immediately.

Jadwiga's Marriage

The Poles meanwhile had set out to find a husband for their young queen. Jadwiga had already gone through a preliminary ceremony of marriage to Archduke Wilhelm of Styria, but that could be annulled easily. Moreover, Wilhelm was unable to lead a sizeable army into Poland to claim Jadwiga as Sigismund had done for her sister. That fact undid him. Despite Wilhelm's youth and obvious military weakness, the Polish nobles still feared that he would be too powerful and that, as a Habsburg, he could involve them in German quarrels. However, there was no one among their number who qualified as a royal consort. As a result, the candidate who most appealed to the nobles was a middle-aged Lithuanian pagan named Jogaila (later more commonly referred to as Jagiełło, 1351–1434), who was currently fighting with his cousin Vytautas (Witold, Vitovt, 1350–1430) for control of the realm that their grandfather and fathers had assembled. The Poles were watching this carefully – in 1376 a Lithuanian raid had reached Cracow. Jogaila could provide troops and the leadership to repel the Golden Horde's attacks on Poland's eastern provinces, Galicia and Sandomir (Sandomierz), and help keep the Hungarians out of Moldavia. Also, the churchmen were excited about the prospect of converting the Lithuanians, a condition they insisted upon absolutely.

At first Jadwiga's feelings were hardly considered. She was clearly in love with Wilhelm, who had slipped into Cracow quietly and arranged to meet her in St Francis's church when she came down from Wawel Castle to worship. When her advisers learned of this, they barred the castle doors. A famous picture by a nineteenth-century nationalist painter, Jan Matejko, shows her, fully mature, axe in hand, ready to beat down the door, restrained only by the entreaties of her aged and well-meaning adviser. The chronicler Długosz elaborated on how her advisers finally sent a trusted observer to look Jogaila over and reassure the queen that he was not aged and deformed, but in fact rather handsome and good-tempered.

In short, there was a remarkable generational change occurring. All the great rulers of mid-century (Louis the Great, Charles IV, Algirdas and Kęstutis of Lithuania, and Grandmaster Winrich of Kniprode of the Teutonic Order) died within a few years of one another, to be replaced by the highly interesting personalities who would dominate political life in the region for the next half-century: Sigismund, Jogaila, Vytautas, Kaributas, Švitrigaila, and Žygimantas. These princes – one German and the rest Lithuanians – were men of genius, however flawed. Alongside them was a series of grandmasters of the Teutonic Order who were competent, but less gifted; they were pious, but also practical and somewhat cynical about the human beings they dealt with.

There would be a similar generational change in the 1430s, but none of those men matched the earlier group in personalities or deeds.

The Grand Duchy of Lithuania

With Poland and Hungary falling into domestic turmoil, the feud between the Lithuanian cousins Vytautas and Jogaila took on increased importance. This mutual hostility was often inflamed, but on occasions it cooled enough for a joint effort to thwart the Teutonic Order's advances into Samogitia (Žemaitija, meaning the Lowlands). However, because their quarrel revolved around who would rule the Grand Duchy of Lithuania, then the largest state in Europe, they could never be reconciled for long. Lithuania was a multi-ethnic state that both princes could claim on the basis of heredity and substantial support from the clans and boyars.

One problem of the Lithuanian state was that it had become intertwined with the debris of Ruś (the term commonly used for the pre-modern states in the territories of modern Russia, Belarus and Ukraine, to differentiate them from the Grand Duchy of Moscow). The thirteenth-century disintegration of Ruś, as a result of dynastic quarrels and Mongol invasions, was followed by the appearance of a gifted pagan dynasty in the Lithuanian highlands (Aukštaitija) which could promise

the dukes of the city-states in Ruś protection from the Mongols and Poles, religious liberty and good government. These states were not technologically backward in the military arts, but division and defeat had eroded their ability to defend themselves.

The Lithuanian state had expanded into Ruś over the years, its warriors providing protection and the new subjects paying taxes. Inter-marriage between the many sons and daughters of Lithuanian rulers and the princely families of Ruś, and among noble families, cemented the arrangement. Because the Lithuanian dukes treated well each of their ethnically diverse subject peoples, they had been able to organise them effectively for the common defence; but they were also sufficiently ruthless to keep the warring factions of cities and provinces under control, thereby avoiding the recurrent dynastic wars of the past that had hindered resistance to the Mongols, then the Mongol–Turkish Golden Horde, and lastly the Tatar khanates on the southern steppes of Ruś. Lithuanian warriors understood that their business was to shed blood on command, and they were good at their job – big, strong, well-trained professionals. They were neither Muslims like the Tatars nor Roman Catholic like the Poles and Hungarians; they adopted eagerly their subjects' religion and language; and even more important, they were not unpredictable, cruel and lacking in a sense of honour – characteristics attributed to all the steppe peoples, incorrectly often, but less so in time of war. Lithuanians shared the values of the subject boyars and burghers – military prowess, ancient genealogies, an appreciation of foreign trade; and all considered serfs useful but of little value for anything except labour.

It was no accident that the greatest expansion of the grand duchy coincided with the drive eastward by the Polish monarch Casimir the Great between 1340 and 1360. There had been a vacuum of power that drew both rulers eastward. The rulers of Ruś wanted help against the khans who ruled the steppe, but they understood and feared the Polish claim to be defending Christendom. They knew that Poles felt themselves culturally and spiritually superior, and they knew that Poles expected them to respond by embracing wholeheartedly everything they offered, including Roman Catholicism; they would probably have been more willing to comply if the Polish armies had been close enough to render assistance when needed. However, the Polish homeland was far away and often the king was more interested in protecting his western and southern frontiers than his distant and lightly settled eastern ones.

The expansion of the Lithuanian grand duchy was due in substantial part to Gediminas (1257–1341), and his sons. The elder son was Algirdas (Olgierd, 1296–1377), who had beaten a Tatar army at the battle of Blue Waters (Sinie Vody) in 1363, driving some Tatars from the steppe into the Crimea, others to the east. He held the title of grand duke (or grand prince) and was responsible for dealing with eastern affairs. His younger brother Kęstutis (1297–1382) faced the Poles in Galicia, Sandomir and Masovia; he protected the heartland of Lithuania from attack by the Teutonic Knights out of Prussia and Livonia. Other sons and grandsons governed cities in Ruś. In general they provided comparative peace, prosperity, and religious liberty.

After Algirdas's death, his lands were divided, with Jogaila and his brothers (sons of Algirdas's second marriage) jealous of the inheritances of their half-brothers from the first marriage. For a while Kęstutis was able to insist that they avoid anything that would lead to a civil war, but there were too many heirs and too few principalities. The dynasty had become powerful by encouraging martial skill, daring and independence, traits that now threatened the unity of the state; and there were clan rivalries that we do not understand well. Moreover, although Algirdas had wanted his children reared as pagans, his widow, Juliana of Tver (Uliana Alexandrovna, 1325–91), encouraged her sons to become Orthodox Christians like her. As a result, they became more and more Ruśian, learning the language and undergoing baptism in the Orthodox Church.

This was complicated by the tradition that sons inherited a claim to the office held by the father at the time of their birth, not on their actual age. Thus, Jogaila had a better claim on the title of grand duke than did Andrew (Andrius, 1325–99), his elder half-brother by a princess of Vitebsk. When Jogaila later asserted that, as a son of the late grand duke, he had a better claim to rule than did Kęstutis, who was merely the grand duke's brother, trouble was bound to come.

Kęstutis, meantime, was trying to maintain peace in the family so that they could defend their traditional homeland from the Teutonic Knights and Poland.

The Origins of the Feud

Jogaila was too realistic to take on Kęstutis prematurely, or even Andrew. In 1375 he sent his brother Skirgaila (Skirgiełło, 1353–97) to make a secret alliance with the grandmaster of the Teutonic Knights, promising to become a Roman Christian later, then sent Skirgaila to speak to Louis the Great of Hungary and Wenceslaus of Bohemia, and perhaps even to Pope Urban VI.

This persuaded the aged grandmaster, Winrich of Kniprode, to drop his support of Andrew in spite of the advantages that gave the Livonian branch of the Teutonic Order in dealing with Novgorod. Next Jogaila made friends with Kęstutis's favourite son, Vytautas.

Jogaila always gave the impression that he was older than Vytautas, but that reflects his having had to take care of himself earlier in life, his dour personality and his mistrust of everyone; he seemed to have been an adult since birth. Vytautas, in contrast, was active, courageous and emotional; in many senses, he remained a boy throughout his life, and at first he greatly admired his independent cousin.

When Kęstutis noticed that the crusaders seemed to know his military plans, he connected that with Jogaila bringing his army too late to trap raiding parties of crusaders. But when he shared his suspicions with Vytautas, he was told not to worry – Jogaila was no traitor. Kęstutis was not persuaded, but he did not want to alienate his wilful son.

Vytautas was already thirty, an age when princes usually begin to think about the succession, and he shared the impatience of all younger men for opportunities and responsibilities. Kęstutis worried that Vytautas was being lured by Jogaila's arguments that they should seek to occupy more Orthodox lands, even if that meant abandoning parts of Lithuania to the crusaders. Kęstutis was too deeply committed to paganism and too practical to agree to that – the princes of Ruś might welcome Lithuanian dukes now, but they had a habit of throwing out their own princes, and would probably not hesitate to expel foreigners.

It was difficult to see a pattern to Jogaila's activities. When he arranged (without Kęstutis's permission) for his sister Alexandra (*c.* 1360–1434) to marry Masovian duke Siemowit IV (*c.* 1353–1426), it seemed as though he was strengthening his ties with Poland; and his support of the Livonian Order against Novgorod seemed the opposite of an eastern policy. But when he expelled Andrew and Kaributas (Korybutas, *c.* 1350–*c.* 1404) from their lands, it became clear that he wanted to acquire a base in the north-east. In 1381 Kęstutis arrested Jogaila and adopted the title of grand duke. This made the aging ruler superior to all his nephews. Soon thereafter, however, worn down by his son's pleas, he released Jogaila and sent him back to his lands. That was a mistake.

Jogaila waited to strike until 1382, when Kęstutis left for Novgorod-Seversk to deal with a rebellion by Kaributas. After seizing Vilnius, Jogaila urged the grandmaster to join him in besieging the island castle at Trakai. When Kęstutis and Vytautas heard of this, they abandoned their campaign and hurried home. Outside Trakai they found themselves surrounded, with no way to escape without a bloody battle that would decimate Lithuanian strength.

Kęstutis and Vytautas agreed to meet Jogaila, only to be stunned by his treachery: he made them prisoners, then hustled them to the fortress at Kreva. He said that he would allow no harm to befall them, then permitted his brother Skirgaila to murder the grand duke, together with his famously beautiful Samogitian wife Birutė. This was a dangerous step, because the victim's three surviving sons and three daughters were sure to seek revenge, but this was a passionate era and nowhere more so than in Lithuania.

While Jogaila allowed Vytautas to have overnight visits by his wife, Anna, he otherwise kept him under strict guard. Meanwhile, he signed treaties with the new grandmaster, Konrad Zöllner of Rotenstein (*c.* 1330–90), promising to convert to Roman Catholicism and cede western Samogitia to the Teutonic Order. That would allow him to expand his empire to the east.

Jogaila's plan failed when Vytautas exchanged clothing with his wife (or one of her maids) and was out of the castle before anyone noticed. By early November Vytautas had made his way to Masovia, where a sister, Danutė (1358–1424), was the wife of Duke Janusz (*c.* 1347–1429); however, the duke was too cautious to offer anything more than momentary refuge. In desperation Vytautas went to the grandmaster in Marienburg. This was a critical moment in regional history. If Konrad Zöllner turned the fugitive over to Jogaila, that would have left Jogaila unchallenged in Lithuania. Dared he trust him?

The Christianisation of Lithuania

Vytautas, understanding the grandmaster's dilemma, offered to undergo baptism and to support him in converting Samogitia – his mother, after all, had been highly revered there. Soon afterwards his wife and daughter were released by Jogaila, who was sensitive to the opinions of his warriors about the sanctity of the ruling dynasty. But Vytautas's younger brother, Žygimantas (1365–1440), remained a captive for two years before managing to escape to Prussia.

Beyond baptising Vytautas and his family, Konrad Zöllner did not know what to do. His career had given him little experience in diplomacy. So he sent Vytautas to western Samogitia, to help prepare the people for conversion, but kept him under close watch. Konrad Zöllner apparently believed that this would keep both princes in check while he subdued the remaining pagans.

Vytautas's subjects destroyed pagan shrines and holy woods, assisted the grandmaster in building log-and-earth forts along the Nemunas (Niemen, Memel) River, and fought willingly against Jogaila and Skirgaila. They admired Vytautas's martial virtues so much that it did not matter that he was nominally a Christian.

Jogaila quickly recognised that Vytautas's reputation was spreading rapidly, while his was declining. This ruled out murdering his rival. Meanwhile, he could not turn back the invading crusader armies. With defeat imminent, Jogaila secretly contacted Vytautas, offering to restore his father's lands (and certainly warning him not to trust the grandmaster). For the good of their nation, they had to bury their grievances and join forces against the German enemy.

Vytautas carefully organised a revolt, all the while pretending to be the grandmaster's loyal ally. In July 1384 his people rose as one against the Teutonic Order. Because the castles had contained garrisons with more Lithuanian warriors than Germans, Vytautas's followers had no difficulty seizing most of them. Many of the rest fell to Jogaila's army. This reversed all the crusader gains of recent years.

Then Jogaila reneged on his word again. He made Skirgaila regent of Lithuania, including Samogitia, while sending Vytautas to the Polish border. Vytautas was undoubtedly furious, but he kept his famed temper in check

Jogaila's behaviour is partly explained by the debates in Poland over Jadwiga's future. There is little doubt that he had arranged to have his name placed in consideration as a bridegroom. In fact, he had already got the support of Pope Urban VI by offering to make Lithuania Roman Catholic, but there would be no point in discussing the matter without peace at home. Therefore, he kept Vytautas virtually a hostage; then, to make sure of his cooperation, he took him along to Cracow for the wedding.

In February 1386 Jogaila married the young Polish ruler – after a baptismal service for all the Lithuanians present, in which each received a Christian name (his was Władysław, which English-speakers call Ladislas). He then led a small band of priests to Vilnius, bringing along thousands of Polish knights to intimidate dissidents. He named as bishop of Vilnius a Polish Franciscan who had once been bishop of Halych, but soon withdrew to a safer position as an auxiliary bishop in the diocese of Gniezno. (This was a common phenomenon on the frontier. Prelates who lacked sufficient income to sustain themselves served wherever needed in more settled dioceses. This one had also become confessor to Louis's queen, Elizabeth.) The bishop immediately ordered a new cathedral built on the foundations of a former cathedral that had been replaced long ago by an unroofed pagan cult centre with a sacrificial altar. Jogaila distributed clothing to everyone who came forth to be baptised, a great attraction for people who viewed wool as a luxury item.

Franciscans had long demonstrated sympathy with the Baltic pagans – indeed, with all non-Christians. They had once been well-established in Vilnius, but their last missionaries had been slaughtered by pagan fanatics. (In those days martyrdom had its attractions.)

Jogaila then announced that there was no reason to continue the crusades; after all, Lithuania was now a Christian state, ruled by Christian dukes. The Teutonic Knights were sceptical – they had heard this story too often. There was no union of Poland and Lithuania, which remained separate states, joined in the person of the monarch – or in this case, the persons of the queen and her consort. But the subtleties of the situation eluded most observers.

Reconciliation

King Ladislas, as Jogaila was formally titled, was thereafter known by his Polish name – Jagiełło. Not yet the ruler, but only the consort of Jadwiga, he had little time to worry about the formalities. His skill as a leader of warriors was needed in Moldavia and Wallachia, where Hungarian influence was growing and Turkish raiders were appearing; closer to the capital, in Galicia, Tatars were rampaging. He succeeded. Before the end of 1387, Ladislas-Jagiełło had restored royal authority at home and on the frontier. Some of this was thanks to papal mediation and Sigismund being too busy with rebels and Turks to do anything beyond complain.

However, his absence from Lithuania meant that Jagiełło could not mediate between Skirgaila and Vytautas. He did warn them that if they could not get along, one would have to go, but each thought he meant the other. By the spring of 1389 the dispute was so tense that Skirgaila said to Vytautas, 'Beware of me as I of you.'

Not long after that Vytautas sent Konrad Zöllner a message via two captured knights, Marquard of Salzbach and the count of Rheineck, that he was open to peace talks. He offered hostages – including his brother Žygimantas – and promised to convert all remaining pagans to Roman Christianity; in addition, he would make an alliance against the Polish king. The grandmaster was sceptical, but Marquard persuaded him to receive a delegation led by Vytautas's brother-in-law. The situation was tense: Skirgaila was aware of Vytautas's communications with the Germans, and Švitrigaila (Jagiełło's younger brother, *c.* 1373–1452) was unhappy with his share of the inheritance. As Konrad Zöllner lay dying, he agreed to a new alliance and sent forces to attack Vilnius.

For the next three years, while Vytautas accompanied crusader armies on their rampages through western Lithuania, the new grandmaster, Konrad of Wallenrode (*c.* 1330–93), forbade him any contact with Lithuanians except in the presence of Marquard of Salzbach or other Lithuanian-speaking knights.

King Ladislas-Jagiełło was meanwhile losing his hold on Lithuania. His brothers were incompetent and untrustworthy, and many of his subjects, even Samogitians, seemed willing to forgive Vytautas for having gone over to the enemy. The only places Jagiełło held were manned by Polish knights – his governor of Vilnius from 1390 to 1392 was Jan Oleśnicki, a knight from Cracow whose baby son Zbigniew was to become one of the greatest figures in Polish history. The defence of Vilnius in September 1390 against the Teutonic Knights was the decisive moment in the civil war. Volunteers from France and England, including a future king of England, Henry Bolingbroke (Henry IV, 1367–1413), and the marshal of France, Jean II Le Maingre (Boucicaut, 1366–1421, one of the era's great travellers) had joined in the siege; Vytautas's brother Tautvilas died in the failed assault on the Crooked Tower.

Meanwhile, Sigismund of Hungary was strengthening the position of the Polish Palatine, Ladislas Opole. King Louis had appointed Ladislas to govern key provinces in the north of Poland and given him possession of a castle near Thorn (Toruń) that protected Dobrin (Dobrzyn) and Kujavia (Kujawy) from pagan assault. When Jagiełło revoked those appointments, it was a cruel mocking of his governor's long career in the service of the Polish crown. Ladislas Opole took revenge by mortgaging the castle to the grandmaster, then, when the king sent Polish knights to take the castle, the Teutonic Knights intervened to drive the Poles away.

In hope of resolving the border disputes here, Grandmaster Wallenrode sought to purchase the disputed lands outright. The negotiation led to an offer to sell the Neumark as well, but Konrad of Wallenrode was reluctant. It was awkward to purchase Polish lands, but even more so to acquire a German territory. Nevertheless, possession of the Neumark would guarantee that crusaders would not have to travel through Poland. Therefore, though the grandmaster said that he could not do anything inconsistent 'with God, Honour, or Justice', he was willing to improve the defensive position of Prussia while simultaneously pleasing the Hungarian king. Those purchases, though perfectly legitimate by contemporary standards, challenged the growing pride of Polish patriots.

Sigismund briefly hoped that he could dismember the Polish kingdom, taking the richer southern parts for himself, while rewarding his fellow conspirators with the less valuable northern territories. But while Sigismund was always dreaming up impractical enterprises, he rarely concentrated his energy on any one project long enough to finish it, and he always had problems severe enough to distract a more talented man.

Jagiełło in contrast, was able to focus his energies and outwit all his enemies. In early August 1392 he sent as his emissary to Prussia Bishop Henryk of Płock (1368–c. 1393), who used the opportunity to hear Vytautas's confession. At that moment the bishop passed on his master's proposition.

Vytautas was willing to change sides again. In Prussia he would be secure, but politically impotent; in Lithuania his future would be uncertain, but potentially rewarding. Under the pretext of allowing his wife to make a visit home, he sent her to negotiate with the king. He also managed to secure the release of many hostages who had been kept in honourable captivity in scattered fortresses. Then he gave his sister Ringalė (Rymgajla) in marriage to Bishop Henryk (who had conveniently never taken orders or been ordained – in fact his entire life had been a tragedy, his mother having been accused of adultery by Siemowit III of Masovia and then strangled, while he had been sent to live with a peasant family until his sister, Margaret of Pomerania, rescued him; his impressive physical strength and the resemblance to his father led to his being recognised as legitimate). Vytautas dismissed the English crusaders who had just arrived to join another invasion of Lithuania – an act that should have aroused suspicions – and in June Vytautas sent orders to his subjects in Lithuania to revolt, then supervised the seizure and destruction of several undermanned castles before he hurried into Poland.

This time his cousin honoured the promise to give Vytautas authority over all of Lithuania. It was a small sacrifice, because Jagiełło was fully occupied persuading his very devout and somewhat sickly wife of his loyalty, while periodically leading military expeditions to the south-eastern part of the kingdom. This was necessary, but risky, since his absence meant that his rivals for influence could speak regularly with the queen without his being able to defend himself. He had no sons yet, or even daughters; but the Polish nobility and clergy were accepting him as more than his wife's consort – he was clearly the powerful ruler the kingdom needed. Having cast his lot in Poland, he had neither time nor enthusiasm for continuing a losing struggle for control of the grand duchy.

Vytautas, meanwhile, though giving primary personal attention to defending Lithuania against the incursions of the Teutonic Knights, was establishing his supremacy over the nearest states in Ruś. By the end of 1393, there was little opposition left; and when Vytautas's forces won a major battle at Kremenets in 1394, crushing the Volhynian, Galician and Moldavian dukes, Jagiełło completely abandoned his brothers to their fate: Kaributas went into exile in Cracow; the Moldavian ruler fled there too, only to be thrown into prison; Skirgaila died in Kiev in 1396, probably poisoned. Švitrigaila fought for the Teutonic Order briefly before being reconciled with Jagiełło. The former bishop, Henryk, died, unmourned, of poison – suspects included the Teutonic Knights, Orthodox priests and his wife. Peace talks with the Teutonic Order began. These culminated in September 1398 in the Treaty of Sallinwerder, which surrendered Samogitia to the Germans; soon thereafter Vytautas led his army to Kaunas, where the last pagans surrendered to the Teutonic Order.

The decade that followed would be marked by moments of peace and cooperation between Poland, Lithuania and the Teutonic Order. Why this failed to mature is one of the puzzles that fascinate historians of this era.

The Polish Kingdom

Jadwiga was the monarch. At first she had to rely upon experienced advisers for counsel. This meant courtiers and ecclesiastics for domestic affairs, and her husband for dealing with the Tatars, Moldavians and Hungarians. As she matured, she took an ever greater personal role in the administration of the country and even its foreign policy. By 1397 she was conducting negotiations personally with Grandmaster Konrad of Jungingen (1355–1407). That made sense. Her consort's support of Vytautas's war against the Teutonic Order threatened to involve her kingdom in an unwanted conflict. Moreover, she was more interested in religion than in spending time with her cheerless husband.

Jagiełło established himself in Cracow, a site well suited to protecting Polish interests in Silesia (part of which was in the Bohemian kingdom) and dealing with crises on the Hungarian and Galician borders. But that meant that he was too distant from Prussia and Lithuania to monitor activities there. Moreover, the intervening provinces were ruled by Masovian relatives of his wife who thought themselves better qualified to be king than he was. The fact that the Masovian dukes had Lithuanian ancestry themselves was of little importance when it came to an ambition to wear the crown; and it can be safely supposed that even Jagiełło's sister Alexandra in Masovia would be more ambitious for her children (she ultimately had thirteen) than for her brother.

Jagiełło's greatest fear was that he would be suspected of having remained a secret pagan. That was a charge that the Teutonic Order and its friends never let die, in spite of the fact that he had been an Orthodox Christian for years before becoming a Roman Catholic. Consequently, he never missed a religious observance, whether it be a Mass or a fast. Jagiełło was not a man for feasts: he ate little and drank no alcohol at all. A thin, powerfully built figure of average height, he kept his own counsel at all times; by avoiding drink, he avoided the rash slip of the tongue, the wounding remark, the inappropriate curse. He was not one for idle conversation, perhaps partly because his command of Polish developed slowly, but also because that was simply his nature – he had no interest in music or art, and he preferred chasing wild game to dalliances with women. It helped that Poland's huge forests, like those of Lithuania, were filled with deer, elk and wild boars; there were even a few aurochs, that gigantic relative of the bison then on the verge of extinction. He remained superstitious, but he abandoned some of the pagan folk wisdoms of his youth for the hardly more sophisticated ones of Poland and Roman Christianity.

Thanks to an influx of German and Jewish immigrants, Poland was changing from a frontier country to one with towns and villages. The new urban centres made it possible for the nobles to sell the grain that grew so abundantly on the rolling plain, grain that merchants shipped down the slowly moving rivers to the Baltic Sea, thereby earning the money that paid the taxes the royal government so desperately needed. Awkwardly, the mouths of the rivers were controlled by the Teutonic Order and its allies.

The Church was a powerful institution, thanks to the early donation of huge empty stretches of land that prelates had recently filled with settlers. Rich, self-confident, proud of its art and architecture, the Church was led by the archbishop of Gniezno, regional bishops, and an ever-growing number of abbots and abbesses. The best way to understand the religious life of that era is through the art. This was the gothic era, and Poland shared fully in its glories.

Rural life in Poland was dominated by an abundance of petty nobles, knights who were once necessary to defend the sparsely populated plain against a host of mounted enemies. As the population grew, the numbers of petty knights kept pace, but their military importance did not. They divided their lands among numerous sons, provided mutual protection of their rights and privileges through a clan system that theoretically integrated them into the families of the great landowners – the magnates – and provided maximum freedom from feudal obligations. This swarm of warriors comprised perhaps 10 per cent of the total population. As might be expected, once the lands of the dukes, the magnates and the Church were taken into account, what remained for the knights after a few generations of dividing the inheritance among numerous sons were plots of land sometimes too small to sustain a warhorse or equip its owner with armour and weapons; what remained for peasants was little indeed. The knights, rich and poor alike, defended their rights fiercely; they often considered themselves free of any theoretical obligation to anyone, even to the king. Their loyalty and support had to be requested, courted, even bought.

It was not that there was no immediate threat to the Polish state. In 1392, Sigismund of Hungary, upset by Jagiełło's penetration into Moldavia and Wallachia, persuaded Wenceslaus of Bohemia and the margrave of Meissen to propose a scheme to Konrad of Wallenrode for dividing Poland between them. The grandmaster declined, but Sigismund persisted in proposing various plots – hoping at one time to organise a united resistance to the Turks, while at others keeping Poland and Venice away from the lands he wanted for himself. Sigismund faced a serious crisis in 1395, when his wife died in a hunting accident. Heavily pregnant (goodness knows how, because Maria hated Sigismund, who refused to allow her to participate in the governance of her kingdom, and whose resources were being wasted on light-hearted women and light-headed politics), she miscarried after her horse fell. Fortunately for Sigismund, everyone agreed that the danger of invasion by the sultan was too serious to permit the luxury of a civil war. Sigismund thus retained power.

Jagiełło, meanwhile, was spinning off plots of his own: Jadwiga made a claim on the Hungarian crown after her sister's death, and Jagiełło made an alliance of mutual aid with Wenceslaus of Bohemia, an alliance that could only have been directed at Sigismund. Jagiełło also took great advantage of Sigismund's troubles after his crusading débâcle at Nicopolis in 1396 – Sigismund had lost control of his army, which dashed into a Turkish trap and was totally destroyed. Sigismund barely escaped.

Sigismund's enraged Croatian vassals confronted him at a *sabor* (parliament) in February 1397; feelings were already high because their leaders had reacted to the defeat by calling upon Ladislas of Naples to become king, a plot that failed when Sigismund landed in Dalmatia, rounded up the leaders and murdered them. The Croatians had left their weapons at the entrance to a church, while Sigismund's men had hidden theirs inside their cloaks, so that when Sigismund accused the Croatians of treason, a scuffle broke out – and the armed men won. Afterwards, this was cursed as 'the Bloody *Sabor*'. Sigismund fled to Hungary, where he awarded his enemies' lands to Hermann of Celje (Cilli, *c.* 1360–1435) and ordered the slaughter of 170 Bosnian rebels.

The Hungarian king was sufficiently chastened by this experience to change his attitude towards Poland. In July 1397 Jagiełło and Jadwiga visited him in a castle on the southern slope of the Carpathians south of Cracow. All smiles and friendship, they signed a peace treaty. Amid the vague promises of support were some important specific points: Jadwiga withdrew her claims to the Hungarian crown, and the aged Ladislas

Opole agreed not to sell Polish lands to the Teutonic Order. The contrast between the two kings could not have been stronger. Jagiełło's policies were difficult to predict. He was taciturn, neither bragging nor musing in public; but there was a consistency to his actions that indicated he had clear and achievable goals in mind, even if they could not be realised immediately. Sigismund, in contrast, had neither permanent friends nor long-term programmes, only ambitions which might change from week to week. When Sigismund offered to resolve the 'tiny differences' that remained between Jagiełło and the Teutonic Order, both parties declined the lightly made offer. (The need to offer ever-higher bribes would have exhausted their treasuries.)

Such implausible plots make it easy to underestimate Sigismund, but he was making headway in his efforts to bring order to his Hungarian kingdom. Some still refused to be governed by a 'Czech swine', a reference to his father having been the king of Bohemia, but others were cowed by his ruthlessness. Both friends and enemies understood that the one constant element in his policies was to accumulate power into his own hands.

Political life was much more orderly in Poland. Jadwiga and Jagiełło had little in common, but each was committed to the Christianisation of Lithuania and each preferred a life of simplicity and informality. Jadwiga had been reared at one of the most magnificent courts in Europe, that of Louis the Great, though by temperament she did not enjoy entertaining; Jagiełło was comfortable in a comparatively chaotic and informal environment. They provided ample entertainment for courtiers and visitors, without doing more than the obligatory personal appearances.

Jadwiga kept a separate court, with a separate budget, that included ladies-in-waiting, western musicians, artists, poets and friends; as much as possible she lived far away from the court in Cracow. Jagiełło surrounded himself with Lithuanian friends and relatives, Ruśian musicians, Ruśian artists, huntsmen, hawks, dogs and horses. He did not like the popular jousts – they took time away from hunting! Town life was not for him, either.

Jadwiga ate little, which gave additional importance to the office of royal chef, who was expected to keep her healthy. Neither was Jagiełło much interested in banquets. Except for the occasional important visitor, such as Sigismund or Jagiełło's sister, royal feasts were no longer affairs to boast of, especially for westerners unused to the rude manners of Jagiełło's men, or to his fastidious personal cleanliness (Lithuanians loved saunas). Usually the king and queen dined separately and modestly. The queen was a saint, at least in behaviour and in the eyes of her subjects. She was constantly accompanied by a bevy of priests and scholars and, being well educated, she could converse with them knowledgeably.

His entourage also included numerous clerics, but some of them were surely there to watch him for signs of deviation from the faith. Most clerics must have been puzzled and unnerved by their first experience of the multi-confessional nature of the king's courtiers, but those who came to understand what they were seeing had brilliant careers ahead of them. For Jagiełło, of course, it was important to keep his ties to Lithuania. He could never know how long he would remain royal consort. Should the frail queen die without children, the Poles might turn to one of her relatives rather than entrust him with full power. He was clever enough to pick brilliant men to be his secretary, because, being illiterate, he was dependent upon them to read to him his secret correspondence.

A well-informed chronicler of the Teutonic Knights summarised the life of the royal pair as formally correct, but lacking in passion. Her religious habits verged on fanaticism, but those were considered attributes of sainthood: she wore plain clothing, turned away from entertainment, made her bed in a coffin and sat on the floor. She tried to avoid sex, becoming so angry at her confessor's reminding her that this was her duty that she remained silent at confession. She seems to have plotted to be reunited with 'her true husband', Wilhelm of Styria. The chronicler Długosz said that they had consummated their marriage; but that was disallowed because of her extreme youth.

The truth of the matter is not easy to arrive at. Traditional Polish patriotism focuses so intensely on Jadwiga's personification of the nation's Christian mission and the Piast dynasty's virtues that even the best of historians end up writing hagiography and propaganda. It is no surprise that novelists have loved Jadwiga, and that they have transformed her relationship with Jagiełło into true love. If that was so, the royal couple did an excellent job of hiding it. Medieval Christianity emphasised extreme modesty, fasting, chastity, the sad and suffering countenance. It may be, as most historians assume, that Jadwiga was moved more by piety than by a dislike of her husband or a longing for her first love. Her clerical advisers had a fine path to lead her along, keeping her sufficiently concerned for the salvation of her soul (and the many in Lithuania) to follow the policies they recommended, without having her turn into a recluse who refused to conduct any worldly business at all.

For all the court's seeming disorganisation, it was the centre of political life, the training ground for future administrators, and where Jagiełło began to win grudging acceptance from the nobles and prelates who worked with him. He was a hard taskmaster, and for all his reputation as a schemer and double-dealer, he did nothing untoward in Wawel Castle. Court life went on without unusual violence, crime or scandal.

Vytautas's Domains

In many ways Vytautas was Jagiełło's mirror image. They shared a love of the hunt and politics, but their personalities were not at all alike. Vytautas learned guile and subterfuge, but it had not come naturally to him. He was a warrior-king. Of course, technically he was not a king, nor were his warriors knights. But the Lithuanian soldiery who earned their living as garrison troops in Ruśian cities or possessed country estates loved him. He won them fame in battle, provided offices and lands, and filled their villages with serfs. In return, they offered their loyalty and every so often had to go through the motions of having accepted Christianity. How sincere that had to be, no one dared inquire: Lithuanians loved outwitting their enemies as much as they valued their own reputations for honesty, loyalty and courage; they did not allow anyone to question their honour.

Vytautas was comfortable in his extraordinary multi-cultural environment. Like all his relatives, he was multi-lingual. He knew Lithuanian, of course; the Ruśian language in its local variants was also essential for anyone wanting to rule in Eastern Europe; some Low German for speaking with merchants and burghers from Riga; High German for dealing with the grandmaster and his knights; and Polish that improved over time. He dealt with Lithuanian pagans, Tatar Muslims, Roman Catholics from several nations, Orthodox Christians and Jews. He lived among warriors, haggled with merchants (and inquired of them whatever news they had acquired) and argued with city councils and priests. He employed as governors Poles, Germans and Ruśians, and he gave Tatars prominent roles in his armies. In short, without much regard for national origin, he selected men who seemed most likely to carry out his wishes effectively and swiftly. Of course, he preferred to use relatives, believing in the doubtful proposition that they could be trusted more than vassals or strangers. He had tremendous vitality and energy, was often swollen with pride, and was equally filled with ambition for himself and his homeland. His subjects recognised his heroic qualities, and for those they forgave him everything else.

Vytautas's one vulnerable point was not having sons who could be entrusted with the governance of important cities and fortresses. Brothers and cousins were too independent-minded and ambitious for themselves to be trusted completely. His one ally was Basil I of Moscow (Vasily, 1371–1425), who had been a hostage among the Tatars until he escaped from his 'hosts' in 1386, then made his way to Lithuania via Moldavia and Germany.

Six years earlier, Basil's father, Dmitri, had led the Ruśian princes to victory over the Tatars at the battle of Kulikovo Pole on the Don, winning thereby the title Dmitri Donskoy. Andrew of Polotsk and Kaributas of Briansk had fought bravely for Dmitri (according to a tradition which some historians reject), while Jogaila, their rival for control of eastern Lithuania, had been part of the Tatar coalition. Jogaila arrived, suspiciously, just too late to participate in the fighting, but was close enough to have been able to say to the khan that he had hurried as swiftly as he could. He could make a plausible case to his Ruśian subjects that he had only been leading the khan along, so that Dmitri's coalition could bring him to battle. (Alternatively and more persuasively, Dmitri had skilfully thrust his army between the two enemies and defeated the Tatar forces before the Lithuanians could arrive.)

The khan who had lost that great battle was soon supplanted by another, Tokhtamysh (*d.* 1406), who then led a punitive expedition against Moscow. The Tatars, enraged by drunken citizens mooning them from the walls, cleared ramparts by accurate, concentrated archery fire, then assaulted the fortifications. Tokhtamysh, his troops driven back by a deluge of boiling water, offered to discuss peace, then murdered the Lithuanian commander of the garrison when he came out to parley. He immediately resumed the attack, this time successfully. Once his men were inside the walls, Tokhtamysh allowed them to murder, pillage and rape, then set fire to the city. He granted peace to the grand duke (who had wisely taken refuge farther north) only on the condition that he pay a heavy tribute and give hostages who would guarantee his vassals' good behaviour. Dmitri sent his son Basil.

Basil came close to being the son that Vytautas never had. He fell in love with Vytautas's sixteen-year-old daughter Sophia, and asked to be allowed to marry her when circumstances allowed. In very early 1387 Basil returned to Moscow with an honour guard of prominent Lithuanian boyars. This created a personal attachment so strong that Basil ignored as best he could Vytautas's encroachment on lands that belonged to Kievan Ruś, lands that he could easily imagine being subject to himself. But he could not remain quiet for ever. He, too, had subjects whose wishes could not be ignored.

The apple of discord over the decades was Smolensk. In 1387 the duke, Yury Svyatoslavich (1355–1407), invaded Lithuania with the intent of revenging his father's death in battle against Skirgaila the previous year, but was held up at a border fortress; his troops demonstrated that they had learned much (but nothing good) from the Tatars. The fortress, under the command of the youthful Švitrigaila, held out until Vytautas and Kaributas came 'with a multitude, with numberless Lithuanian forces, marching swiftly across the fields towards the fortress'. The Ruśians fled in panic from the slaughter, abandoning their boyars. Vytautas followed the fugitives to Smolensk, exacted a high ransom from the terrified citizens, and imposed tribute on the city. They left Yury as ruler, but since soon thereafter a plague struck the city, for some time it ceased to be a major force in regional politics.

Basil's travels through the Hungarian realm of Sigismund, perhaps to Bohemia, perhaps through the lands of the Teutonic Order, suggest the existence of another of those plots and intrigues by which Sigismund and Grandmaster Konrad Zöllner had played on Vytautas's dissatisfaction with Jagiełło's imperious ways and his hatred of Skirgaila, who now ruled in Kiev and Volhynia. However, the momentous events of 1386–7 in Poland and Lithuania filled the western chroniclers' pages without leaving room for the movements of an obscure Ruśian prince. Nor are Ruśian sources more informative. What is clear is that Vytautas's growing influence in Ruś had been one of Skirgaila's main complaints. When Vytautas fled to Prussia in 1389 with all his closest relatives, to become the crusaders' ally, he was able to send Sophia to Moscow, leaving on a Hanseatic vessel sailing from Danzig to Novgorod, whence she went overland to Moscow. Sophia and Basil were married the following year; they eventually had nine children, including an heir.

When Vytautas returned to power in 1392, he quickly eliminated most of his competitors. After defeating Kaributas in battle, he sent him to Poland; that prince was later appointed governor of Kremenets and worked effectively with Vytautas until his death in 1404. In 1394 Vytautas released Jagiełło's half-brother Andrew from prison where he had been held for seven years; Andrew went to Pskov to live with his son-in-law. He, too, became a loyal supporter, dying in battle in 1399, fighting for Vytautas in the battle on the Vorskla River.

Vytautas celebrated his new authority symbolically, though cautiously enough that Jagiełło could not claim that he was striving for total independence: Vytautas kept Jagiełło's 1384 denars in circulation, but began to mark them with a V on the reverse; in addition, he began to issue a new silver coin with a *vytis* (knight) on the face and the Lithuanian doubled cross on the reverse. He wanted everyone who handled those coins to realise that Lithuania remained an independent realm. Even so, he cautiously avoided using the title, supreme prince – that title was reserved for Jagiełło, should he need to return to Lithuania – but Vytautas exercised extensive powers.

Vytautas's reconciliation with the Teutonic Knights was yet a further demonstration of his independence from Polish supervision. He needed peace with the Germans to pursue his plans in the east, but expeditions south and east of Kiev would be possible only with Jagiełło's assistance. He wanted a guarantee that there would be no attacks in his absence, and he needed Polish knights to reinforce his light cavalry. He also recruited a force of Teutonic Knights that included heavy cavalry and artillery. Perhaps nothing demonstrated Vytautas's diplomatic skill better than his success at making allies out of crusaders he had betrayed twice and a cousin whose ambition to rule in his place was restrained only by the need to be present in Poland, and gaining the support of Moscow when he moved into lands that its ruler could reasonably make claims to.

Vytautas saw opportunity in the Golden Horde's disintegration from internal power struggles and outside attack. Plague had reduced the Tatar numbers. Moreover, the overland trade in luxury goods was disrupted when the Chinese expelled the Mongol dynasty and the Genoese had established themselves on the Black Sea coast. Then Ruśian princes, led by Moscow, refused to pay tribute or serve in the Tatar armies, and civil war divided the loyalties of the khans. Lastly, the weakened victor, Tokhtamysh, was attacked by Timur (Tamberlane) in 1391; the Turkish–Mongol army took the eastern half of the steppe, then came back in 1395 for more. Timur's armies left the Golden Horde a shambles. This was no surprise, since they had slaughtered millions in their rampages across Central Asia, Persia, the Middle East and the frontiers of China. But these armies could not be everywhere at once, and there were richer areas to the south to loot.

Given this situation, Vytautas's star certainly seemed to be in the ascendant. In September 1395 he had taken Smolensk. Pretending to be en route to the east, he arrested the prince and his leading boyars when they came out of the gate to greet him; then he entered the city in style, with a Latin cross borne before him. He dispersed the prisoners throughout his realm, later executing some whose loyalty he doubted. When Basil of Moscow visited him there, he brought along the metropolitan of Moscow, who apparently approved the plans to make war jointly on the Tatars. Basil went to Kiev, where for the next year and a half, he directed the military effort on that front.

Kiev was governed by Skirgaila, who had been Vytautas's greatest foe and could, therefore, have disrupted the campaign. However, at this point he died suddenly. Rumours spread that he had been poisoned by Orthodox priests. But nobody knew the truth.

Subsequently, in late 1397 and early 1398, Vytautas took his army as far east as the Don River, where he defeated the Tatar forces and was proclaimed 'king of Lithuania' by his boyars. The new title could not be assumed permanently without Jagiełło's approval, of course, but it was an indication of his popularity. When Tatar khans, including Tokhtamysh, came to Vytautas in Kiev and asked for his protection, it appeared that Vytautas would become master of all those lands which make up modern Ukraine.

At the same time Vytautas sent envoys to Novgorod, warning the people there to accept Basil as their prince; as a compromise, the Novgorodians accepted Basil's younger brother, Andrew, perhaps because he was only seventeen and therefore likely to accept local advice. When Sophia visited Vytautas for two weeks in Smolensk, bringing her children to see their grandfather, he was able to shower her with impressive gifts, among which was a piece of the True Cross.

It was at this moment, just as he was reaching new heights of self-confidence and enthusiasm for his eastern ventures, that Vytautas was informed by Jagiełło that all Lithuanians would be expected to pay an annual tax to Poland and that the queen had doubts about the wisdom of challenging the Tatars on the steppe, doubts so serious that she would strictly limit the number of Polish knights who could participate in the next campaign. Vytautas had no doubts what his Orthodox subjects would think of that! They had just escaped paying heavy tribute to the Tatars. They were not about to begin paying a tax to Roman Catholic Poles, who might go so far as to share it with the hated popes. Moreover, Polish help was not guaranteed. What was the use of an alliance with Poland if knights would not be available when most needed?

The Poles, of course, saw the matter differently: Lithuania was a Polish province, to be dealt with as they pleased. This meant that a new conflict between the cousins was building up, looming far away over the flat horizon, but with no geographical obstacle to prevent its winds from sweeping over the region. Therefore, Vytautas took steps to assure his own safety and his control over the grand duchy.

Vytautas settled some Tatars in Trakai, near his favourite castle, in order to provide himself with a dependable bodyguard. The extended

Lithuanian ducal family was as ruthless as a Mafia one, and as practical: why fight an expensive and time-consuming civil war to rid yourself of enemies if assassination would do the trick? Everyone knew that Švitrigaila had been behind an attempt on his life in 1394, and a repetition was almost assured.

An additional safeguard lay in the clan loyalties of Vytautas's Samogitians; they would certainly retaliate against anyone who might harm him; but the Samogitian reach was short. Thus, in spite of every precaution Vytautas took, he could not feel secure. He had to contend with Tatars on the steppe, rebellious relatives, Jagiełło's ambitions, and, of course, Konrad of Jungingen, who now held the Samogitian lands that Vytautas considered the symbolic heart of his patrimony. However, at the moment his alliance with the grandmaster was more important than Samogitian feelings – the military order had the artillery and the engineering know-how to build fortresses on the steppe frontier. By using the proper mix of Rusian troops, Lithuanian cavalry, Tatar and Moldavian horsemen, Polish knights and German artillery, Vytautas just might be able to defeat the hitherto invincible Timur and the Tatars under his command on the steppe that ran from their base in the Volga Valley to Galicia.

Prussia

The grandmaster was in a position to drive a hard bargain for his aid. He possessed a powerful military force, one that could make its way to Vilnius should he choose. Prussia would not have been considered large by most medieval princes. Moreover, it was relatively poor in natural resources and did not have a sizeable population. But over the decades Konrad of Jungingen's predecessors had organised the people and the resources effectively. By grants of land, promises of low rents and few taxes, they had attracted hard-working peasants, knights and burghers, who made the sandy soil, the fir forests and the rivers flowing from the interior produce grain, wood and commerce. Compared to neighbouring states, Prussia was rich indeed.

Konrad of Jungingen's state was managed by competent administrators: officers supervising castles, advocates overseeing the rural districts and financial officers keeping waste and corruption to a minimum. Most of these men were knights, brought up both to make war and to administer estates, then given increasingly difficult jobs to test their suitability for promotion. They wore white clothing, with a white cloak bearing a black cross; they were kept ready for battle by training and hunting; all wore beards. The army was composed of a combination of the order's own well-trained knights and men-at-arms, secular vassals of German, Prussian and Polish origin, burgher and peasant militias, and an ever larger number of mercenaries. The castles were stocked with food, clothing and weapons – even cannons.

The preoccupation with supplies reflected the essentially tranquil nature of governance. War was rare, but preparation for war dominated the daily routine. There was plenty of time for supervising the stud farms and practising with missile weapons – the knights preferred the crossbow over spears for fighting in forests. The grandmaster's role was general supervision – presiding over meetings, making periodic inspections of junior officers' performance, asking for lists of equipment and livestock, and holding military reviews that also served as entertainment and propaganda.

The decentralised nature of the order's administration and the inevitable loss of records over the centuries make it difficult to estimate the order's resources as well as we would like, but specialised studies are filling the gaps in scholarship very quickly. The grandmaster had a good income from taxes, tolls, the sale of amber (a monopoly he guarded carefully, because it often brought in more revenue than anything else), trade, court costs, profits from the mint and interest from loans; in addition, he had some estates in the Holy Roman Empire. The officers and advocates concentrated on raising animals and grain on their estates, collecting taxes from peasants and burghers, tolls from merchants and travellers, and assuring that mills, taverns and other regulated public services paid the proper fees and taxes. Contemporaries considered the order's revenues immense.

The grandmaster's castles had once hosted annual, even semi-annual influxes of crusaders from Germany, France, Bohemia, Austria, England, Scotland and Italy. Those which have survived to today are impressive monuments to the wealth of a military–religious order that had found its niche in the popular imagination, the expanding commercial world and in furthering the interests of both the pope and the Holy Roman emperor.

The symbol of this powerful state was the fortress at Marienburg (Malbork), an edifice that was actually three castles in one. More than a military structure, being so obviously impregnable that it was never attacked, it was the representation of chivalric knighthood at the highest level yet attained. Even the fabulously rich Burgundians admired it. Marienburg contained central heating, spacious banqueting halls, numerous saunas, and commodious lodgings for guests. Grandmaster Konrad's free-standing residence alone was the size of a fine castle, and it lacked nothing that counted as contemporary luxury. Even the best wines were on the grandmaster's table – those were imported from estates in Germany, because only inferior grapes grew as far north as Prussia.

The thousands of documents which survive testify to the order's preoccupation with careful record-keeping. Among these are short notes to the effect of 'Lithuanians are coming', which suggest more widespread literacy than might otherwise be expected. Certainly, the knights and serving brothers of burgher origin who kept the account books were literate. The saunas (and bloodletting) were popular and some knowledge of local languages was essential.

Literacy did not mean that the knights enjoyed literature. Their approach to reading was practical – they listened to readings at meal times and were entertained by storytellers, but these did not match their love of hunting or training for battle. All that differentiated them from secular knights was not having women and children around. Ageing knights in the convents probably reminded them of parents and relatives that they would never see again.

Nineteenth-century German historians exaggerated the modern nature of the grandmaster's state, just as Polish novelists overplayed the tyrannical, bureaucratic governmental regulation of every aspect of life. Germans liked to think of the medieval Prussian state as the germ of early modern Brandenburg, with the Teutonic Knights becoming the modern Prussian *Junker*. That was not so, but that still does not prevent the public from continuing to believe it.

So ready was the educated public to think of Marienburg as the *capital* of a Prussian state that numismatists long sought to locate the mint which surely must have been there. In fact, coins were first minted in Thorn, then later in Danzig. Similarly, the view of the Teutonic Knights as essentially secular is another example of our era's central anti-clerical bias. This has distorted our understanding of the organisation. The major officers (*Großgebietiger*) were like a grandmaster's council in that they were entrusted with the most important posts and were expected to speak first at assemblies, but they were not like modern government ministers or cabinet members whose titles indicate specialised duties. In fact, most of the order's officers had responsibilities for regional government and convent discipline that were similar to the commanders of small districts. The major difference came on those rare occasions when they gathered at formal meetings, at which time they were expected to speak on issues reflecting their titles; but they were not expected to be, say, bookkeepers, only to see that bookkeeping was done. Also, there would be no question that the marshal was in command of the army when the grandmaster was not present.

Modern studies of castle designs demonstrate the importance of convent life and liturgy to the knights and their servants. Of course, any cursory reading of the order's chronicles and correspondence would demonstrate this adequately, but some historians find it easier and more enjoyable to cite the order's enemies and whisper 'hypocrisy'.

This was an era in which words were spoken loudly, in which self-righteousness was considered a virtue, and scholarly detachment was rare. Struggles for office and influence, whether based on political, personal or religious motives, may not have been pretty, but they were impressive in their scope and ruthlessness; traces of these disputes ran through every discussion of policy, though they could be suspended for impressive rituals of friendship with erstwhile foes.

The Changing Scene

The rapid changes occurring in the European world had special consequences for the crusading movement. Nobody saw a way to revive the crusades to the Holy Land, and few even discussed seriously the means by which Constantinople could be rescued from the Turks. Islam was on the advance, while Christendom was retreating everywhere except in Spain and north-eastern Europe.

That fact had important implications for the Teutonic Knights, whose expeditions against the Lithuanian pagans seemed to be approaching an end, the victorious conclusion of sixteen decades of bitter warfare. Recent grandmasters had made this possible by playing Vytautas against his cousin, extorting from each formal concessions of Samogitia in return for military aid in their struggle for supremacy. Had the grandmaster been a secular ruler or a member of the secular clergy this would have been an understandable exploitation of his neighbours' troubles; however, the Teutonic Order was part of the regular clergy and therefore held to a higher standard – a higher standard even than expected of secular clergymen like bishops. Polish spokesmen were saying that since the Lithuanians had converted to Christianity, the Teutonic Knights should leave the Baltic and go and fight the Turks.

This argument did not yet apply to Samogitia. It still remained pagan years after the other Lithuanian districts became Roman Catholic. After the 1398 Treaty of Sallinwerder guaranteed the cooperation of the Lithuanians and Poles in pacifying Samogitia, the Teutonic Knights used the need to defend Livonia as a justification for continuing the crusading tradition in the Baltic, for in Livonia the Teutonic Knights faced the Russian Orthodox warriors of Novgorod (and eventually Moscow). The Teutonic Knights were represented there by the Livonian Order, supervised loosely by the grandmaster. The two organisations cooperated closely in military ventures against the Samogitians and with Vytautas against Novgorod and Pskov.

Distant observers doubted that this was sufficient reason for maintaining the military order in Prussia. Nor were these observers persuaded by secret warnings that the consort of the Polish queen was only a superficial convert, one sufficiently dangerous that the Teutonic Knights had to be ready to fight him at a moment's notice.

The knights of the military order were confident of success in any encounter with local enemies. They had experienced efforts by popes, emperors and neighbouring rulers and prelates to direct their actions and take their lands, so often, in fact, that they were cynical about the ambitions and interests of both hostile neighbours and supposed friends at great distance. Remembering the fate of the Templars, the Teutonic Order thought for itself and acted in its own defence; death at the stake had no attractions for the knights and officers of the Teutonic Order, nor were they impressed by policies formed hundreds of miles away by poorly informed bureaucrats who could not have found Lithuania on a map, if they could have found a map with Lithuania on it.

Jagiełło Becomes King

At no time was the difference between a military order and a secular monarch more obvious than in late 1398 when the queen of Poland found herself, to almost universal surprise and delight, pregnant. Jagiełło wrote to the queen to decorate the bedroom with gold and finery to guarantee future pregnancies, but she responded that she had abandoned such secular pomp as sterile evils. Fertility, she said, came not from jewels and gold, but humility. Not much evidence of a joy in life there, certainly no suggestion that she was eager to see him again soon. The child, a daughter, was delivered prematurely on 22 June. On 17 July, Jadwiga died.

The Poles saw the queen's death as a tragedy. Thinking members of the Teutonic Order did too, because she had told the commander of Thorn, 'As long as I am alive, the order need not be concerned, but once I am dead, you will certainly have a war with Poland.' Jadwiga was widely regarded as a saint. She supported education (willing her fortune to the small new university in Cracow), the spread of Christianity into

Lithuania, and peace with the crusaders. Her marriage to Jagiełło at the age of twelve or thirteen was a self-imposed martyrdom designed to further these goals. Earlier in 1398 she had negotiated with the grandmaster over the return of Dobrin and other occupied lands, and she had excluded her husband from these talks, lest he undermine her efforts. She had gracefully entertained Sigismund of Hungary, who made a short visit to Cracow, where she had arranged for a tournament that allowed her guest and his new armour to shine with exceptional brilliance.

The queen's contemporaries mourned, and modern scholars have joined them. All considered Jadwiga far more than a young monarch. For some she was the spokesperson for, perhaps the creator of, far-reaching policies designed to extend Poland's influence eastward while maintaining peace on all other frontiers, a noble personality who went beyond private morality to speak on behalf of an enlarged concept of public service. Although 'the application of Christian ethics in politics' was not an unusual goal in the medieval world, it had been so long absent in Poland that its advocacy by an attractive, intelligent and personable ruler, who had the quiet authority and the patient will to enforce her wishes, made a lasting impression on her people. This was made all the deeper by the contrast to her successor. However one might admire Jagiełło for his sagacity, forcefulness and perseverance, no contemporary ever mistook him for a saint.

While Vytautas and Anna hurried to Cracow for the funeral ceremonies, they must have been uneasy about what this meant for the future. Would Jagiełło have to abandon Poland and return to Lithuania? He was not happy in Poland. He could not participate in serious discussions with western rulers without a translator; he was illiterate, and he took astrological predictions very seriously. However, Vytautas certainly did not want him back in the grand duchy; therefore, he probably argued that Jagiełło was indispensable in Poland, that only his presence in the kingdom could prevent a Polish move eastward to challenge Lithuanian hegemony in Ruś.

Polish churchmen certainly spoke to Jagiełło about the good that Poland could do in civilising the east. Strengthened in his resolve, Jagiełło assumed the role of king/regent, telling his supporters that he would be an active ruler in Poland's interests, assuring his enemies that he was only governing on behalf of his daughter, the heiress to the late queen. When the daughter followed her mother to the grave within a month, Jagiełło began to look rather desperately for an unmarried female with Piast or Angevin blood.

His advisers quickly found a suitable bride in Anna (1381–1416), the young niece of Hermann of Celje, a granddaughter of Casimir the Great; awkwardly, she spoke only German and had to learn Polish before she could be introduced to the nobility and clergy. Her more attractive cousin Barbara was soon thereafter espoused to Sigismund of Hungary. This undoubtedly made Jagiełło's foreign policy easier, at least for the moment. His daughter had lived just long enough for him to make arrangements with the clergy and magnates to assume power; it now remained for him to govern in such a way that he could retain his office.

War on the Steppe

Vytautas was soon engaged in the east, in Smolensk at the start of winter 1398/9, in Polotsk in February, then in the summer on the steppe, rallying to him all the khans who were frightened by Timur's ruthless methods. Tokhtamysh became a vassal prince, eagerly supporting Vytautas's drive towards the Crimea. In this Vytautas was joined by several prominent Ruśian princes, but not by those eastern rulers who had learned from Timur's earlier march on Moscow that they had to give priority to their own defences.

Vytautas's advance from Kiev towards the Crimea in August 1399 was joined only by the western Ruśian dukes. This force, together with Polish knights, the grandmaster's artillery, and a papal call for crusaders to aid him – a fact unlikely to be mentioned to his Orthodox supporters – was sufficient for Vytautas to demand haughtily that the chief Tatar khan offer his submission and pay an annual tax:

> The Lord has submitted all lands to me, and you should also submit to me. Then you will be as my son and I will be to you as a father, and you will pay me every year the taxes and duties. In case you do not want to do thus, you will be my slave and I will put your entire horde to the sword.

The grand plan had been first to liberate Ruś from the Tatar yoke, then open the way to the Black Sea, and finally – perhaps – march against the Turks in the Balkans. Relying on a wagon fort, the wagons bound together with chains to stop charging horsemen, Vytautas planned to use the longer range of his artillery to offset the enemy's archery. By campaigning in August, he would avoid the wet weather that could make the gunpowder useless. When he made camp near Poltava (where the great battle of 1709 was fought) by the Vorskla River, a tributary of the Dnieper, it appeared that he could obtain his goals by diplomacy. This plan went awry when Vytautas was taken in by Mongol–Turkish guile – Timur's khan proposed a three-day truce; when reinforcements arrived, he offered battle, then feigned a retreat that lured the Lithuanian horsemen into pursuing him. On the steppe, away from the wagon fort, Vytautas could not employ his artillery effectively. When horsemen appeared suddenly from ambush, Tokhtamysh's men fled the battlefield, leaving the Christians to fight their way out as best they could.

The Mongol–Turkish horsemen surrounded the Lithuanian army, shot the knights' horses out from under them, then closed in for the kill; they took the wagon fort without much difficulty, since most of the defenders had fled, leaving the shattered Christian forces no place to rally. The slowest Christians were slaughtered or taken prisoner for sale, but this probably delayed the pursuers only for the time necessary to loot the dead, round up the horses and captives and look for new victims.

Vytautas's army bled to death in the massacre, some perishing on the battlefield, more dying during the rout. Nine Teutonic Knights failed to return home, lost also were their two trusted Samogitian translators, Hanus and Thomas Surville. Vytautas fled to Kiev in the company of one brother and Marquard of Salzbach. Apparently, the enemy was not in pursuit of Vytautas, but of Tokhtamysh, who plundered his way across the country to feed his forces and to leave little food or fodder for his pursuers.

The Chronicle of Novgorod summarised what Ruśians learned from all this: that God had brought the Muslims to punish Vytautas and his subject princes for having converted to Roman Catholicism rather than to the true faith, Russian Orthodoxy.

Vytautas's plans had ended in disaster. The battle on the Vorskla cost the lives of thousands of Lithuanian warriors, several Lithuanian dukes, possibly the ruler of Moldavia as well, and hundreds of cavalry from Poland and Prussia. Vytautas was never again to wade his horse in the Black Sea. Moreover, his eastern subjects immediately began to plot rebellion, renewing the long struggle over Smolensk that he had considered finished. Basil, for his part, faced rebellion in Novgorod. This made it absolutely necessary for Vytautas to seek an immediate reconciliation with the Poles, lest Jagiełło turn on him as well.

A New Coalition in the East

Vytautas was never one to take a defeat for a setback. He knew that central Lithuania would remain loyal to him. Moreover, he lost remarkably little prestige from the disaster on the Vorskla River – no previous ruler had even dared challenge the steppe khans so boldly. Nor had the enemy followed up their victory.

Within a short while Vytautas turned his eyes to places where he would not encounter Timur's Mongols and Turks. Once he had stabilised the situation in Smolensk, he looked again at the bargain he had made with Grandmaster Konrad of Jungingen, by which he had given the crusaders Samogitia in return for peace and technical assistance.

In 1401 Vytautas and Jagiełło settled their remaining differences in the Vilnius–Radom Union. The Lithuanian boyars and the Polish nobles, meeting simultaneously but separately, voted to acknowledge Vytautas as Grand Prince (*magnus dux*) during his lifetime, then to accept Jagiełło as Supreme Prince (*supremus dux*) and his heir. Once there was no question as to who was the senior partner in the relationship, it was possible to formulate a joint policy concerning Samogitia. Vytautas built Roman Catholic churches in Gardinas (Grodno, today in Belarus) and, somewhat later, Trakai, and perhaps two or three other fortresses, thereby taking western Christianity beyond Vilnius to provincial centres.

Although there were complaints about what the crusaders were doing in Samogitia, it is not easy now to see how the government was particularly onerous. The Teutonic Knights seemed to be well aware of the cumulative effect of past accusations of misgovernment, and they had long found it difficult to defend their policies to foreign courts or the Papacy. They knew that someone would complain no matter what they did. If they imposed Christianity and Christian taxes, the liberal faction of the Church would complain that they were oppressing the natives; if they did not, the conservatives would raise a cry that they were not carrying out their Christian duty to save the endangered souls. Consequently, the Teutonic Order tended to rely on experience and common sense. Having learned early that sudden innovations in native life provoked uprisings, they made relatively modest demands – abandon polygamy and cremation of the dead, pay taxes and perform military service. They applied these lessons to Samogitia.

While they especially refrained from forced baptisms, they did insist upon opening the villages to western contacts, especially visits by western merchants, who were supposed to demonstrate that Christendom had more to offer than fire and the sword. This 'hands-off' policy had worked well earlier, despite having been bitterly denounced by every generation of clergy, especially the archbishops of

Riga and Gniezno, whose conflict of interest with the Teutonic Order was so obvious that they had not been able to persuade any pope to support them, or to enforce penalties laid upon the military order by visiting legates for refusing to agree unconditionally with whatever they wanted. What most clergymen argued for was, first, a drastic intervention in the life of the native peoples in order to impose upon them western customs and mores; second, less oppression of these subjects; and third, giving the lands and administrative responsibilities to the more benevolent and less grasping representatives of the Church, who would somehow fill the land with churches and pious subjects without raising taxes and tithes or injuring the rights of the native peoples.

To put the problem in a nutshell, Christian ideals were in conflict with Christian experience, the idealism of outsiders versus the practical knowledge of the military order.

The Future of the Crusades

Not all the difficulties the Teutonic Knights encountered came from their political opponents. The plague struck Prussia with devastating effect in 1398: entire villages and cities were depopulated and eighty knights of the order died. In 1399 the cold was so fierce that the Baltic froze. Nevertheless, crusaders continued to participate in expeditions against the now-desperate Samogitians (who were probably hard hit by disease and harsh weather as well). The grandmaster's effort was directed at crushing the military resources of the pagans, not towards making them into Christians immediately. This policy of avoiding forced baptisms created considerable difficulties for the Teutonic Order, since it ran counter to the expectations of contemporary churchmen, visiting crusaders and probably most modern readers.

The Teutonic Knights had achieved the essential goals of their crusades in Livonia and Prussia: they had converted some native peoples by persuading them of the advantages of a western alliance (these were usually weak tribes which had been oppressed by stronger ones); they had assisted bishops and monarchs in forcibly converting others (who remained potential rebels, as the Estonian experience in 1343 demonstrated); they had encouraged the conversion of native rulers (as in Lithuania in 1251 and 1386). They had welcomed the first conversion, but had denounced the second as a cynical manoeuvre to disrupt the crusade. But the war had left an unpopulated wilderness along the entire frontier, the inhabitants fleeing attack by both sides. This made efforts at peaceful conversion difficult.

The policy adopted in Samogitia after the tribesmen had surrendered was to encourage rather than force them to accept Christianity. This was controversial because at the time there was little readiness in theological circles or secular society to accept the idea that ordinary people should be given choices in such matters. The representatives of the grandmasters found it very difficult to argue that a policy of rewarding vassals who adopted western practices, of allowing priests to preach but forbidding them to make demands on their hearers, and of using the military talents of still-pagan or semi-pagan subjects against their former rulers was wiser in both the short and long run than an effort to flood the country with priests who were not available and episcopal tax-collectors who were.

Everyone acquainted with east-central Europe knew that there were almost no Lithuanian-speaking priests who could be placed in Samogitian parishes (the university at Cracow which Jadwiga had proposed for training priests had not yet even been founded) and that the quality of priests of any nationality who could be recruited to serve in the Baltic was poor almost beyond description. Hence, the 'ideal' policy was clearly impractical. As a result, in the short run the Teutonic Knights were successful in meeting every challenge to their Samogitian policy, especially when they could speak to prelates with experience in the real world of people and politics; they were less able to persuade intellectuals and idealists, many of whom stubbornly held to the notion that the pagans were eager to embrace the Christian message, if only the Christians would stop killing them. For the moment, the Teutonic Knights' explanations still carried the day in every debate, but the world of ideas was changing as rapidly as the political constellation was rotating.

Evolution in the Concept of Crusading

While the Teutonic Knights stubbornly held to their traditional method of recruiting crusaders and leading them into the Samogitian wilds for elaborate chivalric entertainment, elsewhere in Europe there was a groundswell of interest in new crusades. Numerous individuals proposed plans by which the larger goals of Christendom could be advanced by military action.

The most important of these writers was Philippe de Mézières, a French crusader turned monk, who in 1389 published a plan to reorganise the military orders and revitalise efforts to defeat the enemies of the Cross. In the years that followed, he urged English and French knights to make a two-pronged attack through expeditions to Prussia and a crusade against the Turks in the Balkans. The fact that the public was more drawn to the Balkan situation than that of the Baltic was sufficient reason for the Teutonic Knights to disassociate themselves from such projects. In any case, the Teutonic Knights knew well how difficult it was to make chivalrous playboys attend to serious business. During the last siege of Vilnius, the French crusaders had wanted to joust with the Polish knights in the garrison. As long as the grandmaster was in command, as Konrad of Jungingen was in Prussia, he could control such anarchistic tendencies; in the Balkans, where the order lacked a strong territorial base with numerous auxiliary warriors, it would be impossible to impose such discipline. Even in Prussia French knights complained, while English and Scottish knights resented their hosts' refusal to allow them to brawl in bars. Only the Genoese crossbowmen, famous mercenaries sent by the fabulously wealthy duke of Burgundy, seemed to be truly disciplined.

Meanwhile, as foreign knights began to lose interest in Baltic crusades, the burghers and secular knights of Prussia were becoming less willing to perform military service, pay taxes and put up with the rapidly waxing arrogance of the Teutonic Knights. As long as the burghers and knights saw their hardships as military necessities, they suffered in silence. Now that the war seemed won, they began to grumble, and they bristled more easily when confronted with insults and discourteous behaviour. This did not go unnoticed. Grandmasters Konrad Zöllner (1382–90), Konrad of Wallenrode (1391–93) and Konrad of Jungingen (1394–1407) sought to discipline their officers and knights so that they would not antagonise their subjects, but the task was too great. Everywhere in Europe nobles looked down on their inferiors and resented efforts by assemblies and parliaments to moderate their behaviour; what the knights had been taught growing up in Germany could hardly be unlearned in Prussia.

The approaching end to the frontier warfare was probably viewed with mixed emotions by the native warriors. On the one hand, they would worry less about the loss of property, family members and serfs. On the other, they would lose the opportunities for personal enrichment, gaining status in the eyes of their peers, and winning admiring glances from pretty girls. Even more important in the longer run, their talents in irregular warfare, scouting and looting were no longer as highly valued by their lords, who were already wondering how to convert military service into cash payments. This hardly differed from practices long since introduced elsewhere. In England, for example, the old Saxon warrior class had been divided into a few who became lower nobility and the many who became taxpayers; while the upper nobility was composed of Norman foreigners.

The last great moment of cooperation between the grandmaster and his subjects was at this point, when pirates based on the island of Gotland threatened all their interests.

Chapter 2

Piracy, Saintly Visions, and Challenges from Germany

War over Gotland

The island of Gotland lies near the middle of the Baltic Sea, somewhat closer to Sweden than to Livonia. Seventy miles long and twenty-five wide, it is the largest of the islands found along the trade route between the Hanseatic cities in Germany and the mercantile cities of Novgorod, Pskov and Polotsk. Gotland was only lightly populated in the medieval period, and it had only one town worth noting, Visby. Nevertheless, its bays provided havens for sailing vessels on windy days. In those times, when all sea travel was done in small sailing ships, Gotland was important strategically, but produced little of value.

The German cogs, squat sailing vessels with a comparatively large cargo capacity and small crews, had almost completely replaced the Viking longboats for international trade. Moreover, a cog could be easily converted for military operations: it could carry up to a hundred soldiers with their equipment, or horses, and even siege machines; its high sides overlooked longboats, allowing the crew to sweep enemy decks with crossbows and primitive firearms, then board them. On the other hand, while the clumsy square rigging worked well in good weather, that was not true during summer storms; at the earliest sign of bad weather, captains sought the protected waters of a harbour or bay. As for winter, nobody dared venture onto the Baltic Sea.

For these reasons merchants tended to sail from one city to the next, making landfall at regular intervals along the coast where, if necessary, they could anchor safely, obtain fresh food and beer, and trade part of their cargo. No less important was the need for warehouses where they could pick up and deposit goods, for their voyages were profitable only if they remained under way, moving merchandise from one place to another; a cog was too expensive to be used as a floating department store.

In the twelfth and thirteenth centuries Visby supplied all these needs to the merchants from the Hanseatic ports, especially Lübeck, Rostock, Stralsund, Danzig and Königsberg (Kaliningrad), merchants carrying salt, cloth, grain, iron, wine and beer to Stockholm, Finland, Livonia and Novgorod to exchange for furs, beeswax, and other northern products. Through those years even Ruśian and Baltic merchants from Ruś and the nearest coasts visited Visby to exchange goods at the international market. It was there that the regional rules for commerce were developed and also where merchants of various cities and nationalities first became aware that they could act together for their common benefit.

The kings of Denmark and Sweden also realised the island's strategic importance. Unfortunately, the constant warfare – whenever their armies could be freed from the contest for Scania (modern southern Sweden) – undermined the island's frail local economy. In addition, merchants from Ruś decided that they had to give their primary attention to protecting commercial interests closer to home. When the Swedish king seized Gotland just before 1300, the German merchant community called a meeting at Lübeck to plan ways that would make it possible for them to trade freely wherever they wished. That meeting did little to benefit Visby, but the loose union of cities later called the Hanseatic League grew out of it, usually meeting in Lübeck.

The united merchants always resisted efforts by a Scandinavian monarch to tax them. Sometimes they raised a superior navy, then in alliance with his rivals attacked his realm; alternatively, they imposed an embargo. These options were not always successful, because the Hanseatic cities could not afford to maintain a fleet long and because it was difficult to blockade harbours effectively. Consequently a rough parity of forces existed in the Baltic Sea.

As improved navigational techniques and better knowledge of the waters reduced fear of shipwreck, merchants preferred to stay at home rather than to accompany their merchandise abroad. Their captains stored their trade goods in *Kontors* (a combination warehouse, inn for foreign visitors, and chapel) and relied on local partners to deliver goods from those warehouses to customers. This spread the risk, increased profits and reduced uncertainties about market conditions. As a result, there was ever less need for merchants to visit Visby.

This slow decline in Visby's fortunes accelerated quickly after Waldemar IV of Denmark (Valdemar, 1320–75) seized Gotland from his Swedish rival in 1361. His defeat of the local forces outside the city walls was so complete that the island's economy never fully recovered. Although Waldemar spared the city, captains henceforth used the island only as a landfall.

As the wars between the Danish and Swedish kings continued into the 1390s, the Hanseatic League attempted to protect its own interests

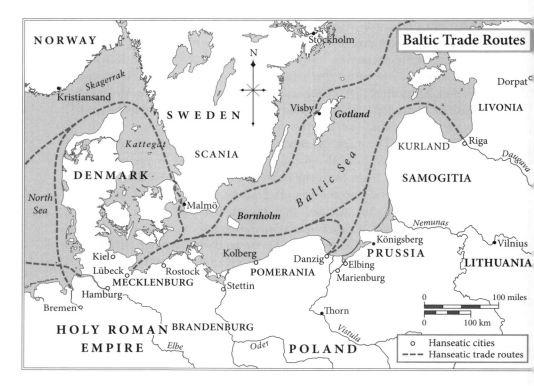

by controlling privateering. Each king had authorised subjects and allies to attack the other's ports and vessels, but neither had any means to prevent this from becoming simple piracy. As a result, Prussian and Livonian cities began asking the grandmasters to do something about the problem. Although successive grandmasters urged their diplomatic agents to impress the monarchs with the seriousness of the situation, each maintained scrupulous neutrality. That had to change in 1396, when the ferocity of the wars escalated beyond previous experience, threatening every merchant who took his ship onto the high seas and complicating the Livonian master's efforts to tame his independent-minded bishops.

The reasons for all this are unusually complex, so complex that even contemporaries had difficulties following them. The rude outline is that in 1390 there were two contenders for control of Scania and Gotland – Queen Margaret of Denmark and Norway (1353–1412) and Albrecht of Mecklenburg, king of Sweden (1338–1412). Margaret was the only child of Waldemar IV, and although her only son, Olaf, had died three years before, she was nevertheless pressing forwards to unify all Scandinavia and pass the three kingdoms on to her heir, Eric of Pomerania (1381–1459), the only surviving grandson of Waldemar IV.

Albrecht of Mecklenburg had been king of Sweden since 1363, but in 1389 he and his son Eric of Mecklenburg (*c.* 1359–97) had been taken prisoner in battle and held against either a huge ransom or the surrender of Stockholm. Albrecht's interests in Stockholm were ably represented by a cousin, Albrecht the Elder, one of the most capable members of the dynasty that had divided the Mecklenburg duchy among themselves. Albrecht the Elder kept the Danish forces at bay, though he could not prevent the siege lines from being drawn tighter and tighter around the Swedish capital. Only the many waterways saved the city, because the Danes could not stop smugglers from bringing food to the garrison and citizens.

The Hanseatic League had not relished the prospect of Margaret's taking Stockholm because that would make her dangerously powerful. Moreover, the cities of Rostock and Wismar sympathised with their Mecklenburg lords. So those cities supported the smugglers.

Grandmaster Konrad Zöllner had followed these developments carefully, talking personally with Queen Margaret when she crossed Prussia in 1390 on a pilgrimage to Rome; and he supported her successful efforts to canonise Brigitta of Sweden. However, he also had reason to be concerned: he had heard that she had considered joining a grand coalition with Poland and the archbishop of Riga to seize the lands of the Teutonic Knights and the Livonian Order – presumably to recover Estonia, which had belonged to Denmark until the peasant uprising of 1343. Also, Wenceslaus of Bohemia was urging him to support the Mecklenburg claims in Sweden, and the citizens of Danzig and Elbing (Elbląg) were pressing for action against the pirates. In short, the Hanseatic cities, the emperor, and the grandmaster's own fear of Jagiełło all combined to make Konrad consider intervening in the Scandinavian wars on the side of the imprisoned Albrecht of Mecklenburg. That he did not was largely the fault of Mecklenburg supporters.

In the summers of 1390 and 1391 the Mecklenburg fleets stopped at Gotland on their way to carry supplies to Stockholm. There they plundered the villages and sallied out to capture passing ships. The grandmaster concluded that, as long as the war lasted, Prussian and Livonian ships would be taken by both sides, but the freebooters called Vitalien Brethren were particularly annoying because they attacked coastal districts belonging to the Teutonic Knights. They even raided Novgorod territories for booty, actions the Hanseatic merchants who sailed up the Neva River for trade had to promise to stop.

Negotiations for Albrecht's ransom reached a critical stage in 1393 when the Hanseatic League imposed an embargo on trade with Denmark, then offered its services as a mediator, promising to hold Stockholm in pawn until both the queen and Albrecht had fulfilled any agreements they made with one another. This was an important step forwards, for it established the machinery for transferring authority in Sweden from Albrecht to Margaret with minimum turmoil, while guaranteeing the rights of Albrecht's partisans and protecting Stockholm's citizens and merchants from reprisals. Still, progress was slow.

Although Konrad of Wallenrode was highly skilled at planning and supervising the development of Prussian resources, he never felt comfortable in foreign policy. It is not surprising, therefore, that he achieved no more in Gotland than he had in Lithuania. (The historical person had but superficial resemblance to the one portrayed in Adam Mickiewicz's 1828 Polish-language poem, *Konrad Wallenrod*, in which a Lithuanian-born grandmaster deliberately leads his army to defeat – 'patriotic treason'. Its nationalist tone contributed to the 1830 rising against Russian occupation.)

Wallenrode's successor was a man more willing to take direct action. Konrad of Jungingen was determined to protect Prussian and Livonian merchants by force if diplomatic means failed. In May and June 1394 he hosted diplomats and representatives of the contending parties, who debated proposals for resolving the matter. It was such a successful meeting that a year later the parties met at Lindholm in Sweden to sign a formal peace treaty.

The main point of the treaty was that Albrecht would be released until 1398, at which time he promised to surrender himself to the queen. Margaret would then decide whether to accept his ransom or to resume the war. Meanwhile, Stockholm would be held by the Hanseatic League, with the promise that it would hand the city over to the innocent party if either Albrecht or Margaret broke the truce. The better to fortify the city, the Hanseatic League raised a large sum that was to be repaid by Margaret and Albrecht jointly; arrangements may have been made with the local convent of the Teutonic Knights, just south of Stockholm, to supply food for the garrison, though this is not certain.

Although Margaret released Albrecht and Eric, and the Hanseatic League took possession of Stockholm, almost nothing else went as planned. The pirate menace did not go away, but became worse once the privateers had no employer. As soon as Gotland's ports were ice-free, the pirates sailed out to plunder the surrounding coasts, even raiding Livonia. Some sailed up the Narva River to Dorpat (Tartu, in modern Estonia) and entered the service of Bishop Dietrich Damerow, who was allying himself with Jagiełło and Vytautas against the Livonian Knights.

The pirates, it seemed, had become an international power themselves, equal in importance to any monarch.

Konrad of Jungingen was very concerned about the Dorpat problem, representing as it did another of those far-fetched schemes beloved of monarchs and their advisers. In this case it was the aforementioned combination of Poland, Lithuania and Denmark to 'protect' the archbishop of Riga by crushing the Livonian Knights and then dividing their lands and those of the Teutonic Order between them. Like many political daydreams, this one had some potential of realisation until the victim took steps to deal with it.

Konrad used his influence with the Papacy to quash Pomeranian suggestions that the duke provide a son who could be named archbishop of Riga, with the understanding that he would then call for help from the surrounding monarchs. The grandmaster then arranged instead for the pope to appoint the late grandmaster's nephew, Johannes of Wallenrode (1370–1419). The new archbishop immediately became a member of the Teutonic Order and promised to tame Riga's unruly citizens, nobles and clergy. Wallenrode was not yet thirty, but no matter – age counted for less than high birth.

Meanwhile, Konrad of Jungingen was keeping one eye on Sigismund's crusade against the Turkish sultan who had crushed the Serbs seven years earlier and ever since had been crossing the Danube into the Hungarian borderlands. He was not willing to commit knights to the crusade, but he knew the French crusaders well from their 'journeys' (*Reisen*) to Prussia.

The Crusade to Nicopolis

Although the Hungarians had been sufficiently successful south of the Danube in 1390 and 1394 to persuade the king of France and the pope that a larger crusading army might be able to drive the Turks from the Balkans and rescue Constantinople, in late 1394 the Turks had managed to cross the Danube into Wallachia. This threat not only to the Hungarian kingdom, but also to trade via the Black Sea, prompted King Sigismund to reverse the decades-old alliance of Hungary with Genoa in favour of one with Venice. With Byzantium in obvious decline, it seemed logical to take sides with the now-dominant seapower. He also courted the duke of Burgundy, who had the resources to raise a large crusading army.

In the summer of 1395 Sigismund sought to stop the Turkish raids on his kingdom by attacking the fortress of Nicopolis on the south bank of the Danube. However, his failure left the Turks in position to attack Transylvania, Moldavia, or even Hungary whenever they chose; also, they could block Christian forces hoping to drive the Turks from Bulgaria.

In the late summer of 1396 Sigismund recruited a large force of Burgundian, German and Hungarian crusaders, promising to lead them along the north bank of the Danube to join the Transylvanian forces, then rendezvous with a Venetian fleet that would transfer them across the river.

In this, Sigismund was emulating his grandfather, Johann of Bohemia, perhaps the most daring and colourful adventurer of his age – and also an enthusiastic supporter of the Teutonic Order. With the aid of his half-brother Wenceslaus, Sigismund recruited prominent men who had fought in Prussia; among them were the marshal of France, Jean Boucicaut, a veteran warrior; Enguerrand de Coucy; and Jean de Nevers. There was also a large but undependable Wallachian force, and knights from Poland, Germany and Bohemia, with a small number of volunteers from England, Spain and Italy.

The crusaders assembled in Buda in mid-summer, then marched down the Danube to the Iron Gates, where the Venetian fleet awaited, together with Hospitaller reinforcements. Once across the river, they proceeded to mistreat Serbian and Bulgarian Christians they were supposedly rescuing and to murder garrisons which surrendered. Stories of these misdeeds stiffened the courage of the Ottoman garrisons, particularly at Nicopolis. Here it became apparent that they needed siege machines, but capturing the fortress quickly became less important than drinking and gambling. The Burgundian knights, whose influence was dominant in the crusader camp, were not taking the Turks seriously in any case – they were the most famous warriors in France, and surely they could beat anyone in the world.

The French and Burgundians were dressed like 'little kings' and so confident of victory that they neglected to watch for the approach of the Turks, who appeared two weeks later under the command of the sultan himself. Bayezid (1354–1403) was an experienced warrior who had defeated Turkish rivals to unify his empire, besieged Constantinople, and completed the conquest of Serbia that his father had begun in 1389. His light cavalry and mounted archers were numerous and accustomed to victory. His army was also more colourful, with bands playing martial music, and included 'Ghazis', fanatical Islamic volunteers.

Nevertheless, the crusaders from beyond the Rhine were confident that they could beat any army in the world. After all, they said that they had as many as 100,000 men with them. The reality was that the crusaders numbered perhaps 16,000, roughly as many men as the sultan commanded.

Although Sigismund had performed brilliantly in organising the expedition, he had no control over the Frenchmen and Burgundians in their 'Gallic frivolity and petulance'. They ignored the advice of men experienced in Balkan warfare; and Sigismund, who understood the Turkish tactics, could not persuade the revellers to allow local troops to occupy the front line of battle. He warned that his own troops would remain in a defensive posture until he could see what the Muslim dispositions were, but that made no impression on the other crusaders – they were quite content to win all the honour of the victory for themselves; after all, in the first skirmish they had annihilated a Turkish scouting force.

In their chivalric pride the French and Burgundians charged the first troops they saw, unaware that sharpened stakes were behind the Muslim irregulars who then stepped back to let the charging horsemen impale themselves. The knights dismounted to remove the barrier, then charged up a steep slope (or clanked along on foot) until they approached the crest. There they met the main Turkish force.

By now the rest of the Christian army had followed along, but was too far behind to help. The French and Burgundians realised their danger too late. Sigismund, too, had been swept into the fray as though seeking to win his spurs like a common squire. Soon it was his turn to be routed.

Meanwhile, the Wallachians withdrew, unnerved by the sight of riderless horses galloping away from the noise of the distant battle, abandoning exhausted fugitives to their fate. Sigismund's life was saved by Hermann of Celje and Friedrich of Hohenzollern (1371–1440). They had managed to find a small boat on which they could escape to the Venetian vessels, but, according to rumour, refused a place to a prominent Polish noble (who somehow managed to swim to the opposite shore in his full armour) and cut off the hands of crusaders hanging on to their overloaded vessel.

After Sigismund assessed his situation, he chose to travel home by sea via Constantinople, Rhodes and Venice rather than risk the overland journey through territories filled with Turkish and Tatar raiders. As he sailed from Constantinople through the Dardanelles, the sultan mockingly lined up captive crusaders on both banks, so that they could plead for him to come to their rescue.

Only prominent prisoners would be ransomed, and then only after being paraded throughout the Turkish domains; the rest were murdered or sold into slavery. Meanwhile, Turkish raiders roamed Wallachia and the Hungarian frontier almost without resistance.

The enterprise was not a complete failure, however. First and foremost, opposition to Sigismund's consolidation of royal authority almost vanished. The nobles acquiesced in his demand that a census be taken to determine how many warriors were available in the kingdom and who would be responsible for bringing them to the royal levy. They also agreed that for the duration of the emergency (for ever, it turned out), there would be no exemptions from military service; and they allowed the king to confiscate the estates of hostile barons, then give them to his friends. The Church gave him half its annual incomes for his expenses. After a failed uprising in 1401, when the nobles actually took Sigismund prisoner briefly (and offered the crown to Jagiełło, who wisely declined), he was able to act effectively in domestic affairs and foreign policy for the rest of his life. Prominent among his rescuers was the Polish noble he had abandoned at Nicopolis.

A second success of the entire enterprise was in disrupting Bayezid's siege of Constantinople. When Timur defeated the Ottoman army in 1402 and captured the sultan, Byzantium received an additional half-century of existence. Had Sigismund been luckier in his timing, with his offensive coinciding with Timur's onslaught, the history of the Balkans might have been much different: the Turks might have been driven back to Asia Minor, at least temporarily. But no one could have foreseen Timur's attack. In 1396 Europeans knew only of his intention to dominate the steppe north of the Crimea.

A few nobles approached Jagiełło, proposing that he claim the Hungarian throne, but since Jagiełło was only the consort of the Polish monarch, he was too cautious to accept. Unity among monarchs was strong when everyone felt threatened, and at this moment Jagiełło was no more secure in his position than the Bohemian or Hungarian kings. The defeat of the crusaders had almost been a fatal blow for Wenceslaus because he had invested so many German resources in first assisting Sigismund to acquire Hungary, then in backing the failed enterprise. The German electors began to talk about impeaching the emperor and replacing him with one of their own number. The disaster was also a severe setback for the Teutonic Knights, despite their having taken no part in it, because French knights never appeared in Prussia again in significant numbers, and Sigismund and Wenceslaus had too many problems of their own for them to pay attention to Prussia and Samogitia.

To everyone's surprise, the Turks did not follow up the victory by advancing farther north. Very likely the sultan regarded the Danube as the best frontier he could defend easily. Of course, he did not tell the Christians that, and had he done so, who would have believed him? It was easier for the Christians to believe that Muslims were impossible to understand or that they had suffered badly in the battle too, so much that they had no strength left for the sieges of border castles and towns that a conquest would have required.

Piracy in the Baltic Sea

Baltic politics became more complex when the two Erics claimed the Swedish crown. The first in point of time, in 1395, was Eric of Mecklenburg, who ignored his father's promises not to interfere in the affairs of the kingdom until 1398; from his stronghold in Gotland he declared himself king of Sweden. The second was Eric of Pomerania, Margaret's heir apparent. Since Eric of Mecklenburg had few ships at this time, he relied on privateers who found Gotland ideally situated for attacking commercial vessels, many of which belonged to cities in the Hanseatic League. This was a mistake on the part of the Mecklenburger because the victims should have been his natural allies, but his mistake can be understood, since Hanseatic policies at the moment seemed to favour his rival.

His closest pirate allies, the Vitalien Brethren, even sailed into the Vistula River, taking fourteen vessels as prizes almost under the grandmaster's very walls. This was a direct challenge to Grandmaster Konrad, who didn't want to hear arguments about the differences between privateers and pirates. He wanted the attacks stopped.

At the autumn 1395 meeting of the Hanseatic League, the Wendish and Prussian representatives promised to send ships to join a Danzig fleet the next summer and together seek out the pirates and destroy them. As it happened, the pirates slipped away beforehand, just before a small Danish squadron arrived in Visby. As the queen's fleet sailed on towards the Neva River in Russia to search for the pirates, it ran into the Danzig armada. The Prussians immediately attacked, and although most of the queen's captains evaded them, two did not. The Danzig commander, refusing to believe that the Danes were not pirates themselves, treated them brutally, confiscating their ships as prizes and heaving all seventy-four members of the crews overboard into the freezing waters.

When the seamen in the Danish fleet learned that their comrades had been murdered, they were furious. Not long afterwards, when sailors of the two fleets encountered one another in the streets of Visby, a bloody riot broke out. Eric of Mecklenburg, who was on the spot, was unable to stop the violence.

The story might have ended there, with the pirates dispersed and the contending forces stalemated, if Eric of Mecklenburg had not died of the plague during the summer of 1397. Queen Margaret immediately announced the union of the three Scandinavian kingdoms (Denmark, Norway and Sweden) for herself and her heir. Given time, she could break the Hanseatic efforts to monopolise Baltic trade, perhaps even force Danzig and the grandmaster to open the Prussian market to her merchants. Meanwhile, the Vitalien Brethren seized Gotland for themselves, putting forth Johann of Mecklenburg (1370–1422), a nephew of King Albrecht, as the new candidate for the Swedish crown. This gesture meant little in practice, but it was required by medieval custom, since every land had to have a nominal lord, even if he had no authority.

The pirates attempted to negotiate with the grandmaster, even sending a delegation via Johann of Mecklenburg to ask for his aid in sustaining Swedish resistance against the queen. Konrad of Jungingen refused, but he came to understand that the Hanseatic fleet could defeat the pirates at sea, though it had no land army to besiege and capture their fortresses on Gotland.

The Conquest of Gotland

The representatives of Danzig, Culm (Chełmno), Elbing and the other towns used the next meeting of the Prussian estates to plead for help. Although we do not have the text of the arguments, doubtlessly they reminded the grandmaster of the close relationship of trade and taxes. That was something he could understand. The merchants must have been very persuasive because the grandmaster decided to send a force of Teutonic Knights to Gotland in early 1398 with orders to eliminate the pirates in one hard, swift blow.

Konrad of Jungingen prepared his strike carefully. He first warned neighbouring princes not to give escaping pirates shelter, as they had so often done before. Then he ordered the Prussian towns to prepare ships for a spring campaign and assigned the command to Johann of Phirt, the commander of Schwetz (Świecie). Phirt set a very early date for the fleet of eighty-four ships to sail, hoping to catch the pirates still waiting for the ice farther north to melt. As the order's chronicler summarised it: 'God's knights set out from Prussia with many ships and a great host to Gotland.'

The fleet landed the knights on 21 March 1398. Despite the difficulties caused by the weather, especially the cold rain, the troops moved siege machines into position beneath Visby's walls while the fleet pressed into the harbour and small detachments captured several outlying pirate nests. On 7 April, as the besieging forces were preparing to attack, the defenders began to quarrel among themselves. When the citizens took up arms to save their town from being destroyed, the Vitalien Brethren fled as best they could. By some accounts only about 400 escaped, but more likely most of them did. Some made their way to the northern reaches of the Baltic; others sailed to the North Sea and joined the charismatic Klaus Störtebeker, whose name indicated that he could empty a four-litre mug of beer in one gulp. In 1401 another Hanseatic fleet captured him, put him on trial in Hamburg, and beheaded him and seventy-four accomplices.

In April 1399 the Teutonic Order, the Hanseatic League and Queen Margaret sealed a formal treaty of friendship. Though this was not a military alliance, it was of sufficient importance to be commemorated in the church of St Mary in Elbing by a large painting containing the portraits of the queen, Eric of Pomerania, Grandmaster Konrad and St Dorothea of Montau, all praying to the Madonna.

To everyone's surprise, the grandmaster did not turn Gotland over to the queen. His reasons are not absolutely clear, though the correspondence shows that Margaret formally requested him to do that. Perhaps he chose to obey the order of Ruprecht of the Rhine (1352–1410), the pretender to the imperial crown worn by Wenceslaus of Bohemia, to defend Albrecht's rights; the German master, who was among Ruprecht's strongest supporters, probably also encouraged him not to turn over the island to the Danish queen. However, he could not hand the island over to Albrecht either, because the Mecklenburg prince lacked the men and ships to prevent it from becoming a pirate lair again.

As it happened, Albrecht proved to be absolutely unreliable. In November 1401 he did not appear as promised at a summit meeting of the Hanseatic League, Mecklenburg and Schleswig-Holstein. Margaret thereupon told the assembled delegates that the island clearly belonged to her. Under these circumstances, the best the grandmaster could do was to keep his garrisons on the island. Perhaps he hoped that the Hanseatic League might find a solution to the problem, but more likely he was leaving the matter in God's hands – people died young in those days, even monarchs.

Time for waiting ran out in 1403. When Albrecht sought Hanseatic aid to recover the island, Margaret sent the grandmaster an ultimatum demanding the cession of Gotland by 12 November. Meanwhile, she was gathering a fleet and an army. Jungingen misjudged her determination and daring. She had made complaints and threats before, but she had never acted on them. Moreover, experienced men had told him that it was already too late in the season for the Danes to undertake a large-scale naval operation. As a result, he reduced the Gotland garrison just as the danger became most acute.

The grandmaster was caught off his guard. He had been concentrating on Samogitian affairs when Margaret's fleet arrived the day after her deadline passed. The small garrisons on Gotland were able to defend their castles, but only with great difficulty because it was not optimum weather for the early cannons used by the Teutonic Knights; and the garrisons knew that no relief army was likely to come for months, because sailing in December and January was too dangerous.

The grandmaster hesitated for several weeks, apparently seeking to obtain both a diplomatic resolution of the principal issue – possession of Gotland – and a consensus among his advisers. Eventually, he was encouraged by the German master and Ruprecht to recapture the island and give it to Albrecht of Mecklenburg; also the Vitalien Brethren had reappeared in Margaret's employ.

Reorganisation and Religious Life

Before issuing orders, Jungingen reorganised his government, a normal procedure, one followed every few years. There was a tendency in all religious orders (as perhaps in all organisations) for aged and infirm leaders to hold on to office too long. Jungingen's predecessor, Wallenrode, had inherited a geriatric administration, and neither he nor Jungingen had made great changes. Perhaps it had seemed best to rely on experience and proven skill, without noticing the extent to which the physical abilities and stamina of the men holding the highest offices had declined. Perhaps, too, their secular-minded, hard-boiled pragmatism had turned into cynicism and laxness towards religious observation, a shortcoming that would have troubled the pious grandmaster.

The Teutonic Order, like all other religious orders, was always on the alert for tendencies towards worldliness and the formation of cliques. That was a part of monastic life everywhere. Shortly before her death, Dorothea of Montau (1347–94) had complained about the worldliness of the Teutonic Knights, and while her statements reflected her own otherworldly – saintly – beliefs, the nun's visions were believed by many of the knights, including Konrad of Jungingen.

There is some indication that at least part of the grandmaster's programme was to make his knights observe their religious obligations more fully. One of his critics complained that he should have been a nun rather than the grandmaster of a military order.

The Second Gotland Campaign

The chroniclers' accounts of the subsequent Gotland campaign are far too short to tell us much, but the treasury books allow us to determine that about 5,000 troops from all the convents in Prussia boarded the ships, reinforced by city militias and secular knights. The force also included some Lithuanians sent by Vytautas in adherence with the recent treaty at Sallinwerder and repayment for the Teutonic Knights having aided him in his wars against the Tatars and Ruśians. The force was so large that the fleet could not transport it all at the same time. Moreover, the grandmaster ordered it to sail in February, a very early date for any operation, so that his men would get onto the island before Danish reinforcements could arrive. The cold and wetness resulted in many deaths and the loss of hundreds of expensive horses.

Under such circumstances, it was difficult to put on a chivalric show. Nevertheless, the grandmaster did what he could, The account books indicate that he provided appropriate music. There certainly was not much else to listen to in the cramped conditions below the decks of a tossing cog.

Thanks to a fresco commissioned by the grandmaster for a church on Gotland – the Baltic equivalent of the Bayeux tapestry – we can see the course of the conflict cartoon-fashion, panel by panel. The artist showed the Teutonic Knights pushing back the defending forces at the landing site, then attacking smaller fortifications. In the month this took, they readied siege machines for an assault on the city walls. Towards Easter reinforcements landed, rather later than planned. Once those knights were on shore, the fate of the Danes was fairly well decided, unless the queen could land reinforcements.

As expected, Queen Margaret was encouraging her commanders to slip past the Hanseatic squadron watching for her fleet. The gamble failed. A Danzig-led fleet found the Danes at anchor near Kalmar, attacked immediately, and captured a hundred vessels while burning sixty more. When the royal forces on Gotland heard of this in late June, they capitulated.

One of the order's chroniclers summarised the campaign against the Danes thus:

> Their arrogance was stilled, for they refused to deal with the Order respectfully, nor would they entrust anyone to mediate, neither prince, lord nor the Hanseatic League. Great was their woman's war, but they came away from it with little to rejoice about.

The grandmaster's officers set about establishing a proper civil administration, making no pretence that their presence was temporary. Noticeable in this effort was the particular care given to the long-neglected peasantry so that they could survive without importing food and would have a battle-ready militia. Not that this could be achieved quickly. The commander also set about rebuilding the fortifications and stocking them with firearms and armour, ready to repulse any effort to recapture the island. Renewing the contest, however, was far from Margaret's mind. She complained, but she made no effort to challenge the grandmaster again.

Jungingen was interested in doing more than merely supporting international trade by providing safe harbours and suppressing piracy – he was determined to exploit the natural resources of Gotland, especially stone. Prussia had little suitable building stone, and transport costs were high, but limestone could be quarried from Gotland's coastal cliffs and transported throughout the Baltic at reasonable cost. Subsequently, large quantities of stone were sent to Prussia to build castles and churches, and broken pieces were processed into mortar. Even more important were falcons, which had been a traditional export; now he wanted these large birds as impressive gifts for the order's friends. In doing what he could to make the Gotland enterprise pay for itself, Jungingen prepared to hold the island for ever.

This policy came to an end on the grandmaster's death in 1407. Eric Christiansen, in *The Northern Crusades*, reports a later story that he had hastened his death by rejecting his doctor's advice that his gallstones could be cured by intercourse with a woman; also that he warned (unsuccessfully) against electing his brother, Ulrich (1360–1410), to succeed him, because he hated Poland excessively. Christiansen was properly sceptical of both stories, preferring to believe that Jagiełło no longer feared to confront the Teutonic Knights on the battlefield and that the grandmaster no longer had allies willing to support him – not even the master of the Livonian Order.

Ulrich of Jungingen had been the marshal and commander of Königsberg, so he was well aware of the political, economic and military situation. The total cost of the recent war over Gotland had been well over 20,000 marks, and there was no end of special expenditures in sight. Everyone was complaining about the tax burden; even the merchants, who had demanded strong measures against the pirates, now wanted tax relief. Moreover, Ruprecht, his hopes to be crowned emperor shattered by an Italian fiasco, no longer had any interest in northern affairs. Lastly, Ulrich needed the knights and the money for a growing crisis in Samogitia.

The best way out of the situation, Ulrich believed, was to return the island to the Danish queen. In June 1408 he sold Gotland to her for 9,000 nobles, a treaty of eternal friendship, and a promise that the queen would prevent any pirates from using any of her lands as a base for raiding Baltic shipping. The Gotland affair thus came to an end. So, too, did the Teutonic Order's almost uninterrupted string of diplomatic and military successes.

The Religious Culture of the Crusade

The fourteenth-century expeditions of the Teutonic Order in Samogitia reflected the military practices and the religious enthusiasm of the era of high chivalry. It was the combination of the two that produced a regional crusade which had little to do with the earlier crusades to the Holy Land. Honour and display were important. Not all-important, perhaps, but the more important the noble who took the cross, the more significant the concept of honour and the more impressive the display. This cost money and, unlike the wars at home, there was little booty to take, and whatever cattle and horses were rounded up had to be herded back to Prussia or Livonia and protected by dint of hard fighting; best to leave that to the native irregulars who knew the country.

At this time armies did not yet routinely employ large numbers of mercenaries and, while the grandmaster tried to make their service honourable, he had to reserve greater praise for volunteer crusaders, men who chose to risk their lives in the service of the Virgin Mary – knights, squires and burghers. They expected to earn eternal rewards, perhaps also receive knighthoods in a brilliant ceremony, but certainly to return home with a reputation as daring fellows who had gone into dark swamps and wilderness in search of human beasts who worshipped idols and burned prisoners alive as sacrifices to the devil.

Less prominent 'guests' received a bit of financial aid and a cut-rate dubbing into knighthood. While the crusaders might have disparaged the profit motive, they rarely hesitated to accept money when it was offered 'honourably'. After all, who can give liberally unless someone is willing to accept graciously? When medieval men encountered individuals who truly disdained earthly riches, they immediately proclaimed them devoutly saintly or exceptionally chivalrous, depending on the circumstances.

It was not the knights alone who shared this attitude. In Prussia the German merchants, artisans and peasants, and their wives and children, were part of a culture that did few things by halves. When they scoffed at wayward or slovenly clergymen, they were cruel; when they were moved by a saint, they wept profusely; and when they witnessed impressive ceremonies, they joined in enthusiastically.

There was one saint in Prussia who experienced both public ridicule and veneration, a middle-aged woman whose cult spread rapidly in the early fifteenth century.

Dorothea of Montau

Dorothea was born in 1347 in the village of Montau, near Marienburg, the seventh child of a Dutch immigrant family. Her father died when she was ten. Her mother was extremely religious, so fervent in her prayers that even in winter she would be covered with perspiration. Dorothea had to share in the hard work, care for her two younger siblings and earn money for the family; her only escape from daily drudgery was to join her mother in church.

It was very common at the time to tame the flesh by self-inflicted punishment, physically whipping oneself. Dorothea not only flailed herself until she was covered with blood, but she held her hands in steam and over candles until fearfully burnt, believing that the pain would make her worthy of her heavenly bridegroom. However, entering a nunnery was impossible, because she could not provide the customary dowry.

When Dorothea was sixteen, her brother arranged for her to marry a swordsmith named Adalbert. In the course of the years she bore him nine children, half of whom lived past infancy. However, hers was not a typical housewife's life. Although she could not continue the self-flagellation, she did not give up her extraordinary religious devotion. Once Adalbert even kept her in chains for three days to keep her from straying away in rags to join the beggars at the church. Once she emerged from a church, having stayed overly long in prayer, to hear the voice of God commanding her to hurry home. She arrived to find the house was in flames. She had neglected to put out the fire before leaving for worship. She barely saved the building and her children.

Adalbert was pious too, though not to Dorothea's degree. He had gone on pilgrimages to Rome and to Aachen, leaving Dorothea at home with the children. Consequently, the marriage was no mismatch. He was as good and tolerant a husband as could have been found. When the plague carried away three of their children, Adalbert began to share his wife's austere devotional practices. In the summer of 1384 he took Dorothea and their surviving daughter on a pilgrimage to Aachen, a long journey to the other side of the Rhine, to the shrine of Charles the Great. Afterwards they decided to devote their lives to God, not by entering a cloister, but by living a worshipful existence in the secular world.

Dorothea, soon dissatisfied with such half-measures, gave herself so fully to prayer that she earned a wide reputation – not all good. Neighbours thought she might be insane, a poor woman mourning the loss of eight children. Dorothea was not thinking of the past, however. She was deep in mystical experience in January 1385, when she suddenly felt that Jesus had physically ripped out her old heart and given her a 'warm heart' in its place.

The next year Adalbert sold their home and set out with his family for Aachen. In the Neumark they were waylaid by bandits who stole everything. Adalbert himself was badly wounded, but he was sufficiently in control of his mind to reject Dorothea's wish to become a beggar and live from the charity of strangers. When he heard that officials of the Teutonic Order had arrested the robbers, he sent his wife to claim their belongings. She obeyed unhappily.

For a year and a half they lived in a small religious community near Aachen, but on the outbreak of war there, Adalbert decided to return to Prussia. Dorothea begged to remain there, to live as a beggar from the alms of pilgrims. Only by the intervention of a friendly priest could Adalbert persuade her that she had to follow the wishes of her husband. The journey home was long and dangerous, their sled breaking through ice on one occasion, and the last leg of the trip being a hazardous sea voyage from Lübeck to Danzig.

Now Dorothea was often lost in meditation and prayer. Repeatedly she left the house uncared for to visit churches dedicated to Mary, spending ecstatic hours in prayer. Common people began to mock her, and a few suggested that she was a heretic or a witch. Fortunately for Dorothea, her confessor, Nicholas of Hohenstein, spoke to Prior Johann of the cathedral at Marienwerder (Kwidzyn) – one of the oldest churches in Prussia, south of Marienburg. He investigated her visions and ruled that they were in perfect accord with the teachings of the Church.

In 1389 her confessor led a large party of pilgrims over the Alps to Rome. Adalbert was too ill to go along, but Dorothea went. In the six-month stay she visited all the churches of the Eternal City. At one point, when she was desperately ill for seven weeks, she learned of Adalbert's death in Danzig. She briefly considered entering a Roman convent, but in the end she decided to return to Prior Johann, a man with a distinct sympathy for her divinely inspired gifts.

As she revealed more of her visions to the astounded prior, he became aware that he had something very unusual in his care. Her visits to Marienwerder became ever more frequent until the day Dorothea's wagon overturned, injuring her severely. Unable to travel, she asked permission to be walled inside a cell in the cathedral, to live in that confined space for the rest of her life. The prior, who dared not give such permission himself, asked his superiors what he should do.

While awaiting permission to immure her, the prior found her housing in Marienwerder. During this time she received new revelations almost daily. Many concerned politics. The prior wrote them down, hiding his actions from Dorothea, who did not want her predictions made public before her death. Meanwhile, he asked for permission to build a small cell adjoining the cathedral, to be constructed according to long-established church procedures for such cases: the cell was to have three windows, one looking to the sky, one to the outside for food, and one to the inside of the cathedral for communion.

Konrad Zöllner had not favoured this, but his successor, Konrad of Wallenrode, must have done so, because the bishop and canons of the cathedral were all members of the Teutonic Order and would not have proceeded without consulting his wishes. Dorothea was doubtless aware at the time of Konrad Zöllner's hostility, for she reported a vision of him sitting in hellfire.

In November 1393, with all possible ceremony, the cathedral chapter led her into the church and walled her into the cell. She spent her remaining months under constant supervision, often mourning with many tears, often in great joy. She hardly slept. When she died in the summer of 1394 she was hailed by the local population as a saint. Soon afterwards, Konrad of Jungingen was persuaded by personal experience that she had been given insights into the future.

After her death, pilgrims streamed to Marienwerder by the thousands to look at her cell, touch her relics and pray at her grave. Konrad of Jungingen began the process of having her formally declared a saint.

Discontent with the Organised Church

It is not known why Konrad Zöllner had not been enthusiastic about Dorothea's religious experiences. He had been quarrelling with the Marienburg canons about property, and with little doubt this issue came into the prayers of Sister Catherine Mulner, a nun of the Teutonic Order and Dorothea's constant companion. More likely, the grandmaster mistrusted Dorothea's tendency to comment on politics, as had other contemporary female saints. However, it is also possible that his scepticism regarding visions and miracles was unwittingly reinforced by proposals for religious reform that were circulating through Central Europe. There was a widely voiced discontent with contemporary ecclesiastical practices, a popular outrage eloquently summed up by scholars as widely separated as John Wycliffe in England and Jan Hus in Bohemia.

The English reformer John Wycliffe (*c.* 1335–84) had denounced everything even remotely connected with the scandalous papal government of Avignon which Petrarch had characterised as the Babylonian Captivity of the Church. Wycliffe's hatred of Avignon's corruption went so far that he rethought much of the contemporary theology and practice that hindered church reform; he concluded at last that the entire approach to religion through the outer forms of sacraments, pilgrimages and relics was in error. Instead, he taught, true Christianity consisted of a piety reflected in daily behaviour. Under his influence the English Parliament passed legislation that curbed the rights of the Papacy, legislation that was not enforced until Henry VIII wanted to make himself head of the Church of England. Wycliffe also argued that the Church should give up its property and that clergy should live in apostolic poverty.

Many Englishmen were already angry that the Avignon popes had favoured the French in the Hundred Years War. But they became even angrier after the Great Schism began in 1378, with one pope in Rome, another in Avignon, because each began raising money to conduct war against the other. With revenues divided, each employed dubious financial measures that further diminished their prestige.

In England pious people influenced by Wycliffe's ideas emerged from the congregations to wander about the country preaching an individualistic approach to Christ that bypassed the hierarchy of the established Church. That call for renewal was very popular, for many parishes had no priests or only very incompetent ones. Wycliffe helped 'Lollard' preachers by providing them with an English translation of important parts of the Bible; he believed that the most important duty of Christian teaching was to be found in such preaching. However, as time passed, the Lollards went beyond denouncing the pope and clerical superstition; they began to preach social justice.

When the peasants revolted in 1381, they defended their uprising partly by scripture and partly by citing important Lollard spokesmen. After King Richard II (1367–99) crushed the peasant uprising, he suppressed the heretical teachings, dug up Wycliffe's body and burned it, and sought to round up more Lollards, so that they would never again stir up trouble in England.

A Scandal Originating in Bohemia

Wycliffe's teachings next appeared in Bohemia, where they accelerated a reform movement already under way. As was true in England when Wycliffe first began preaching, his ideas were initially welcomed in the royal court and found an echo in the development of national feeling, especially in expressing local resentment against the exploitation of the natives by foreigners. The main difference was that in England the foreigners were French clergy, while in Bohemia they were Germans.

It is believed that the ideas of Wycliffe were first brought from England by members of the entourage that had accompanied Wenceslaus's half-sister to England to marry Richard II. Later, Czech nobles and clergy gave refuge to Lollards who fled from England to escape royal persecution. In Bohemia the reformers' insistence on preaching from Bible texts in colloquial Czech took on a special colouration – the German-speaking clergy, burghers and nobles who dominated the kingdom insisted upon using Latin in church services. The Hussites, as the Czech radicals became known from the name of their leader, Jan Hus (1370–1415), had one strong supporter, King Wenceslaus, who was quarrelling with his churchmen and with those Germans who did not sympathise with the reform movement.

Jan Hus was an important personality in Prague, where students from Prussia were currently studying at the university, and at Wenceslaus's court, which had close ties to the Teutonic Order, but he was even better known for his Czech sermons in the Bethlehem Chapel. The split between traditionalists and reformers had not yet occurred; therefore, it is possible that a certain obscure 'Leander' brought to Prussia ideas learned in lectures and discussions in Prague. We do not know even who he was, but reputedly he was among the closest advisers of Konrad Zöllner. That this Leander would denounce the 'unnatural asceticism' of Dorothea was as natural as her calling his attacks 'the barking of a mad dog'. This did not mean that the grandmaster and his associates were social revolutionaries, only that they were not exempt from the influences of the times, and that the spirit of the times was, as always, complex.

Contemporaries could see in St Dorothea both the most conservative aspects of mystical religious expression and a rejection of the existing ecclesiastical order. Thus, in resisting her influence one could believe oneself either to be upholding traditional worship or undermining it. In general those who wanted to reform the Church were somewhat sceptical about saints; they looked for ways to live better lives in the world, not ways to escape it.

The knights of the Teutonic Order were not theologians. They were pious, practical and earnest. Their attitudes towards the Church and its hierarchy were divided between a conservative caution and a desire to see moderate reforms, between a respect for rightful authority and a disdain for the Papacy's oft-demonstrated ignorance and folly, between a hope that the Church would take more interest in their concerns and a wish that it would simply leave them alone. In short, there were aspects of the Wycliffe/Hus message that everyone from the grandmaster down to the lowliest sergeant could understand and appreciate. And since the anti-German aspects of Hussite practices were not yet fully evident, there seemed to be little threat in them. At least, little that anyone but a theologian might see.

As time passed, of course, informed men began to suspect the presence of Hussite ideas among the native Prussians. Some time before, the bishop of Ermland (Warmia), Heinrich III Sorbom (governing 1373–1401), had established three Augustinian convents in his territory, and at Heilsberg (Lidzbark Warmiński) a school designed to prepare twelve native boys at a time for the priesthood, staffed by teaching monks of the same order that Luther later joined. Other schools had scholarships for one or more native boys as boarding students. The bishop later asked Johann Merklin to prepare a book of instructions for 'simple priests' who would have to deal principally with the special problems of people whose ancestors had been pagan and who consequently understood the Christian faith only as filtered through questionable concepts handed down from generation to generation in a language still tinged with a pagan vocabulary.

Although long Christian, the Prussians understood their faith only superficially. Preaching in the vernacular, as the Hussites advocated, would help rectify the local situation. This was potentially dangerous, as later experience demonstrated – seemingly harmless concerns for the common people could provide religious justifications for armed uprisings designed to eliminate present injustices and to establish a perfect society based on Christian doctrine. Konrad Zöllner, of course, did not see that as likely to happen.

Rebellions had not been experienced in Prussia for many years; they were something of the past, something that the order's good government and strong discipline had eliminated. Konrad, like the bishop of Ermland, was more concerned with promoting his subjects' welfare than worrying about anti-German revolutions. His order's religious practices were austere enough, sufficient to the needs of a military organisation with a wide variety of secular business to attend to. He did not need a religious fanatic, however divinely inspired, to advise him. After all, what did a widow know about politics, especially one determined to be walled into a cell where she could starve herself to death?

In the end, Dorothea won. As time passed, the dangers of the Wycliffe teachings became apparent in Bohemia, where the interests of the German Order were important, but Konrad of Jungingen was more impressed by the apparent accuracy and force of her predictions. A man of his time, he probably believed she was indeed a saint – and one who could reach out from her well-visited grave to help her friends and harm her enemies.

Though under pressure from the German master to suppress every thought and action which might have roots in Hussite ideas, Konrad of Jungingen could only see in the thoroughly German Dorothea a safely dead saint friendly to him who could divert thoughts and energies from present problems into mystical expression. Men and women who were going on pilgrimages were unlikely to be plotting uprisings or demanding change. Moreover, St Dorothea had an amazing effect even on her former enemies.

Many of the people closest to the saint, like the canons in Marien-werder, had been priests of the Teutonic Order; foremost of these was her biographer, Johann of Marienwerder. These individuals quickly won over some of her bitterest opponents by sharing her revelations about their personal lives: Konrad Corhusen, a hard man never known to shed a tear, obtained from her the highly prized ability to weep profusely, after which he withdrew into a purely religious community. The knight Jodocus, commander of Rehden, who had scoffed at St Dorothea's miracles, saw her in a dream reproaching him, and when he awoke he had a key in his hand which he could not release until he had visited her grave and repented of his sins. Many of the witnesses interviewed by clergy at the request of the grandmaster reported similar experiences. Lastly, she had warned the grandmaster that he would face four great dangers on his expedition into Samogitia – on the sea, on an island, at a castle, and in a forest – and Konrad of Jungingen believed this had come true in his 1394 campaign. Whatever tendencies towards Hussitism may have existed inside the order in 1390 vanished before the new century arrived, thanks at least in part to Dorothea of Montau's reviving traditional mysticism.

As a result of the predictions, the personal experiences, and the massive response of the local population to the cult of St Dorothea, the grandmaster and his bishops sought to have her declared a saint.

The formal process was begun in 1404; within two years 200 witnesses had been interviewed, and 300 miracles had been reported. But only slow progress was made, despite the waxing number of pilgrims who journeyed to Marienwerder; and over the centuries the matter of canonisation was taken to the popes again and again, without results – until 1976, when Pope Paul VI formally recognised the cult of St Dorothea of Montau.

Elisabeth of Marienwerder

St Elisabeth was not as well known as St Dorothea, understandably so, because she was only a simple nun, one of many intensely devout women who began demanding to be immured in a cell in the Marienwerder cathedral similar to the saint's. The canons had many duties to perform, one of which was to persuade these petitioners to go home to their families or stay in their nunneries. They had little time and perhaps less patience for the difficult task of separating the truly inspired from those who had become unbalanced or were caught up in mass hysteria. Elisabeth was first mentioned in 1404 by Catherine Mulner, who was then collecting documentation that Dorothea was performing miracles. Elisabeth was quietly reporting visions and warning individuals of dire fates they should avoid. Her influence on grandmasters Konrad and Ulrich was limited, perhaps because they were already well aware of the dangers of a 'great war'. Her visions lacked supporting details (such as when and where, as is common in such cases), so that their 'accuracy' was only recognisable after the fact.

Later grandmasters found her visions politically useful, especially the one remembered after the Battle of Tannenberg in which she saw Christ and Mary weeping profusely at the sight of the crusading army in defeat and Prussia being ravaged.

The Grandmaster's Quarrel with the German Master

In 1396 Konrad of Jungingen quarrelled with Konrad of Egloffstein, the German master. Since Germany produced almost all the knights and much of the order's money, the officers there were jealous of the great attention drawn to the fighting knights on the frontier. But the immediate crisis stemmed from the electors in the Holy Roman Empire, who were quarrelling over whether or not to replace Wenceslaus of Bohemia with Ruprecht of the Rhine, who had imperial blood in his veins from Friedrich II (Hohenstaufen) and Louis IV (Wittelsbach) and possessed an important territory – the Palatinate, north of Bavaria and stretching from the Rhine to Bohemia.

In Egloffstein's opinion, Germany was more important than
Bohemia for recruiting knights, seeking out crusaders and raising
money. The grandmaster, in contrast, believed that the Teutonic Order
had profited greatly from its long and close relationship with the
Luxemburg dynasty and would do so again. Even though Wenceslaus
of Bohemia was neglecting his duties and quarrelling with practically
everyone, the grandmaster could point to Sigismund of Hungary, a
promising monarch who was the only hope for stopping the advance
of the Turks in the Balkans and rescuing Constantinople. In addition,
Sigismund was known to the Poles, a fact that might become significant
for Prussia if the childless Jadwiga continued to undermine her
health with excessive fasts and prayer; Jagiełło was still an unpopular
foreigner, and there was no rival candidate in sight.

Rivalry was part of the dispute between the grandmaster and
German master, but the question was whether it was worse to suffer
longer under Wenceslaus or to risk civil war to remove him. This
issue had been under discussion for several years. The grandmaster
felt that he had good reasons for opposing the efforts by officers in
Germany to undermine the Luxemburg dynasty, good reasons that
the personal rivalry with Egloffstein only made more pertinent. It
had not helped him that Sigismund's claim to Poland diminished in
value in May 1395, when the pregnant Queen Maria died in a hunting
accident, making an unhappy end to an unhappy life. But it did help
when Sigismund turned his gaze to Bohemia, where Wenceslaus was
declining in health and popularity. Moreover, the emperor had no
male heir. The crown could devolve on Sigismund, seemingly any
day now.

Sigismund's Troubles and Triumphs

Wenceslaus's grant of the title of vicar of the Empire to Sigismund had
seemed to assume that Sigismund would eventually become emperor,
but the disaster at Nicopolis changed everything. He seemed to be
unlucky. Everyone admitted that Sigismund was genial, handsome
and intelligent. Everyone was impressed that he had mastered seven
languages and was eloquent in all of them. But he had no strong sense
of morality, no ability to manage money, and his military skills were
limited. It was clear he lacked sensitivity. Of course, he believed in
astrology. Everyone did. And he had a sexual magnetism that attracted
women. Just as girls and women of any era have thrown themselves at
athletes, musicians and politicians, the ladies and maids-in-waiting of
this time lusted to sleep with this attractive, powerful man.

Men could be found who would excuse his disaster at Nicopolis, but there were others, like Egloffstein, who thought that the Holy Roman Empire needed better leadership than that, and it needed it now – it needed German leadership, not Hungarian.

Removing an emperor was not easy, of course, and it would be dangerous for the Teutonic Order to support a challenge to Wenceslaus. Bohemia held numerous convents and hospitals belonging to the military order. Moreover, Wenceslaus, however inebriated he might be, was still emperor and the order's sovereign lord (a right and responsibility he shared with the pope). Then there was the matter of the Czech reformers, which the German master was more aware of than the grandmaster. Konrad of Jungingen could not please the emperor without antagonising the German master, and he could not satisfy the German master without angering Wenceslaus. He was caught in the middle.

In addition, family politics inside the Teutonic Order had severely hindered effective governance. There had always been some nepotism and abuse of power by important officials, who conducted business in ways which favoured their relatives, or even, as in the case of Johannes of Wallenrode, advanced them to high office. This was less noticeable in Prussia than in Livonia, and there less than in Germany. However, before the 1390s no one family had been able to dominate an entire region, and in order to guarantee that no one would dominate Prussia, the Teutonic Knights avoided recruiting members locally, concentrating instead on attracting knights from central and southern Germany.

Egloffstein's election represented a significant shift in the political balance in the German convents because his powerful Franconian family had contributed many sons to the order, and, since the clan was very capable and ambitious, it had many followers and admirers.

The heart of the dispute was the form that the Holy Roman Empire itself should take. First of all, there were many German princes who had feared that the growing power of the Luxemburg dynasty would lead to despotism. (Some nobles and towns were so afraid of even the comparatively impecunious Ruprecht that they formed a league to protect themselves against him.) Secondly, in the current scheme of things, eastern European affairs took precedence over German ones, especially over German concerns about the prolonged schism in the Church. When Wenceslaus supported his brother Sigismund, in his efforts to drive back the Turks, both were blamed for the débâcle at Nicopolis.

Similarly, Hungarian barons had wanted Sigismund to remove his foreign advisers. Sigismund weathered the crisis by confiscating the estates of his enemies and awarding them to his foreign friends. A little over a decade later he signalled the completion of this task by creating a special chivalric order for his nobles, the Order of the Dragon; thereafter everyone who hoped to be anyone in Hungary knew that admission to that order was the first step to promotion. But that was still far ahead, and meanwhile Sigismund had many problems to deal with.

His position was further undermined in 1400 when the German electors declared Wenceslaus deposed as Holy Roman emperor. Then, a year later, Sigismund was taken prisoner by rebels and held for six months. He obtained his freedom only by promising to marry Barbara, a daughter of the powerful count of Celje, whose cousin had recently married Jagiełło. In 1402 he 'sold' (pawned) the Neumark to the Teutonic Knights for 63,200 ducats to raise money for his armies. Such measures allowed him to improve the condition of the castles on his southern frontier and thereby discourage Turkish attacks.

Sigismund's New Adventures

Sigismund's marriage was not a love match, but neither had his alliance with Maria been. Marriage was a political arrangement. In Barbara's case, it assured him a base in Croatia that guaranteed Hungarian merchants could reach the Adriatic Sea, a means of intervening in Bosnia, and of securing communications to Italy. He also gained occasional access to one of the great fortunes of the era. However, Barbara was not one to waste money. She became an astute manager of estates and investments; year after year she added to her lands through pawn and purchase; she was able to give money to her spendthrift husband when he needed help most because she generally refused his requests.

Barbara had been so very young when the marriage was contracted that it was not consummated until 1406 or 1408, and it produced only one child, Elisabeth, born in late February 1409. But Barbara was a beautiful and talented woman in her own right. Her slim figure and snow-white skin, her sense of humour, her astute judgements of men and women, and her political skills made her a fitting companion for her handsome and gregarious royal husband. Sigismund, recognising that she had something worth saying, whether she was speaking in German, Hungarian, Czech, Polish or Latin, gave her an important role in the administration of his eastern lands. Unfortunately, Sigismund's prolonged absences and notorious philandering soon put the marriage under great strain. Sigismund had his own priorities, and his wife was low on the list.

Sigismund's most constant worry was the Angevin claim on the Hungarian crown that went back to 1308, when Charles Robert (Károly Róbert, 1288–1342) was invited to bring an end to a chaotic civil war; his grandmother had been a Hungarian princess, but the wealth and power of Naples may have been more important, and the connection of the two realms had never been fully severed. The current rival, Joanna II of Naples (1373–1435), had in fact been born in Hungary. She returned to Croatia briefly after Maria's death, where she found adherents to her cause. Croatia was filled with restive nobles who resented Hungarian domination – they disliked performing military service in Wallachia and Galicia, especially when they could see a Venetian threat on their coastline and the Turkish danger in Bosnia. In 1402 Joanna married Wilhelm of Habsburg, the same handsome youth who had courted Jadwiga; now he promised to fight for Joanna's right to rule Hungary. His Steierland possessions were perfectly located, lying as they did on the northern border of Croatia and to the west of Hungary. Unfortunately for him, his forces were too small to do anything except tip the balance in a closely contested fight; they were not sufficient to offset the advantages that the Celje family gave to Sigismund.

In 1403 Joanna sailed home to Naples, where she did not lack for titles – Queen of Jerusalem, Sicily, Croatia, Dalmatia, Bulgaria, countess of Provence, Piedmont, and other places – leaving her husband to do the best he could until his death in 1406. Wilhelm did very little, in fact, though if Sigismund had suffered another débâcle, he could have been dangerous. Sigismund, however, concentrated on Hungarian affairs until his rival was off the scene; without her Habsburg consort, Joanna II was no threat. Her later behaviour made her the central figure of tales of lewdness and cruelty that overshadowed even her predecessor as queen, Joanna I.

Wenceslaus, meanwhile, found himself in greater difficulties each year. His political sins were greater than simply wasting German resources in Hungary – he was suspected of complicity with the anti-German Hussite agitation in Bohemia. Ruprecht proposed to concentrate on German problems and the associated crises in Italy and with France. To keep eastern influences at a minimum, he proposed to return authority to the electors, who would see that no innovations disturbed the traditions of the Holy Roman Empire. Ruprecht's proposals were reflected in debates inside the Teutonic Order. The Egloffstein faction wanted to concentrate on preserving the wealth of the convents inside

Germany, and, if possible, expand their local holdings. This meant, in effect, that less money would be used to support the crusades in Prussia, Livonia and Hungary. Presumably the conversion of the pagans would be left to the Polish king, Jagiełło, who was not trusted by anyone in Prussia who had ever dealt with him. Still, Prussia was far from central Germany, and when they looked abroad German eyes were always on Italy.

Konrad of Jungingen found this approach to the crusade and to imperial policy totally unacceptable. Therefore, though he conceded Egloffstein's main point (that Ruprecht might be a better emperor), he tried in every way to reduce the influence of the new German master. He increased the number of administrative units in Germany, raising thereby the number of voting participants in the annual assembly, which made it more difficult for Egloffstein to obtain a majority. He took the administrative regions of Alsace, Swabia and Burgundy for his own financial exploitation. He allowed his own advisers, whose origins in the mountainous southern regions of Germany conflicted with the Main River families supporting the Egloffsteins and Ruprecht, to carry out policies benefiting their own families. Lastly, the grandmaster continued to maintain garrisons in Samogitia and to occupy Gotland until his death in 1407.

The result was predictable: the German master strove to defend his office, his supporters and his family. Tensions rose among the members, paving the way for future disputes, ultimately to a schism in the order. Nevertheless, many contemporaries believed that Konrad had displayed the most successful diplomatic and military skills of his era. He placated the Egloffstein faction by allowing them to speak in assemblies on Ruprecht's behalf, and he moderated his Gotland policy to fit Ruprecht's wishes. This latter concession, however, came only in a period when Wenceslaus was drawing close to Jagiełło; otherwise Konrad remained at heart an imperial loyalist, true to the Luxemburg dynasty.

Even so, when the electors removed Wenceslaus as emperor in 1400 and selected Ruprecht to be German king, the grandmaster acknowledged Ruprecht as the legitimate candidate to be crowned emperor. Later it became obvious that the Palatinate was an insufficient base to support an imperial presence in Italy, and since Ruprecht could not resolve the problems there, he could never persuade the pope to crown him emperor. Similarly, the problems of Germany were beyond his ability to resolve. Thus, Ruprecht's ambitions were already frustrated before his death in 1410. After the battle of Tannenberg that same year the Teutonic Knights had reasons to regret that they had not put their services at the command of Sigismund of Hungary earlier and less ambiguously. However, the prestige of the military order had never been higher, its possessions never more secure, never more extensive, than under this grandmaster's leadership. Some may have wondered if the finances were not overstrained, the population too heavily taxed, and the manpower spread too thin, but there was nothing to suggest that the problems could not be surmounted. Quite the opposite. In almost every way Konrad of Jungingen could have been proud of his achievements. He had won victories abroad while preserving peace and prosperity at home. Few politicians accomplish more.

Sigismund emerged from his troubles stronger too. His wife's family had secured Croatia and Bosnia for him, allowing him to deal with Hungarian problems, then, after 1406, providing access to Italy and Germany. As Ruprecht's star sank, Sigismund's rose. When the German electors looked around for a potentially effective emperor, they could not find a better candidate to replace the disreputable Wenceslaus than Sigismund. Whatever Sigismund's faults and shortcomings, he was a Luxemburg, he had in the Hungarian kingdom the means to support an Italian campaign, and he was too far from the German heartland to be a danger to the electors themselves. The fate of the Holy Roman Empire seemed to lie in Italy, where a divided Church – with one pope in Rome, another in Avignon – worsened the traditional political chaos. Italy was a helpless, attractive prize, or prey, to any prince with the strength and boldness to seize it.

Sigismund declared himself interested. He proceeded to win adherents south of the Alps, not with force – which would not have worked – but through his powers of seduction. In those he had few equals.

Chapter 3

The Samogitian Revolt

The End of the Samogitian Crusade

As the fourteenth century came to an end, so too, it seemed, would the crusade in Samogitia, informally, of course, since the annual call for volunteers was rarely authorised by the pope (or now, either of them). This point has been noted by critics, but practical people have long since recognised that the crusader states in the Holy Land had never asked permission to defend themselves or to conduct offensive warfare; nor had the Spanish monarchs; nor the Christian states facing the Turks. But what was the reason now to urge Christian warriors to hurry to the defence of Prussia?

The Grand Duchy of Lithuania had been Roman Catholic for fourteen years, with no sign of the rulers lapsing even into Orthodoxy, much less back into paganism. In an era of large states held together by trade and ever more complex administrative systems, it was not in the interests of the dynasty to encourage a revival of the old religion. Through their contacts abroad, Catholic prelates could aid in diplomacy and commercial exchange, and their experience in royal service enabled them to give valuable advice and assistance in governing.

In 1398 both Jagiełło and Vytautas had agreed that the long-disputed land of Samogitia should belong to the Teutonic Order. Moreover, they had assisted in occupying the main centres of resistance and promised to withhold any aid, moral or physical, to any warriors who continued to fight for the pagan gods. As a result, in early January 1401, the crusaders and knights of the military order observed a sight that justified for them all the generations of warfare:

> On the Sunday after Epiphany, the leading nobles of Samogitia came to Marienburg, allowed themselves to be baptised, and received the Christian religion. [We] sent with them some priests and monks who were to baptise their wives and children and teach them the Christian religion. Not long before, at their request and wish, the grandmaster had caused their children who were held as hostages to be baptised wherever they were kept, scattered here and there among the castles of the land.

Two decades after the formal conversion of Lithuania, Christianity seemed to be firmly established in the towns, at least to judge from the example of Grand Duke Vytautas, who had not wavered from his new faith. The Teutonic Knights still believed they had reason to mistrust him, though. He had betrayed them not once, but twice; and no one had forgotten the precedent of King Mindaugas, who had relapsed into paganism before being murdered. However, the intensity of that memory was fading.

In the summer of 1400 Vytautas visited Samogitia, while his wife, Anna, made a state visit to Prussia to pray at the shrines of St Catherine in Brandenburg, St Barbara in Aldenburg, and St Dorothea in Marienwerder. While her visit was primarily a pilgrimage, it had all the trappings of a great occasion: each stop along the journey was marked by a gala reception and the presentation of rich gifts. The tour was climaxed by an extravagant welcome at Marienburg in which Grandmaster Konrad of Jungingen outdid his legendary hospitality by an escort of 400 horsemen, then presenting her gifts and mementos. Among her escorts was Vytautas's younger brother, Žygimantas. It seemed as though he could cement a lasting friendship with the Lithuanian ruler.

Although the grandmaster entertained Anna with all the famous pomp and ceremony that the rules of his order allowed (there were limits on how much contact with women was permitted), he proceeded with plans to reorganise the administration of Samogitia. This involved changes in recognising as warriors only rich peasants who could afford armour and a horse – with everyone else paying taxes – appointing new leaders of the militia units, and changing the holders of minor offices. By winter many Samogitians were in open rebellion.

Meanwhile, the grandmaster was negotiating a final purchase of the Neumark from Sigismund of Hungary to replace the lease arrangement that could be revoked at the royal will. The Neumark and the associated territory of Stolp (Słupsk) in eastern Pomerania lay between Prussia and Brandenburg, so that the purchase of the Neumark and an alliance with the dukes of Stolp would secure the overland connection from Germany just as the occupation of Samogitia assured communications between Prussia and Livonia. Similarly, possession of Gotland and the alliance with the Hanseatic League guaranteed the security of the seaways. The Poles had looked at the Neumark as rightfully theirs, and so they keenly resented its sale to the grandmaster. However, Jagiełło was not yet secure on his throne, and so he cautiously refrained from provoking a confrontation that he was unlikely to win. It seemed that nothing could prevent the Teutonic Knights from acquiring a solid band of territories along the shores of the Baltic Sea that would make their position impregnable and deny Poland direct access to the Baltic.

This perhaps distracted attention from Samogitia, where the rebellion spread quickly. There were more Lithuanians in the garrisons than Germans, so the castles fell easily to well-organised uprisings.

Rebellion

The rising of 1401 began in March and was out of control by April. The Samogitians captured the castles at Kaunas and Friedeburg, taking the garrisons captive so that they could exchange them for the hostages held in Prussian castles. As the hostages heard the news, they reacted with mixed fear and pride, the first for their lives, the latter for the daring of their people. To free their families from indecision, two hostages in Thorn tore off their clothing, ripped it into strips, and hanged themselves. Presumably, officers in other locations took preventive steps to assure that they would have live captives to exchange, rather than corpses to send home for pagan cremations.

Unquestionably, the reaction of the Samogitian hostages demonstrates how unpopular German rule was. The Teutonic Knights were not worse rulers than most contemporaries, but the Samogitians had even resisted the efforts of Lithuanian rulers to impose order and taxation on them, and they would for ever remain famous for their independence of spirit and local patriotism. The Teutonic Knights' policy of '*lasset Preussen, Preussen bleyben*' ('let Prussians stay Prussian') was intended to make the landed warrior class feel respected and valued, but the knights were proud to an extent that encompassed arrogance. Such pride characterised noble demeanour everywhere; there was a swagger to a warrior's very words as well as his walk. German knights admired this. At the same time they did not need reminding of recent betrayals, or of friends who had perished when Samogitian garrison troops rose in near-perfect coordination across the entire country, with no word of warning.

Nor did Samogitians needed reminding of the crusaders' sword and fire campaigns, or the ancient feuds with clansmen who had gone over to the Germans, become Christians, and who now expected to be rewarded for their loyalty. In short, Samogitians needed no special reasons, at least no new ones, for hating the Teutonic Knights. The foreigners were there, in their homeland, and they wanted them gone.

The crisis expanded to Lithuania when some Samogitians fled there. According to the treaties, the Teutonic Knights argued, peasants went with the land and, therefore, the refugees should be returned to them. Vytautas retorted that this applied to peasants, but not to warriors. In any case, he said, the Germans were responsible for their own problems – if they had governed better, the people would not leave their homeland and come to him.

Vytautas added that he had not been party to the uprising in any way and promised to help the crusaders subdue the rebels, but Konrad of Jungingen nevertheless suspected him of having been somehow involved. Since Vytautas had ended his quarrels with Jagiełło in January 1401 and was guaranteed full possession of Lithuania and the undisputed title of grand duke, his alliance with the crusaders was more a convenience than a necessity. Later, in mid-May, when Vytautas went to Kaunas, the centre of the uprising, Polish knights were in his army. However, he held the castle only until his men could carry away the guns and equipment.

There seems to have been little, if any, resistance on the part of the Samogitians. This led to scepticism that Vytautas's professions of admiration and friendship for the military order were genuine. He could point to his expedition down the Nemunas River as proof that he was honouring his commitments, but the doubts remained. The grandmaster had to pretend still to trust the grand duke, but henceforth he chose to act alone.

Marshal Werner of Tettingen (*c.* 1350–1413) sailed up the Nemunas in September 1401 in hopes of frightening the rebels away from Kaunas and Gotteswerder (at Old Kaunas, where the Neris [Viliya] flows into the Nemunas). His many ships contained but few men, but they gave onlookers the impression of being a much larger force. He reached Gotteswerder unopposed and relieved the hard-pressed garrison there. He found Kaunas abandoned and burned.

The marshal learned that some Samogitians had remained loyal. Whether this was due to fear, cool calculation about the ultimate outcome of the war, desire for revenge upon local enemies, or religious persuasion is impossible to say. Not even the Samogitians could predict how all their fellow tribesmen would behave. When two rebel leaders serving in the garrison at Gotteswerder slipped away to warn Vytautas that the marshal's force was nearby, they went to a nearby village to ask where he was. However, instead of being helped to find the grand duke, one was slain by the tribesmen and the other only narrowly escaped capture. Vytautas's local commander, hearing of this, hurried with his men to take revenge on the traitors, who fled panic-stricken towards Prussia. He overhauled the fugitives and killed a few, but he lost some of his men too, and was unable to catch the rest.

The grandmaster was not certain how to deal with Vytautas. There was little doubt that the grand duke was not discouraging the rebels, but there was also the possibility that the grandmaster could keep Vytautas from moving closer to Jagiełło to make possible a joint intervention on the side of the insurgents. The grandmaster bought time by aiding Vytautas in an attack on Novgorod that winter, a move that benefited the Livonian Order. In addition, he refrained from making any accusations that could bring about a rupture of relations. Perhaps he hoped that Vytautas's difficult war over possession of Smolensk and control of Novgorod would make him realise that an alliance with the crusaders was more advantageous than drawing closer to Jagiełło. By winter this hope failed. In January 1402 Konrad of Jungingen decided that it was time for war with Lithuania again.

This was not a radical change in policy. Vytautas was a mercurial personality, whose next mood, whose next undertaking, could hardly be foreseen. Since 1386 grandmasters had been at war with him one moment, signing a peace treaty the next, making war again shortly afterwards. The only consistency was fluidity.

War with Lithuania

The adventures of Švitrigaila, Jagiełło's younger brother, are almost as amazing as they are obscure. A life-long enemy of Vytautas, whose lands he had once hoped to make his own, he saw himself as the representative of Orthodox interests. He had been deprived of Vitebsk by Jagiełło because his ties to the Livonian Order were too suspicious, then he had been defeated by Vytautas when he tried to regain his inheritance by force. Taken to Cracow in chains, he had agreed to go into exile in south-eastern Ruś; however, when Skirgaila died in 1396, Švitrigaila claimed that he was the heir to his lands. Defeated in that effort, he slipped away to Bohemia to scheme with Sigismund. Soon he was back in Ruś, where he fought for Vytautas at the battle of the Vorskla. Finally, he was in Cracow.

Residence at Jagiełło's court did not improve him – he was in too many ways his brother's opposite. He was brave beyond reason and 'staunch in battle', but he lacked patience, prudence and perseverance. In short, he was the kind of leader that hot-blooded young Lithuanian warriors loved. He hated Vytautas – who was like him in too many ways. He hated him so deeply that he refused to attend Jagiełło's wedding to Anna of Celje when he heard that Vytautas would be attending.

In fact, that wedding had not been a happy occasion for anyone – Jagiełło was disappointed in her looks, in her not knowing Polish, and in her inexperience. Anna had only the advantage of genealogy, belonging to the powerful Celje clan and being a granddaughter of Casimir the Great. For her part, Anna found the king repugnant; after all he was thirty years older and interested only in war and hunting. Jagiełło had more to worry about than his youngest brother's absence. This was a mistake.

On 31 January 1402, Švitrigaila appeared in Marienburg in the disguise of a merchant to offer his services to the grandmaster. He was too late to join the marshal's raid on Gardinas, deep in Vytautas's lands, but he promised that if the grandmaster would help him to recover his lands in southern Ruś, and support his claim to be the grand duke, he would allow the crusaders to govern their territories undisturbed, including Samogitia. Without hesitation he ratified the Treaty of Sallinwerder.

Grandmaster Konrad decided to put all his hopes on Švitrigaila. Without warning Vytautas, the Prussian and Livonian Knights struck simultaneously into Lithuania in March 1402; subsequently, they announced that Švitrigaila was henceforth recognised as the legitimate grand duke of Lithuania. There seemed to be some support for him among the boyars, though few were so rash as to express it openly. Konrad's decision was a coldly political calculation with no perceivable religious overtones. Perhaps a long-lingering desire for revenge, a memory of Vytautas's two acts of treachery, was Konrad's real reason; twice Vytautas had abandoned the crusaders to make common cause with Jagiełło, who had seemed at the time to be his death enemy.

Who could predict what any Lithuanian duke would do? Most of all, the grandmaster feared Vytautas's intrigues, his next reversal of policy. All his many enemies considered Vytautas unprincipled and untrustworthy, a dangerous foe to be put out of the way by any means, fair or foul. Konrad let Vytautas's many relatives know that they would be welcome in Prussia or Livonia at any time. He also knew from reports, especially from the reliable Marquard of Salzbach, that while Vytautas was immensely popular with most Lithuanian boyars, he had to take precautions against the rest, and against Švitrigaila. That was why Vytautas surrounded himself with a fiercely loyal Tatar bodyguard.

Marquard of Salzbach had become a major figure at court, a knight known for his prowess and sound judgement, and his knowledge of Lithuania was unmatched. He had lived at Vytautas's court while a prisoner and now spoke fluent Lithuanian. Vytautas liked him, and had entrusted him with diplomatic missions, and eventually released him. Marquard subsequently commanded the important castle at Ragnit (Neman, Ragainė), from which he had led a force of 1,600 men in support of Vytautas's 1399 campaign against the Tatars – he escaped the disaster with a handful of men, and perhaps saved the grand duke (or the other way around). Thereafter, however, his relationship with Vytautas was strained.

As for the grandmaster, his support of Švitrigaila reflected a time-tested tactic of backing rebels; he also rewarded lesser nobles who were willing to serve him. He did not think that Lithuanians were any less loyal or trustworthy than any other nationality – nobles often opposed their ruler. He had only to look at the unrest in Hungary and Wallachia to see the lengths to which political factions would go. Moreover, unstable political conditions tempted fearful, vengeful and ambitious individuals to betray their oaths. Lithuania was still a young state, one with tribal foundations, and few members of the ruling dynasty were immune to the call of ambition.

However, with Vytautas momentarily weak because of his failed Smolensk adventure, there was some hope that a coup would be supported. Vytautas had taken the city, but lost it in August 1401 to Prince Yury Svyatoslavich, who had put the governor and much of the garrison to the sword, then later, when Vytautas laid siege to the city, he had slain everyone suspected of pro-Lithuanian sentiments. When plague broke out in both the besieging army and the city, Vytautas accepted a truce and retreated. It appeared that the grand duke was vulnerable.

As a result, the grandmaster's meeting with Jagiełło in late May 1402 was noted for nothing more than some well-prepared meals, some enjoyable music, and a pleasant sail upon the Vistula. However, it was an important meeting in that it indicated the king was ready to negotiate personally rather than through intermediaries.

Vytautas struck back at the grandmaster by ravaging the environs of the castle at Memel (Klaipėda) in May, destroying the town and almost capturing the keep. Then he stormed Gotteswerder, carrying away the cannon and then burning the place. Clearly, he had learned to use the cannon captured earlier in Samogitia (and more that he had obtained from Poland). It was also proof that Švitrigaila's rebellion had failed.

Nevertheless, the Teutonic Knights did not give up. In July their grand commander (*Großkomtur*), Wilhelm of Helfenstein, led a huge force estimated by a contemporary chronicler at an unlikely 40,000 men towards Vilnius. (Forty generally meant 'many,') He remained on one bank of the river, ravaging and burning, while the Lithuanians kept pace on the opposite shore. The order's navy controlled the river, its galleys being too large for the Samogitians' canoes to challenge. The galleys also carried ample provisions, so the crusaders were not dependent on foraging. If Vytautas had attempted to protect both sides of the river, the crusaders would have been able to overwhelm whichever force seemed weaker.

Vytautas thus could do nothing but watch helplessly as one village after another went up in smoke – their inhabitants had presumably fled already. He did place a defensive force farther up the river that gave him time to rush to Vilnius and round up conspirators who might open the gates for Švitrigaila. The crusaders, not equipped to assault a well-defended city, retreated after learning that their friends had been beheaded.

In October 1402 there was an exchange of prisoners, captive knights for hostages. This was a great improvement over days when Christian prisoners were likely to end their days atop a grill, a sacrifice to pagan gods, and hostages dangled by the dozens from gallows at the crusaders' castle gates. This was a step towards peace, but only a small one.

Vytautas's rapprochement with Švitrigaila was a second step – he went south to an enlarged appanage in Podolia (in modern Ukraine).

The Teutonic Knights now ravaged the Lithuanian highlands almost without resistance. Crusaders from the Lower Rhine plundered from Trakai to Gardinas, destroying two major castles, then returned through miles of fields burned to deny them fodder for their horses. They carried away seventy-two nobles and 3,000 other captives during the thirteen-day raid, retreating via Kaunas down the Nemunas. The commander of Ragnit meanwhile raided Samogitia, joined by knights from Livonia.

Vytautas struck back in April 1403, first raiding Livonia, capturing the strategic fortress at Dünaburg (Daugavpils), then returned to the Nemunas Valley and took the lightly garrisoned castle at Georgenburg (Jurbarkas). He turned back from Ragnit only when he discovered that the marshal was waiting for him with an army of crusaders, some of whom had come all the way from Italy.

Negotiations for peace began, but meeting together was a long step from finding an agreement. In July 1403 the Lithuanian negotiators came to Marienburg to hear a proposal for a summit meeting on the Dubissa River (Dubysa) in September. Although again prisoners were exchanged, the negotiations almost collapsed because Marquard of Salzbach accused Vytautas of being an evil man and a traitor. The heralds took these accusations back to Vilnius. Although Marquard apologised so that the peace talks could resume, he proposed a formal duel, a joust, to settle the question of honour. He knew Vytautas well, and Vytautas knew Marquard's skill as a warrior. The grand duke did not lack for courage, but he was not foolish enough to believe that he could prevail in a sport he had never trained for. The joust was never mentioned again, but honour was satisfied. Negotiations resumed.

In September the grandmaster went with some bishops and priests to the Dubissa River, a tributary of the Nemunas, where he was joined by the Livonian master. However, Jagiełło and Vytautas did not appear. The grandmaster then offered the Samogitians one inducement his opponents could not meet: food. The Samogitian harvest had failed that summer, as was the case in the Baltic every few years, and the Teutonic Knights were shipping large quantities of grain to feed those natives who had surrendered. With little doubt, the success of the crusaders in winning over starving natives was not lost on the grand duke and the king.

Vytautas, meanwhile, was concentrating on Smolensk. In 1403 he sent Jagiełło's brother, Lengvenis (c. 1360–c. 1431) to Viazma, where he captured two rebel leaders and delivered them to the grand duke.

(Lengvenis, once governor of Novgorod, had married Basil I's sister in 1394; hence, he was an important man, trusted by both sides.) In early 1404, Vytautas summoned Lengvenis and Švritrigaila to assist him in what became a seven-week siege of Smolensk. He did not capture the city outright, but while the rebel prince was in Moscow to plead for help from Basil, his boyars surrendered the city. Vytautas executed everyone who refused to give an oath of loyalty, then exiled others to scattered locations in Lithuania where he could watch them.

It was not until May 1404, when Konrad of Jungingen met Jagiełło at Racianz (Raciąż), just west of Gardinas, that a breakthrough in negotiations was achieved. This was due in part to the grandmaster's willingness to renounce claims on Dobrin, a strategic province just south of Thorn which had belonged to Płock. This small land thus was part of Masovia, then ruled from Warsaw by Vytautas's brother-in-law, Duke Janusz of Masovia.

Recently Janusz had given aid and refuge to Samogitian rebels. When the Teutonic Knights besieged and captured one of the frontier posts suspected of being a base for raids, they found the Masovian duke among the prisoners they had taken. When the grandmaster released him from captivity, the way was open for a renewal of the Sallinwerder treaty. Vytautas may not have been present throughout the meeting, because he denounced the terms that Konrad and Jagiełło had agreed upon. His stubbornness provoked the spokesmen of the Teutonic Order, especially Marquard of Salzbach, to accuse him of deceit. As mutual accusations flew, Marquard made insulting remarks about Vytautas's parentage, even disparaging the virtue of his murdered mother. This was an insult that the grand duke could not overlook – Biruté had been a beautiful and powerful woman, a former pagan priestess of noble ancestry.

Jagiełło broke the impasse by ordering Vytautas to give way. The grand duke pled his case to the king in a tearful voice, but in August he came to Ritterswerder near Kaunas for the formal confirmation of the treaty.

Interestingly, Vytautas's mistrust of his royal cousin was still such that he asked the grandmaster to protect his wife's interests in the case of his death. The grandmaster responded with a promise to do everything possible – it was not in his interest to have Lithuania and Poland united under one hostile ruler. Indeed, when Anna died in 1418, requiem masses were held in all the churches of the Teutonic Order despite the vastly changed relationship of the grand duke and the grandmaster's successor by that time.

The relationship of the three rulers was undoubtedly more com-plicated than surviving records indicate, but any effort to interpret events against that background is likely to be misleading. Misinformation is not a modern invention, nor is play-acting. Lithuanians were much more creative and versatile in their politics than the monkish officers of the Teutonic Knights, who were themselves famous for their subtle and sly diplomacy.

Crusader Victory in Samogitia

The resistance of the Samogitians slowly melted away once they lost the backing of the king and grand duke. Told by Jagiełło and Vytautas to cease fighting, most of the rebels laid down their arms and accepted the Teutonic Knights as lords. When some did not, Vytautas and the new Prussian marshal, Ulrich of Jungingen (1360–1410), joined forces in January 1405 to subdue them.

Winter was usually a good time of the year for campaigning in the swampy lowlands of Samogitia, since the rivers and lakes were transformed into ice highways and it was easier to follow the footsteps of cattle and people to their hiding places. 1405 had a warmer winter than anyone could remember, with no snow, but it was apparently still cold enough to allow the armies to move around easily, forcing captives to give hostages.

The crusaders returned in July to build a wooden castle named Neu Königsberg, leaving behind a garrison of sixty Prussians and 400 Lithuanians. In September the marshal brought in supplies, accompanying the transport with a large army. Nevertheless, the last rebels held out. When they felt safe to do so, they attacked the new castle, advancing into the ditches under the cover of large shields. The garrison waited with cannons and crossbows at the ready. When the Samogitians reached the walls, the defenders rose up to mow them down in masses, then sallied out to kill or capture great numbers of the routed rebels.

This was the decisive blow. In the winter of 1405/6 the last Samogitians surrendered and brought in hostages to guarantee that they would not take up arms again. Konrad of Jungingen rebuilt some of the castles and named a new governor for Samogitia, the genial Michael Küchmeister of Sternberg (c. 1360–1423), whose experience had largely consisted of acting as a supply officer, most recently in Königsberg, where he had organised peasant labour, supervised commerce, and overseen tax collection. He was now expected to introduce western farming practices to the former pagans by bringing together the scattered farmers and serfs onto manors, teaching them how to plough with teams of oxen, weed the fields collectively, and to share the harvest. Introducing the three-field system was essentially collectivised agriculture and about as popular.

The Teutonic Knights argued that the standard of living would eventually be higher for all concerned, but that was irrelevant to the Samogitian anger at the accompanying change in social status – Samogitians believed that a real man was a warrior. It did not matter that the poorer warriors herded cattle and horses and grew only a bit of rye; they still thought of themselves as potential boyars. Though they were far below the boyar class in Russia, or even Poland, they refused to be mere peasants.

Küchmeister was not about to entrust expensive animals and equipment to such people without guarantees. He moved the poorer free farmers into villages and collected hostages. From those he classified as boyars he expected only regular military service, but he took hostages from them as well. Vytautas did not protest at any of this. What happened in Samogitia was no longer his business, he said. But when the Samogitian boyars proved reluctant to join the order's forces for the grand duke's march on Moscow, Vytautas told Küchmeister to spread the word that it was his wish that they render military service in this campaign. The warriors then appeared at the mustering places on time. That episode left no doubt who the real ruler of Samogitia was.

Grandmaster Konrad's relationship with Jagiełło remained tense as well. Both declared that they wanted a further reconciliation, but neither was willing to renounce legitimate claims to minor territories in Great Poland. On the one side Polish nationalism was inflamed, on the other the Teutonic Order's pride was tested. Vytautas, who needed help from both parties, attempted to mediate.

The Teutonic Order paid off its debt to Vytautas by assisting him in military expeditions in 1406, first against Pskov and Novgorod, then a fifteen-week campaign against Basil I, who had been invited to become overlord of Novgorod. Prominent in the forces sent into Ruś were the experienced Count Friedrich of Zolr, commander of Ragnit, and Michael Küchmeister, the governor of Samogitia. Polish knights sent by Jagiełło fought alongside the Germans, Lithuanians and Samogitians. The Ruśian chroniclers blamed the war on the rash counsel of young warriors, who had neither sense nor experience, and on the clever intrigues of the Tatar khan, Edigu (1352–1419), who now led a great horde that ruled from the Crimea to the Ural Mountains. He promised to aid Basil in subduing the other princes, then spread suspicion about Vytautas's motives. Very likely the chroniclers were correct: it is rarely a mistake to credit the Tatar khans with great skill in war and diplomacy.

Edigu soon arranged for Tokhtamysh's assassination – revenge for his having murdered Edigu's father – and he himself would eventually die at the hands of one of Tokhtamysh's sons. Steppe politics were ruthless.

It was only marginally better in Ruś. War brought in its wake plague, famine and unrest. Amid signs and portents, the armies slaughtered the population of one another's lands, storms devastated harvests, and important churchmen died. In the minds of the chroniclers all these events were closely connected. God was punishing Ruś for the sins of its rulers.

The Roman Catholic presence in Vytautas's armies, especially the Livonian Order's assistance in his 1406 campaign against Pskov and the presence of Polish priests, disturbed the grand duke's Orthodox vassals. This was on top of Vytautas replacing prominent boyars with members of his family or his officials. One by one important vassals began to defect to Basil I of Moscow.

A New Grandmaster

Konrad of Jungingen died in early 1407. It was not unexpected. He had been in poor health for some time. Tettingen was selected by the Council to govern the order until the electors could be assembled on St John's Day (24 June), and summons went out to Germany and Livonia. The electors' choice was the marshal, Ulrich of Jungingen, Konrad's younger brother. Ulrich's career in Prussia had already spanned twenty years, so that he was neither inexperienced nor youthful. Yet there was something about him that has always reminded historians of a teenage hot-head. Undoubtedly, this judgement reflected later events. Ulrich actually involved his order in fewer wars than his brother had, and when Ulrich did make war, he was relatively well-prepared. However, one could properly say that he was less wise than Konrad. At least, less patient.

Konrad had ignored Jagiełło's increasingly provocative activities, especially Polish scouts and hunting parties crossing the poorly marked border in the wilderness. Some of that was a side effect of the king's effort to improve communication with Lithuania, building roads and castles, clearing obstacles to river traffic; these were clear threats to Prussian interests. More to the point, however, as the king felt more secure on the throne, he was becoming more willing to respond to requests by hot-headed patriots that he do something about the arrogant knights on the kingdom's northern border – the purchase of Neumark had been a provocation, but the order's influence in Masovia was an outrage. In fact, the very existence of the order's state was felt by many to be a violation of Poland's natural frontiers on the Baltic Sea. Although hardly anyone remained alive who could remember Poland's last war with the Teutonic Knights (1339, followed by the Peace of Kalisch [Kalisz] in 1343), everyone had heard stories of past conflicts.

Ulrich of Jungingen's response was to make peace with Queen Margaret and pull his forces out of Gotland. He tried to keep the friendship of Vytautas by assisting in his Rusian campaigns, and he increased the rate of pacification in Samogitia. What he was thinking and what his council advised are difficult to separate. Prussia was not a monarchy, so the grandmaster could not adopt policies contrary to the advice of the experienced men who sat in Königsberg, Balga (Veseloye), Elbing, Danzig and Marienburg. In the past these men had helped minimise potential conflicts. Now, perhaps because they could see that Jagiełło was clearly in charge of Polish policy, they remembered stories from their youth, when the name Jagiełło was synonymous with deception, guile and betrayal.

In short, the grandmaster emphasised the alliance with Vytautas. As long as the grand duke was busy in Ruś, he would not take much notice of Samogitia and the Neumark. Poles might mutter or bluster that they should have got more land back from Prussia in 1404 than Dobrin, but Jagiełło would do nothing without Vytautas' help. This cautious approach seemed all the more correct when Švitrigaila went over to Moscow in 1408.

Švitrigaila had perhaps been inspired to treason by the powerful duke of Starodub, who had shared his prison cell after plotting to kidnap the grand duke. Both were released about the same time and both quickly joined Basil. Švitrigaila was given the important region of Vladimir to rule – in effect about half of Moscow's territory. In that same year Vytautas marched on Moscow. As Posilge, one of the order's better chroniclers, summarised it:

In this year in the summer Witold [Vytautas] made a great expedition against the king of Moscow, and our lords sent many knights with him, and the king of Poland a huge force. And with them went many princes, counts, knights and soldiers. They went an immense distance towards the said king, but they accomplished nothing and had to retreat to safety. On the return the vast distances and poor roads wore out the horses. When they could no longer carry the weapons, they threw some into deep water, burned others, and buried others; and thus, having left horses and weapons behind, they were barely able to escape by foot.

Vytautas was not dismayed by the setback any more than his love for his daughter hindered his making war on her husband. The next year, perhaps at his instigation, the Tatars ravaged all the possessions of Moscow from one end to the other. Rusian chroniclers denounced the faithless and cruel pagans, mocked the confusion and flight of Švitrigaila's *brave* warriors when confronted by the steppe horsemen, then bemoaned the sins of their own dukes.

Švitrigaila, who could read the signs of the times as well as anyone, switched back to Vytautas at the right moment. However, he was unable to change his character; within a year, he was detected communicating with the grandmaster. When Vytautas saw the letters, he threw his cousin in prison again, this time to hold him prisoner for nine years. It apparently never occurred to Švitrigaila that anyone who would enter into a conspiracy might also be swift to change sides when it was to his advantage, or even be a double agent. Jagiełło did not complain. His brother was lucky to be alive.

Despite Vytautas's successes, it was becoming clear that all was not well in his realm. Moreover, he was unhappy with the grandmaster's complaints about his seeming encouragement of Samogitian rebels, his support for the rebellious citizens of Riga and the bishop of Dorpat, and his imprisonment of Švitrigaila. Vytautas and Marquard of Salzbach ended a conference in 1408 shouting at one another. The grand duke realised that his hold on power was far less secure than it had been.

Vytautas made peace with Basil, then drew closer to Jagiełło, perhaps anticipating an opportunity to settle accounts with the crusaders. He visited Samogitia once in the winter of 1409, twice in the spring. Clearly, something was going to happen. Since he would not back down, the grandmaster had to, or else.

Crusader Government in Samogitia

The Teutonic Knights, meanwhile, seemed to be oblivious to what Vytautas was doing. Ulrich of Jungingen and his advisers apparently believed that he needed their military assistance so badly that he would overlook whatever disagreements they might have. That was Ulrich of Jungingen's first mistake, but it was not to be his last. He was new to responsibilities, but he was confident in his ability to manage them. Not for him the quiet and cautious policies of his elder brother.

Arrangements to transform Samogitian society had proceeded slowly, for it was a larger land than the handful of men at the advocate's disposal could supervise. Michael Küchmeister was a competent manager, not a warrior; as such he seemed the perfect man to introduce modern agricultural methods to poor farmers. Also, his linguistic ability was notable – he knew Lithuanian so well that he could speak to Samogitians without an interpreter.

Although Vytautas boasted of Samogitia as the breadbasket of Lithuania, farming practices there were backward. Cattle were the basis of the local economy. In the past crusaders had so little regard for the value of the crops that they had rarely bothered to attack during the harvest; instead, they had concentrated on driving away the herds. When the Samogitian nobles came to Marienburg in 1407, the grandmaster persuaded them to ask to be governed by Culm law, which was used for the German immigrants in Prussia, and not by the less advantageous Prussian treaties, which were designed to allow agriculturally backward peoples to continue their outmoded techniques. When the Samogitians complained that they could not pay the higher taxes, despite the greater amount of land distributed through this law to each freeman, he arranged for them to be excused for three years from payment of that tax and the special border defence tax. Moreover, he saw to it that oxen and ploughs were brought into the country, so that the three-field system could be introduced.

One could hardly expect that the native population would give thanks for the advocate's efforts. This was, after all, only a step towards restoring some of the prosperity that had been destroyed by crusading expeditions. Long ago agriculture had been better established in Samogitia than in the highlands, but now the reverse was true. Nor could anyone fail to notice that military service was being required from fewer warriors, and that they were the men who received the gifts of fine cloth and salt.

All other free men were relegated to the role of taxpayers, expected somehow to make their traditional beekeeping, hunting, herding and fishing provide an excess beyond that needed for their families' subsistence until they could learn the skills of grain farming. When called to perform military service they were assigned to carry equipment, or, perhaps, to mow the hay and bring in the boyars' harvests as was already customary in Lithuania.

Ulrich of Jungingen took a great personal interest in Samogitia, becoming ever more intrusive. He disliked buying loyalty with gifts. Power and prestige, he seemed to reckon, would impress primitives more. He listened to his marshal, Friedrich of Wallenrode (the younger brother of the late grandmaster and the current archbishop of Riga), and less to Küchmeister.

Jagiełło saw opportunity here. He was taking up the patriotic maxim that Pomerellia (West Prussia) was by right Polish land; and he wanted it, wanted it even more than he wanted any other land that had ever been associated with or belonged to Poland (which, as far as the more extreme patriots were concerned, amounted to the same thing). The same was true about the Neumark. Vytautas, as far as Jagiełło was concerned, was too narrowly focused on Lithuania. One had to think large, to keep Poland, Lithuania, and Ruś – and more – in mind, and to think of ways to obtain one's goals without taking risks. Vytautas was much too ready to grasp the sword and slash away at his enemies.

Jagiełło knew that marriages and dynastic claims worked better than war, and that he could achieve more through enemies' mistakes than through his own cleverness. Earning trust was essential to Jagiełło's policies, but that was difficult to achieve, given the betrayals that had brought him to power. Ever since, he had been working to win over sceptics and doubters, Vytautas most of all. Nevertheless, there was reason to believe that the king had not reformed completely. He was eager to have the crusaders preoccupied with Samogitia, and he was jealous of Vytautas, whose exploits had won the hearts of his subjects and who, he feared, would rob him yet of the opportunity to rule over his homeland.

He reminded Vytautas that giving Samogitia to the Germans had been a mistake. At the same time he called on the pope to support crusades against the eastern Christians, which would involve the Livonian Order in wars with Novgorod; and he encouraged ventures that could result in the Teutonic Order being sent to fight the Turks. These proposals from Jagiełło's sophisticated and clever Polish advisers were like a double-edged sword, the one edge weakening Prussia, the other protecting Poland's south-eastern borders.

Ulrich of Jungingen met Jagiełło and Vytautas in Kaunas in January 1408, holding secret talks amid great public festivities and chivalric display. Nevertheless, he did not trust Vytautas. He knew the day would come when the Samogitians would have to pay the full tax, and tithes as well, and that day would probably be marked by armed resistance which would call on the grand duke for help. Therefore, he prepared for war, abandoning the old castle at Neu Königsberg and building new castles at Friedeburg and Tilsit (Sovetsk) near Ragnit. In 1409 he began to expand the fortifications of Memel. Those costs born down heavily on Prussia, and the grandmaster lacked enough troops to garrison the castles properly. He had established a new government, but its reach did not go into the hinterland or affect daily life significantly.

He rebuilt the fortress at Ragnit too. Already in 1403 the foundations of a new stone and brick fortress had reached a point where the old earth and wood castle could be torn down. Engineers had brought stone from Königsberg, cut wood locally, baked bricks nearby, and hauled limestone from Gotland for mortar. A small mountain of nails, 5,000 pounds of white glass, and even a few small panes of coloured glass went into the construction. A dam was built nearby for the moat and a mill. The work was not completed until 1409, but long before that Ragnit was the most modern fortress on the frontier, a square convent-like brick structure with an impressive keep and a fine *Danzker* (a tower-like toilet facility beyond the walls). Ragnit lacked nothing for comfort or defence. Moreover, it was not quickly outmoded by technology. If the grandmaster could build more fortresses of this type, the order's hold on the frontier would be unbreakable. Nevertheless, he did not rely on brickwork as much as on his field army, which had not been beaten in living memory, and his diplomacy was based on the ability to use this army effectively.

Aside from the Samogitian question, there seemed to be no good reason for peace not continuing. At times the Teutonic Order seemed ready to accept the king and grand duke as Christian monarchs rather than secret pagans. However, there were suspicions that the traditional double game was being played by all sides with more than the usual vigour and enthusiasm. Ulrich of Jungingen, who certainly had contacts in both courts, may have believed that someday he would have to settle matters with his order's old enemies; but he assumed that he would be able to deal with them one at a time.

Whenever the grandmaster made an incautious statement, it was undoubtedly quickly reported to Vilnius and Cracow; Ulrich probably relied upon that. It was always possible to deny a spy's report, or say that he was misunderstood; but it got his message out. However, it is easier to start rumours than to control them, or to counteract their impact later; and Ulrich was dealing with proud and sensitive men.

Ulrich had been in Prussia for twenty years, holding responsible offices much of that time; but he still seemed to lack the *gravitas* of a grandmaster. Moreover, since he was not an absolute ruler, his efforts to sway his knights towards more aggressive policies met with resistance regarding the Samogitian crisis.

The Growth of Trade

Many people believed that the way to peace and prosperity, and ultimately, the conversion of the pagans, was through international trade. One of the attractions of paganism, especially for young men without the means to establish themselves as householders or even boyars, had been its encouragement of warfare against Christian neighbours. Young men could count on a share of the booty and prisoners, more established warriors could expect grants of land and serfs. The less militant aspects of paganism – superstition (as moderns generally think about predicting the future from the flight of birds or throwing sticks), traditional rituals for birth, death, achieving manhood or the age to marry, or marriage – could often be accommodated with Christianity, with the exception of cremation (which priests considered a sign that the deceased had died a pagan) and polygamy. These were all obstacles, but none so great that it could not be overcome. Some difficulties were expected from pagan priests who warned that their gods would be displeased; certainly, there would be resistance from women whose status would decline from wife to concubine. But more important was the instinctive hatred of being ruled by outsiders.

The Germans may not have been the worst foreign rulers in the history of the world (not as long as there were Tatars), but Samogitians believed that they would be better off under fellow Lithuanians. Still, even rule from Vilnius by men who spoke their language was less desirable than self-government.

There was little the Teutonic Knights could do about being foreigners. But they could provide some of the products that hitherto were available only through war, and by providing an outlet for Samogitian produce, they would encourage the development of peaceful skills that hopefully would eventually supplant the ancient military ones that were associated with paganism. Christianity had to be patient, the knights believed, though it was as hard to persuade the popes of this as it was to convince the Samogitians of the necessity to change.

German merchants had long made their way through Poland into southern Ruś, through Livonia to Pskov and Polotsk, and via the Gulf of Finland to Novgorod; now they followed the Nemunas River past Samogitia into central Lithuania. However, their trade with the Samogitians never became significant. The treaty of 1390 had opened border traffic, allowing the Samogitians to visit markets in Memel,

Ragnit and Georgenburg, but the unpredictability of local politics – war, peace, war again, and finally a tenuous peace – discouraged western merchants from risking their lives and property there.

Likewise, the treaty of Sallinwerder had promised freedom of travel and exemption from new customs duties, but this, too, had little effect. Surviving records from the era indicate only a small increase in the number of merchant ships sailing to Ragnit: nine in 1374, thirteen in 1379, thirteen in 1402, and sixteen in 1407. Merchants tended to go farther north, to Riga, where citizens had enjoyed mercantile rights in Lithuania since 1323.

Long standing ties gave Rigan merchants in Vilnius great advantages over those from Prussia. Many commercial treaties testify to the importance of the Riga–Polotsk trade to Vytautas and his subjects. Nevertheless, the Nemunas River was a more convenient route into central Lithuania for bulk cargo such as western grain and salt, than bringing cargo on small boats first up the Narew River from the Vistula, then through the braided channels of the lake district to streams flowing towards Lithuania. Even Jagiełło sent bulk supplies to Vytautas through the crusaders' lands, down the Vistula and up the Nemunas.

Still, the records on river traffic kept at Memel indicate that small boats were most common, craft suitable only for protected waters. The Baltic Sea was dangerous, especially the Curonian Lagoon (Kurisches Haff) at the mouth of the Nemunas – which was known as 'the wild gulf.' Ships were lost there every summer; and winter ice stopped sailing between late autumn and early spring.

Because it was necessary to send supplies and trade goods from Königsberg to the Nemunas River valley, the order's officers were intrigued by the number of watercourses flowing into the Pregel (Pregoła) River, streams that were navigable almost to tributaries of the Nemunas. That suggested the possibility of linking the two rivers by canals. Before 1376 the engineers of the Teutonic Order had completed a small canal along the Deime (Deyma) River east of Königsberg to Labiau (Polessk); in 1395 they deepened and widened this waterway and installed locks. They also proposed extending the Deime canal to the Gilge River, which would have made it almost forty miles long. However, only a third of the work was finished by 1410, after which there was no money available. Another canal, from Labiau to the Nemunas, a distance of only eleven miles, was started in 1409, and by the summer of 1410 three miles were completed. It was not finished for many years, but eventually it became a major trade route.

Merchants needed more than convenient routes; they had to have towns and markets as well; and the Teutonic Order did what it could to provide them. This, too, was in the interest of Vytautas, who in 1408 founded a town at Kaunas, giving the German merchants there permission to live and trade under Magdeburg law. He also allowed them to build a warehouse/hostel complex to distribute their goods up all the rivers that converged on Kaunas like spokes on a wheel.

Magdeburg law differed sufficiently from the law codes of Culm and Lübeck commonly found in Prussia that the Kaunas merchants were less likely to feel part of the Hanseatic League or an extension of the merchant communities in Vilnius and Riga. Also, the burghers would pay the grand duke taxes and provide goods at lower prices. The Teutonic Knights were apparently not consulted. Later, Danzig merchants complained that they were being required to deliver salt in bulk quantities rather than in barrels, which resulted in them being eliminated from more lucrative retail sales. That was a technical matter, not a cause for a fundamental change in policy; therefore, Jungingen did nothing about it.

Vytautas did not have to worry about the citizens of Kaunas being mostly Germans because that did not mean they shared the interests of the Teutonic Order, as the long friendship between the Lithuanians and the rebellious burghers of Riga demonstrated. Though few in number, the new settlers of Kaunas exercised an effective monopoly over local trade, which they owed to the special privileges granted by the grand duke. The Lithuanian boyars did not react strongly against this, nor against the new taxes.

For years the Teutonic Knights had lured Samogitian warriors to Prussia, giving them lands exempt from taxes in return for military service and duties such as tax collection. Those petty nobles, first of all, escaped death and destruction by crusading armies and local rivals; second, they could look forward to returning to Samogitia some day to take up larger estates with more serfs. Necessity and opportunity thus went hand in hand. Taxes were ultimately paid by commoners, who were relatively unimportant in political or military matters.

This policy failed in Samogitia because the grandmaster introduced the taxes in a famine year. Combined with the exclusion of poor warriors from the boyar class, and possibly Vytautas's manipulation of the general discontent, followed by the interruption of the import of grain, the taxes provoked an uprising of 1409.

Starving peasants sought to flee to Lithuania, hoping for food and recognition of their boyar status. Meanwhile, an unnamed prominent

Lithuanian noble visited Samogitia (without his permission, Vytautas said) and gave advice on how to organise the revolt. When the order's diplomats complained, Vytautas is said to have roared that the knights of the Teutonic Order had no proper homeland, but had taken lands which once belonged to Lithuania, and that he was ready to take Königsberg from them and drive them into the sea.

The Teutonic Knights needed several years of peace for their policies to work, but peace was always just out of reach; and the only way they could sustain their war effort was by collecting taxes and requiring their subjects to perform military service. Vytautas found it easy to stir resentment into rebellion.

Failure to Convert the Samogitians

The military order's administration did not reach far inland from the castles along the Nemunas River. Officials dared not settle among their new subjects or even travel except in large parties. With armed resistance never completely stamped out, and Vytautas alternately encouraging rebels and assisting in the suppression of new uprisings, the grandmaster and his officers were in no position to insist that the Samogitians listen to missionaries, much less undergo baptism.

Not only did canon law forbid forcible conversion, but most missionaries realised that it was a vain gesture. If the Samogitians (or, more to the point, the Samogitian women) continued pagan practices in the household or in their rural communities, who was to know? But also it was too dangerous to do anything more than cut down the trees in sacred woods (and then usually only in the company of Vytautas). Only after the Samogitians had become accustomed to paying annual taxes, to working on fortifications, to serving in the army, might it be safe to insist on conversion. One had to be far away – say, in Rome – to believe that this was going to happen soon.

There was a shortage of Lithuanian-speaking friars and priests. Even in Vilnius, Jagiełło had initially done little beyond building a private chapel for the court and for foreign merchants. It took two years after he appointed a bishop before Polish and German Franciscans and Benedictines were able to organise seven parishes around Vilnius and establish a few schools to train native youths for the priesthood. Many years passed before the new priests established parishes in the Lithuanian highlands, where the boyars were always eager to please their lord (even when some preferred Orthodox Christianity).

Vytautas was often present personally to see that religious instructions were obeyed, but he was satisfied with superficial conformity.

In his frequent visits to Samogitia he was even more easily satisfied. Thus, there was little reason for Samogitians to take their new religious orientation seriously. A friar or two in the castles, a chaplain accompanying the advocate on his rounds, were hardly likely to make any significant number of conversions.

The polite refusal of the Teutonic Order to pressure its bishops to move more aggressively in sending missionaries into Samogitia was probably wise. Hard-core pagans were known to be extremely dangerous. Nor was their sentiment exclusively anti-German: when the first group of Lithuanian-speaking priests entered Samogitia under Vytautas's protection in 1413, they confined their activities to the churches in the few fortified centres. As soon as they tried to collect taxes and tithes, outraged peasants forced them to flee for their lives. The bottom line was *no new taxes.*

The grandmasters adopted a hands-off policy, satisfied to have pacified the country, to have ended the raids into Livonia and Prussia, and to have eroded the prestige of pagan priests who promised that the ancient gods would provide military victories and great booty. They knew that at any moment the discontents could flare into revolt and war. They had seen it happen before, and they knew it could happen again. Therefore, they proceeded slowly and carefully, conferring often with Vytautas, for everything depended on his good will.

If the grand duke remained true to the Roman faith, the Samogitians would eventually accept their fate. But if a Samogitian rebellion spread into the highlands, he might have to choose between joining the rebels and assassination. That had been the fate of King Mindaugas in the thirteenth century, and the knights were well aware of how he first abandoned Christianity, then was murdered by a rival, thanks to the practice of having the order's chronicles read aloud at the evening meal. There was no point in risking the loss of Samogitia by hurrying into a missionary effort which could not be properly staffed. Let distant clergy complain if they wished. The knights of the military order were accustomed to ignoring them.

Conditions in Prussia

Despite the tensions with Poland and Lithuania, the Teutonic Knights could be very satisfied with their status in early 1409. Jungingen could take pride in the completion of his order's historic task: bringing Christianity to the Baltic, most recently to Samogitia. In recent years his knights had beaten every foe to challenge them. They had an enviable international reputation among the cream of west European chivalry and their castles, chapels and cathedrals were admired by connoisseurs. Moreover, the discipline and morale inside the convents had never been higher.

The advanced conditions in the Prussian state may be judged fairly by two rather insignificant details. The first was the number of clocks. The purpose of the clocks was principally to regulate the hours for prayer, so that the bells could be rung to summon the friar-knights, priests and servants to worship; naturally, the businessmen and artisans of the towns came to rely upon the ringing of the hours too. In the dark winter months of Prussia telling time was more difficult than during the long summer days. Consequently, it was surely the priests who persuaded the convent officers to introduce mechanical clocks into the dayrooms and even to mount huge clock faces upon the towers. The time rang out automatically, announcing the hours, so that in the correspondence one often finds phrases like, 'finished just as the clock struck seven'.

The second was the issuing of gold coins. First struck in 1394 in Danzig, the *Gulden* made the payment of international debts easier. In place of the relatively heavy and cumbersome *Pfennige* (pennies), *Halbschroter*, and *Schillings* was a small and handsome coin which could circulate easily abroad. How many gold coins were struck in subsequent years cannot be determined – only two examples survived the melting pots of later generations – while the silver coins, most importantly, the *Schilling* – are so common that almost any modern collector can afford them. The records of the Teutonic Order, so excellent in many ways, did not extend to supervising the private enterprises of the minters. These artisans were merely obliged to provide a specific number of uniform coins of full weight from each amount of silver given to them, a financial arrangement not entered into the account books.

We learn from the treasurer's book in Marienburg that between 1399 and 1409 the bell founder in the city was manufacturing cannons by the lost wax process. There was no standardisation of calibres yet, and therefore stones or lead balls had to be manufactured separately for each weapon; this gave at least one stonecutter a livelihood. The production of powder, in itself a skilled process and a dangerous one, was entrusted to the bell founders' wives who lived and worked in Danzig and Elbing. They were sometimes brought to Marienburg at the order's expense to mix gunpowder. The quality of the powder was unfortunately variable, since it was considered too expensive to test. Moreover, it tended to settle during transport, so that remixing was often necessary, and humidity – a serious problem in the Baltic – often decreased its explosive power.

In the hands of unskilled gunners, cannons were almost useless. Moreover, most western knights considered learning the practical – in other words, dirty – details of firearms demeaning and their use unworthy of their status. Thus it was only slowly that cannon came into widespread use in France, England and Germany. In Prussia the early acceptance of this weapon and its placement in all the large castles and endangered border posts indicates that the attitude of the Teutonic Knights was far different. Cannon made it possible for a few hundred knights in their shining white cloaks, supported by a much larger number of grey-clad sergeants, their native infantry and light cavalry, the militia from the towns, and a small number of crusaders to defeat formidable foes.

Equally essential to the success of the government of the grandmasters was the support of the estates. The bishops, secular knights and burghers participated in the making of laws and edicts both through informal consultation and the holding of assemblies. Taxation was of greatest interest to the burghers who had complained about Konrad Zöllner's high tariffs and interference with trade. These complaints became increasingly insistent in the following years. It was a point that should have concerned the members of the military order more. But people always grumble about taxes, and it is easy for administrators to become inured to complaints and to react with exasperation at the apparent expectation that the defence of the frontiers, the suppression of piracy, the maintenance of law and order, and the encouragement of commerce should somehow not cost money.

During this time the knights and gentry of Culm also formed an association called the Lizard League, an organisation later suspected of pro-Polish sympathies. The Lizard (or dragon) symbol was popular at the time – Sigismund founded an Order of the Dragon for his most important Hungarian nobles (this honorary organisation, similar to the Order of the Garter, later admitted Jagiełło to membership); the Wallachian ruling dynasty adopted the word for dragons (*Drache*) as their name and later produced Dracula (Vlad the Impaler).

Secular Prussian knights, of course, did not move in such rarefied circles; their Lizard League was more like a fraternal order or a noble guild. It is likely that the members wanted what was later called 'Sarmatian' freedom, an exemption from obligations to the state such as those that the Polish nobles were beginning to enjoy. This was a sign that the rigid government of the war years was relaxing. To some knights and officers, this was a bothersome development; they understood how quickly the skills and instincts necessary for military victory rust away when unused.

There is no question that the government of the Teutonic Order was nevertheless still rigorous. The nobles and burghers would have liked more liberty for themselves, but they also wanted a strict enforcement of the laws protecting them. In 1394, for instance, they approved this ordinance:

> If anyone comes into a hostel whom the manager does not know, the manager shall go to the mayor and say that he has a stranger staying there; and if the mayor finds the stranger's statements and answers unsatisfactory, he shall take him prisoner until the matter is investigated. Whoever delays or does not do this, and if the stranger commits some harm, whoever housed him shall pay the same fine as the criminal. Moreover, no crusader shall wander around the countryside until he has proof from his lord that he knows him and is in his army. We especially forbid anyone to wander around in beggar's clothing in parishes where he is not known.

Such detailed laws were not uncommon in medieval Europe. What was uncommon, especially in Germany, was the grandmasters' ability to enforce them over a large area.

It appeared, in short, that the grandmasters had managed to create such an effective state that the Prussian borders had not been crossed by hostile armies in many decades, that internal unrest was minimal. Peace allowed agricultural and commercial prosperity to be fostered beyond the imagining of earlier generations. Such complaints as existed seem to be minor, generated by that indomitable impulse in human beings never to be satisfied with anything short of Utopia. Those complaints existed because the inescapable nature of human beings to fall short of perfection was not sufficiently offset by a perception that everything possible was being done; and it was magnified by the human tendency to go to extremes either of liberty or authoritarianism.

A middle course was especially hard to find and follow in medieval Europe, and extraordinarily difficult in medieval Germany. The medieval mind encouraged enthusiasms and provided few means of escaping deep depressions of the spirit or the economy. The Teutonic Knights seem to have been more successful in locating and holding to a moderate policy than anyone else. If the moderates in the military order could maintain the peace through the decade beginning in 1410, the Teutonic Knights might be able to consolidate their hold on Samogitia and look to the future with confidence. If not, there was no way to restrain Ulrich of Jungingen from demonstrating that the military order of old had found its calling again: war against the open and the secret pagans in the east.

1409: The Samogitian Revolt

Famine struck north-eastern Europe following the summer of 1408. Winter had lasted from Christmas into April, then dry weather set in. The growing season so far north was short in any case, and because the rye and wheat could not be planted at the right time, the harvest was meagre. Prices rose to unprecedented levels. The grandmaster forbade the export of grain from Samogitia, hoping to keep such supplies as existed available to his subjects. Yet Jungingen was undoubtedly tempted to take advantage of the situation, to feed those who had proven loyal, and to withhold stocks from those who had refused to cooperate.

As the winter of 1408/9 came to an end, hungry Samogitians discussed their choices – to flee the country, to hope for charity, or to attack the castles where grain was believed to be stored. The situation in Lithuania was not much better. Vytautas had arranged for Jagiełło to send him grain, but then a border commander reported that Samogitian warriors were planning an uprising. Suspecting Vytautas of giving secret support to the rebels, Ulrich ordered all ships carrying Polish grain to Lithuania stopped and searched. When officials found some weapons, or claimed to have done so, Jungingen ordered the vessels and cargo confiscated; afterwards, he told the outraged Jagiełło and Vytautas that he would forbid future shipments until the rebellion in Samogitia was subdued.

This pressure on a famine-stricken Lithuania only made Vytautas and Jagiełło angry. Not only did the blockade fail to stop the rising, it may even have encouraged its spread.

Vytautas accused the Teutonic Order of having made war on Christian Lithuania and of oppressing the Samogitians without making any effort to Christianise them. He compared the Teutonic Knights to serpents masquerading as doves. The grandmaster, concerned about western opinion, warned gravely that Vytautas would lapse from the faith a third time, then invade Prussia with a huge force from Tatary and Ruś. In Lithuania, he alleged, Roman Catholics were few and the clergy poor, Orthodox believers numerous and their prelates rich. For every Lithuanian baptised into the western Church, he said, a hundred entered the Orthodox. As a consequence, Roman Christianity was in danger. To Vytautas he sent another message, one of peace.

The grand duke rejected it, well informed about everything that the grandmaster did.

Surprisingly, when the Samogitians did revolt, they found the Germans unprepared: officials, merchants and fishermen were acting as though it were peacetime, and the castles were undermanned. Presumably, Vytautas's outbursts were so common that Michael Küchmeister did not take them seriously. The rebels burned the outbuildings at Christmemel – near Georgenburg on the north bank of the Nemunas – stole the horses and carried away the villagers; then they raided other castles and began a siege at Friedeburg. Vytautas appeared in Samogitia in April, disappeared, then reappeared in May. No one knew what that meant. He came back in August and remained several weeks, at least once reviewing the progress of the siege at Friedeburg.

Jungingen's response that May was to send two knights on a secret mission to recruit 200 *Spieß* – a miniature military unit comprising a knight or man-at-arms accompanied by a warrior with a crossbow and a young man leading the warhorse – from the closest German states. These were insufficient to overawe the rebels.

When Küchmeister hurried to Jungingen to describe the seriousness of the situation, the grandmaster sent him immediately to Hungary, to explain the crisis to Sigismund. One might have expected the grandmaster to be angry. After all, Küchmeister had allowed himself to be deceived by Vytautas, had misjudged the mood of his subjects, and had failed to have his castles battle-ready. However, Küchmeister was an intimate friend of the grandmaster, he was famous for his talent at explaining away failures, and no one doubted his courage, military skills or his administrative ability. If the Samogitian policy had not worked out, that was unfortunate; but the grandmaster does not seem to have suggested that anyone else could have done better. As soon as Küchmeister returned to Prussia, he was assigned to be governor of the Neumark.

This means that Jungingen now believed that the strategic situation could hardly be changed radically by sending more expeditions up the Nemunas into Samogitia. Victory there had been achieved before, but only with Vytautas's and Jagiełło's help; never when the Samogitians had Lithuanian and Polish help and encouragement. That seems to have been why Jungingen asked Jagiełło to send representatives to Marienburg to discuss a joint intervention in Samogitia.

The result was not what the grandmaster expected. On 1 August the archbishop of Gniezno warned Jungingen not to attack Lithuania – Jagiełło would regard aggression against Lithuania as an attack on his own kingdom. That threat was more than a bit presumptuous and may have been the last straw. The grandmaster seems to have decided to cram it back down the royal throat.

Jungingen began to recruit mercenaries from Silesia – 800 *Spieß* at a total cost of 46,000 Prussian marks. (Sven Ekdahl notes that these were '*soldener im kryge ken Polan*' ['mercenaries in the war against Poland'].) The total cost of mercenaries for 1409 may have been four times that much. He chose to hope that the garrison at Friedeburg could hold out without reinforcements. Meanwhile, he would strike at Poland. If he could make the king back down, he seemed to reason, the rebels would fall silent.

The advantages of attacking Poland directly were clear – the kingdom was comparatively rich (there not having been war along the Prussian border in almost three generations), so that invading armies could supply themselves off the country. That would attract mercenaries, who generally regarded the prospect of loot and ransom as more important than their wages. Moreover, the damage inflicted would be real rather than symbolic and it would be aimed at a single enemy – Jagiełło – while Vytautas was in the east. Lastly, it would take Jagiełło completely by surprise. Why, indeed, should he expect an attack now? For two years the grandmaster had ignored provocations, and the order's situation in Samogitia was more dangerous now than ever. According to one chronicler belonging to the Teutonic Order, and therefore presumably well-informed, the king had interpreted the inaction along his frontier during the past years as fear.

Jungingen remarked to his knights that the king would never suspect what was going to happen, and indeed the declaration of war caught the Poles by surprise. Jagiełło, in fact, was so confident of his kingdom's security that he had gone hunting, so far out of contact with his advisers that no one even knew where to look for him when the first invaders crossed the border.

The armies of the Teutonic Order broke into Poland ten days after the declaration of war. The marshal burned the castle at Dobrin; the grandmaster besieged a nearby castle for fourteen days, eventually breaking down the walls with his powerful new artillery train; troops from West Prussia invaded Great Poland, sacking several towns and burning them; and an expedition from East Prussian convents ravaged Masovia.

Jagiełło's counterattacks proved so ineffective that he soon sent the archbishop of Gniezno to ask for a truce. That seemed to confirm the views of that faction of Germans who had predicted that strong action would intimidate the Poles, whereas soft words would encourage them to behave yet more arrogantly. In short, the way to peace seemed to be through war. Moderation and concession, Ulrich of Jungingen thought, was not a way to create conditions for a lasting peace. Military strength was.

As long as nobody considered the steps beyond forcing Jagiełło to seek a temporary truce, that policy seemed very practical. Even the next step, perhaps, was obvious – to send an expedition into Samogitia. But what of the years to come? Would the grandmaster have to occupy parts of northern Poland indefinitely? Could he make war effectively on Lithuania without the participation of western European knights? And, lastly, how would the Church and the Holy Roman Empire react? At a time when Christendom was challenged by a new Turkish onslaught, would its leaders approve a military order making aggressive war on a front-line kingdom? Ulrich of Jungingen undoubtedly thought about these issues, but not for long. His attention span was best suited for immediate, pressing matters.

When representatives of King Wenceslaus came to mediate the peace talks, the grandmaster cooperated fully. Jungingen wanted to turn against the Samogitians who had recently captured Friedeburg, and to do that he needed a cessation of hostilities with Poland. The truce with Jagiełło, signed in October 1409, contained these significant words: 'Also we promise by our royal words, that we will not give the Samogitians or any other non-Christians or their helpers advice, aid, or money, and also that we will not receive them in any way.' The grandmaster's practice of standing up to enemies and tolerating no insult seemed to have been successful once again. As a result of his no-nonsense policies, it seemed likely that in the near future the Teutonic Order would be able to reassert its authority over Samogitia. However, that was not to be the case.

The grandmaster's aggression was a fatal leap into the unknown, aligning two adversaries whose ability to work together had always been strongest at a distance. But now he had challenged two proud peoples to an unnecessary war, without a plan for achieving victory. Did Ulrich of Jungingen really believe that Jagiełło would again assist him in suppressing the Samogitian uprising and that the Polish Diet would countenance this commitment so soon after this devastating attack on the kingdom? Prussia and Poland had been at peace almost without interruption since 1343, and many Polish nobles and prelates had not been eager to confront the battle-tested forces of the Teutonic Order unless they could see a better opportunity for victory than was present in 1409. They knew well the reputation of the crusaders and the strength of their many fortresses. In retrospect, one can see that Ulrich should have let sleeping dogs lie, but even when the hot-blooded grandmaster kicked them in the ribs, it was not immediately clear that the suddenly awakened enemies had sharp teeth.

Chapter 4

The Battle of Tannenberg

War Clouds

The Teutonic Knights did not expect a great war in 1410, much less a great battle. While wars were common, great battles were rare, since the weaker party usually fell back on castles and walled cities, knowing that sieges were likely to be brief. Invading forces feared being trapped by relief armies coming from a distance, and losses from disease and bad water could be high. In addition, the grandmaster expected that Jagiełło would be too worried about Tatars and Sigismund of Hungary to do more than bluster. Also, he knew that Polish nobles were likely to fight bravely against invaders, but were often reluctant to cross borders. And he had a famed, almost undefeated army.

That judgement was probably true in the past, but much had changed in recent years. Polish nobles and clergymen were feeling increasing self-confident, and they had become accustomed to following the wishes of their Lithuanian-born king. Jagiełło, for his part, knew how to play on these emotions and those of his rash opponent as well. This led to the great battle in the Prussian wilderness, known variously as the battle of Tannenberg, Grunwald or Žalgiris, that has been retold countless times in histories and fiction, becoming thereby a centrepiece in the historical memory of Germans, Poles and Lithuanians.

Political Manoeuvring in 1409–1410

When it became apparent that war was likely, both sides called on outside powers for support. Nobody was surprised by this. Such appeals were conventional, and usually some important mediator managed to find a way to bring an end to the crisis. Each side could go home in honour, then complain and plan for a later resumption of hostilities.

Each pope (Rome and Avignon) issued a call for peace so that Christendom could restore unity in the Church and take collective action against the Turks, but that meant little. They were probably more concerned that a new (third) pope elected by the Council of Pisa, Alexander V (1339–1410), would use the crisis to enhance his reputation. That did not happen either. Everyone assumed that if anything of importance took place in the Church, it would occur in Italy and

Germany, far from Prussia. In any case, Alexander would die within months, leaving the Church in crisis again.

This left the way open for the former Holy Roman emperor, Wenceslaus of Bohemia, to recover the prestige he had lost when removed from office a decade earlier for general incompetence and extraordinary alcoholism. His successor, Ruprecht, would die in mid-May 1410. In any case, he would have been too weak to provide leadership in the crisis and too far away to act as an intermediary. That left only Wenceslaus.

Both the Germans and Poles approached the king with oral and written explanations of the matter, and each made complaints about the other party; but everyone knew that they could not even rely on Wenceslaus to show up at meetings. That is why representatives of the parties met without him for five days in early October 1409, going home with a truce that was to last until St John's Day of 1410; this truce was later extended to 4 July.

One article in the agreement authorised Wenceslaus to propose terms for a permanent settlement, terms to be announced before Lent. That not only allowed negotiations to continue, but practically guaranteed that both sides would flatter the king and offer bribes – Jungingen gave him 60,000 *Gulden*. Each side had reason to expect Wenceslaus's help, Jagiełło because of his military alliance with the king, and the grandmaster because years before Grandmaster Konrad had spoken out against Wenceslaus's deposition as emperor. There were also the military order's ties to Sigismund of Hungary, which were especially strong at this moment.

The grandmaster sent Wenceslaus a short history that laid out the order's case, a strongly worded indictment of the Lithuanians as apostates who had violated every agreement they had ever signed. Moreover, that the Lithuanians who were Christians belonged to the Russian Orthodox Church and that many Samogitians were still pagans. In December Jungingen sent a large delegation to Hungary which obtained an assurance of support for the grandmaster in return for making a payment of 40,000 *Gulden* towards the purchase of Neumark. As a result, Wenceslaus proposed a return to the *status quo ante bellum* and threatened to make war on anyone who rejected his plan. This was a complete triumph for the grandmaster.

This announcement was, of course, too one-sided. Within a month Jagiełło sent a delegation to Prague to complain. This merely infuriated Wenceslaus. The Poles left the court certain that war would follow. On 20 December 1409 Sigismund promised to come to the grandmaster's aid if the king of Poland employed 'unbelievers' – a vague formulation aimed at Lithuanian subjects. Jagiełło, however, was not intimidated. He rejected the decision and announced that there would be no further negotiations. When Wenceslaus summoned him to a conference in Silesia in May 1410, he sent word that he would not be coming.

Meanwhile, both Jungingen and Jagiełło began energetically hiring mercenaries. The typical mercenary unit was the *Spieß*. The armoured horsemen (often called men-at-arms to distinguish them from knights) were assigned to groups (*Gesellschaften*) that could be combined into larger formations (*Rotten*) commanded by prominent mercenaries called *Rottmeistern*. The crossbow was a deadly weapon, especially in close quarters and woods, but when a formal battle loomed the crossbowmen dismounted to join others to provide volley fire. The youths withdrew to the rear with the horses used for travel. Men wearing armour preferred to mount their fresh warhorses just before the combat began; the young men were also expected to safeguard any booty or captives the horsemen took.

Additional men-at-arms were provided by regional lords who had long-standing contracts with the military order, but the conditions of service were onerous for the grandmaster. Since they were obliged to fight only in defence of Prussia, this precluded using them offensively without wearying negotiations, and the mercenaries expected that they would be reimbursed for the loss of their warhorses and armour, as well as being ransomed if captured. This, too, was unacceptable in principle, though in practice grandmasters had done that in individual cases. More often the pay was cut in half, in return for a promise to replace lost equipment and animals.

Jungingen had the initial advantage in recruiting Bohemian mercenaries – the best in Europe – because of his close ties to Sigismund and Wenceslaus – but he lost this when it appeared that war could be averted. He had, in fact, planned a surprise attack on Poland for 1 June. With Sigismund tying down Polish forces in the south, the order's men, together with those of the Pomeranian dukes, would surely have caused more destruction than the 1409 raid. However, he cancelled the incursion in April, when Sigismund met Vytautas on the Polish–Hungarian border, with Jagiełło close nearby. Sigismund offered to make Vytautas a king, thus Jagiełło's equal, but the grand duke rejected the idea. Having failed to break up the alliance, Sigismund proposed a summit conference in Thorn on 17 June. All parties seemed in agreement. Jagiełło even sent Sigismund a long safe-conduct (*Geleitsbrief*) so that the Hungarian king and 1,500 horsemen could safely cross Poland to Prussia.

Hearing this, Jungingen ceased recruiting, then waited in vain for the royal participants to appear. In those two weeks many Bohemian mercenaries who had gone to Prague expecting employment accepted offers from Polish recruiters, tipping the balance between the two armies. Jungingen's understandable reluctance to spend money unnecessarily turned out to be a critical mistake on his part. Those fine warriors were not to serve in the grandmaster's army, but his enemy's.

The grandmaster had made extensive preparations for the summit conference. He went to Thorn with 600 *Spieß* and several prominent German lords, but neither the king nor the grand duke appeared, and the Hungarian delegation was a mere 200 horsemen without their king. The plans were, in Sven Ekdahl's words, 'a fiasco'.

When Jungingen realised that the peace negotiations had failed, he hurriedly authorised a resumption of recruiting. But it was too late – those mercenaries were unable to make the two-week journey to Prussia before the war began. Jungingen had been out-manoeuvred by the Polish king. It was a bad start for his campaign.

The Armies Gather

Jagiełło and Vytautas agreed to meet in western Masovia in the middle of June, then, as soon as the truce expired, they would march on Marienburg. That was an extremely ambitious undertaking. Until recently it would have been difficult for Vytautas to cross the wilderness with an army, but new roads, as well as boats on the Narew River, had changed that. Moreover, the king had sent small forces ahead to prevent the grandmaster from seizing key fords and thereby stalling the Lithuanian army.

This was something that Jungingen had not expected. He had reinforced the garrison at Rheden to block any invasion down the Nemunas River as had happened the previous year. As it was, those forces were left hanging, completely out of the campaign that followed.

Vytautas moved quickly, assembling his army in Gardinas, and thus disguised his direction of march. He reached Płock on the Vistula about the same time that Jagiełło began sending his men across. Holding the Polish army west of the river until then might have been a ruse to keep the grandmaster's scouts and spies in the dark, but that was unnecessary, since Jungingen did not learn that the king had constructed a pontoon bridge until a Hungarian peace delegation told him about it. That same day the Masovian forces under Siemowit IV and Janusz I joined the Polish army.

With reinforcements coming daily, there were soon an estimated 30,000 cavalry and infantry in the royal army, more than could be supplied for long, and the chances of epidemic disease increased the longer they camped together. Moreover, there were opportunities for individual knights or entire units to take revenge on other Poles and allies for past grievances and for alcohol-induced quarrels. (The chroniclers do not usually mention drunken brawls, though all the peoples involved in the war were heavy drinkers.) Jagiełło reduced some of these dangers by stationing some Polish units along the border of West Prussia to watch for raiders and to threaten the Neumark, but he took most of his army across the river with him.

There were heavily armoured Polish knights, but most Polish cavalry were too poor to afford the best equipment. Besides, lighter armour was more appropriate for fighting in the eastern borderlands. There were a few thousand foot soldiers behind whose ranks horsemen could take refuge; some were archers. There were Bohemian and Moravian mercenaries – the best in Europe – among whom may have been the future Hussite hero, Jan Žižka (1360–1424). Light cavalry were brought from Smolensk by Lengvenis, from Starodub by Žygimantas, and Tatars were led across the steppe by a future khan, Jalal al-Din Khan (1380–1412), the son of Tokhtamysh. No contingent was more feared than this one, because the stories of Tatar cruelty had long been heard throughout the region.

In addition there were cavalry units from Moldavia led by its prince, Alexander the Good, whose long reign was already ten years old. (Alexander's sister would give birth to Vlad the Impaler, which should remind us how enemies were treated in this era.) Moldavians were experienced in fighting Turks, Tatars, and occasionally Poles and Hungarians; and their region was famed for the savagery of its politics and warfare.

Naturally, there was a large force of Lithuanians, more experienced in combat against the Teutonic Knights than anyone else on the campaign. They were known for extremes of valour and panic, and therefore were better on the attack than in a defensive position. They knew that they could not stand up to heavy cavalry, but the knights' advantage in armour was paid for by lessened speed and endurance.

The chronicler Jan Długosz recorded the number of banners under which each cavalry unit fought as fifty-one for the Teutonic Knights, fifty for the Poles and forty for the Lithuanians, but he could not say how many horsemen were in each banner. He later composed the *Banderia Prutenorum* (fifty-six battle flags of the Teutonic Order and its allies, illuminated by Stanisław Durink), now displayed in the library of the Jagiellonian University in Cracow.

There was no unified command for the Polish–Lithuanian army, though Vytautas led the Lithuanian forces and during the combat took command of Polish units as well. Zyndram z Maszkowic (*c.* 1355–1414), the swordbearer of the crown, headed the banner of Cracow which contained the best horsemen; but overall command of Polish units was probably exercised by Zbigniew Lanckoroński, (*c.* 1360–1425), the royal marshal. Jagiełło, considered too old for exhausting hand-to-hand combat, remained to the rear – this was a day when commanders usually fought at the head of their troops.

The grandmaster raised perhaps 20,000 men. About half were well-armoured knights on specially bred steeds, vassals and allies armed as heavy cavalry and light-armed Prussian horsemen. About half were 'pilgrims' – a few crusaders among 6,400 mercenaries, who were given spiritual credits for the length of their employment. This wing was led by Marshal Friedrich of Wallenrode, the other by Grand Commander Kuno of Lichtenstein (1360–1410). The grandmaster would remain in the third line with the reserve, ready to charge when the moment was right. The army was well equipped, experienced and confident. Their record spoke for itself – they had fought superior numbers in difficult terrain and usually prevailed. They also had better cannon and more experienced engineers than their opponents.

If the Livonian Order had sent its army, Jungingen's force would have been significantly stronger; but those knights would have had to travel overland through Samogitia or sail along the Baltic coast. Moreover, since Jungingen had approved the Livonian master's recent truce with Vytautas, those knights could not even raid Vytautas's northern regions. Thus the grand duke could summon warriors from all parts of his domain without worrying unduly about the Livonians falling on poorly defended towns and villages.

The grandmaster was pleased that Wenceslaus had permitted him to recruit mercenaries in Bohemia – those were among the best warriors in Europe, some speaking Czech, others German. But his hope that Sigismund would invade southern Poland did not come about – the Hungarian king was generous in making promises and commitments, but stingy in carrying them out.

Contemporary estimates of the armies' sizes varied wildly. Modern estimates are probably quite accurate, but the number that finally arrived on the battlefield was less than that which began the campaign. This is almost always the case in warfare. Similarly, contemporary accounts of the battle varied widely in detail and accuracy; only by comparing them side by side can we get a proper overview of the event.

What has changed most in recent years is the lessened reputation of the chronicler who wrote the most exciting narrative of the campaign and the battle, Jan Długosz (1415–80), who obviously was not an eyewitness. He was prejudiced against Germans, Lithuanians, and anyone who was not a Polish patriot. Sven Ekdahl, a Swedish historian who has spent his career writing about military history in this region, came upon an important alternative source in 1963, one that influenced his subsequent research (and was printed in Poland in July 2015 in the periodical *Mówią wieki*). In 1982 he published *Die Schlacht bei Tannenberg 1410*, then spent almost two decades in winning over critics to his viewpoint. He argued that past historians had found it too easy to rely on Długosz without comparing his narrative with others – even other Polish accounts – and with contemporary correspondence. Long ago this omission was understandable, but after edited collections of letters, petitions and treaties became available, it was inexcusable. Other errors piled up, such as when historians failed to determine accurately even where the two armies had lined up against one another. Archeologists have helped correct this – using metal detectors in 2015, then with more studies in 2016 and 2017 – to show that the main battle took place to the south and east of Grunwald (Grünwald or – more correctly long ago – Grünefelde), not south and east of Tannenberg (Stębark).

Interestingly, no matter what estimated numbers are assigned to the armies by various scholars, the ratio of forces usually works out as approximately three to two in favour of the Polish king and the Lithuanian grand duke. Also, while a few of Jagiełło's and Vytautas' men had served together in campaigns, the rest were untested in fighting in an alliance. In contrast, Jungingen had disciplined knights who knew and trusted one another; he was also fighting on the defensive and could fall back to castles where food, water and weapons were stored; and his men were better informed about local conditions, including roads and fords. That made the odds fairly equal.

A chronicler belonging to the Teutonic Order described the pre-liminary manoeuvring for advantage in vivid detail:

[King Jagiełło] gathered the Tatars, Russians, Lithuanians and Samogitians against Christendom … So the king met with the non-Christians and with Vytautas, who came through Masovia to aid him, and with the duchess [Alexandra of Masovia] and Poland and Wallachia there was so large an army that it is impossible to describe, and it crossed from Płock towards the land of Prussia. At Thorn were the experienced diplomats, Nicholas II Garai [Garai II Miklós, *c.* 1367–1433] and Stibor of Stiborzieze [1348–1414], whom Sigismund had sent especially to Prussia to negotiate the issues and controversies between the order and Poland; but they could do nothing about the matter and finally departed from the king, who followed his evil and divisive will to injure Christendom. He was not satisfied with the evil men of the pagans and Poles, but he had hired many mercenaries from Bohemia, Moravia and all kinds of knights and men-at-arms, who against all honour and goodness and honesty went with heathendom against the Christians to ravage the lands of Prussia.

Contrasting Strategies

Whether in war or sports, the attacker has the advantage in knowing where and when the first contact will occur. The defenders, in contrast, must rely on obtaining sufficient warning to gather forces, then move quickly to engage the invaders. Jungingen was frustrated here because Lithuanian and Tatar advance units prevented his scouts from determining where the royal forces were or where they were headed.

This was no surprise. Not even Jagiełło's commanders knew. Each night they would camp in the dense forest, often unsure where they were and unclear as to where they were going, travelling on tracks rather than roads, with paths that wandered around obstacles and towards unseen fords. Making camp must have been a logistical nightmare, but the warriors were accustomed to privation. The Polish historian Stephan Kuczyński (*The Great War with the Teutonic Knights, 1409–1411*), whose views once dominated all discussions of the battle, argued that his movements were based on the idea of 'concentric blows against the capital of the foe', a Mongolian principle unknown in the west. This is only one of many issues where good historians disagree, partly because, while the route did lead in the general direction of Marienburg, there were thick forests and swamps to cross before reaching that fortress; and the invaders were not bringing siege engines with them.

Meanwhile, the grandmaster waited for reports from his scouts. Apparently believing that Jagiełło had sent only a few units to the east bank of the Vistula as a feint, he had kept his main army in place, sure that the king would cross back over. When he learned from the Hungarian envoys that the king had indeed sent his army across the river, he ordered his forces to hurry east to take up positions on the fords across the Drewenz (Drwęca) River that ran westward into the

Vistula near Thorn. If he could prevent the royal host from reaching more settled lands, their numbers would work against them – they would exhaust their food and fodder more swiftly than his army would.

It would become important later that the grandmaster had left 3,000 men at Schwetz in West Prussia under the command of Heinrich of Plauen (c. 1370–1429). Though not among the most valuable officers, Plauen was a good choice because he was an experienced warrior not afraid to make quick decisions. But Jungingen took his senior officers with him. He relied on men who knew the wilderness well for advice about where to station his forces and what the invaders' strategy was.

Jagiełło similarly relied on experienced local men. He does not seem to have known what the grandmaster was doing, so he was careful not to stumble into an ambush. When he learned that the grandmaster had taken up a position on the Drewenz River, he must have been relieved; but he could not have been happy to hear that it would be difficult to force a crossing there – Jungingen had built a log barrier on the far bank, with sufficient men to repel any attempt by horsemen to cross.

Both commanders did well in moving their forces – together with the wagons and pack animals, reserve mounts, and cattle – towards camp sites with water and grass. The men in the armies could not have known what lay before them, and only a few Germans and Poles had been in a pitched battle on the scale that would result if the armies actually came together. There had not been a major combat between the Teutonic Knights and the Lithuanians since 1370 or between the Teutonic Knights and the Poles since 1332. Both veterans and neophytes probably took consolation in storytelling, boasting, prayer, drinking and speculating about what would happen next.

The Lithuanians, on the other hand, had campaigned on the steppes and in the forests of Ruś, as well as in the woods of Prussia and Samogitia with their hills, rivers and swamps. While some of those campaigns had ended in disaster, one had reached the Kremlin in Moscow; Vytautas had come away with a favourable peace treaty. He was confident of his army's ability to move through a wilderness that others considered impassible, and he counted on his Tatar scouts discovering any ambush by the heavily armed knights of his opponent.

The Polish forces were better equipped for battle with German knights, but they lacked confidence. Długosz complained about their lust for booty, their independence and their tendency to panic. It was not true, as has been occasionally claimed, that their equipment and tactics were 'oriental', but those did reflect local conditions and the general poverty of the knightly class. However, Jagiełło did not need to send any of those horsemen into the woods to look for Germans – the Tatars did that while pillaging the countryside.

The advancing forces must have trod portions of the roads and tracks into muddy morasses – this was wet country then, and forested, in contrast to the beautiful rolling countryside of today; other portions were dry, but the temperature was warm. Horses must have tired, and men who dismounted to lead them would quickly have become exhausted. But as they observed Jagiełło's calm and sober demeanour, they would have been reassured. He drank no alcohol himself, and usually spoke little; his love of hunting had prepared him for the long hours on horseback in dense woods. In contrast, Vytautas was an inspirational leader who customarily exhorted his men loudly and denounced his enemies passionately. No one would have doubted his abilities or his determination, and he was always ready to advance whenever Jagiełło's caution said to take care.

When the invading force arrived at the ford across the Drewenz, it was obvious that further progress would not be easy. The best choice was to move eastwards and upstream, where the river would be less of an obstacle and the once thickly forested countryside was now dotted with villages. However, the tracks and roads between the settlements were narrow and winding, so that even the best of guides could lose their sense of direction. Fortunately, many villagers spoke Polish and must have been relieved to be able to communicate with some of the invaders. All must have been terrified of the smoke that marked the progress of the Tatar raiders, and fear must have helped persuade prisoners to give information about the roads.

Polish knights soon began complaining to Jagiełło about the Tatars, who hauled women into their tents, then raped them repeatedly, who slaughtered even peasants who spoke Polish, and generally mistreated captives. Eventually the king ordered all prisoners released and warned the Tatars to stop their outrages. This did not seem to be very effective, and in any case, he wanted Jungingen to weaken his position by sending knights to protect rural communities. However, Jungingen was too good a commander to make a sentimental error.

Jagiełło faced a problem. He could not sit still, his men warily watching the Germans across the river; but the way to the east and north through the swamps and woods was unfamiliar territory and the knights of the Teutonic Order who had hunted there knew the roads well and might block his progress. Retreat was out of the question; that would be too embarrassing. At length, his prayers were answered – and the king had been very devout, never missing an opportunity to hear Mass – when Lithuanian scouts found roads leading towards Osterode (Ostróda) that could be used if he acted before Jungingen learned what he was up to.

The March to Tannenberg

After meeting with his council Jagiełło gave orders to move quietly and quickly. No one was to give any sign of preparations to leave until the trumpeter awoke the camp, but immediately afterwards each unit was to move out in order without fanfare. He hoped that this would give him a head start of several hours, but to gain more time, he sent a herald to request a meeting to discuss peace.

Jungingen must have been sceptical about the offer to parley, but he nevertheless called his officers together to discuss it. As expected, they rejected the invitation. Then scouts reported that the Poles had abandoned their camp, perhaps retreating.

Immediately, Jungingen ordered pontoon bridges thrown across the river and set out in pursuit, hoping to overtake the last units and destroy them. But when he learned that the royal host was moving north-east in two columns, he ordered his men back across the river – there was no point in following the enemy though the woods, witness to torched villages and risking ambush. He needed to get ahead of the invaders.

Jungingen's army responded quickly, moving over better roads on interior lines. This almost caused him to go too far east, but the swift movement caused the Polish scouts to lose contact with him. Consequently, Jagiełło was surprised when he did find units of Teutonic Knights blocking the roads.

Jagiełło had taken a significant risk in taking his army farther into the forest, whence it would be difficult to retreat if he suffered a setback; he had also divided his forces, sending the Lithuanians on a parallel road. Jagiełło must have assumed that the grandmaster could not move quickly enough to attack one force or the other before he could bring his armies together again. But bring them together where?

It was a great gamble because Jagiełło was aware that many Poles still thought of him as a Lithuanian – a disaster would have them howling for his hide, and they would get at least his crown. Ulrich of Jungingen understood this as well, that a decisive battle could eliminate his foremost enemy once and for all, and perhaps Vytautas too. Jagiełło brought his armies together between the two villages that gave their names to the battle – Tannenberg on one side for the Germans, on the other Grunwald for the Poles or Žalgiris for the Lithuanians.

Up to this point Jungingen had conducted a careful and apparently successful campaign, but he lost his temper when scouts reported that Tatars had burned the frontier town of Gilgenburg (Dąbrówno). Jungingen then abandoned positional warfare in favour of striking the invaders at the earliest opportunity. The best-informed German chronicler summarised this in horrified prose:

> The grandmaster with his forces and the guests and mercenaries rode against the king to the border near Drewenz, near Kauernik, and the two armies camped opposite one another. Because the king of Poland did not dare cross the Drewenz, he went towards Gilgenburg and took that city and burned it, and they struck dead young and old and with the heathens committed so many murders as was unholy, dishonouring churches and maidens, and women, cutting off their breasts and torturing them, and driving them off to serfdom. Also the heathens committed great blasphemies on the sacraments; whenever they came into the churches they ground the host in their hands and threw it under their feet, and in that way committed their insults. Their great blasphemies and insults went to the hearts of the grandmaster, the whole order, and to all the knights and men-at-arms among the guests; and they rode with righteous indignation against the king from Lubov to Tannenberg, to the village in the district of Osterode, and came upon the king without warning, having come in great haste fifteen miles by daybreak on the 15th of July. And when they could see the enemy, they formed their ranks and held the enemy in sight for more than three hours. The king meanwhile sent the heathens out to skirmish, but the Poles were altogether unready. If [the Teutonic Knights] had attacked the king immediately they would have won honour and booty, but that, unfortunately, did not happen; they wanted to call him out to fight chivalrously with them. The marshal sent the king two unsheathed swords with the heralds.

The heralds were proudly dressed, one bearing the arms of the emperor, the other those of a Pomeranian duke. The king, according to Długosz, was about to put on his helmet when the emissaries were escorted to him by Polish knights. The heralds delivered their message in German, which was immediately translated for the king by one of his retinue.

The presentation of the swords – one for him, the other for Vytautas – was a western tradition unknown in Poland, but it was meant as a provocation; and the heralds accusing him of hiding in the woods was an insult. Jagiełło responded with tears (of anger?) in his eyes, addressing the heralds with harsh words undoubtedly improved by Długosz, calling on God, the Virgin Mary, and numerous Polish saints to support him in his just cause. He nevertheless accepted the swords, later placing them in the treasury at Wawel castle – to be displayed in later coronation ceremonies of Polish kings, only to vanish in 1853 after being confiscated by tsarist authorities looking for potential revolutionaries.

These events have been told and retold over the centuries, but the best summations of today's viewpoints are in the proceedings of the international Grunwald Conference of 2010 (*Conflictus Magnus apud Grunwald 1410. Między Historią a Tradycją*) held in Malbork and Cracow. There were far too many events in 2010 commemorating the battle to hold a scholarly conference on the actual 600th anniversary. That date had drawn 200,000 spectators to what was the largest reenactment of a medieval battle ever, with 2,200 horsemen and 3,800 peasants and camp followers. This was not the nationalist celebration it might have been. The communist government that would have used the occasion to whip up feelings against West Germany was twenty years in the past; and the German–Polish textbook commission had long since removed the most propagandistic passages from school books of both countries, but Poles still took great pride in the event.

The Armies Prepare for Combat

Jungingen had sought to take the royal array by surprise, but his army could not make its way through the woods quite fast enough. By the time they could see the Poles and Lithuanians, it was daylight. It was impractical to withdraw, even if he had wanted to, so the grandmaster lined up his men on the long field between the villages of Tannenberg and Grunwald, their faces to the foe, and perhaps had them dig camouflaged pits for charging cavalry to fall into. Jungingen's plan was to make a decisive counterstroke after repelling the initial charge – that was a common strategy and was usually effective when conducted by a disciplined army – but his opponents were slow to emerge from the woods where they had camped.

The royal tent and chapel could have been easily seen, if they were on the rise above the nearby lake and stream from where the king later watched the battle unfold; but more likely they were in the woods, with the supply wagons. But such points were minor compared to the competing nationalisms of the early twentieth century. Then, after the Second World War, Marxist historians stressed the importance of the lower classes, making it necessary to introduce a 'people's army' into what the sources indicated was largely a battle between mailed horsemen.

The Polish public learned the story from the very popular 1960 movie *Krzyżacy* ('Crossbearers', with the English title, *Knights of the Teutonic Order*) based on the patriotic 1900 novel by Henryk Sienkiewicz. After 1945 the German public learned to avoid subjects that might suggest a revival of militarism.

According to Sven Ekdahl, Jungingen had also planned to have the sun shining in the face of his opponents, but as the hours passed, he realised that the sun would soon blind his own warriors. With the Polish and Lithuanian horsemen showing no signs of moving forwards, the grandmaster ordered his army to withdraw a distance at the moment the heralds presented their challenge so that the Poles and Lithuanians could form their lines in the open field. His artillery was no longer stationed where it could be most effective, but that does not seem to have mattered – only a few shots were ever fired, and those at the start of the combat, suggesting that the morning rain shower might have ruined the powder. Hours had passed, his soldiers standing in battle formation without food or drink, men and horses exhausted from the night march. Steam must have been rising from damp clothing. It was a hot midsummer day, and everyone wore wool.

The size of the armies – surely smaller than the forces that began the campaign – is still disputed, but most likely Jagiełło had 20,000–25,000 men, Jungingen 12,000–15,000. Though the armies were small by modern standards, each probably was as large as any commander could have directed across a wide battlefield. Minimal communication was possible by flag signals, and messengers could deliver directions, but most commands were given by the officers on the spot.

It is unlikely that any participant ever forgot the sight of the armies forming up for battle, each in three deep lines – a process that was stage-managed to encourage and intimidate, with music, shouting and singing. The grandmaster's white-clad knights gathered around his large banner with the black cross; there were also the colourful flags of the officers and bishops; Jagiełło's crowned white eagle on a red field; the archbishop of Gniezno's white cross on a red field; the commander of Cracow's crowned bear; the royal marshal's lion-head breathing fire against a blue background; the Lithuanians' knight on a white horse, and the geometric symbol for Vilnius – those banners were all necessary for the distant commanders to know where the units were. The infantry filed into place to music, while artillery was hauled to whatever rise was closest. Messengers rode back and forth, ordering units to shift their positions, and officers exhorted their men to fight valiantly.

Meanwhile, Jagiełło delayed making an appearance, staying in his tent, hearing Mass after Mass. He was apparently content to allow his opponents to feel the effects of their hurried march and lack of food, then stand in the sun in full armour for hours, but he was also notoriously pious – and if he was ever in need of prayer, this was the moment.

Jungingen, meanwhile, was reluctant to send his knights charging into the woods where many of the Polish and Lithuanian forces waited. To hurry the king along, he sent a chivalric challenge for battle – two swords. Until then Jagiełło seems to have given no orders, nor answered his commanders' requests for instructions. Historians have debated the reasons for this, but there will probably never be complete agreement as to what his motivations were.

Jungingen prayed as well. His troops sang their anthem, the oldest hymn written in German (and one later adapted by Martin Luther).

Christ ist erstanden	Christ is risen
von der Marter alle.	from all his martyrdom.
Des solln wir alle froh sein;	We should all be happy about this;
Christ will unser Trost sein.	Christ wants to be our consolation.
Kyrie eleison.	Lord have mercy!

The Poles and Lithuanians responded with their battle-song, the haunting hymn to the Mother of God:

Bogurodzica dzewica	Virgin Mother of God,
Bogem slawena Maryia!	Maria, chosen by God,
U twego syna, Gospodzina,	Lady, implore your Son,
Matko zwolena Maryja,	Mother Mary,
Zyszczy nam, spuści nam	To love us, to assist us
Kyrie eleison!	Lord have mercy!

The Battle

By the time the heralds had presented the two swords, most of the Polish and Lithuanian forces were moving into place on the field. After the heralds had left, Jagiełło gave the signal for the battle to begin. At first little happened. The Poles on the left wing apparently wanted the Teutonic Knights to charge first, because only the first line advanced, slowly, still singing. On the right the Lithuanians spurred their horses forwards and scattered the skirmishers facing them. Then the armies settled down for an extended combat at less than full engagement, the Lithuanians more committed than the Poles, who withheld their next two lines, apparently still hoping to draw a German charge.

At this point armies usually assessed one another; then the one that was outmatched retreated. Nothing like that happened.

The grandeur of the moment struck everyone. The king, who was about to return to the chapel with the priests, was persuaded to turn around and look, because this was a sight that would never be seen again. Thus he was witness to the moment that the men on both sides raised a great cry and rushed at each other, the Germans going downhill moving the swifter. There were onlookers in six great oak trees in the middle of the battlefield, though nobody knew if they were Germans or Poles.

Historians continue to revisit the battle, though there is more agreement today than in the past. The early fighting was on the grand-master's left, where he had stationed the crusaders, mercenaries and vassals. Probably he would have preferred to have his battle-tested knights there, facing a known opponent; but he could not have foreseen how the king would dispose his forces. On the other hand, he might have believed that crusaders would be more eager to fight pagans and Tatars than a Christian monarch. We know that the grandmaster received a letter before the combat began – probably from one of the mercenary commanders – warning him to keep his forces disciplined because the Lithuanians would feign a retreat in hope of causing his battle line to break up in pursuit.

The traditional account of the combat was that of Jan Długosz, later considered the Polish national historian. While Vytautas and the Smolensk regiments continued to fight, Długosz said, the Tatars fled the field, followed by the Lithuanians, some of whom did not rest until they reached their homes to report a great defeat. Długosz glorified Polish courage while interpreting the Lithuanian flight as cowardice. Certainly, one can understand Polish knights thinking that – they could not have known the battle plan, if there was one that intricate.

The German crusaders and mercenaries, believing that they had routed their enemies, took off in pursuit. The Poles, meanwhile, had engaged the Teutonic Knights all along the line, and especially on the Polish right, which had been exposed by the retreating horsemen. There some of Wallenrode's banners drove directly at the banner of Cracow, assuming that they would find the king nearby. As the Teutonic Knights pressed on, threatening the Polish flank, Vytautas rode back and forth, making adjustments to ward off threats. Meanwhile, the king sent his second line forwards.

Soon the Polish knights were pressing the Germans' main battle force hard, though when some of the crusaders and mercenaries returned to the battlefield with booty and captives, they abandoned these to join in the fighting. However, other crusaders had ridden on and fallen into a Tatar–Lithuanian ambush.

As Jungingen saw the fight turning against him, he had to make a decision. If he ordered a retreat, his forces would fall back against the forest and could not have filed thorough the paths without having the rear formations cut to pieces. Choosing to risk everything in a decisive charge by his best units, he gathered sixteen banners in a wedge formation and sent them against the supposedly weakened flank, directly at the slight height where he expected Jagiełło would be watching the battle. That was, at least, where the royal banner was posted.

As it happened, Jagiełło was off to one side, standing with a small group of bodyguards and courtiers. Some Germans seemed to recognise him because they pointed their spears at the king. This caused the bodyguards to remove the small royal banner – a white eagle on a red field – so as not to call attention to him. Also, they sent the king's secretary, a young priest named Zbigniew Oleśnicki (1389–1455), to summon nearby units to protect the king, but he was told to get out of the way: the knights had a battle to fight and could not break the line.

The king wanted to join the combat, but was restrained by his bodyguard and friends. Vytautas, seen at the centre of Jan Matejko's famous painting, now seems to have hurried over to the king and urged him to commit his last reserves. In any case, that is what Jagiełło did, stopping the German charge just short of reaching him. The giant royal banner with the white eagle did fall briefly, and one German knight was about to strike the king when Oleśnicki seized a broken spear and hit him on the helmet, knocking him to the ground. The king touched the knight with his speartip, indicating that he was a prisoner, but his bodyguards intervened, dispatching him. The king wanted to make Oleśnicki a knight on the spot, but he repeatedly refused the honour, preferring to fight for Christ rather than an earthly king. Jagiełło, impressed, promised to make him a bishop someday. Oleśnicki subsequently became a trusted associate in all royal business.

One German commander shouted, '*Herum, herum*' (retreat), but it was too late. Jungingen himself was surrounded and cut down, most likely by Mszczuj ze Skrzynna, a knight in the royal household cavalry. The rest of his army then fled in disorder. The West Prussian knights of the Lizard League had already recognised the danger and turned their warhorses onto paths leading to safety. The units that followed were not so lucky – they were pursued by the Poles back to the wagon park, where some tried to make a stand, but were hindered by the camp followers looting their unprotected possessions. Others tried to flee down the crowded narrow roads, while the Poles killed the slowest or drove them into the woods to hide. Some drowned attempting to cross the large pond, pulled down by their heavy armour.

The wagon park, according to Sven Ekdahl, was at the site of the 1411 chapel, not by the stream where Polish experts – following Długosz – had traditionally located it. To date, with ever more information coming from ongoing scientific studies, Ekdahl seems literally to hold the field.

Meanwhile, as Lithuanians returning from the ambush joined in the general attack, the disorganised mass of men and horses at the wagon park was quickly overwhelmed. Some became prisoners, but many more were slaughtered. The fate of the prisoners was gruesome – common soldiers and knights who did not seem likely to pay ransom were killed straight away; others must have been stripped of everything valuable and kept under strict guard, perhaps wearing the chains they had brought to bind their prisoners.

While some Polish knights sacked the camps, others broke into the wine barrels, wildly drinking it from their helmets, boots, and even gloves. This ended when the king arrived and ordered the barrels smashed so that his army would not be incapacitated by the combination of heat and strong drink. The wine flowed down into the stream so that stories later circulated confusing this with blood. Even so, there was much blood shed there.

By nightfall the last German units had fled or surrendered. After Jagiełło and his commanders had inspected the carnage, he had the captured mercenaries and several nobles brought to him and ordered them to report to Cracow to arrange the terms of their ransom – this was especially convenient for the Czech mercenaries. Vytautas located Marquard of Salzbach among the prisoners. After denouncing him, he ordered him beheaded. This was not a surprise, given Marquard's prominence in crusader expeditions that reached right to Vilnius and because he had taunted Vytautas with slurs about his beloved mother. Marquard would have fetched a heavy ransom, perhaps one higher than for any other captive, but he understood that there was no advantage to being Vytautas's *former* friend. He died with courage and dignity.

Długosz's account of the battle became the accepted story because it emphasised Polish valour, and Germans agreed with it because it credited them with routing the pagan wing of the enemy. There was no personal combat between Jagiełło and Jungingen, but that myth fitted well into the new Polish national narrative.

The losses were almost beyond calculation. The oldest and also the lowest estimate was that 8,000 men died 'on both sides', but it is unclear whether that meant in each army or the total. Given the length and desperate nature of the combat, casualties would have been high in both armies, but those of the Teutonic Order were catastrophic: most of the knights on the battlefield perished. Those few who managed to escape took refuge in the nearest cities and castles, exhausted, perhaps wounded, and unsure what to do.

The March into Prussia

There was no doubt that such a victory had to be followed up, but Jagiełło and Vytautas were unable to do so for three days. Their own losses had been heavy, their men were fatigued and the horses exhausted. Some of the pursuers had ridden ten miles, cutting down those they overtook or driving them into the woods. Without much question many of these pursuers were Tatars. Meanwhile, there were decisions to make – to look through the corpses on the field, to finish off those too wounded to survive, to determine which of the remaining prisoners could pay ransom and to pardon those whose favour would be needed in the future. They ordered the infantry to gather weapons, money and jewellery from the bodies before burial.

The number of slain and slaughtered was so great that it was impossible to dispose of the bodies properly. After a few days the decomposition so outpaced the ability of the burial squads to dig graves that they began to burn the corpses – a desperate measure to prevent the outbreak of pestilence.

The following year an imposing chapel was constructed on a rise easily seen from all parts of the battlefield and dedicated to Lady Mary – it was first built of wood, then of stone after it was burned in the 1414 invasion. In 1412 the antipope John XXIII approved an indulgence for those who prayed there on designated days, mentioning that 18,000 men had died in the battle. For many years the chapel site was believed to have been where the grandmaster fell, but experts now agree that it was the site of the grandmaster's tent, where a great slaughter took place as panicked troops sought safety. For centuries pilgrims came there to pray for the souls of the fallen, but today only the thick foundations remain.

Everyone needed rest, and some who would have fought more could not until their mounts were fed and rested. While camp followers combed the battlefield, robbing corpses and prisoners, the Tatars and Lithuanians with stout little ponies raided defenceless villages, robbing and raping, killing and burning, creating panic. The Teutonic Knights who survived could not make sense of the situation. Who was to take command? The highest ranking officers had all fallen: the grandmaster, the marshal, the grand commander, the treasurer and more than 200 knights. A chronicler of the Teutonic Order wrote:

> The army, both cavalry and infantry, was routed completely, losing lives, goods, and honour, and the number slain was beyond numbering. May God have pity on them.

Contemporaries did not immediately believe the news. Such disasters were rare – Nicopolis was an exception, and that was against a highly respected Turkish foe. Everyone wanted to know how the invincible Teutonic Knights could have been brought so low, so instantly, by enemies hitherto considered so weak. The Teutonic Knights mentioned treason, the numbers of the enemy, and bad luck; the Poles boasted of their courage, skill at arms, good generalship and God's favour. Aeneas Silvius Piccolomini, writing a half century later, said that the Germans had become so exhausted from slaughtering Tatars and Lithuanians like cattle, then fighting the Poles, that when the king had sent in fresh units, the battle turned into a rout.

Jagiełło rested his men and horses, then ordered them north at a measured pace, taking time to accept the surrender of cities and castles. He believed that once he reached Marienburg, the grandmaster's seat would surrender, then he could occupy all of Prussia at leisure. It seemed that everyone was hurrying to him, declaring themselves eager to become Polish subjects. All he had to do was promise to guarantee their former rights and privileges. The garrisons of castles, without commanders and most of their knights apparently dead, were not resisting. Cities whose officers urged resistance, such as Osterode, Christburg (Dzierzgoń), Elbing, Thorn and Culm, expelled the garrisons and surrendered. The bishops too – Ermland, Culm, Pomesania and Samland – acknowledged Jagiełło as king. All this delayed his progress northward.

Meanwhile, Mszczuj ze Skrzynna had shown the king where to find the body of Ulrich of Jungingen and to prove his case displayed the grandmaster's cloak and the reliquary case that he had borne on his breast holding holy wood from the cross. The body was sent to Osterode for burial; later it was brought to Marienburg to lie with his predecessors in St Anne's Chapel.

Heinrich of Plauen

Jagiełło and Vytautas must have been overjoyed. Their grandfather had once claimed everything to the Alle River, which meant the wilderness between Prussia and Lithuania; Jagiełło's royal predecessors had claimed Culm and West Prussia. Each of those dreams now seemed too modest.

At this moment there appeared the one person whose leadership equalled theirs. This was Heinrich of Plauen, whose temperament and talents had seemingly limited him to mid-level positions in the military order. He was about forty years of age and had first come to Prussia twenty years earlier with Saxon crusaders. He had been so impressed that he later took the vows of poverty, chastity, obedience and war against the enemies of the Church. His birth guaranteed him a responsible post, but it was his demonstrated competence that earned him the important command at Schwetz, a castle on the Vistula south of Marienburg. He had been charged with the defence of West Prussia, but the fact that the grandmaster had not taken him along against the Polish–Lithuanian forces makes us wonder if this was an honour. Plauen's later actions show that he was a man who acted swiftly, overriding all objections, careless of what others thought. In short, he did not have the *gravitas* and caution expected of senior commanders. Of course, neither did Ulrich of Jungingen.

When Plauen heard the panicked news of the defeat, he ordered his 3,000 men to abandon Schwetz and hurry north. Nothing else mattered if Marienburg fell – he had to save the grandmaster's fortress, and he knew that it was not prepared to resist attack. As it happened, the order's traditions worked for him. Since everyone was trained to wait for orders, with almost every high officer dead or in captivity, there was no one to dispute his right to take charge.

Once in Marienburg, Plauen began to issue commands: to garrisons that had not surrendered: fight on; to the sailors in the warships in Danzig: come to Marienburg; to the Livonian master: send troops; and to the German master: raise mercenaries. By the time the first Polish scouts arrived at Marienburg's walls, they found defenders there, ready to fight. Cannon were in position, and the fields of fire cleared. As for the city outside the wall, a place the besiegers could have used for supplies and comfort, it was gone – Plauen had ordered it burned.

As soon as the Polish scouts withdrew, Plauen ordered his men to bring in supplies, to drive pigs and cattle into the castle, together with fodder from nearby storehouses and fields, until he had stores for a siege of eight to ten weeks. That was food and fodder the Poles and Lithuanians themselves needed, and it was unlikely the royal coalition could remain together long.

When the main units of the royal army arrived on 25 July, the king realised that he would need cannon and other siege machines. He had left these behind because they did not seem necessary, and until now there had not been any reason for hurry.

The Siege of Marienburg

Plauen knew that he had to replace as many of the battle losses as he could. He wrote to Germany:

> To all princes, barons, knights and men-at-arms and all other loyal Christians, whomever this letter reaches. We brother Heinrich of Plauen, commander of Schwetz, acting in the place of the grandmaster of the Teutonic Order in Prussia, notify you that the King of Poland and Duke Vytautas with a great force and with Saracen infidels have besieged Marienburg. In this siege truly all the order's forces and power are being engaged. Therefore, we ask you illustrious and noble lords to allow your subjects who wish to assist and defend us for the love of Christ and all of Christendom either for salvation or money, to come to our aid as quickly as possible so that we can drive them away.

Plauen's call stirred the German master, Egloffstein, to send knights to Neumark, where Küchmeister had been stationed with a sizeable force; and officers in the Holy Roman Empire began recruiting mercenaries.

Jagiełło recognised that no rash assault could scale those successive high walls, but he was also reluctant to order a retreat. His compromise was to have his army hammer away at the defences with whatever siege weapons could be found or constructed, while Lithuanian raiders burned and ravaged the countryside, sparing only those regions which surrendered promptly. A part of his force he sent into West Prussia, to capture castles that had been stripped of their garrisons: Schwetz, Mewe (Gniew), Dirschau (Tczew), Tuchel (Tuchola), Bütow (Bytów), and Konitz (Chojnice). But he could not take the two greatest fortresses – Königsberg and Marienburg – and when dysentery broke out among the Lithuanians (too much 'delicate food'), Vytautas announced that he was going home. He was followed by the Masovians, and the mercenaries demanded to be paid so that they could leave, too.

Jagiełło refused to be hurried. He rejected offers of a truce, demanding the surrender of Marienburg first – this was a preview of his later negotiating strategy. For eight weeks he remained in place, hoping that Plauen would run out of food, then give up the fortress.

Plauen persevered, and, as he expected, help was on the way. The Livonian army arrived in Königsberg, relieving the garrison there to clear the nearest provinces of whatever raiders remained. When Hungarian and German mercenaries arrived in Neumark, Michael

Küchmeister took to the field and routed an equal number of Poles, capturing the opposing commander. To be sure, these were not the best royal troops, but they had not expected a response so quickly. Küchmeister then marched east. By the end of September there were no Polish forces in West Prussia. Moreover, warships of the Hanseatic League were in the Vistula River.

By then, Jagiełło had designed a fallback plan – literally – a plan to maintain a presence near Marienburg after he withdrew. The king's knights were complaining that they had already rendered their promised military service; and while he might have been able to persuade them to remain longer if there were any likelihood of achieving something, his vassals recognised that the siege was a failure. Also, supplies were short and disease was breaking out.

The king first built an improvised fortress at Stuhm (Sztum), just south of Marienburg. He put his best men there as a garrison and filled it with all the food and fodder that he could before burning all the fields and barns roundabout to make any siege difficult. Obviously, he hoped to prevent the loss of everything he had gained in the recent weeks. He made a brief stop at the shrine of St Dorothea in Marienwerder, then continued his way south.

When Plauen gave orders to pursue the royal army, it was the Livonians who moved first, recapturing Elbing, then recovering most of the cities in the province of Culm. The commander of Ragnit led his men to Osterode, clearing the Poles from all the towns and castles on the way. By the end of October Plauen had recaptured every town except Thorn, Nessau (Nieszawa), Rehden (Radzyń Chełmeński), and Strasburg (Brodnica) – all located right on the border. Then Stuhm surrendered after a siege of three weeks, the garrison giving up the fortress in exchange for free passage to Poland with all their possessions.

Meanwhile, Sigismund of Hungary had declared war on Jagiełło. He clearly feared that defeated Teutonic Knights would be unable to pin down Polish troops when he needed help. Moreover, he was ambitious to become Holy Roman emperor. To abandon the 'German Order' would ruin that hope. Therefore, though he lacked the authority to call the electors together, he did so. In Frankfurt am Main he urged them to send help to Prussia immediately. Not much happened, of course.

More effective help came from Bohemia. Originally, King Wenceslaus had done nothing. No one was surprised at this because Wenceslaus was often listless when decisions had to be made and was not much interested in work even when relatively sober. But the order's representative, Georg of Wirsberg, the commander of Rehden, knew how to interest him – he made lavish gifts to the royal mistresses, bribed lords and mercenaries, and suggested that Prussia might become a part of the Bohemian kingdom. That got Wenceslaus's attention. He not only gave permission for his subjects to go to the order's aid, but he loaned Wirsberg more than 8,000 marks to pay them.

It seemed at this point that Heinrich of Plauen had saved his military order. There was, of course, the loss of lives and property, and an even greater loss of prestige; but the enemy had been driven out of Prussia. While later generations of historians would see the battle as an incurable wound from which the order would bleed to death, that was not apparent at the time.

As Stephen Turnbull remarked in *Tannenberg 1410*, the decisive battle in a fifty-year war was fought at its beginning, not at its end. He then added, 'There can also be few other examples of a battle so decisively won and a subsequent campaign that so singularly failed to achieve its aims.'

Significance of the Battle of Tannenberg

As each side presented its case to public opinion, each described the battle in very different terms. Plauen had the more difficult task, in that he could not say that the Poles were better warriors, or better led, or even that their numbers were too great. Instead, he argued that the Teutonic Knights had been stabbed in the back by the Lizard League group of secular knights of Polish descent. Their leader, Nicholas of Renys (1360–1411), had lowered his banner to signal a retreat, thereby causing a panic among those horsemen who saw them fleeing. Ulrich of Jungingen had died trying to reverse the consequences of this treason.

Conflicting views of historians about the battle and its aftermath make for interesting if confused reading. One could summarise them by saying that until the 1960s each interpretation reflected a nationalist narrative more than facts. Since then historians have become both more polite and less certain of their infallibility. Archeology has shed light on the battlefield, giving promise that problems left by the literary sources may be more fully resolved. Political issues in Germany and Poland that seemed to depend on every imaginable historical justification have disappeared with the political parties that sponsored them, so that at last a quiet discussion about the past is possible.

One truth everyone can agree upon is that Sigismund and Wenceslaus saw the plight of the Teutonic Order as an opportunity to extort money from it. But Plauen had spent everything saved over the years and the invaders had impoverished his taxpayers. Though at first his subjects cooperated as best they could, they were unable to give what they did not have.

The plight of the captives was on everyone's mind. Knights and mercenaries might be languishing in dungeons, and thus would be too weak to return to service when released. Some, as we know from later documents, were employed as labourers in distant Lublin, building a cloister church dedicated to St Brigitta.

If Heinrich of Plauen had time to reorganise the shattered economy, recruit more knights and win the support of German leaders, the effects of the military disaster could have been overcome. However, his subordinates believed that peace had to be obtained immediately, at any price.

Chapter 5

The Peace of Thorn

The First Peace Treaty

Heinrich of Plauen never allowed anyone to think of the disaster at Tannenberg and the subsequent ravaging of Prussia as fatal. Those defeats were merely difficulties to be overcome: *the more enemies, the more honour.* He called for more men and money from Livonia – in vain, since the master there had exhausted his resources; he summoned money, men and mercenaries from the German convents; then he sent representatives to the emperor, to Sigismund and to the rulers of the neighbouring states to ask for military aid, loans and alliances. When his subordinates asked him to seek a truce, he responded that the Poles and Lithuanians were exhausted too, and victory would go to whoever was willing to endure the longest. Moreover, a prolonged truce could become an unbearable burden because the order would have to hire mercenaries each summer, while the king could summon unpaid feudal levies to appear whenever he believed that the Teutonic Knights were weak. A few years of heavily armed inactivity would bankrupt the grandmaster; there would not even be booty to offset part of the mercenaries' wages.

On the other hand, if Plauen was allowed to prosecute the war, the king could not keep his knights in the field for as long as the grandmaster's mercenaries would serve, and, if victorious, the order's troops could plunder the rich provinces of northern Poland. At the least, the Prussians could restock some of the lost herds of cattle, sheep and horses.

Plauen would consider only one kind of peace acceptable, one that guaranteed the security of Prussia, a peace based on defeating Jagiełło. Was such a peace possible? Perhaps. The Teutonic Knights had been defeated by the united hosts of Poland and Lithuania, but if Plauen could bring his resources to bear on Poland alone, attacking the king's westernmost possessions, he had reason to hope for battlefield successes.

Plauen relied on his will for victory being stronger than that of his enemies. Vytautas and Jagiełło had other concerns that demanded their attention, and they might be more intent on holding on to their reputation as victors than in risking defeat in a second contest. In short, only Plauen could concentrate on the matter at hand, reversing the verdict of Tannenberg.

Plauen was ready to attack Poland as soon as he could rebuild his forces. But first he had to summon a general chapter to elect a new grand-master, select replacements for the fallen officers, and install officers in the convents. After that he planned to collect new taxes and raise new levies of troops. Then he would exact retribution. But in the meantime he was immersed in paperwork, that unpleasant side of conducting diplomacy by letters.

In early November 1410 the officers in Prussia met with repre-sentatives of the knights, priests and sergeants in Marienburg; they were joined by the Livonian and German masters and their entourages. With no dissent they elected Plauen grandmaster. This gave him the authority to make war on Poland.

Plauen's Offensive

Immediately after his election, the grandmaster took the visiting representatives on an expedition to Thorn, winning back many of the small castles in that neighbourhood. Plauen's most recent military venture, in October, had gone awry when Marshal Michael Küchmeister was defeated at Polnisch Krone (Koronowo) and captured. Długosz considered this a greater victory than Tannenberg, harder fought, and more consequential. It was a strangely chivalric three-part contest, in which the combatants took breaks to watch individual combats, to rest, to recover the wounded, and to exchange gifts of wine; it ended after a Polish knight unhorsed the bearer of the order's battle flag and carried it away. As often happened, most prisoners were taken during the retreat, when their horses were exhausted and those who continued to fight were easily overwhelmed. The French-born knight who had lost the banner later wrote to Jagiełło to request a letter for his family absolving him from shame, confirming that he had acquitted himself valiantly. The king complied.

The marshal and many other knights who were later exchanged or ransomed returned with the conviction that continuing the war was impractical; they argued that peace had to be made, cost what it may. Many others who had escaped from the battlefield or who were not there at all agreed with them. This put immense pressure on the grandmaster. Plauen was the first among equals, and while he appeared to be a potentate with the trappings of absolute power, in reality he governed according to the wishes of the membership. At this moment the membership in Prussia wanted peace.

As a result of the order's traditional semi-democratic practices, the peace talks were soon almost out of Plauen's hands. He had no desire to conclude hostilities, but his officers did. He believed that the financial and military situation of his Polish adversary was almost as desperate as his own – and perhaps even worse, in that Jagiełło had more enemies. However, some nobles in the Prussian countryside were rebellious, and burghers were complaining that they were being bankrupted by heavy taxes and the interruption of trade. Moreover, the mercenaries were demanding their pay, the levies were frightened by the numerical superiority of the Poles and wanted to go home, the 'guests' from Germany and the Livonian master were advising against combat, and – at the last moment – Vytautas arrived with a large reinforcement to Jagiełło's already impressive army. Ultimately, the Livonian master, watched closely by the grandmaster's cousin, Heinrich Reuss of Plauen (1370–1429), conducted the negotiations with Vytautas, Lengvenis (governor of Novgorod), Rimbaudas (*Seniūnas* of Samogitia, the equivalent of palatine), and the Polish representatives.

Plauen remained in Thorn, available for consultation; King Jagiełło took up residence nearby. Pride prevented the king from conferring with officers of the Teutonic Order personally because they were inferior to him in rank, but necessity required him to give negotiating instructions regarding each article of the treaty as it was proposed. Jagiełło insisted on stiff terms, requiring territorial concessions and a heavy indemnity. Eventually these terms were revised to provide for a large payment combining an indemnity and a ransom for the prisoners with a penalty clause for late payment. Coerced by his officers, Plauen signed the peace treaty, though he believed it was a mistake. Known as the Peace of Thorn (later called the First Peace of Thorn), it was signed on 1 February 1411, on an island in the Vistula River.

The First Peace of Thorn

The peace treaty violated the order's March 1410 agreement with Sigismund not to conclude hostilities without his permission. But since Sigismund's bluster about defending German interests was unlikely to save Prussia, Plauen had to ignore his complaints.

Sigismund was fighting desperate wars with Austria and Venice, holding a stretched defensive line against the Turks, negotiating with German princes and Italian prelates about the future of the Holy Roman Empire and the Papacy, and now that the Teutonic Knights had made peace, Poland would be able to fall on his rear. He left the governance of Hungary to his wife, who, overwhelmed by the multitude

Germany, Poland and Lithuania in the 1400s

of regional problems, became unhappy with his prolonged absences. In short, Sigismund could not take time to deal with events in distant Prussia. Sigismund was also fully involved in calling the general council that could resolve the Great Schism. Until that was done, it would be impossible to drive the Turks out of the Balkans.

Vytautas, in contrast, was close enough to the Teutonic Knights to matter, and he was not pleased with the terms of the peace treaty. He wanted control of the mouth of the Nemunas River, which the knights still retained; and, of course, immediate possession of all the castles in Samogitia, which Plauen was not about to evacuate until the boundary had been set. It was also unlikely that Pope John XXIII and Sigismund would approve the treaty – all three popes and all claimants to be Holy Roman emperor would oppose any weakening of a religious order with important military resources. An informant told the grandmaster that Vytautas had boasted to the garrison of one of his new castles in the disputed borderland that he would take first the fortress at Ragnit, then Königsberg, since those lands had once belonged to Lithuania and therefore were his patrimony.

The Polish king had his own reasons to be dissatisfied with the treaty, most importantly that the only territorial gain went to Vytautas. Although Jagiełło was named lord of Samogitia for his lifetime, it was Vytautas who was to take actual possession. After their deaths Samogitia was to return to the Teutonic Order (and since both rulers were aged men, no one expected this to be a long wait; in fact, the odds were good that both could die before they ever obtained possession). The grandmaster renounced his claims to Dobrin and Kujavia, but those territorial disputes were relatively empty ones now. In return, the king had renounced all the oaths of fealty which had been made to him by secular knights and towns in Prussia.

The Teutonic Knights retained West Prussia and Culm. An international commission was to decide all border disputes and future disagreements. The borders were to be reopened to trade, a point benefiting Prussian cities more than Polish ones. Because Jagiełło had made concessions on these points, he had demanded a high monetary payment: a combination ransom of prisoners and war indemnity of six million *Groschen*. This was 20,000 kg (44,000 lb) of silver. This amounted to 150,000 marks at a time when a crossbow cost one mark, a helmet one mark, a warhorse eight to twenty marks, and a skilled doctor earned thirty marks a year.

The grandmaster's officers, overwhelmed by the losses in personnel, were willing to pay almost anything to obtain the release of the order's imprisoned knights. They simply had to have experienced men to manage the convents and lead the mercenaries in battle. Jagiełło, of course, promised much and delivered little; he delayed releasing the prisoners, always pointing out that the ransom had not been paid fully or promptly. Meanwhile, Plauen had to replace not only men, but also the order's costly warhorses and the artillery. Doing this required some financial sleight-of-hand that would displease both lenders and taxpayers. However, it was now time to dance. Paying the piper would come later.

Financial Problems

The Teutonic Knights knew from past experience that the sum promised was not impossible to raise. But the grandmaster no longer had the resources of the recent past because his lands had been devastated, a few towns were still held by royal forces, and the cash reserves were gone. Plauen may have assumed that Jagiełło had demanded this astronomical sum only to assure that he would reject the treaty and fight on – and thereby annul the territorial parts of the treaty that were favourable to the order. Also the grandmaster may have overestimated his resources, and he might not have realised that his agents were giving huge sums as bribes to Wenceslaus and Sigismund. More likely, he was waiting for events that would allow him to avoid paying the entire sum.

Plauen could have paid the ransom if he had dismissed the mercenaries and abandoned his ambitious plans for revenge on Jagiełło, but he was unwilling to disarm because that would leave him vulnerable to a surprise attack. Also, the impressive bribes paid to Wenceslaus and Sigismund, and to the papal court, could hardly be avoided; nor could the grandmaster have delayed replacing lost equipment and horses. Still, all those expensive outlays achieved little beyond weakening the order's financial condition. As a result, the treaty the officers forced on the grandmaster and embraced as their salvation proved to be their ruin. The indemnity–ransom was the most important of many financial blows that were ultimately more deadly than the battle at Tannenberg.

After the conclusion of the ceremonies, the various armies went home, but soon afterwards the principals began to quarrel about the terms of the agreement they had just signed. They could not even agree upon a person to head the boundary commission.

That there were difficulties was not surprising. As happened occasionally in this era, the two parties did not even leave the meeting with duplicate copies of the original. Instead, each chancery made out the treaty in the form it customarily used, so that the texts were similar but not identical. Moreover, the preliminary texts – truces, drafts, suggestions – were of little help in clarifying disagreements because they were all issued unilaterally, without consulting the other parties, and no official minutes were kept.

The announcement of the indemnity must have come as a shock in financially astute circles. The parties to the talks seemed almost oblivious to the side effects that the sudden release of so much money into circulation would cause. As a later Prussian, Copernicus, explained it to the Prussian Assembly in 1522, when there are more coins in circulation than goods available, prices would rise; when prices reached inflationary levels, a devaluation of the currency would follow. Everyone would hoard coins with high silver content rather than make loans, and no one would want to accept debased coins; taxes would be raised for the inflated cost of government, but taxpayers would pay in coins of low value that foreign merchants refused to accept.

The Peace of Thorn was a symbolic victory for the Teutonic Knights in the sense that Vytautas and Jagiełło renewed their promises to convert the pagans in their lands (meaning Samogitia), then to build churches and to fill them with priests. That the sons of Kęstutis and Algirdas would make such a pledge, and keep it, had been the dream of generations of devout knights.

Rebellion

The war indemnity was a severe burden, as Jagiełło intended it to be. Still, the participants in the conference might not have realised how much money was actually involved because there was always an air of unreality connected to high ciphers, and medieval politicians seemed to understand astronomical numbers even less than do modern ones. It appears that they sometimes hunted for figures in a completely haphazard manner, in contrast to burgher accountants who knew exactly what they were doing. (Nothing illustrates this contrasting class concept of mathematics better than the extortionate interest that secular nobles were willing to pay bourgeois moneylenders, believing as they did that a concern for lucre was beneath their dignity.) The Teutonic Knights were less prone to such impracticality, but they were still not able to adjust to their new poverty. Plauen acted as if he still had the resources that had been available to his predecessors. In a sense, this was true: he had sufficient ready money to pay the indemnity, had he been willing to disarm; but since he did not trust Jagiełło, he felt it necessary to maintain a large force of mercenaries. He also spent too much money bribing Sigismund and the pope. But those were necessary measures to get what he really wanted: revenge.

When the first payment was due, Plauen did not have the money ready, but he knew he could get it from the Prussian cities. Since he had no authority to levy a special tax, he called representatives of the towns and knighthood to Osterode in late February 1411. Surely that location would remind the delegates of the recent invasion and impress on them the necessity to prosecute the war to its victorious conclusion? With the exception of the Danzig representatives, the delegates were willing to raise a special assessment of one and two-thirds per cent on their possessions: two *Vierchen* per mark (each *Vierchen* was worth four *Pfennig*, one fourth of a *Halbschroter,* and one third of a *Schilling*). But the decision was not unanimous, and Plauen found it necessary to call a second gathering at a more convenient location, in Elbing, where the Thorn representatives joined the Danzigers in rejecting the proposed tax.

When the two largest cities in Prussia turned down the tax, the grandmaster faced a crisis. If he backed down, his plans had to fail. Plauen was a warrior, with a warrior's contempt for politics and economics, but more important was his memory of Danzig's disloyal behaviour in the days following the disaster at Tannenberg.

There had been a riot in Danzig when a farmer recognised a horse that had been stolen by mercenaries on their way from the battlefield to the order's convent in Danzig. Rumours had spread that the troops were fleeing the city and that some of them were plundering houses and robbing citizens, and the ringing of the city bells seemed to indicate that it was not merely the rash actions of the rabble, but that the city council, too, was involved. The council had made a formal surrender to the king when he approached the city, and when the Polish commander of Kalisch entered the city and announced that he had been appointed the royal governor, the city council had greeted him with drums, trumpets and fifes and escorted him through the streets to show him every part of the city. Shortly thereafter, the council asked the commander of the order's castle to withdraw his troops from the city, which he apparently did. The riot broke out shortly afterwards. Later, when the treaty restored Danzig and all other towns to the grandmaster, the mercenaries made claims for restitution of their lost property and compensation for their injuries.

When the news arrived in Thorn that the grandmaster had ordered strong steps taken against that city, the leading citizens fled into Poland. The merchant aristocracy of Danzig, however, stood firm. They began to arm and blocked the gate leading to the order's castle. But even their strong resolve weakened when a report came that all their goods deposited elsewhere had been confiscated and that the harbour was blockaded by ships from other towns. The city fathers surrendered on 5 April. The commander of the garrison, Heinrich Reuss of Plauen – the grandmaster's cousin (all male members of the dynasty were given the same name) – subsequently invited the mayors and councillors into the castle and arrested them. Although the citizens petitioned the grandmaster and obtained an order for the hostages' release, four days passed without news of their fate. Finally, when the commander responded to pleas for information, the Danzig citizens learned that he had slaughtered all the prisoners on the first night of their imprisonment. It was never clear if this was intentional or happened in a scuffle, but that made no difference.

Plauen made no attempt to reprove his cousin. Quite the contrary. He imposed a fine of 14,000 marks on the city. Then he reorganised the governments of Danzig and Thorn, exercising the seldom-used right to participate in the selection of mayors, then illegally remaining to select the new council. The uprisings were crushed, seemingly for ever.

The event was decisive for Prussian history. Plauen had missed an opportunity to establish traditions of shared government which could be of mutual advantage and which offered the potential to change Prussian *subjects* into *citizens*, loyal primarily to the state rather than to their city or class. But the illegal and immoral measures created an undying hatred for his military order among the thoroughly German citizens of Danzig, whose enthusiastic participation in military activities was absolutely necessary because their city was the largest, richest and most strategically located of all the urban centres in Prussia. Plauen's relationship with the other cities and the nobles was better because he was able to persuade their representatives that his steps against Thorn and Danzig were necessary to save the state. But without Danzig this meant little in the long run.

Still, one lives life in the short run. And Plauen seemed to have a difficult situation under control for the moment. Although his new taxes were high, most of his subjects understood that the situation was critical, and patriotic feeling made the sacrifices bearable. Moreover, the citizens would soon have an opportunity that they had never enjoyed fully before, that of having a voice in important affairs of state. By calling for an assembly of burghers, knights and squires, Plauen was in step with the times. Parliaments were being established throughout Europe, and he was creating one in Prussia. Unfortunately for the Teutonic Order, Plauen's successors could not win back the love of the citizens of Danzig, nor did they continue Plauen's experiment in popular government. The hope Plauen had raised among the upper classes in Prussia that they might obtain a role in taxation and foreign policy faded in the course of time. Only the memory of his violence in Danzig remained.

Plots against Plauen

Plauen had little time to plan. No sooner had he crushed resistance in the cities than he uncovered a plot within the very ranks of his officers. This was led by Georg of Wirsberg and supported by Nicholas of Renys, head of the Lizard League.

Similar fraternities of knights were forming in Germany. No lord liked them, and all were aware of how swiftly ideas circulated across territorial boundaries – in this case, the Lizard League illustrated how close Prussia's nobles and knights were culturally to those of the Holy Roman Empire, or, for that manner, to the nobility in Poland

and elsewhere in Central Europe. Plauen acted swiftly to capture the supposed conspirators, but most escaped to Poland. Plauen did his best to keep the exiles abroad – when the bishop of Ermland wanted to return to his see, after having been seen in the company of King Jagiełło, Plauen warned him not to enter the country. The bishop prudently remained away.

The story behind the plots was confused, rumour and supposition contending with fact, but rested on ambitious plans by Georg of Wirsberg, the officer who had raised money and hired mercenaries in Bohemia. His promises to King Wenceslaus bordered on treason, but he thought that only outrageous incentives would move that monarch to action – he guaranteed repayment of the loans by April 1411 with the promise that, 'You may attack, seize, and hold the order's people in all lands and do with them as you wish.' He then secretly promised to make Wenceslaus the protector of Prussia and to subordinate the Teutonic Order to him.

That was a promise he could fulfil only if he became grandmaster himself and, therefore, he had planned to use Bohemian mercenaries to support his candidacy. Thinking ahead to the future, Wirsberg sent his brother to Hungary to inform Sigismund of the plan; there he apparently obtained the king's silent approval. Then Wenceslaus foolishly wrote letters to the order's officers, instructing them to elect Wirsberg as grandmaster. This alerted Plauen to his danger but does not seem to have affected the election.

Wirsberg's plans fell apart completely when Plauen made peace with Jagiełło and sent the Bohemian mercenaries home. He had dared too boldly. By involving too many people, he made it impossible to conceal what he was doing. The grandmaster acted swiftly – he beheaded Nicholas of Renys without a trial; then he stood Wirsberg before his peers at the general chapter meeting and asked for their verdict. Wirsberg went to prison, remaining there until 1429.

Wenceslaus was understandably furious. He tried to force the grandmaster to release Wirsberg and to subject Prussia to his authority, but in vain. The order's loyalty was to Wenceslaus's half-brother, Sigismund of Hungary, who was seeking to be recognised as the rightful Holy Roman emperor, thus effectively the heir of Ruprecht rather than of Wenceslaus, who stubbornly maintained that he was the rightful holder of the office.

The imperial election that followed Ruprecht's death was confused. Three candidates had presented themselves, with Wenceslaus's brother, Jobst of Brandenburg, prevailing by a vote of 4–3. When he died soon afterwards, poison was suspected. By default, the electors turned to Sigismund, who then began efforts to persuade a reluctant pope to place the imperial crown upon his head. Wenceslaus, acting on Wirsberg's promise and his own courtiers' greed, threatened to confiscate the order's extensive properties in his kingdom and arrest the members of the Teutonic Order there.

This persuaded the grandmaster that the danger was not past. He worried that the conspiracy extended deeper into the ranks of the officers and among the secular knights and gentry; and he wondered if more members of the city councils were involved. When the next group of 'crusaders' and mercenaries arrived, the truce meant that he had no military duties for them to perform. So he asked these supposedly neutral warriors to help determine the extent to which treason was present and whether betrayals had not lain behind the defeat at Tannenberg. He especially wanted help in building a case against the bishop of Ermland, who was currently in exile. Since the crusaders and mercenary leaders had nothing else to do, they happily conducted hearings into those matters.

Among the latest group of crusaders was Duke Heinrich of Bavaria-Landshut (1386–1450). A proud but moody ruler, he was supposedly overcome by guilt for having repressed a rebellion more brutally than even the forgiving standards of the era considered acceptable. The crusade was primarily his means of expiating this sin, but in addition, he was responding to Sigismund's personal request to go to Plauen's aid. Lastly, since Heinrich had not yet attached the title 'the rich' to his name, he was lured by the prospect of payment for his service. His departure had been delayed a few months by local problems, but then he had gone directly to Elbing, where Plauen was holding the hearings.

The grandmaster's suspicion rested on a curious combination of guesses and facts. The bishop was the only prelate in Prussia who was not a member of the Teutonic Order, and that in itself was grounds to doubt his loyalty. Moreover, he had accompanied the Polish king through Prussia after the recent invasion; indeed, he had led a delegation to Plauen to ask him to surrender. Moreover, he had confessed under interrogation to absurd plans to set Marienburg castle ablaze, then fled the country in disguise and complained to John XXIII about Plauen's conduct. However, there were questions that prevented this from being either a simple case of discovered treason or one of imagined treachery.

When the bishop returned to his diocese nine years later he brought with him some of the cultural treasures that the cathedral later displayed most proudly, among which was a Madonna from the middle Rhenish school. By then all his supposed intrigues had paled in comparison to later events, but Ermland was always suspected of being a pro-Polish enclave within Prussia.

The Bavarian duke went home after having spent fourteen months in Prussia, bringing back tales of intrigue and suspicion.

Ghillebert de Lannoy

Among the most famous storytellers of this period was a Flemish knight, Ghillebert de Lannoy (1386–1462), later chamberlain to the fabulously rich duke of Burgundy, Philip the Good. He was also a diplomat in the employ of the duke's ally, the king of England. He was best known for his tales of exotic personal experiences in east-central Europe, the Middle East, and France and the Low Countries during the Hundred Years War.

By 1413, the 27-year-old Ghillebert already had wider experience in the world than almost anyone he met, having fought in England against Henry IV, twice in Spain as a crusader against the Moors, and been a pilgrim to the Holy Land. He probably visited Prussia as a spy under the cover of wanting to be dubbed knight by the grandmaster, to gather information for the Burgundian duke about the political situation after Tannenberg, the potential for increasing grain imports, and whether restrictions on Dutch and Flemish merchants might be eased. It helped that the dukes of Burgundy were traditional patrons of the crusade in Prussia.

Ghillebert arrived in Marienburg via Denmark to find the truce in effect. He presented his introductions from the Burgundian duke and the king of France, then returned to Denmark 'to visit the king and spend some time' until the truce expired. Actually, his visit to King Eric was clearly diplomatic – Denmark wanted Burgundian help to fight the Hanseatic League. After being feted among exalted company, Ghillebert sailed back to Danzig, then hastened to Marienburg; thence he joined the marshal's army in Königsberg, where he was seated at the fabled Table Round. When it became obvious that nothing was happening there, he sailed back to Danzig to join a force of 1,000 knights fighting against 6,000 Poles and Pomeranians. Wounded in the arm by an arrow in a failed assault on a fortified town in Masovia, he was knighted by Heinrich Reuss of Plauen and made a lay brother of the Teutonic Order. When that war came to an end, Ghillebert decided to do a bit of sightseeing farther east.

Because it was winter, he could not travel to Livonia by sea; instead, he went from Königsberg to Memel, crossed a great river, then proceeded through the 'desertes solitudes' of Samogitia to Kurland (Courland) and thence to Riga. After being suitably entertained by the Livonian master, he inspected the frontier castles, went on to Novgorod (where he marvelled at the 350 churches), and back to Dorpat. Because Vytautas was at war with Novgorod at that moment, he adopted the disguise of a merchant, made his way to the seat of the archbishop of Riga at Kokenhusen (Koknese), then directed his sled south into Lithuania. For two days and two nights he saw only a 'grosse forest deserte'. Vilnius impressed him, especially its huge wooden castle where Vytautas's court resided, though he noted that the town itself was not really fortified, that most of the buildings were of wood, and the only brick structures were a few churches. Even the high castle was of wood, like the walled grand-ducal residence. Trakai, he said, had two castles, one a very strong wooden fortress well suited for hunting. The other, in the lake, was made of brick in the latest French fashion. He noted that many Tatars dwelt there, along with Germans, Lithuanians, Russians and a 'grant quantite' of Jews. He praised the enclosed park with its displays of beasts of prey and the hunt, the surrounding forests with their aurochs and boars, and other creatures hardly imaginable in the west. At a great castle on the Nemunas River he met the grand duke and his wife, their daughter, Sophia, and her son, who were spending a full month there enjoying the winter hunting season. He was very impressed by Vytautas, a 'moult puissant prince', who had conquered two or three kingdoms with the sword (his own lord, the king of England, was finding it difficult to take one). Nobody passed through the kingdom, he said, without Vytautas having an opportunity to talk with him.

Ghillebert visited Kaunas, riding in his sled across the ice-covered river, noting that the Samogitian countryside was largely deserted, and returned to Königsberg via Ragnit. He said that it had been a very cold winter, and that many people in Ruś, Lithuania and Livonia had frozen to death. Arriving in Danzig in March, he was able at last to mount a horse again. At Marienburg he arranged to join a party of Teutonic Knights going to Poland to talk with Jagiełło. However, arrangements were difficult to make because the king was insisting that they agree on basic principles before meeting; so he spent the summer and autumn of 1213 in the company of Michael Küchmeister. Finally, obtaining a safe-conduct so that he could take a letter to the Polish king from the king of England, in early 1414 he went to Kalisch, where Jagiełło was hunting. There the king entertained him royally, then gave him a letter to deliver to the king of France.

Charles IV (1316–78), king of Bohemia and Holy Roman emperor, as depicted by an unknown artist in 1371.

Jagiełło, as imagined by the Polish-Lithuanian painter Konstanty Aleksandrowicz in 1790.

Idealised portrait of the Emperor Sigismund (1368–1437), by Albrecht Dürer, painted c. 1511–13.

A 17th-century view of Vytautas the Great. The tent behind him reminds us that he was a famed warrior

Above left: A stylised depiction of the battle of Nicopolis (1396) by a French miniaturist c. 1472–5. The Turkish archers in the first rank are withdrawing behind the sharpened stakes.

Left: In a 1470 illustration for Jean Froissart's *Chronicles* some prisoners are being massacred while others are led away for ransom.

Above: The medieval city walls of Visby are among the best preserved in Scandinavia.

Engraving of Königsberg in the 1600s, strongly fortified for protection from the numerous wars of that era. After the loss of Marienburg to the Polish king, the grandmasters took up residence here.

Jan Matejko's 1878 painting of the battle of Tannenberg. In the centre in red is the triumphant Vytautas, who rode around the battlefield to stiffen the defenders wherever the danger seemed the greatest. To his left Grandmaster Ulrich von Jungingen is being unhorsed and slain.

Jadwiga, daughter of Jagiełło, by a German painter of the school of Mair von Landshut (1485–1510). She fell ill and died in 1431 before she could marry Friedrich II of Brandenburg.

Sophia Jagiellon, daughter of Casimir IV, by an unknown fifteenth-century painter. She married Friedrich II of Brandenburg-Ansbach in 1479. The genealogies are often confusing.

Top right: The view of Marienburg castle from the Nogat River always impressed visitors. To the left is the grandmaster's residence in the Middle Castle, and to the right is the High Castle with its meeting halls and St Anne's chapel. Out of sight is the Low Castle, with its apartments for visiting crusaders, saunas, and stables. The largest castle in Europe, it was four times the size of Windsor Castle.

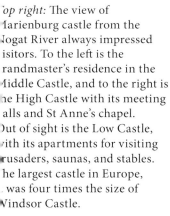

Above right: The island castle at Trakai was a marvel for its time. Although Vilnius was the official capital, Vytautas preferred to live here. He replaced the old wooden fortress with this brick castle shortly after 1400.

Right: The Old Town Hall of Thorn, constructed at the end of the fourteenth century, was the largest brick building in Europe and one of the most beautiful.

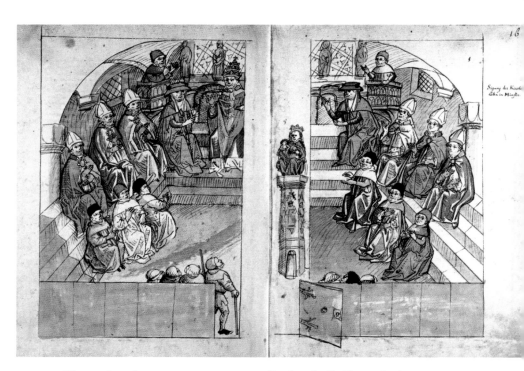

Illustrations from a 1464 manuscript of *Richenthal's Chronicle*, depicting events
at the Council of Constance (1414–18).
Top left: Friedrich of Hohenzollern entering Constance to be named margrave of Brandenburg.
Top right: The great beast brought from Lithuania, preserved in salt.
Above: The pope meeting with cardinals, bishops, and scholars.

Sigismund I of Poland (1467–1548), as envisioned about 1557 by the anonymous painter who signed all his/her works with 'PF'.

St Casimir of Poland (1458–84) by Daniel Schultz the Younger (1615–83), a painter born and raised in Danzig

Martin Truchseß von Wetzhausen (1435–1489), a print published soon after the Teutonic Knights helped in the relief of Vienna from the Turkish siege of 1683.

Duke Albrecht of Brandenburg-Ansbach, seen here in the 1526 portrait by Lucas Cranach the Elder.

Coats of arms of the grandmasters of the Teutonic Order up to Heinrich Reuß von Plauen. He was the thirty-second grandmaster, serving 1467–70. The grandmasters generally put aside their ancestral arms to display the large black cross with the imperial eagle in the centre.

Thence Ghillebert rode to Bohemia to see King Wenceslaus and admire his holy relics (the holy lance, a nail from the True Cross, and numerous heads of saints). Afterwards he returned to England, hoping to visit the St Patrick's Purgatory pilgrimage site in Ireland, but was briefly imprisoned (as a spy?) before being released for the Agincourt campaign in 1415. He fought on the French side, was severely wounded, and captured. Ransomed by Jean of Burgundy, Ghillebert became an important official in the duke's service, negotiating with the Dutch on his behalf and that of the Flemish merchants. There is no doubt that his expert knowledge of Baltic affairs was significant in devising Burgundian trade policies over the next five decades.

In addition to the information Ghillebert gathered for his employer, he undoubtedly passed on a good deal more about east-central Europe to his well-born hosts during his subsequent long career as a diplomat and traveller (which included a later lengthy visit to Prussia, Poland and Lithuania). The underlying reasons for his adventures he blandly disguised from the readers of his memoirs, insisting that he had only the most idle (and noble) motives for his travels. Who knows what impact his table talk had on subsequent political decisions, but his anecdotes of people and places were elaborate, enjoyable and insightful. Surely his listeners got more than mere enjoyment out of his tales. If nothing else, his description of the grandmaster's plight in 1413 must have undermined the Teutonic Knights' pretensions that they were still a force to be reckoned with.

What Sigismund's 1412 delegation to the Golden Horde reported must also have been widely disseminated. One member had been taken prisoner at Nicopolis in 1396 and had written about his experiences, another had been in Turkey. Their reports on the borderlands of Poland and Lithuania must have been appreciated by their master during his later negotiations with Vytautas and Jagiełło.

More Financial Troubles

Plauen found it difficult to pay the war indemnity because his taxpayers in Prussia and the convents in Germany were exhausted. The tax records of 1412 show that many Prussian communities were three years in arrears, an indication that they had not harvested crops successfully during 1410–12. The Polish and Lithuanian armies had done their job of pillage and arson so well that normal agriculture could not resume for lack of draft animals, seed, storage facilities and tools. Since the peasantry were the ultimate source of wealth, their impoverishment implied trouble for the burghers, secular knights and, of course, the Teutonic Order.

The Livonian Order, too, had given all it could without discharging the mercenaries that garrisoned its own castles. The German convents, pressed by Sigismund for help in seeking his coronation, met in Frankfurt am Main to discuss their responsibilities, but in the end offered almost nothing. In fact, the coronation in Rome was so long delayed that although technically Sigismund was only emperor-elect, it became simpler to think of him as the emperor. To make matters worse, this was the moment Wenceslaus chose to express his unhappiness with the order's support of Sigismund's candidacy.

Nevertheless, Plauen made the second payment of the indemnity, 25,000 *Schock Groschen*, on time. Jagiełło released the most important officers. However, he kept 600 lesser captives against the final payment, then demanded that the Livonian Order release the captives it had taken in Lithuania. The Livonian master replied that he could not return the prisoners, as they had already been sold.

Imperial Intervention

When Plauen saw that he would not be able to make the third and largest payment, almost half the original amount, he asked the emperor for help. Sigismund, however, had plans of his own, magnificent plans – he was currently in Italy, trying to end the Great Schism and secure his coronation by a universally recognised pope. He had been named German king in October 1410 by the electors, and that had been confirmed by the nobles and clerics in July 1411, but he had not yet been crowned in either Aachen as German king, or in Rome as Holy Roman emperor. Although he talked of unifying Italy, Germany, Hungary and later Bohemia under his rule, he had the immediate practical problem that he was technically only emperor-elect.

He occasionally dreamt unrealistically of acquiring Poland – perhaps a memory from his youth, when his first wife was to have inherited the Polish kingdom. It was this unlikely hope that caused him to propose an alliance with the grandmaster against Jagiełło. All he wanted, he said, was 600,000 florins from the Teutonic Order! This was the equivalent of 230,000 *Schock Groschen*, more than double the indemnity for the Peace of Thorn. As Sigismund probably explained, elections cost money; and coronations were expensive too. He needed the cash.

Sigismund had expensive habits. He was one of the great womanisers of his era, and his wife's many admirers did not bring the treasury an offsetting income. That went into her private fortune. He was cruel, capable of ordering the deaths of prisoners and the maiming of enemies, of confiscating property and dispossessing ancient families. But he was also an athlete who excelled at the joust, he was multi-lingual, and his command of Latin was excellent, if somewhat erratic grammatically – later, at the Council of Constance, when a cardinal informed him that he had used the word *schisma* as a feminine noun, not neuter, he replied in Latin that the King of the Romans was above grammar. Such moments illuminate why Sigismund was so popular.

Sigismund's Italian adventures were fantastically costly. In truth, there was nothing about Sigismund that was not somewhat fantastic. From his long moustache to his elaborate robes to his complicated political schemes, Sigismund was a ruler who stood out among his contemporaries. It is a tribute to his personality and his political skill that his oft-disappointed supporters rarely lost hope in him. Surely, the *next* time his plans would meet total success, he would be able to carry out the promises he had made, and he would reward his followers for their loyalty. After all, there was the example of Friedrich of Hohenzollern, the burgrave of Nuremberg, who in 1415 he allowed to purchase Brandenburg. (Lands this important did not go on the market often.) This was a reward for his services at Nicopolis and in the recent election. Also, Friedrich's brother had long been married to Sigismund's late sister. Alas, Sigismund generally had the attention span of a spoiled child and even less empathy for others' problems.

The grandmaster's representative to Sigismund was the marshal, Michael Küchmeister, who had recently been ransomed; he wanted a treaty of alliance with the emperor, no matter what the cost, no matter what Plauen's instructions were. This, he believed, might allow him and his order to take revenge on their enemies. In return for imperial aid in making peace and hiring mercenaries, he promised Sigismund 400,000 florins, and he spread bribes around lavishly. Considering Küchmeister's background in the economic management of the Prussian state, this was extraordinary behaviour. If anyone knew the value of a *Gulden*, he did. All in all, he spent more money than was needed to settle the indemnity to Poland.

When the marshal returned to Prussia with two treaties in hand, Plauen refused to recognise them. He made payments of 25,000 florins on debts contracted by Küchmeister, but repudiated all his other promises. The marshal was understandably angry – he was accustomed to traditional diplomacy, which rested on the offering of bribes and presents; and he believed that another war with Poland without an important ally would be a disaster. Better to pay Sigismund, a friend, the fantastic sums of money than to enrich the foe.

Sigismund, meanwhile, continued his own feckless policies, trying first this, then that, pursuing whatever oversized plan appealed to him at the moment. On the one hand, he saw the Teutonic Knights as a natural ally against Poland; on the other hand, he wanted Polish and Lithuanian assistance against the Turks, and Jagiełło and Vytautas had demonstrated at Tannenberg that they were now the dominant military powers in the region. In November 1411 Sigismund met Jagiełło and his queen. Gracious as ever, he was able to establish a cordial relationship verging on an alliance; in December he met Vytautas. Despite the show of friendship, shortly afterwards Sigismund was encouraging the grandmaster to hold fast against the Polish demands.

Plauen delayed making the third payment, using the money to hire mercenaries and rebuild his castles to withstand cannon fire. Jagiełło was angry, and asked what the 'guests' (pilgrims/crusaders, but in reality mostly mercenaries) were doing. Plauen responded softly that the 'guests' were peaceful.

Sigismund sought to mediate personally, a method of diplomacy ideally suited to his personality. He liked nothing so much as public acclaim, and the settlement of disputes to which he was not a party brought him fame and possible advantage. He invited Jagiełło and Plauen to a summit conference, after which a papal legate hurriedly made the final arrangements for a meeting on the Hungarian border in mid-March 1412. Within three days the principals had reached agreement on all the disputed points. Then the party began. Vytautas joined the festivities in mid-April.

The grandmaster did not feel the need to attend the meeting personally, but he sent a respectable delegation: Archbishop Johannes Wallenrode of Riga and Heinrich Reuss of Plauen. The delegates went first to Silesia, then to Buda, where the king was residing. The subjects of the talks – the definition of the Samogitian border, the return of the remaining captives, the payment of the indemnity, and the rights of the bishops in Prussia – were rather overshadowed by the tournaments and hunts staged in Jagiełło's honour. The guests also attended the wedding of the archduke of Austria, Ernst I ('the Iron') to Cymburgis of Masovia. The groom was thirty-five, the bride between fourteen and eighteen. Present were her parents Siemowit IV and Alexandra, Sigismund and Barbara, Jagiełło and Anne, Vytautas and Anna, and Sigismund Kaributas – all related to the bride and groom and to one another in overlapping ways – and a great host of lesser personages.

The delegates of the Teutonic Order arrived in May, led by Archbishop Wallenrode. They managed to spend 10,000 florins without achieving much. There was a moment of anxiety when Sigismund was knocked unconscious in a fall from his horse, but he quickly recovered. Jagiełło and Vytautas went home in June with a mutual defence treaty with Sigismund, each promising not to aid the others' enemies!

Sigismund was content with vague promises to assist him in his three great projects: ending the Great Schism, uniting the Roman Catholic and Orthodox churches, and organising a pan-European crusade that would drive the Turks from Europe. He also enjoyed the parties. Gilt and glitter were more attractive than an iron will and steely determination.

In contrast to the magnificent frivolity and thoughtless play, Plauen decreed that Prussians would fill these days with prayer and penitence. That February the grandmaster and his officers went barefoot from church to church, praying for a favourable peace. Twelve monks were brought into Marienburg so that continual prayer could be offered while the grandmaster watched for the return of his delegation. It was a long and painful wait for the aging and anxious men of the convents, whose only ornament was the black cross on their white robes, but time passed quickly for the bejewelled women and silk-clad courtiers dancing the nights away at the imperial balls.

In August 1412 Sigismund ruled the Peace of Thorn a proper and just treaty, decreed that the exiled bishops must be allowed to return, and ordered a commission sent to determine the border of Samogitia, with the inhabitants of the disputed regions choosing between Vytautas and the Teutonic Order as their overlord. Lastly, he announced that all prisoners would be exchanged within six months and that a reduction in the indemnity would be reached by mediation. It was an entirely fair and just decision – exactly the opposite of that which the grandmaster had hoped to obtain. Why have a German emperor as lord and protector, if his decisions were to be favourable to Poland?

Sigismund's lone concession was proposing to take for himself the money raised to pay the indemnity and to make offers to Jagiełło that would satisfy him. Sigismund suggested that the grandmaster accept the proposal, then pay him 25,000 florins for his efforts on the order's behalf. In addition, there were hints that the order could return the Neumark to Sigismund in lieu of cash payments. Jagiełło also had his eye on that territory, and no one could rule out the possibility that high politics would take precedence over the interests of the Teutonic Order.

Renewed war

Plauen was stirred into action by the fear of losing the Neumark, which had been mortgaged to pay the earlier instalments of the war debt. Although the district was small and unruly, it was the vital link to Germany that permitted reinforcements to come to Prussia. If the Neumark had been in hostile hands in 1410, Marienburg could not have been relieved; if that small territory were surrendered now, the land route would be closed. Plauen called the estates together again, ordered that all silver vessels be melted down, and that all assets be collected for sale. To universal surprise, he made the final payment promptly in January 1413.

Jagiełło was as displeased with that as were many of Plauen's own men. The king had no way to use a large sum of money other than quickly dispersing it among his friends and supporters; he would far rather have had new territories and castles. Some of Vytautas's share of the money went to the imperial commissioner who had been sent to demarcate the Samogitian boundary, which was now more confused than before. The commissioner had been displeased by the order's lack of cooperation, and Vytautas was saying that the marshal was not going to drive him out of his newly constructed castle at Welun (Veliuona). When the marshal tried to show him the documents describing the boundaries, the grand duke finally shouted: 'Prussia is mine from ancient times and I have a claim on everything to the Osse River, for that is my patrimony!'

The marshal understood that this was a very creative reconstruction of historical facts, by which Vytautas claimed all of Prussia that was not to be taken by Jagiełło. (The Osse was the northern border of Culm province.) Samogitia was north of the Nemunas River, and the sandy strip along the Baltic coast had probably been originally Kurish – certainly it had been thinly settled when the Germans arrived and soon became even less populated. In the end, the commissioner relied on recommendations from Vytautas and the exiled bishop of Ermland in awarding all disputed lands to Lithuania. Although this ignored every definition of Samogitia's boundaries since 1252, this border remained unchanged until 1919.

Plauen considered none of these petty disputes worth close attention, since even awards by papal commissioners could be reversed. As soon as the burden of debt was removed, he turned to preparations for war. A few victories, he apparently reasoned, would nullify the treaties and judgments, humble his enemies, and restore the power of the Teutonic

Order. He could also hope that the renewed tensions between Jagiełło and Vytautas would divide his foes. However, at the Horodło conference (October 1413) in eastern Poland, attended by many of the nobles and boyars of both states, the king agreed that Lithuania would have an independent grand duke after Vytautas's death, the king (if still living) was to name Vytautas's successor, and he ordered that the Polish and Lithuanian noble families be consolidated by sharing coats-of-arms.

There is a subtlety here that could easily elude anyone familiar only with the western idea that noble status passed father to son – in Poland noble status came from membership in a clan, a membership that had no fixed geographic centre and which accepted royal appointees and even adoptions by its own members. All shared the same heraldic devices, making recognition easy. Thus, enrolling Lithuanians into forty-seven of the hundred-odd clans was no innovation, and it satisfied Lithuanian objections to being ruled by Jagiełło's Polish successors. The royal promise to appoint local nobles as governors in place of dynastic princes was also popular. Thus the Horodło conference was in every way a major step towards bringing Lithuania into the western world.

The king, whose right to rule as *Supreme Prince* was now even more theoretical than before, left the details of governing to Vytautas and did little in Lithuania beyond hunting. Thereafter he was generally present only in the western, heavily wooded part of his country, usually during the winters. Although he made a visit to Samogitia to urge the people to become Christians, Jagiełło took little interest in that region. Vytautas, meanwhile, fully occupied with his war against Novgorod, could not send help to the king.

All this seemed to work in Plauen's favour. When the Livonian master agreed to provide a small number of experienced knights for service in Prussia, then when more men came from Germany, the grandmaster was ready to fight.

Although many knights, and the secular knights and towns as well, were sceptical about the need for war, they did not object openly. Still, Plauen was sufficiently aware of this sentiment to respond by building a personal party among the knights from the Rhineland and other regions who had been shut out of the high offices and honours. This was noticed by the knights of Westphalian origin, who were accustomed to governing. Civil war was a distinct possibility.

Plauen, a master of propaganda, now spread the prophecies of Elisabeth of Marienwerder, asserting that she had correctly predicted the defeat at Tannenberg and that she had twice said the Poles would not be able to capture Marienburg. The disaster in battle had thus been unavoidable, but ultimate victory was assured. She had spoken to Jagiełło, he said, when the king visited St Dorothea's tomb in Marienwerder, and she had criticised the Poles' unjust and cruel war. Jagiełło's piety would avail him no more against divine prophecy than had the crusaders' noble sacrifices in countless conflicts with the enemies of God.

In the late summer of 1413 Plauen was ready. He had 6,000 soldiers stationed on the Pomeranian front and 15,000 on the borders of Dobrin and Masovia. The king and grand duke were busy in the south and could not send much aid to their vassals in the north. Therefore, the time seemed right to reverse the verdict of Tannenberg.

Plauen ordered Michael Küchmeister to begin the offensive without him until he recovered from a severe illness. The marshal's attack was a success in every way. For sixteen days his forces burned and plundered, inflicting great damage on the homes and fields of the helpless peasantry, without meeting any significant resistance from the local forces.

Küchmeister, however, was not happy. He believed that the war was a terrible mistake and, as he talked with his fellow officers about it, he concluded that he had to stop the invasion. He ordered the army to return to Prussia and commanded Heinrich Reuss of Plauen to halt his attack on Pomerania. When the grandmaster's cousin went ahead with his raid, Küchmeister persuaded his junior officers that it was necessary to retreat.

This rebellion would not have occurred if Plauen had been present or perhaps even if the officers had expected him to recover from his illness, but the ironwilled grandmaster had a mortal body. It seemed that only Plauen could give a St Crispian's Day speech such as Shakespeare provided for Henry V in similar dire circumstances in 1415, only Plauen who could put new heart into men growing accustomed to defeat.

For Küchmeister the issue was simple. He knew that the order could not afford to continue the war. Even if he won the immediate contest with the kingdom of Poland, there was no way to recover Samogitia. Therefore, the logical course of action was to make peace and give up Samogitia for a few years. Better to wait until the aged leaders of Poland and Lithuania had passed away; meanwhile, they should concentrate on restoring prosperity to Prussia. Since Jagiełło professed a desire for peace on the basis of the Treaty of Thorn, the only obstacle to ending hostilities was Heinrich of Plauen.

This was more than a conflict of wills. It was also a constitutional crisis. At the heart of the dispute lay two widely accepted but incompatible concepts of government. First, there was the royalist or autocratic state, by which Plauen could expect unconditional obedience. Such was the ideal of popes and emperors, bishops and abbots. Alternatively, there were the various forms of representative government, by which a ruler was bound to accede to the wishes of his aristocratic inner circle of advisers and vassals, perhaps even to the estates – for example, a parliament. While the Teutonic Order seemed to be an autocracy, it was more accurately an aristocratic corporation. The officers and knights expected to share in making decisions. While the knights were not eager to hear representatives of secular knights and townspeople speak, they allowed them to defend their own interests. When general chapters were called, they insisted on discussing important matters, and there was a memory of previous general chapters having removed grandmasters. While rare and long ago, everyone remembered the precedent.

Poland was experiencing a similar constitutional crisis, kept under control only by Jagiełło's surprising longevity. In the Holy Roman Empire the electors had deposed Wenceslaus of Bohemia. Nor was the Church immune. The Great Schism, with three popes claiming to be the successor of St Peter, led to a call for a general council. The idea that churchmen should decide which of the three claimants would be pope caused some to ask whether the Church should be ruled by a powerful pope or by assemblies of churchmen who met at regular intervals.

Of course, the Teutonic Order's crisis was more than a reflection of the *Zeitgeist*. It was also a reflection of local politics. There was only one basic issue at the moment – war – and that was to be understood in terms of personalities and policies. At this moment Plauen's advisers disagreed with him over the wisdom of making war. Some of them had come to know Jagiełło personally during their captivity and took his expressed desires for peace seriously. All of them understood the gravity of the economic crisis.

Once Plauen had risen from his sick bed, he disregarded his critics' advice and used every constitutional means to remove the most outspoken of them from office. He even called a general chapter to discuss the crisis. Naturally, in the short time available no representatives from Germany could be present. That eliminated the Egloffstein faction from the debate. Since Plauen could expect to win a majority of votes from the Prussian officers, he would be able to do whatever he wanted. In his gruff and impolite fashion he threatened dissident subordinates with reprisals, refused to speak with Küchmeister, and surrounded himself with bodyguards. He would probably have succeeded in his plans too, if illness had not prostrated him again.

On 9 October 1413, five days before the general chapter was to convene, Küchmeister and his friends moved, sending their supporters into the grandmaster's residence in Marienburg. Plauen's efforts to defend himself were ineffective – he had barricaded himself in his room and slept with his armour nearby, but he was too ill to resist. Most knights probably opposed the coup, but they were not enough of them in the castle to intervene and most surely wanted to avoid civil war. Küchmeister briefly addressed the knights in Marienburg who had assembled for the general chapter, justifying his action as a necessary if unfortunate step and naming the *Großkomtur*, Hermann Gans, as acting grandmaster. The knights, having no persuasive alternative, did not object – Plauen was so ill that everyone expected him to die, and without his leadership, nothing could be done.

In January 1414 a formal general chapter with representation from Germany and Livonia met in Marienburg to its predetermined conclusion. Plauen offered his resignation, which was accepted. After that he was sent to an insignificant post at Engelsburg (Pokrzywno) in the distant south-west, perhaps in hope that he would desert to Jagiełło and complete his disgrace. Heinrich Reuss of Plauen was removed to an isolated command where he would be both powerless and easily watched. Then the officers elected Küchmeister grandmaster.

Küchmeister promised to make a permanent peace with Poland and Lithuania on the basis of the Peace of Thorn. He dismissed the mercenaries and offered to negotiate the remaining points of dispute. Since the war-mongering Plauen was now gone, the new grandmaster assumed that he would find Vytautas and Jagiełło ready to make peace on equitable terms. He was utterly disappointed.

Jagiełło announced a programme designed to embarrass the new regime. He demanded that both Plauen and Heinrich Reuss of Plauen be restored to their former offices, and he spread the story abroad that the Teutonic Knights were now managed by an illegal and violent cabal. That so frightened the conspirators that they took another look at the former grandmaster, who had now recovered his health and was being supported by his relative, Count Albrecht of Schwarzburg, then in Prussia. Fearful of a countercoup, Küchmeister ordered Plauen arrested.

Negotiations with Jagiełło

Küchmeister's policy was to adhere strictly to the Treaty of Thorn: peace now, but no renunciation of the order's ultimate sovereignty over Samogitia. Among his first acts was to remind Vytautas of the order's continuing interest in that land by confiscating goods bound for Lithuania, claiming that he was merely retaliating for goods confiscated there. A further aspect of Küchmeister's policy was to bring every diplomatic means possible to bear on Jagiełło, either to persuade him to sign a permanent peace treaty or to so drag out the talks until his order was ready to fight again. If possible, he would delay and delay, waiting for the ageing monarch and grand duke to enter their graves, after which Samogitia was to revert to the Teutonic Knights.

He was disappointed to hear from his diplomats at the peripatetic imperial court and at the church council assembling at Constance that Sigismund was too preoccupied to help. Sigismund was planning his coronation as German king in Aachen, which would be followed in due time by an imperial coronation in Rome, if he could persuade the churchmen to decide quickly which pope was the rightful heir of St Peter. In short – no help was coming soon.

Küchmeister then sent a steady stream of messengers to Jagiełło's ever-travelling court, until he finally arranged a personal meeting near Thorn. Unfortunately for Küchmeister, in April 1414, when he and the archbishop of Riga arrived for the meeting, they found that the king and grand duke had brought armies with them to support their demands for significant territorial concessions.

Küchmeister had only one minor success at the talks – he sat down with King Jagiełło as an equal. He opened the discussions with a statement that he greatly desired Prussia and Poland to be at peace again, that he had demonstrated his peaceful intents by removing from office the one man who wanted war, and that he was willing to demonstrate his peaceful intentions further by signing a permanent treaty that confirmed the terms of the Peace of Thorn. The king responded by asking for additional proof of his desire for peace – the complete renunciation of Samogitia.

From that moment on the discussions revolved around the Samogitian question. Küchmeister himself was willing to give up the land, for he saw no value in possessing it; but his subordinates were of a different mind, and he therefore had to insist on not deviating from the terms of the treaty: ultimate sovereignty lay with the Teutonic Order. He asked Jagiełło if he did not remember confirming him in his office as governor of Samogitia. The king claimed to have no such recollection. The talks continued in this fashion for three hours. Finally, the king demanded that the grandmaster give up all claims to the disputed territory for then and evermore, then added that the order would also have to give up Culm and Pomerellia as well and then pay another huge indemnity to reimburse him for his recent expenses. Küchmeister must have been stunned. As the Polish and Prussian parties rode away in opposite directions, both knew that the unhappy grandmaster's only choices were between fighting and surrender. He reluctantly chose to fight.

Küchmeister was somehow now committed to the war he had sought to avoid, but he now lacked the advantages Plauen had worked so hard to acquire. Moreover, he had dispersed his predecessor's armies and dulled the will for victory. He had learned that the king disliked traitors and despised fools, and Jagiełło had treated him as both. He sought desperately for last-minute aid, writing to the emperor and authorising him to make a final decision on territorial matters, something he had refused to concede earlier. He sent messengers in all directions to plead for troops and money, but in vain. Since he had little money, and that was debased, he could hire but few mercenaries, and the troops in Prussia were too few to risk the pitched battle necessary to defend the frontiers.

The Hunger War

Küchmeister concentrated on defending the province of Culm, where the nobles and burghers had surrendered so quickly four years earlier. He managed to block that route directly into the Prussian heartland, forcing the king into a lengthy siege of border forts that ultimately caused him to move east along the route of the 1410 invasion. At harvest time, in July 1414, the Polish–Lithuanian army approached Osterode.

The royal army contained many more Polish knights than had been present at Tannenberg, and some Moldavians, but there were few Lithuanians present. Nevertheless, prominent among Vytautas's warriors were Ruśian and Tatar horsemen whose atrocities soon won them a special place in Prussian folklore. The armies marched through Ermland to the sea, then moved east and west. Everywhere they burned, murdered and raped. The king was apparently trying to force the grandmaster to bring his forces out of the castles and face him on the battlefield. He was confident that he could repeat his Tannenberg victory. What he earned was the hatred of Prussian nobles, townsmen and peasants who might have become his allies.

All Küchmeister could do was to pray for a miracle. He shared the king's opinion about the inevitable result of any pitched combat, and he was confident that the invaders could not maintain any siege long enough to take a major castle. However, he did have to forfeit the harvest, the villages, the mills and the warehouses; but he anticipated their destruction by burning as much potential food and fodder as he could. The invaders, unable to obtain bread, ate what they could find; the inevitable result was dysentery. The tactic of starving the invaders caused the conflict to be called the 'Hunger War'. That name took on a more sinister meaning after the Polish and Lithuanian forces withdrew, when it was the Prussians' turn to starve. Even Masovia was struck by famine, the result of depredations by the Tatar and Lithuanian horsemen. The herring catch was diminished, too, thanks to the destruction of the fishing fleet, and merchants ceased to call on ports where rumour had it that there was no money to be earned.

The extent of the destruction in the Hunger War can be estimated by the order's detailed records in Heiligenbeil (Mamonovo, in the Kaliningrad region). One subdistrict of twenty-five villages lost in property the fantastic sum of 31,875 marks. Considering that a horse sold for three marks, that a small farm could be purchased for fifteen marks, and an entire church could be built for 500 marks, nearly every building must have been destroyed. That only twenty-seven men were killed and ten youths carried away indicates that the inhabitants must have taken refuge somewhere. Village after village in other districts reported losses of 400 marks, 800, 400, 100, and so on, with total destruction of houses, grain stocks and herds. Only the arrival of foodstuffs from Livonia saved the population from even greater suffering.

The grandmaster's few tactical successes, such as capturing Vytautas's marshal, were of no importance. Jagiełło was single-minded in his pursuit of victory, allowing nothing to distract him from reducing Prussian towns to smoking ruins. The Teutonic Knights had chosen to begin the war; the king was going to end it, not just on this occasion, but by dealing such a blow to the Teutonic Knights as would render them incapable of future mischief.

Küchmeister had chosen to avoid combat, but it did not work tactically any better than his diplomacy had strategically. His plan had all the disadvantages he had pointed out in Plauen's proposal, without the forces needed to fight it or the inspiring personality to direct it. Moreover, since Heinrich of Plauen now seemed more dangerous, he moved him to a prison in Danzig until 1418, then exiled him to a minor post. He sought to imprison Heinrich Reuss of Plauen as well, but the former commander of Danzig escaped to Germany. Such actions were hardly likely either to inspire confidence in the grandmaster's judgement, or to encourage minor officers to take any initiative on their own.

Küchmeister had come into office on arguments that Plauen had ruled like a tyrant, arresting men on inadequate grounds, and raising taxes illegally. Now he found it necessary to do the same. Küchmeister had promised tax relief. Instead, he had to raise new taxes. To raise those taxes, he had to ignore the assembly of burghers and knights that he had promised he would consult for advice and counsel. He had hoped to reduce the size of the army, but instead had found it necessary to hire mercenaries. However, the force he could raise was inadequate to defeat an enemy even more numerous and confident than the one which had triumphed at Tannenberg.

He had promised an honourable and definitive peace, but all he could do was humbly plead for a truce. He had to endure Jagiełło's taunting demands that Plauen be released from prison. This he refused to do, at the cost of consenting to other stipulations before Jagiełło granted even a short truce. When the war ended in October 1414, the matter was given over to papal mediation. Of course, John XXIII and his cardinals had problems of their own at the moment which prevented them from acting. As a result, Küchmeister was limited even in his ability to negotiate the extent of his final humiliation.

For his subjects, however, even worse was in store. Plague broke out in Danzig and spread through the cities, through the villages, and into the countryside. No one was safe. The prelates ordered their congregations to make processions every Friday, to confess their sins, to change their way of living, and to fear the Lord. Eighty-six brothers of the order died in this year, a number of whom were worthy men who would have served the order well. Also a number of officers in Germany died, including Egloffstein.

In short, between Tannenberg, the Hunger War and the plague, the number of knights present in 1410 was reduced by half; and many of the survivors were aged or infirm.

Küchmeister found himself in an impossible situation – honour and the wishes of the membership required that he follow Sigismund's instructions, even when Sigismund ordered him to prepare for wars he did not want and had no means of prosecuting effectively. He learned that the emperor could not be relied upon, but who else could help him? Sigismund may have been crowned German king, but he could not be counted upon to serve 'German interests' when those conflicted with his own personal concerns, the need to defend his Hungarian domains, or his interests in the problems of the Church and Italian politics. At the moment Sigismund was preoccupied with the organisation of the Council of Constance, a frustratingly difficult task.

In short, Sigismund wanted to resolve the problems of the Teutonic Order mainly because they distracted him from his other plans, and he wanted them resolved in such a way that future grandmasters would give him unconditional obedience. If he wanted the order so assist him against the Turks or against Poland, or to secure his claims on the crown of Bohemia, he expected immediate and unquestioning compliance. That was something the Teutonic Knights had never given anyone. Moreover, Sigismund probably did not have specific long-term plans for the military order at this moment, nothing he could promise to sway the undecided. Decisiveness was never a characteristic one associated with Sigismund, but he knew what suited his immediate purposes. Right now that meant preventing Jagiełło from acquiring the Neumark or other territories, as might happen if the Polish army crushed the Teutonic Order again. He assured the grandmaster that he would be there to protect him, even while his immediate actions seemed to belie that promise.

To the extent that Küchmeister had any insight into his dilemma, it was in recognising the danger in submitting to Sigismund. Consequently, he resolutely held to the formula that the Teutonic Knights were equally responsible to the Holy Roman emperor and the Holy Father, and he was determined to follow policies that protected the military order, not ones which sacrificed it for Sigismund's distant schemes. This would not be easy – every time Küchmeister unfurled his great white banner with the black cross, he saw the gold and black imperial coat-of-arms signifying his close relationship with the emperor. Moreover, Sigismund's determination to bend the grandmaster to his will meant allowing him to learn that he could not defend his state alone.

The Papal Legate's Truce

The papal legate, William of Lausanne, arranged for a two-year truce. This Treaty of Strasburg (named for the city on the Drewenz River where it was negotiated, today Brodnica) suspended hostilities, but allowed Jagiełło to start them again at almost any moment. Thus, Küchmeister could not release his small force of mercenaries. He recognised that Jagiełło's intent was to drain his financial resources dry, but there was nothing he could do about it.

The grandmaster melted down whatever silver remained in the churches' treasuries. When he proposed to restore the silver content in the coins to the previous standard, his officers realistically pointed out that they could either mint a small number of good coins or a large number of debased ones, and that right then they needed a lot of coins. They could always require local merchants and peasants to accept them, and while mercenaries would be reluctant, they always earned more from pillage than pay. The grandmaster had to give way, even though he understood that his state's prestige depended on minting good coins, and that the debased currency undermined all arguments that the Teutonic Knights were there to stay.

Küchmeister next tried to detach Vytautas from Jagiełło. The two cousins had never fully trusted one another as much as they had needed one another's support, and Küchmeister remembered that past grandmasters had been able to play on Vytautas's emotions. This could best be done through the Livonian master because Livonia and Lithuania faced the same problems in Ruś: Vytautas was concerned with Moscow, the Livonian master with Novgorod. The ancient antagonism of the crusaders and the former pagans was slowly disappearing; in its place came an awareness of common interests.

However, this process was occurring too slowly to help Küchmeister now. Jagiełło was not as dependent on Lithuanian help as he had been in the past. Thanks to the increasing number of patriots willing to join his army, the king had sufficient resources of his own to defeat in the field any force of mercenaries the Teutonic Order could raise.

Thus it came about that the Peace of Thorn was the deathblow to the Teutonic Knights that the battle of Tannenberg had not been. Even more important was the surrender of Samogitia to Jagiełło and Vytautas for their lifetimes because the knights of the military order had made the pacification and conversion of the pagans there their *raison d'être*. The symbolic end of the struggle against paganism was emphasised by the subsequent breakdown of discipline and then military defeat.

Nor was there an obvious message that the grandmaster could send to the West. The Teutonic Knights now either had to denounce Jagiełło and Vytautas as sly hypocrites and secret pagans, and call the establishment of a bishopric in Samogitia a sham, or admit that their crusade was over. There was no real justification for summoning crusaders from western Europe or collecting money in the German churches and chapels unless there was a clear and present danger to Christendom. Even the Orthodox clergy was now taking a sincere interest in converting the last remaining pagans in Ruś.

In short, paganism was disappearing as an official faith, and the Teutonic Order could have rested its crusade then, had it chosen to do so. The Peace of Thorn left the Teutonic Order in Prussia no more unique as a representative of the Church or of Germany than any other ecclesiastical state in the Holy Roman Empire attempting to defend itself from secular neighbours. This situation was recognised by western Europeans who had been long-time supporters of the Teutonic Order. Fewer gave money, and very few came east as 'pilgrims' or 'guests' on crusade; and those who came were probably disappointed that the festivities did not live up to the splendid reputation they had once enjoyed. Between the intractability of Plauen and the incompetence of Küchmeister, the leaders of the Teutonic Knights had squandered the last resources of Prussia, brought devastation to the countryside and cities, and created turmoil inside the once highly disciplined military order itself. Internal dissension, foreign invasion and economic catastrophe were the products of pride and miscalculation.

Even worse was the thought that the military order had outlived its usefulness in the Baltic. The German knights could not bear to think of the Poles as their military superiors, much less acknowledge that Jagiełło had bested them. Any grandmaster who proposed peace with Poland, any officer who might have wondered if the military order could serve Christendom better on another front, would have been removed by the general membership. The three popes (Rome, Avignon, and the Council pope, John XXIII) could provide no leadership, the Holy Roman Empire no help. Under the circumstances all that Küchmeister could do was to hire as many mercenaries as he could afford, prolong the truces one after the other, and hope that something could be achieved at the Council of Constance to save his order and its mission in the Baltic.

Chapter 6

The Council of Constance

The Schism in the Church

The Council of Constance was the supreme effort of medieval intellectuals to turn the unhappy maelstrom of recent church history back into its traditional, trusted, tranquil bed (as they fondly but inaccurately remembered the past), so that both the Papacy and the Empire might enjoy a long-needed period of rest.

Above all, the intellectuals, together with most prelates, clerics and laity cried out for a resolution of the Great Schism. Since 1378 the Church had been divided: one pope in Rome and another in Avignon. But while their followers quarrelled over who was the proper head of the Church, there was more unity over the need to check clerical corruption that fed on inadequate incomes and less than adequate supervision. More than a few important posts were dual appointments, one from Rome (Boniface IX, 1389–1404; Innocent VII, 1404–6; Gregory XII, 1406–14), the other from Avignon (Benedict XIII, 1394–1417). The choice for physical occupation of a see or abbey was determined by politics, not the quality of the candidate.

Monarchs were using the schism to strengthen their shaky control of their own kingdoms. Intellectuals bemoaned unsavoury but necessary political compromises; they were frustrated by the repeated failures to find a place even to discuss the crisis. Many, in fact, were persuaded that no soul had entered heaven since the onset of the schism. The existence of multiple popes was more than a scandal; it was a crisis that threatened every churchman and Christian, and the Teutonic Order too. The grandmasters had tried to avoid the evil consequences of the controversy by ignoring it, but in the early 1400s Archbishop Johannes of Wallenrode of Riga, having quarrelled with the Livonian master and knowing that the Teutonic Order would be supported by the Roman popes, had brought his complaints before Benedict XIII. This had involved the order in the complexities of Church intrigue.

The procurator-general of the Teutonic Knights, the lobbyist/ diplomat responsible for representing the order to the Roman popes, had carefully observed the efforts of churchmen over a period of years to reunite the Church, but under orders from Marienburg he had abstained from taking part in the discussions personally. The Teutonic Order had remained steadfastly loyal to the Roman popes, but made few statements which might anger the Avignon curia. Because the order had cast its lot with the Roman pope, the grandmaster and his officers had difficult decisions to make when rebellious cardinals from both parties joined together to call for a general council. If they withdrew their allegiance from the Roman pope, and the council failed to unseat him, they risked his displeasure; and the odds were good that the pope was stronger than the churchmen. If they remained loyal to Rome and the council succeeded in deposing him, the order would be vulnerable to a review of all papal decisions made in its favour over the recent decades.

When the procurator-general, Peter of Wormditt (c. 1360–1419), was summoned to Pisa in 1408 to discuss the possible deposition of the two quarrelling popes, he chose to avoid committing to any policy that might later prove embarrassing. Instead, he travelled to Prussia for a conference with Ulrich of Jungingen and his counsellors. Such an important decision could not be made on the basis of written communications, not even when written in code – messages were too easily intercepted. Perhaps the safest course would have been to remain aloof from the discussions, stay nominally loyal to Rome, and await the outcome of the matter. But caution was not in Ulrich of Jungingen's nature. In February 1409 he announced that the Order of Saint Mary of the Germans would be represented at the Church council. By May Peter of Wormditt was in Pisa.

The Council of Pisa

The gathering at Pisa attracted 22 cardinals, 180 bishops, 87 abbots and 41 priors and generals of religious orders. Almost all were more important than the procurator-general who had represented the Teutonic Knights since 1403. Nevertheless, Peter of Wormditt was not a quiet observer. He had seen more of life at the Roman court than the vast majority of clergymen had ever dreamed of experiencing; therefore, his testimony at the hearings for the deposition of the Roman and Avignon popes was of great importance. He spoke openly of papal corruption, citing examples of misdeeds he had either heard about or seen personally. Particularly damning was his account of the sabotage of negotiations for ending the schism. He sought to persuade churchmen that rather than continue efforts to depose the Avignon pope and persuade his adherents to recognise the Roman claimant, they should declare both popes deposed and elect a new supreme pontiff. He was not alone in voicing this distasteful and painful idea, but he helped move the undecided into a majority. The council declared Gregory XII and Benedict XIII deposed, then in June 1409 elected a new pope.

Alexander V was a learned Franciscan of Greek ancestry, noted for his lack of corruption. It was widely hoped that he could not only end the schism in the Roman Catholic Church, but also bring about a reunion with the Orthodox Church. Best of all, he was a well-known friend and supporter of the Teutonic Knights, and would remember the role that they had in his election. The procurator-general congratulated himself on having used discretion and restraint. He had not told the story of the previous pope's borrowing his valuable warhorse and not returning it, nor had he recounted every scandal he knew. His careful choice of the details he chose *not* to relate preserved friendships with officials in the curia who had been as deeply involved in the acts of corruption as the pope had been, including the man who would become pope in 1410 after Alexander V died suddenly. Balthasar Cossa of Bologna, who took the name John XXIII, was widely believed to know more about politics and horses than saying Mass.

The Crisis Deepens

After John XXIII became pope, he was able to bring peace to parts of the papal domains in central Italy, but his moral shortcomings soon became obvious. This increased the difficulty of persuading the two other popes to resign. Frustrated churchmen began to clamour for another council, to meet in a central location convenient to the German, French and English participants, yet accessible to the numerous Italian bishops and abbots.

The location was important because the conciliar leaders wanted to involve all the major clergymen, so that any decision made there would end the schism once and for all. Such a council could then take up the question of Church reform, so that future popes would not fall into corruption as had all the others, including the recently elected pontiff.

John XXIII had been required by the Council of Pisa to call another council, but he had cleverly summoned the churchmen to Rome almost immediately, knowing that few could attend another lengthy meeting so soon. Then he quickly dismissed the handful of churchmen who appeared. This was a sign he was not eager to give reform-minded clergymen a forum to hold him accountable for his actions.

Proposals for reforms offended traditionalists. It was practically impossible to rise to high office through talent alone – family con-nections, compromises, conspiracies, bribery and even occasional threats were necessary to get anything accomplished. Therefore decisions had to be made by the reformers beforehand as to what abuses would be discussed, promises made not to look too deeply into each other's past, and there had to be a general caution against going too far.

Opposed to the details and the general concept alike were the three popes and their closest supporters, who saw in the proposals ideas which would deprive all future popes of time-honoured privileges and incomes. If corruption had crept into the awarding of offices, the resolution of legal controversies and the distribution of money, that was part of the exercise of power. Without power, the pope was nothing. There was no point to a unified Church if future popes were unable to defend themselves and the Church from all the dangers that everyone could see round about them.

The Teutonic Knights had long profited from papal officials being dependent on fees rather than living on salaries. The lawyers, and their procurator employer, knew that bureaucratic functionaries operated in much the same way no matter who was sitting on the papal throne. Routine paperwork went on, sometimes slower, sometimes faster, depending on what incentives were offered. The wealth of Prussia and the German convents had allowed the procurators general to make friends of popes, cardinals and lawyers and thereby win decisions over opponents who thought they had much better cases.

It was not necessary to bribe officials to subvert justice, but sometimes there seemed no other way to persuade them to find time in their busy schedules to hear the order's case. The silent lawyer, the florin, was on their side, yet the procurators general had the weakness typical of human beings to think that they used immoral practices only because that was the accepted and convenient method of doing business. Therefore, they did not demand reform in loud and angry tones, or perhaps not even quietly but firmly; but at no time did they oppose reform. This silence was continued after 1410, when the defeat at the battle of Tannenberg brought a sudden end to their ability to pour out treasure in support of their diplomacy. Now they wanted a strong pope who could help the weaker parties in a dispute.

John XXIII, unhappily for the grandmaster, was not the man he needed. This pope lacked both authority and will. His vision hardly extended past Rome and central Italy. It certainly did not extend to distant Prussia, where the Teutonic Order was fighting for its very survival. There was only one person who might help – Sigismund. Because the Hungarian king was eager to bring another council together, the Teutonic Knights gave their enthusiastic support to that endeavour, in hopes of thus winning his favour on matters that had been submitted to him for arbitration.

Sigismund Rises in Political Importance

The Holy Roman Empire was in no less trouble than the Church. It had suffered under Wenceslaus, who was now best known for having thrown a troublesome cleric from the Charles Bridge in Prague and reputedly setting his hunting dogs on his first wife. But soon people would remember him for encouraging a formidable Czech nationalist movement at Charles University. These professors demanded that German clergy be removed from Czech churches and urged the reform of both liturgical and financial practices. Because the philosophy of this movement was similar to the heretical ideas of the English scholar John Wycliffe, German churchmen had accused the foremost Bohemian scholar, Jan Hus, of fomenting a dangerous heresy that would end, they predicted, as it had in England, in a peasant uprising.

There was a strong connection between England and Bohemia following the marriage of Anne of Bohemia (1366–94, Sigismund's sister) and Richard II of England in 1392. Czech scholars and clergy had accompanied the bride to England, where they met Wycliffe's followers; they were especially impressed by the Lollards' criticism of the established church and their determination to bring the Bible to the common people in a language they could understand. They brought these revolutionary ideas back to Prague, where they sought to substitute Czech for Latin in religious services and homilies, and to replace German prelates with Czech ones. (The popular nineteenth-century Christmas carol, 'Good King Wenceslaus', referred to a tenth-century saint, not the new queen's half-brother.)

The Teutonic Knights, along with other German patriots, had regarded Wenceslaus's political lethargy with dismay. Relatively unconcerned with the Bohemian religious controversies, they concentrated on the monarch's failure to give leadership to a badly divided Holy Roman Empire. Hope for his moral regeneration faded year by year, until at last in 1400 the electors had taken steps to remove him from office. Declaring the throne vacant, a majority of electors chose Ruprecht as their new king and emperor. However, Wenceslaus pronounced their act illegal and therefore null and void; and he retained a significant following among the German princes. Bohemia was the largest and most powerful single state in the Empire and Ruprecht's Palatinate was among the weakest, so the new emperor-elect was unable to establish his authority. For a decade the schism in the Holy Roman Empire paralleled that in the Church. Authority was disputed, leadership was absent, and hope was put in the council that the churchmen would find a means of resolving the crisis.

The Teutonic Order, despite divided feelings on the matter, had supported Ruprecht from the moment of his election. Archbishop Johannes of Wallenrode had served him as diplomat and adviser and represented him before the Roman pope and various secular lords. It was he who urged Ruprecht to rally German nationalist feelings – an effort that failed to overcome local interests. Therefore, even before Ruprecht's death in 1410, Ulrich of Jungingen was already supporting the candidacy of Sigismund, in hope that he might be able to give the strong leadership necessary to reunite both Empire and Church.

Sigismund would probably inherit Bohemia upon Wenceslaus's death, once Jobst of Brandenburg (his cousin) was disposed of. The Bohemian kingdom, together with Hungary, would provide Sigismund with the material and moral base to give leadership. Sigismund had established his military reputation in wars against the Turks and Venice. While no one had forgotten the débâcle at Nicopolis, that battle had distinguished him as the only ruler willing to do more than talk about defending Christendom. The Teutonic Knights could not help liking him. He was their type of man and ruler. His personal shortcomings were not unusual, and until Tannenberg the military order saw what it wanted to see – a reincarnation of the Hohenstaufen dynasty.

Compared to his contemporaries, Sigismund seemed even more attractive. England had an aging king, Henry IV, who had seized power in a civil war and whose heir seemed to have no talents beyond hell-raising. France was misruled by quarrelling factions, Orleans and Burgundy, with the occasional peasant uprising and urban rebellion thrown in. The king was insane and the gouty, obese queen was too frivolous to assist in any way. In the years to come two *dauphins* would die, a third would be kidnapped, and the next English king, Henry V, would seize the northern half of the kingdom. Spain was ruled by quarrelling kinglets, Italy torn apart by feuding city-states, and Scandinavia always troubled by internal and external conflicts. Many observers of the political world despaired of the chasm between potential and reality; yet all that was needed, they believed, was for some leader to come forward, end the anarchy, and unify Christendom once and for all. Sigismund seemed to be the man.

Sigismund's desire to reform church and state had grown out of personal experience. In 1402 he had been presented with an oppor-tunity to accomplish his crusading goals when Timur's legions had poured out of Turkestan into Persia and the Near East, challenged the Ottoman Turks for regional supremacy, and had inflicted such a devastating defeat on the sultan that any sizeable Christian force could have reoccupied the Balkans easily. Sigismund, however, could not raise an army – Christendom was too divided by wars in Italy, conflicts in France, and quarrels in Germany. Before Sigismund was ready to march, Timur had withdrawn to Turkestan to use the captive Ottoman ruler as a stepstool for mounting his horse. The Ottomans chose a new sultan, who reestablished order in his domains, and the opportunity passed.

In any case, Sigismund had his hands full at home. There had been no emperor-elect crowned since Charles IV in 1355, so he arrested Wenceslaus in hopes of escorting him to Rome for his coronation. This would confirm the right of the Luxemburg dynasty to the title, thereby ending the current political stalemate and almost guaranteeing his own future coronation. When that failed, he found himself governing Bohemia for a year. Meanwhile, nobles in Hungary had elected Ladislas of Naples (1377–1414) as king in Sigismund's place; that plot failed after Ladislas proved unable to conquer any cities apart from Zadar, despite significant help from Venice. Though a good-looking youth, he had stuttered after the age of thirteen as a result of being poisoned by the bishop of Arles on the behest of Louis II of Anjou (1377–1417), who had seized control of Naples. Ladislas's sister Joanna II did better, but not enough to acquire more than a nominal title as Queen of Hungary.

Sigismund's fundamental problem was that he was not really qualified to lead. He was not the Holy Roman emperor and, even after Ruprecht's death in 1410, he was not able to gather commitments from a majority of the seven electors. He did not have significant possessions in the empire and, although he stood to inherit Bohemia eventually, Wenceslaus was still alive and healthy enough to hunt enthusiastically – his family's mania. Wenceslaus was a little wobbly on his feet, but other hard-drinking rulers had been known to govern effectively; and Wenceslaus was known for his cruelty, stubbornnesss and determination. More to the point, he might choose to retaliate for his half-brother's presumption in seeking an office that he still claimed.

Wenceslaus was highly unpredictable. In 1411, after defending Jan Hus for three years against the indignant archbishop of Prague, outraging all the German clerics, Wenceslaus turned against him in order to share in the proceeds of an indulgence declared by Pope John XXIII. When Czech students rioted in protest, he had three beheaded and allowed the pope to excommunicate Hus. Whether Wenceslaus was drunk, or insane or merely unstable did not matter – without his

Bohemian knights, Sigismund might not be able to defend Hungary against a Turkish attack.

As a result, it was difficult for Sigismund to bring into Italy an army sufficiently powerful to compel the competing popes to end the schism and to cooperate in reforming the Church through a general council. Venice was a strong and formidable enemy of the Hungarian kingdom, and Ladislas of Naples still regarded Sigismund as a usurper. Nevertheless, with the aid of the duke of Celje – since 1408 his father-in-law – who controlled the passes between Germany, Hungary and Italy, Sigismund entered Italy in 1411 and established a reputation as a diplomat. Some ridiculed the small size of his army, which contrasted strongly with the amount of debt he was accumulating; but he was the best candidate to be emperor available, and it had brought considerable joy to the German princes to witness his coronation in Aachen because that was the essential first step towards restoring order and national prestige.

Sigismund was also so busy pursuing beautiful women (or not so beautiful, but willing), that he was often up late at night, moving through the bars of whatever city he was in, 'disguised' by masks but revealed by his joy in jokes and amusing retorts. This often preoccupied him through the day as well. It is said that his butler travelled to Ireland to seek out young beauties for him, and down in St Patrick's Purgatory he had a vision of young lasses waiting for Sigismund there with a red-hot bath and a bed of fire. On hearing this, Sigismund is supposed to have exclaimed, 'then we must have that bed shifted to heaven'. He then raised money for a new church in Ofen (the German name for Buda), making this a famous pun on the word 'oven'. His apocryphal sayings appeared all over Europe, each revealing that the public considered him to be clever rather than wise. Yet he once chided a learned doctor who, while being rewarded for his services, said that he would prefer to be enrolled among the nobles than among the scholars. Sigismund, referring to his authority to dub knights, retorted that he could made a thousand gentlemen in a day, but could not make a scholar in a thousand years.

Sigismund's philandering ways were almost equalled by the conquests attributed to his wife, Barbara, whose ribald comments became part of regional folklore. As Aeneas Silvius, a brilliant and notorious Renaissance gossip, put it, 'She spared her gallants the trouble of courtship.' When Sigismund locked her away, she wiled the time by improvising entertainments with her maids-in-waiting and making fun of holy virgins. She was not as scandalous in her behaviour as Queen Joanna II of Naples, but only because she did not rely on the dagger as much as the queen did. Joanna became a central figure in the world of gossip and conspiracy theories that entertained her age.

Sigismund found it difficult to separate the appearance of power and the reality of it; and thus he often sacrificed real advantages in order to make a good show. He relied on a handful of dependable friends; in 1415 he would reward one of them, the Nuremberg burgrave Friedrich of Hohenzollern, by selling him Brandenburg – an event with great significance for Prussia in the future. With Sigismund thus having an elector of the Holy Roman Empire in his debt, he was more confident that he could tame the political unrest that had marked German politics in recent years. This was important because Sigismund often failed to pursue policies once serious opposition developed. Fortunately for western Christendom, there were many important men who could help him keep his mind on business, men who knew how to appeal to his vanity and keep him working on what must have often seemed to be a hopeless task. But he never lacked for self-assurance that he could accomplish any goal he set his heart on.

He took up the matter of the schism immediately after his coronation in Aachen. In 1413 he promised to protect the frightened John XXIII – then in a panic after Ladislas of Naples occupied Rome – if he would call for an assembly of churchmen. Then he won the papal ambassadors over to the plan of holding the meeting on German soil, at Constance (Konstanz), where his own influence would be the greatest.

Constance was a beautifully situated city with the resources to house and feed thousands of visitors for a long time; it was also not dominated by any of the powerful neighbouring princes, such as the Wittelsbachs in Bavaria or the Habsburgs in Austria. There was an immediate scramble to book housing because everyone understood that choices would be limited and prices high; participants began to arrive in late October 1414. Even today visitors to Constance can easily visualise the scene since the Old Town is largely intact or restored, as is the huge warehouse where Council meetings were held.

The Teutonic Knights at Constance

The defeat at Tannenberg in 1410 was only the first of a long series of setbacks for the Teutonic Order. The procurator-general, who had been instrumental in blocking the efforts of Jagiełło and Vytautas to take sole responsibility for the conversion of the Lithuanians, was at the court of John XXIII, desperately raising money to hire mercenary troops for use in Prussia. Peter of Wormditt raised little in Italy, of course, because the pope had need of every coin he possessed for his own war against Naples.

By 1413 King Ladislas, the son of the late Charles of Durazzo, had recovered from earlier defeats and gone on the offensive. He broke into the Papal States, causing the pope to flee for his life – into the arms of Sigismund and the supporters of a general council. The procurator-general did not join in the flight from Rome, but placed his trust in the promises of King Ladislas and his supporters in the city that he would be safe. That was a mistake. The king had not forgotten that the Teutonic Knights were allies of both Sigismund and John XXIII, and he had no reason to favour the military order with his protection. His soldiers sacked the convent–embassy, stole the order's treasury, and held the procurator-general for ransom. Although the king soon freed Wormditt, he did not return his possessions or money – but then the king died unexpectedly of a genital infection and was succeeded by his sister, Joanna II. Thereafter the lawyer-diplomat was in financial difficulties. Appeals to Prussia and Germany helped little because the Teutonic Knights were near bankruptcy. As a result, his diplomatic activities were limited.

Still, the Council of Constance offered the Teutonic Knights an opportunity to regain favour with Sigismund, John XXIII and the influential men of the Church. Moreover, if the recommended reforms were truly accomplished, the military order might fare better at an honest curia than in one where money was power because the Polish king was now rich and the order was poor. The attendance of the German master and the archbishop of Riga emphasised the importance of the council's actions.

The chronicler Richenthal, who lovingly described every pageant performed in the city during these years, well remembered 13 January 1415, the day that nine officers from Prussia arrived with 150 horsemen to take up lodgings in a house and a hotel. The order spent as much as it could afford to make a great impression.

The Poles had arrived three days earlier. Led by the archbishop of Gniezno, they asked the council to take up the matter of the Prussian war immediately. Although they were allowed to make an initial presentation of their case, everyone was too busy with the trials of John XXIII and Jan Hus to give their problem further attention. The hearings were adjourned.

The knights of the Teutonic Order did not tarry long in the expensive city. Only the wealthiest of states could afford to house and feed delegations, and even they complained about the cost. The contemporary

Minnesinger (poet-musician) Oswald of Wolkenstein, wrote about his 1414 visit to Constance: '*Denk ich an den Bodensee, tut mir gleich der Beutel weh*' ('When I remember Lake Constance, my wallet hurts'). That may have referred more to the numerous local brothels – where prices were set by the city – than to anything else because that was probably where he met Sigismund, who soon employed him as a diplomat.

Since there was no pending business of importance to Prussia, everyone except the archbishop of Riga and the procurator-general returned to their convents. Of course, the servants and staff of the archbishop remained behind, and Wormditt scraped along as best he could.

The presence of Johannes of Wallenrode was important because, unlike Wormditt and the other members of the Teutonic Order, archbishops had an uncontested right to a seat in the council and a voice in all important debates. The procurator-general was no more than an advocate representing a client who was technically a servant of the pope. Although the Teutonic Knights possessed great territories and had once led an important crusade, they were now only a mid-sized monastic order. Also, they had suffered a recent humiliating military defeat. The minor bishoprics in Prussia and Livonia occupied by priests of the order were, in the eyes of most churchmen, beneath notice; but even those prelates were better qualified for seats at the council than the Teutonic Knights' representative. Only the archbishop of Riga possessed sufficient status to demand a hearing and command respect for whatever he said.

Unfortunately for the Teutonic Order, Wallenrode did not serve them well. Many years earlier, after quarrelling with the Livonian master over the limited authority granted to him, he had gone into virtual exile. Technically he remained a member of the order, but in practice he was on his own, though he had been employed by Ruprecht of the Rhine. That decade of experience in diplomacy made him a valuable man at the council, however – he knew the leading churchmen and nobles. He understood the problems; and he saw that he himself might profit by taking a leading role in the proceedings. For personal reasons he stood in the ranks of the Teutonic Knights, but he was really no longer one of them. The grandmaster knew this, but he could not avoid allowing the archbishop to speak for him. It was similarly to the archbishop's advantage to represent the military order rather than a distant diocese he had not visited for years. Therefore, although the personal goals were different, there was no open disagreement about proposals or procedures, no public displays of contempt. Nevertheless, all was not well in the crusader camp.

The Deposition of John XXIII

The churchmen organising the council divided the delegates into *nations* to counterbalance the many Italian prelates and to make it easier to debate problems of regional interest. Following the university custom of dividing students into nations named after the largest country or region located in the cardinal directions, Constance was to have Italian, French, German and Spanish nations. But since Spain was not participating at first, that place was taken by England; countries which did not fit into this scheme were assigned to the smallest or nearest nations. Thus, Poland was assigned to the German nation. That was not a devious plot on the part of Sigismund or the fathers, but a logical decision. It also gave great power to the archbishop of Riga, who was called upon from time to time to chair its sessions.

That did not seem important as long as the churchmen were principally concerned with persuading Pope John XXIII to resign. That was difficult because he had been instrumental in calling the council together, and he would never have cooperated if he had not hoped to be acknowledged as universal pope; or, at a minimum, to be given a post of honour. By March 1415, however, John saw that the council would force him out of office unless he somehow escaped to some place where he could declare the council dissolved. He slipped out of Constance by night with Archduke Friedrich IV of Austria and made his way toward Alsace, then Burgundy. The archduke was known to contemporaries as Friedrich of the Empty Pockets because of his expensive strife with the nobles in Tyrol. That slur should have no longer applied after he had divided the family lands with Ernst the Iron, acquiring Alsace, but he undoubtedly expected to turn around his financial situation if he could rescue John XXIII from what appeared to be certain removal from office.

The dissolution of the council was frustrated by Sigismund, who commanded everyone to remain in Constance while he hunted down the runaway. He caught John XXIII within a few days and turned him over to the archbishop of Riga, who guarded him carefully on the road back to Constance. That was a particular pleasure for him because John XXIII had been so receptive to Polish arguments that he could see the matter ending badly.

Among the witnesses who testified at John's trial was Peter of Wormditt. His testimony confirmed the most damning accusations levied against the pope: that he had destroyed churches and monasteries; that he had murdered a barber so as to conduct an affair with the deceased man's wife; that he had sold offices and justice; that he had been a sodomite and a deflowerer of virgins; and that among his other crimes he had poisoned Pope Alexander V and his doctor. Wormditt had apparently not wasted his time at court. He must have been an indefatigable collector of gossip (although his lengthy reports to the grandmaster stand as proof that he knew how to separate hard facts from idle chatter). For the conciliar cause, he was now ready to tell everything he had ever heard against John XXIII.

More significant than the recitation of vicious rumours was the detailed list of specific abuses of papal authority in the daily management of Church affairs. The sale of high office in the Hospitaller Order to the five-year-old bastard of the king of Cyprus was notorious, but few were aware of the manipulation of prices in Rome, or how Roman street urchins were in the habit of calling out to strangers: 'Where are you going? Do you want to buy a benefice from the Pope in the curia?' How the pope practiced simony on a smaller scale was also less than common knowledge. But Wormditt knew. He had been assisting the pope and the cardinals in these practices for many years. Now he revealed selected examples such as would not embarrass the order or his friends, presenting a picture of the corrupt ex-soldier pope which would help the solemn churchmen arrive at their predetermined verdict.

The weeping John XXIII, held in captivity by Friedrich of Hohenzollern, was formally deposed in 1416, then transferred from prison to prison until the churchmen declared their meeting adjourned in 1418.

Jan Hus

The trial of Jan Hus, the event for which the assembly at Constance is most commonly remembered today, was one of the most controversial in the history of the Church. Hus had been invited to present his ideas on radical reform to the churchmen, an invitation he had accepted gladly. Though his friends warned him not to go because his arguments had already been declared heretical in 1412, he was confident that Sigismund would honour the safe-conduct to and from Constance. Moreover, he had to defend himself. Not going to Constance would suggest a combination of cowardice and uncertainty about his beliefs.

Hus had a martyr complex. He was persuaded that he was right, and would not compromise, not even when a mild condemnation of Wycliffe might have saved him. Most churchmen were equally sure that they were right and he was dangerous. As for the trial, the accusers were technically correct, but the process was chaotic, one-sided, and influenced by fear that the Council itself would be considered heretical if it was too soft on heretics.

Nothing went as anticipated by either Hus or Sigismund. Though Hus was housed comfortably in the city, he was not allowed to defend himself. Instead, at the end of the process he was asked only whether he would subject himself to the judgment of the Papacy and the council. This was a crucial point, for any Christian who rejected out of hand the central role of the supreme pontiff and an ecumenical council in determining doctrine was *ipso facto* a heretic. Hus reflected over his answer, then gave what eventually became the classical Protestant response: he could not go against his conscience and the teachings of Christ. Hus was doomed.

Sigismund nevertheless wanted to send Hus back to Bohemia, but when told by many German clergymen that they would go home in protest, he relented. If those bishops and abbots left Constance, the council would break up. Sigismund, therefore, reluctantly allowed the churchmen to arrest Hus and condemn him to death. As Jesus had put it: gather up the tares among the wheat and burn them (Matthew 13).

The archbishop of Riga was responsible for holding Jan Hus during his trial and, in July 1415, delivering him to the executioner. He did not seem to have any enthusiasm for the task. He left the accusations and prosecution to prelates from the Czech lands. The elaborate ceremony, mocking the victim's claim to have insights into religious truth, ended at the stake, where the authorities prevented him from addressing the crowds in German, lest gawking onlookers enter into mortal error, losing their souls to the devil. Hus's ashes were thrown into the Rhine, the authorities falsely believing that his followers would otherwise give them the same reverent significance as Catholics did holy relics.

The council members from Bohemia urged immediate military action against Hus's followers. But Sigismund was hesitant. The fact that 452 Czech nobles were willing to sign a defence of Hus and his theological position was a warning that action, if taken, would have to be taken with overwhelming force. Sigismund could not leave the council at this moment, and he could not assign anyone else the task. King Wenceslaus was incapable of acting in any way.

The Teutonic Knights versus Jagiełło

Soon after the trials the Teutonic Knights asked for payment. They had given Sigismund full cooperation; now they wanted him to demonstrate his appreciation. The grandmaster feared that the truce with Poland would not be renewed and that Jagiełło would fall upon Prussia again. Küchmeister knew that Sigismund would soon leave for Spain to seek the adherence of the Spanish kings to the council and to negotiate for the resignation of Benedict XIII. He wanted Sigismund to act immediately, before he was out of reach. The question was when and how to approach him.

The council created a special committee to hear the grandmaster's plea. At a crucial moment in the meeting Sigismund interrupted to ask the procurator-general and the Polish delegation if they would submit unconditionally to a ruling by the Church, the Empire and the council. This was the same question that had tripped up Jan Hus. Wormditt agreed immediately, but the Poles hesitated to put their kingdom under the authority of the Holy Roman Empire in any way. They had no authority from their king to negotiate a binding peace treaty, and they were unwilling to leave the decision to politicians and churchmen who had been noted for their corruption, partiality and self-serving ambition. If they acknowledged the right of the emperor to act in this matter, they would compromise the sovereignty of their state; but if they refused, they would deny the competence of the tribunal. The Polish delegates, unwilling to emulate Jan Hus, but equally unwilling to act without instructions, could not formulate a reply; nor could they think of cogent arguments against a resolution that the truce be continued until Sigismund could return to Constance.

When Sigismund left the city, Wallenrode accompanied him. Not only would Sigismund try to keep a trusted and capable adviser beside him, but for his part, the archbishop had to be well aware of the proverb, 'Aus den Augen, aus dem Sinn' ('Out of sight, out of mind'). This applied particularly to men in Sigismund's employ. For the protection of his order and for his personal ambitions, Wallenrode was determined to be remembered. The procurator-general was left to care for such minor disputes as might be submitted to the council. Two such cases were immediately presented, much to the disgust of the other delegates, who were being overwhelmed with petty problems they neither understood nor cared about.

The first case was that of the cloister of St Brigitta in Danzig, whose nuns (all middle-aged or older and mostly widows) were being harassed by brothers of their order for not accepting young virgins into their ranks, for not electing an abbess or prioress as the rules prescribed, for not practicing proper seclusion, and for not permitting visitations by their order's officers to check on their behaviour. The council ruled that the nuns must either conform or choose another order, one with rules more suited for widows who wished to live together and govern themselves without outside supervision (or the presence of giggling teenage girls).

The second case was an appeal by the bishop of Salisbury (who had a leading role in the council) on behalf of four councilmen of Braunsberg (Braniewo). He accused the grandmaster of having suspended the city charter that had been given by the bishop of Ermland and subsequently of having driven the councillors and the bishop out of the country. Wormditt explained that the legal problems here were complex. A prominent man had been found drowned in a lake near Braunsberg. Since stones had been tied to his neck and feet, murder was suspected; and there were grounds to believe that the councillors had been accomplices to the crime. The principal dispute was jurisdiction, the local knights and gentry wanting the trial be held in the episcopal court, but the councilmen insisting on hearing the case in the city court. Küchmeister had become involved only because the bishop had fled the country to escape imprisonment on a charge of treason. The grandmaster had sought to arrange a compromise by summoning a special jury of twelve knights and twelve burghers to meet in his presence, to witness the oaths of the accused before the body of the deceased, to see if either the corpse (by bleeding) or the accused (by nervousness) would give some sign of guilt. As soon as the council heard his order to attend, seven fled the country.

After the delegates to the council had listened to the arguments gravely, they ordered the grandmaster to turn the matter to the new bishop as soon as he was confirmed in office, and that the new bishop was to swear to uphold the city charter. The Teutonic Order then gave the exiled councilmen a safe-conduct to travel home.

Meanwhile, the Polish delegation had made several spectacular announcements designed to attract the attention of the council. Vytautas claimed to have converted the Tatars to Christianity, and Jagiełło announced his ability to bring about a union of the Greek and Roman churches. Confirmation of these claims would take time, but until that could be done, the churchmen would remember that the Poles and Lithuanians were powers to be reckoned with, states uniquely placed to advance the cause of Christendom in the east. Therefore, it was advisable that the churchmen be careful not to favour the Teutonic Order unduly.

When Wallenrode decided to travel to Prussia to discuss strategy with the grandmaster, he first needed to conclude the talks with the antipopes. Only Gregory XII agreed to resign. Made a cardinal, he lived another two years, performing useful tasks for the Church. The Avignon antipope held out longer, in exile in Catalonia.

The Samogitian Delegation

In December 1415 a special delegation from Poland, Samogitia and Ruś arrived, announcing that Lithuania and Russia had been converted, that their lands were now full of Catholic churches, and that the conversion of the Greeks, Tatars and the few remaining pagan Lithuanians was to be expected in the near future. Referring to the Samogitians, the spokesman said,

> Inspired by the Holy Spirit, the said princes and brethren have by their own right faith and unblemished conduct brought this valiant and invincible people through all their wide provinces and the dukes and duchies subdued by force to their dominion, and other enemies of the faith, to approach the knowledge of the true God and from approach to belief and from belief to love . . .

This was truly an inspiring moment for the council's members who had long followed the crusades there, to see those former pagans standing before them, acknowledging their allegiance to Roman Christianity. Wormditt was present at that session with two lawyers, but since the Poles did not mention the Teutonic Knights directly, he did not speak. It was a good moment to hold his tongue; besides, the archbishop of Riga had not yet returned from Avignon. It would not be wise to say anything in such a sensitive matter without instructions.

Wormditt wrote to the grandmaster:

> The delegates of Duke Vytautas . . . are still in Constance and wait for the Roman emperor, and they brought gifts and Russian hats with them and give them to the entire world. Many people who favour the order think that we make unnecessary payments on the order's behalf for the many horses, which are of no use, and that we do not make a friend for our case, but with our miserliness we lose the friends we have. They say that unless one sends much money here, all will be lost . . .

The grandmaster was almost simultaneously writing to the procurator-general that Jagiełło had agreed to submit to the judgment of the Council of Constance, if he were first guaranteed Pomerellia (West Prussia) and Danzig in any settlement that might be reached. The grandmaster had rejected the king's proposal and now requested that the entire matter be taken before the council.

The military strength of the order in Prussia was exhausted. The army could defend the fortresses but not the countryside. Another year of plundering by the Polish and Lithuanian armies would ruin the peasantry totally and make it impossible to reestablish agricultural productivity and collect taxes for many years. Without food and taxes, the order was doomed. The Council seemed to be the only alternative to surrender; and surrender was impossible because the king might take revenge on the order's knights for the many wrongs and injuries of the past. Rightly or wrongly, the knights saw Jagiełło as an unregenerate but secret pagan who sought only their destruction. The fate of the Templars was ever in the minds of the German crusaders – arrested *en masse* by the king of France, their property confiscated, and their grandmaster burned at the stake along with many of his knights.

The matter was never presented to the council, however, except as a tactic to buy time. The Teutonic Knights did not want a decision at Constance because it was too likely to be against them, while their opponents, the Poles and Lithuanians, pressed for a permanent settlement that would secure the gains they had made.

Delay and Controversy

Although the situation of the Polish king looked good, it was actually not much better than that of the Teutonic Order. A war of attrition wears everyone down, and it was not easy for the king to raise armies to fight in Prussia. He could not tax his state effectively or command his proud and independent vassals against their will; nor did he have much interest in, or energy for, the details of governing. He could never count on Vytautas unconditionally. Although Vytautas needed him now, he might not need him later. Therefore, Jagiełło dared not forget that Vytautas remembered well the causes of their former hatred and their long-lived mutual mistrust. That meant that the king could not rely on the safety of even one frontier. He had to watch the Lithuanians about as much as he did the Tatars, the Hungarians, the Bohemians, the minor German dukes and the Teutonic Knights. Jagiełło was a major figure in international politics, but he had his troubles; and he saw the Council of Constance as a means of resolving some of them. Equally important, the council being the most important arena of political activity at the moment, Jagiełło did not dare allow the Teutonic Order to disseminate its propaganda unopposed. If he was clever enough, he might even hope to win advantages for himself.

Polish and Lithuanian policy, however, remained a hope rather than an actuality due to the skill of Peter of Wormditt, who wrote in

February 1416 that he had frustrated another Polish attempt to present the Prussian matter to the council, routing his diplomatic opponent 'to the great honour of the order'. He boasted further that, 'In all the time that we have been in Constance, we have never had to bring our business and justice before the council.' It was a difficult task for the procurator-general, especially when the Polish representatives were lavishly distributing gifts so as to obtain a hearing for their arguments. Since preliminary debate was confined to the German nation, and not to the council as a whole, Wormditt was able to win some sympathy. He did not press the order's claims to Samogitia, as had been the practice in the past, but rather argued that it would be unjust to give lands held by Germans time-out-of-mind to foreigners.

This tactic can be viewed as sheer opportunism, the practice of a *Realpolitik* of a particularly callous and cynical nature, and filled with internal contradictions; but it was not dishonest. The Teutonic Knights desired the conversion of the Samogitians even though that would undermine the reason for the order's existence. It might have been hypocritical when Wormditt said publicly, 'May God make them good Christians!' But he also wrote the same thing to the grandmaster in their private correspondence. The problem was in the argument that pagans could be kept from backsliding into evil habits or going over to the Orthodox Church only when their conversion was overseen by trustworthy Germans, not by Poles. To save the military order so that it could accomplish its God-given mission, the procurator-general had to argue for maintaining Prussia's territorial integrity and defensible frontiers. To that end he dedicated all his skills and guile.

The Poles were not greatly interested in the procurator-general's chimerical fears and nightmares. They trusted their king to act justly and in the interest of Christendom, which was essentially the same as the interests of their kingdom. After all, by this time Jagiełło had been a Roman Catholic for thirty years, and the lands in question had been stolen from the crown as far back as 1309 and earlier. If some claims were exaggerated, that was merely a part of the process of bargaining. If the grandmaster would put his order's services to the use of the kingdom, they said, its officers should not fear the future. When that argument failed to persuade the German nation, the Polish delegation set off for Paris to present their arguments to Sigismund in person. He was then visiting the French and English monarchs in an effort to end the Hundred Years War and unify Christendom for a great crusade which would expel the Turks from all their conquests of recent centuries – in short, a Hungarian project. The Poles hoped for a favourable hearing because they, and the Teutonic Knights as well, would never be able to participate in this quest until the territorial issues were settled.

The Teutonic Knights were represented during the archbishop's absence by the commander of Thorn, Johann of Selbach. The result was another deadlock. Sigismund had, he said, no authority or power to compel obedience outside the empire. Meanwhile, the truce should be extended.

Sigismund eventually ordered two competent people to investigate the situation: Friedrich of Hohenzollern, the new margrave of Brandenburg, who in any case wanted to visit his purchase and meet his new neighbour; and the archbishop of Riga. They met the grandmaster to discuss the truce and other problems, but clearly the margrave's major interest was to determine how much money the Teutonic Order had available for imperial interests. Without question, Sigismund still believed that the grandmaster possessed an inexhaustible supply of treasure.

In June a rumour arrived in Hungary that Vytautas had made an alliance with the aged ruler of Wallachia, a vital territory on the north bank of the Danube in modern Romania. Both Hungary and Poland were striving to hold each other off there while driving back the Ottoman Turks; this was an impossible task for a disunited Europe – therefore, it was a matter that required Sigismund's immediate attention. Archbishop Johannes of Riga, having recently returned to Constance, rushed this news to Sigismund in England, dispatching the count of Holland to carry the documents to him.

Sigismund took the news coolly, replying that he would soon return to Constance, where he could better judge the matter. As it happened, the alleged alliance proved to be no danger to him, but it provided a temporary propaganda advantage for the Teutonic Order. Aside from this rumour, however, the order found little about which to be encouraged. Its delegates could not pay their daily expenses; the grandmaster had nothing to send them; and being in debt for thousands of florins made it impossible to borrow more. Moreover, the grandmaster's refusal to hand over several pawned villages to the new margrave of Brandenburg threatened to undermine the carefully cultivated friendship with Sigismund, who would surely have favoured his Hohenzollern friend over the order. As bishops in Prussia died, there were complications. The grandmaster did not like the cathedral chapters' nominees; the procurator-general lacked money for bribes; and there was no pope to confirm the elections. The archbishop of Riga was spending money freely, with an eye on improving his own image rather than that of the

Teutonic Order. In all these matters Wormditt complained bitterly to the grandmaster, but not to the feared archbishop. In the end, he obtained a loan of 3,000 florins from the Florentine Alberti bank.

When Wallenrode informed the grandmaster about Sigismund's demands, he added a demand of his own – for the archbishopric to have authority over the Livonian master! The grandmaster summoned the German and Livonian masters to Marienburg; in the end they rejected both Sigismund's and the archbishop's conditions. The Teutonic Order was thus left in the weakest of all possible positions, relying on the justice of their cause. The Poles, meanwhile, after reminding the council that nothing had been done for the Samogitians, received a letter filled with rigmarole about the Holy Spirit, the duty to baptise the heathens, to build churches and cathedrals – and the inability of the council to do anything at the moment.

In October the Polish delegation appeared before the council, this time with a new approach – announcing that Tatars had raided Poland. Although their king had driven the invaders away, he expected them to return in greater numbers. Therefore they asked Christian princes and lords to come to his aid. This speech hardly pleased the representatives of the Teutonic Knights at the council because it was almost a call for a Polish-led crusade against the Tatars. The Poles had similarly warned that the Turks were planning another advance into the Balkans and reported that their king had sent an embassy to the sultan in an effort to persuade him to make peace. Was it any coincidence that at this moment a rumour swept Constance to the effect that Jagiełło had promised his daughter in marriage to a son of the sultan? Sigismund wrote to Jagiełło about the rumour, but he did little else. Imperial interest in the east was so small that even Wormditt began to complain.

Sigismund had only one goal in mind at that moment, the election of a new pope. Many participants had already gone home, impoverished. Pressed by local problems, many of them returned to Constance only as Christmas approached. The imminent return of Sigismund, sparkling with the success of his visits in Spain, France and England, had a magnetic influence on the prelates who had dispersed, drawing them back to the beautiful city on the lake.

Banqueting at Constance

Whatever Sigismund may have lacked in perseverance, he made up in personality. He was pleasant, affable, chivalrous and a warrior. Moreover, he was Holy Roman emperor-elect, the acknowledged leader of western Europe, and the apparently indispensable man. Men flocked to his presence, hoping to obtain an office or alliance, or merely to bask in reflected glory.

The midsummer just past had seen no work in the daytime heat and only partying by night. (On the day that Pope John had chosen to slip out of Constance unnoticed almost the entire population had been watching a joust on the other side of town.) The churchmen, in short, represented the usual human mixture of seriousness and levity. The spirit of the Avignon papacy had not vanished, nor had personal and family interests given way to larger concerns.

The feasts were especially memorable during the Christmas season, perhaps because others paid the bills. The English gave several magnificent banquets, thereby setting the precedent; the festivities continued into January, assisted by the legendary temperate weather of the region between Lake Constance and the Alps. The holiday reached its climax with Sigismund's triumphal entry into the city. Two weeks later, another arrival impressed the churchmen. It was described thus by a contemporary:

> On Tuesday before St Valentine's, a great beast arrived for our lord King. He was captured in Lithuania and sent by the king of Poland, who ordered three of them sent from Lithuania alive as gifts. But when the three reached Cracow, they were so weak from captivity and restiveness that they could not be brought alive from Cracow to Constance. So the king had all three of them killed and two salted down in herring vats and sent to the bishops and lords of his realm who were at Constance . . . The third beast, which is the largest, he had salted in its own skin and preserved with good spices. This beast was like a great black ox, although it had a larger head than an ox has and a thicker neck and a heavier chest and two little pointed horns on its forehead, a shoe's width apart, and a short tail. It looked like the oxen they call buffalo. Its entrails were taken out of it. When it arrived in Constance, King Sigismund had new spices put in to preserve it and sent it down the Rhine to the king of England. When they took it out of Constance, he had the trumpets blown before it so that everyone might see it. The carrier who brought it from Lithuania said that the cost of it as far as Constance was over four hundred Hungarian *Gulden*.

That same day that the great carcass of a wisent (*Bison bonasus* or European bison, often confused with aurochs) entered the city, the Polish delegates presented a list of complaints against a Dominican friar, Johann Falkenberg. His own order had already confined the defendant to forestall the embarrassment of having him arrested. Hearings were soon scheduled in all the nations, and the Dominicans were determined not to link their fate with Falkenberg's – they had a reputation to protect.

Falkenberg and Vladimiri

Falkenberg was a German-born Dominican who had been educated in Prague and Vienna in civil and canon law. When Jagiełło had refounded the University of Cracow (now Jagiellonian University), Falkenberg was recruited to teach theology. As was customary among academicians, he sought to enhance his reputation by publishing his lectures; but his books were not well received at the royal court, as might well be imagined from his thesis that a Christian king could not have pagan nobles in his service or employ pagan warriors. Also, in an age when many scholars held that the Church should be governed through periodic general councils, Falkenberg argued for a papal monarchy. He was, to put it bluntly, a fanatic out of touch with his times, insisting that church law be enforced to the letter, no matter what results that might have in practice. He was accused of heresy in Poland, but after he was found innocent Jagiełło ordered him exiled. Falkenberg then made his way to Prussia, where the Teutonic Knights were blaming their defeat on their opponents' use of pagans, Saracens and 'schismatics'.

Had Falkenberg not already been cleared of the charge of heresy, he might have been in real danger. Hus had come to the Council expecting a fair hearing of his ideas and had ended at the stake. But unlike Hus Falkenberg had powerful supporters in Constance: the Teutonic Knights and the Dominicans. This alliance was not new – the Teutonic Knights had long been opposed by the Franciscans, whose sympathy for non-Christians ran contrary to Dominican legalism; indeed, Dominican friars had long performed the missionary work in Prussia because the knights of the Teutonic Order were barred from such activities.

Falkenberg's trial was significant mainly because the ideas he had put forward were not unlike those long expressed by the Teutonic Knights. The charges were based on his *Satire*, a polemical tract accusing Jagiełło of being the greatest enemy the Church had ever had, of being an idol worshipped by idolaters, and of being a servant of the devil. Falkenberg's proof had been Jagiełło's military victories using pagan and 'schismatic' warriors and his alleged lies about their conversion. Temperance was not a virtue that Falkenberg practised.

As Eric Christiansen, one of the most insightful historians to study the Teutonic Order, remarked about Falkenberg, he was a clever man, but he was too clever by half. It was one thing to attack other scholars, but another to attack the king, and attacking him gratuitously was folly.

On the other hand, it did not help the Polish case that Jagiełło was petitioning for a dispensation to marry Elisabeth Pilecka who had already been married three times – a fourth marriage was usually forbidden. Moreover, there were rumours about her associates and her relatively low birth, jokes about her weight and concerns about her health. These gave plausibility to the stories told by the Teutonic Knights about Jagiełło's distant and only vaguely understood kingdom. Consequently, the Polish delegation wanted to have Falkenberg not merely admonished, but to have his thesis demolished altogether.

The bitterness of the invective in the so-called *Satire* reflected Falkenberg's unhappy experiences in Cracow. He said there was no such creature as a peaceful heathen; therefore they must be stripped of their arms and possessions so that they could pose no danger to Christians. Since the Polish king was unwilling to do that, his reluctance was proof that he was Satan's tool. Therefore, it was incumbent upon all Christians to punish him and his subjects by destroying the Polish state! This was an argument that the Poles had to rebut.

One other nation was taking this argument seriously, France. Shortly before, in 1407, the duke of Burgundy, Jean sans Peur (John the Fearless, 1371–1419), had murdered his rival, Louis of Orleans. This was an unusual way to conduct politics, but no innovation. What was new was his attempt to justify the murder as an act of tyrannicide. The French brought charges against Jean's publicist, Jean Petit (1360–1411), and asked the council to declare his thesis heretical. Such was the superficial similarity of the Petit and Falkenberg cases that the Burgundians sought to use Falkenberg as a test – introducing the Falkenberg case in the French 'nation' in hope of obtaining a precedent they could use against Petit's thesis. No decision was reached, however. Because the French clergymen were too closely divided into Orleanist and Burgundian factions, the other nations, baffled by the complexity of the arguments and not really interested in them, wanted to take up more pressing issues. The matter of tyrannicide was left to the German nation.

The debate in the German nation reached a high level of sophistication when Paulus Vladimiri (Paweł Włodkowic, 1370–1435) presented his case. The rector of the University of Cracow, a member of the Polish delegation, Vladimiri was a scholar of great erudition. He needed all his scholarly experience and force of personality because justifying the royal case before a sceptical audience that wanted to move on to other matters was almost impossible. In fact, it took most of his remaining years and became an absorbing passion. Ultimately, no one knew the documents of the Teutonic Order better than he. It was not his knowledge of the facts, however, that made his tracts important; it was his original thought, his attacks on the fundamental assumptions about the crusades.

Paulus Vladimiri went beyond the concept of holy war to offer a challenge to the right of popes and emperors to exercise authority over pagan peoples and to decide matters between sovereign states. He said that only international congresses, such as the Council of Constance, could bring quarrelling parties together and make peace. He wanted nothing less than an international tribunal that could make decisions concerning the justice of disputes and enforce its rulings. Only in that way, he said, could peace come to a troubled world. That argument did not appeal either to Sigismund or to potential popes because it implied sharp limitations to their authority; and more than a few of the council's members felt the same way – almost everyone had already listened to more revolutionary statements than they wished to hear. Therefore, his arguments were heard only reluctantly by the churchmen. Still, when he was given his opportunity to speak, he made the most of it.

This gifted spokesman concentrated on the concept of the just war as it applied to the Samogitian Crusade. He could not safely say that a just war was impossible, but he emphatically denied that what the Teutonic Order had conducted against Lithuanian pagans had any resemblance to such a concept, much less their present justifications for waging wars against Christian states. He cited Hostiensis as the principal authority on the just war, which was a satisfactory choice that everyone, including the Teutonic Order, could agree upon. He also used the definitions of St Augustine and St Bernard, which was surprising, since the former had defined the elements of a just war and the latter had organised the first military order. What he did with their teachings was to argue that they did not apply to the Teutonic Knights.

There are five conditions pertaining to a just war, according to Hostiensis: 1) the person fighting must be legally qualified, such as a warrior or a party to the case; 2) the object of the war must be proper, such as righting a wrong, protecting oneself or others, reestablishing the peace; 3) the cause of the war must be just, such as self-defence; 4) the means must follow church degrees and be directed solely against military enemies; 5) the war must be authorised by a proper authority, such as the pope or emperor.

Paulus Vladimiri argued from these conditions that first, the knights of the Teutonic Order were members of the regular clergy and were therefore legally barred from bearing arms, even if the cause were just.

Second, the knights were fighting not to protect Christians, but to steal land, an unjust cause. Third, there was no need to defend Christians since all pagans had been converted. Fourth, their means of warfare were beyond what was permitted to Christians. Lastly, the pope and emperor had not properly authorised this war.

He emphasised the fourth point, heaping citation upon citation, quoting from such witnesses as kings, bishops, abbots, clerics and papal legates. He levelled accusation after accusation against the Teutonic Order: enslavement of peoples, slaughter of prisoners, torture, executions without trial, violations of treaties, attacks on Christian princes. All this, he said, was to keep the Samogitians out of the Church so that the knights could take away their lands and property.

He spoke from personal experience and from a wide variety of sources, writing with great passion, expounding the peaceful nature of the Polish king and the criminal nature of the Teutonic Order. He interpreted the sending of two swords at the battle of Tannenberg as a provocation to shed blood. He lumped the hiring of mercenaries and the imposition of trade blockades together with murdering prisoners, desecrating the dead, stripping women *en masse*, and slaughtering children, old men and clerics. He depicted the knights as the lowest form of human beings, a band of murdering criminals.

The logical question that followed was, if the Teutonic Knights were indeed as evil as he described, what should be done with them? Here Vladimiri lost his audience. He suggested that, first, the order be condemned for heresy, the heresy of conducting illegal war. Second, that the order restore the territories stolen from others – including Prussia to the Poles. Lastly, since the order could not be expected to obey the council, that war be made against it. The Teutonic Order had to be dissolved and destroyed, the very root of its vices dug up and thrown away.

Hearers were dismayed at some of Vladimiri's statements, for example, that the earth had been divided up by God so that each people had a permanent right to that portion which had been assigned to them. It was just, therefore, that the pope or emperor undertake crusades to recover Jerusalem because that would be to reclaim the heritage of Christ from those Saracens who had illegally seized the holy city, but it was wrong for anyone else to conquer other places. In this latter case he meant Prussia and Samogitia, but his listeners could make their own list of places which their monarchs and peoples had taken. This may have occurred centuries ago or very recently, but, according to Vladimiri, that did not matter.

The churchmen became exasperated. One side seemed to have arguments about as good as the other, and each seemed to be slightly insane. The disputation was a mass of citations, ingenious arguments, terrible accusations and denials of one another's statements. There was no way to get at the truth of the matter, if there was indeed a final truth to be found in the mass of rubbish that both sides were dumping on the bored audience. Finally, Vladimiri's proposals were set aside, to be continued for several years in discussions at the papal and imperial courts, so that the council could concentrate on the more immediate question of Falkenberg. Perhaps his guilt or innocence could throw some light on the groups he represented.

Unfortunately, this proved a vain hope. The facts in that case proved hardly clearer than in the previous debates. The trial became an ordeal of exhaustion. Hearing followed hearing; postponement followed postponement. Falkenberg languished in prison and was soon almost forgotten. The basic problem was that churchmen could not find any easy way to distinguish between condemning the crusade against pagans and condemning crusading in general, and few Catholics were ready to abandon every crusade.

A Truce in Prussia

By this time a new complication had arisen. Sigismund wanted the Teutonic Knights to sever their ties to the Church and to become his vassals. This blackmail reflected Wirsberg's offers to Wenceslaus after Tannenberg. But it was also Sigismund at his most typical, an opportunist who took advantage of weaknesses. But his suggestion that he had no right to mediate between two states which were not subject to him was suddenly welcome to both the grandmaster and the Polish king, who had begun to think that it might be better to settle this matter themselves than continue to entrust it to foreigners.

Sigismund eventually wrote to Jagiełło that he would support him in his cause and that he had ordered the new margrave of Brandenburg, Friedrich of Hohenzollern, to bar mercenary soldiers from travelling through his domains to Prussia. This additional extortion did not change the grandmaster's mind, but with such friends the Teutonic Knights hardly needed enemies to hold a paranoid view of the world.

As for Jagiełło and Vytautas, they understood that the best means to influence the churchmen was actually to do something about converting the Samogitians. In late 1417 they installed as bishop a German born in Vilnius who knew Lithuanian and the Samogitian dialect, donated lands and incomes for his support, encouraged him to start his work immediately, and then wrote to the council to describe their achievements.

The Election of Martin V

The Teutonic Order was not completely ignored. There was some consolation in the honours given the archbishop of Riga, who was president of the German nation. Also, it was wittily said that MARS (Milan, Antioch, Riga, Salisbury) ruled the council, but for whatever advantage that gave the order, it was paying royally. In 1416 alone the delegation cost 13,800 florins, a fortune in view of the order's reduced income. That made it all the more important to elect a new pope quickly and dissolve the council.

Archbishop Wallenrode was not worried. In September 1417 Sigismund secretly promised him the bishopric of Liége, a rich diocese that would give him the means and the opportunity to bestride the diplomatic scene for years to come. He might even become pope. Understandably, he looked forward to the council adjourning, so that he could travel to his new see and be installed in office. However, that had to await the election of a new pope.

This had been repeatedly delayed by the obstinacy of the Spanish support for Benedict XIII. Wallenrode was frustrated because he had visited Spain in late 1415, trying to impress the king of Aragon with Sigismund's desire for unanimous action, lest the unhappy experience of Pisa be repeated. Even the mocking title given to Benedict, 'the pope of the Moon', based on his family name, de Luna, had no effect for the moment. (After the election of Martin V, Benedict, now an excommunicated antipope, remained in isolated exile until his death in 1423.)

Wallenrode now kept the churchmen in session, endlessly debating in the nations and in the commissions the myriad problems of church reform, territorial disputes, accusations of heresy and money. The last question was no small one, for almost every delegation (and even Sigismund himself) was in desperate straits. There was simply too little money in the world, and life in Constance was very expensive. Meanwhile, the council was always on the verge of dissolution. Rumours of secret flights by night circulated, and angry quarrels broke out in the debating chambers by day. Months passed and anxiety grew. Few decisions were reached and many participants became convinced that the schism would not be ended, nor the Church reformed, nor heresy stamped out, much less that their own personal complaints would be heard.

The cardinals were determined to retain their authority no matter what, and they believed that refusing to participate in the election process would defeat all reform proposals. At length, Sigismund, realising that he could not persuade the cardinals to cooperate, proposed that he would cease to champion reform if they would aid his efforts to become master of the Hungarian Church. The cardinals agreed, seeing that his powers there would be no different than those enjoyed by the French monarch in his kingdom. When the Spanish arrived and formed a fifth nation, a conclave was organised, the cardinals and other electoral officials were sequestered, and the electoral process begun.

The Teutonic Order was not given any post of honour at the election, as were the Hospitallers, whose grandmaster was made doorkeeper. But the archbishop of Riga shared with the archbishop of Gniezno the responsibility of going from elector to elector and urging each one to join with the others in selecting a pope, whomever they might choose. That a Pole and a member of the Teutonic Order were chosen to perform this important task together was an expression of the desire for solidarity in ending the schism. Such unity of purpose did not last long, but it sufficed. In November 1417 Odo Colonna (1369–1431) was elected. He quickly took holy orders, making himself eligible to be bishop of Rome, and took the name Martin V.

Wormditt began to work immediately to impress the new pope, sending presents 'as are honourable and good', namely silver cups and Siberian furs. In return, the new pope confirmed the election of the bishops of Culm, Ermland, Samland and Pomesania. He also expressed a wish to keep the costs of confirmation low and did not seek to extort advantages from his exercise of authority. That was a sign that the old days of corruption were over, at least temporarily, which was a welcome development because Wormditt lacked the means to vie with the Polish representatives in the giving of gifts and bribes.

Papal Favour

The diplomatic position of the order improved immediately. Because the Teutonic Knights were a military order directly subject to the pope, Martin V was inclined to offer it more protection from the king of Poland than he would have provided to a secular state. In late December 1417, when Sigismund sent Martin V a letter describing the problem of making peace in Prussia, the new pontiff rejected the proposed conditions, saying that they were too hard on the Teutonic Knights; and he ordered both sides to observe the conditions of the 1414 truce until he could study the matter more thoroughly. The pope then asked the procurator-general privately what his true wishes were, and that these should be communicated to him orally and secretly, while he required the Poles to make a written statement.

The pope said that he would be willing to instruct the king to abstain from warring on Prussia, but he doubted that the command would be obeyed. Therefore, the grandmaster should put the castles and fortresses into condition for war, provide them with garrisons and supplies, and not to be surprised if there were a sudden invasion. This message was forwarded immediately to Marienburg. The pope then wrote a note to Jagiełło, urging him to concentrate on converting the schismatics subject to his rule, on planting the true religion among those Samogitians who were wandering in the darkness, on walking on the paths of peace and light, and on and on, until at length he could bring the schismatics and infidels into the Holy Mother Church. Fine words, but there was no indication that the pope would give close personal attention to eastern problems soon.

The Polish delegates tried to reach a settlement before Sigismund and the pope left the city in February 1418. This time when the procurator-general was called before the pope, he said that he had no authority to make negotiations concerning land, but that he could submit to arbitration regarding the payment of reparations. Wormditt reported that three cardinals and two archbishops were appointed to hear this matter, and he counted the exclusion of the Samogitian claims as a notable success. Still, he complained that he was finding it difficult to present his arguments.

The procurator-general did not usually speak directly to Pope Martin and the cardinals, but communicated through the cardinal-protector – the cardinal of Pisa, Alamanno Adinari – who had been very effective in performing his office. When the pope dispatched the cardinal on diplomatic business, Wormditt complained privately to the grandmaster that his replacement was woefully incompetent. Still, he maintained a public silence and duly presented the new protector with gifts of a silver cup and a cape of Siberian silver fox.

Wormditt approached Sigismund for help again when the truce was extended for more than another year, offering him a profit for transmitting the war reparations of 100,000 florins and for keeping certain disputed villages until ownership could be determined. Sigismund then rejected the archbishop of Gniezno's request that this matter be arbitrated by princes chosen by the two parties; instead, he reserved to himself the right to issue decisions at some future date. Wormditt remarked in a report that Sigismund 'is terribly poor, and with a thousand florins, which the Rigan person receives in ten weeks, you could make him a friend as long as he lives, to protect the order and keep him in friendship'. The pope, in contrast, rejected payments, but he expected that all legal taxes would be paid. Nevertheless, the procurator-general suggested that a gift be offered 'so that the pope keeps us under his protection'.

This complaint about the archbishop demonstrates how far he had drifted from the rest of the delegation. Wallenrode had, in fact, not been a committed member of the order for almost fifteen years. His position was much like that of previous archbishops of Riga who had opposed the Livonian Knights on almost every issue of importance. Within a short time he resigned his office to hurry to Liége, leaving behind a mountain of debts and much unfinished business.

This defection, abandoning the poor northern archbishopric for a rich Flemish bishopric, reopened the yet unresolved issue of Rigan independence. The pope had the right to appoint the archbishop, but past appointments had almost invariably gone to strong-minded men who refused to subordinate their interests and ambitions to those of the Livonian master. Since renewed civil war was a distinct possibility if Martin V named the wrong man, the grandmaster and the officers were greatly relieved when the pope swore that 'he would never abandon the order but would stay by it and protect it to the death', and then appointed the man suggested by the procurator-general, Johannes Ambundi (1384–1424), a person the grandmaster criticised as being too close to Sigismund.

The Falkenberg Case Ended

The trial of Johann Falkenberg concluded in April 1418 in scandal. Although the Polish delegation had obtained the Dominican's condemnation in the German nation, the new pontiff had insisted that the matter be heard by the entire council. The Poles were naturally perturbed because they had met great resistance even in the German nation, where they represented a considerable part of the membership and had the backing of Sigismund. In the larger body the influence of the Dominicans would be much stronger and papal authority much greater. Therefore, although obeying the command to transfer the question to the assembly of nations, the Polish delegates appealed to a future council against an adverse judgment. When Paulus Vladimiri asked the assembly to declare Falkenberg's *Satire* heretical, an immediate tumult resulted, as representatives from the Spanish and English nations jumped to their feet to protest that the book had not been condemned in their nations as was necessary to bring the matter before the assembly.

Vladimiri then grabbed the petition and began to read it aloud. Finally, Pope Martin interrupted, commanding him to silence. The pope spoke briefly to the point, briefly because he was interrupted by Vladimiri, whom he now admonished to keep quiet under pain of excommunication. Another Polish delegate appealed this order, whereupon Pope Martin thanked the delegation with the remark that he held King Jagiełło and Grand Duke Vytautas to be good and true Christians, after which he set a date for another formal hearing. With that, debate ceased on the Falkenberg case.

A few days later the pope held a meeting to hear the Falkenberg question. To his surprise, the Polish delegates brought Sigismund with them to support their case. The pope was much displeased, but there was little he could do about the matter without offending the emperor-elect. The learned doctors read the decision of the German nation condemning the *Satire*, after which Wormditt addressed the assemblage. He stated that although Falkenberg had written the book in Prussia, when he had shown it to the grandmaster and the prior of Braunsberg (now the bishop of Ermland), they had recognised that the statements were libellous and dangerous. When they ordered him out of the country, Falkenberg had gone to Paris and published the treatise. Therefore, he argued, whatever might be said against Falkenberg, the same could not be said against the Teutonic Order.

The Dominicans protected themselves in a similar manner, remarking that they had imprisoned the offender and destroyed his books. Therefore, no present and dangerous heresy existed in the ranks of either religious order. Since there was no one to convict except Falkenberg, who was already in prison, and there was no direct evidence of heresy, since the statements in the book were perfectly orthodox, the pope then dismissed the case.

The Polish delegates were furious. They shouted and stamped their feet, waved arms and pushed, until the pope called out: 'In the name of Christ, let us be quiet.' Then he threatened to excommunicate anyone who persisted. All of this was glorious to Wormditt, who wrote that the Polish delegation 'suffered great shame at this time and our Order got great honour from it'.

Whether the Teutonic Knights got much honour is questionable, but it is undeniable that the Polish delegates hurt their own cause. Soon they added to the scandal by breaking into the papal residence, pushing aside the guards to reach the outraged pope. Martin V did not change his verdict as the noisy protestors demanded, but ordered a special consistory to decide upon a proper punishment for the rioters.

This meeting resulted only in the pope announcing a date at which the delegates would be tried as 'perjurers, disturbers and a danger to papal freedom'. Then he assigned several cardinals to hear the charges and ordered the accused to be held in prison or on parole.

Soon afterwards the pope reversed a 1412 decision that had awarded reparations to the bishop of Poznań (Posen) for damages committed in earlier wars. This was so unexpected that Wormditt recommended special celebrations and masses throughout Prussia. The pope also told the bishop of Ermland privately to warn the grandmaster of the danger of a sudden attack by the Polish king. The angry Polish delegates departed for home, leaving the Teutonic Order temporarily triumphant at the council.

The Council Dissolves

Everyone was tired. Many had spent a fortune; all had other business to attend to. Wenceslaus of Bohemia had died while hunting in August 1419, probably of a heart attack. Soon afterwards Sigismund learned how great a mistake the burning of Jan Hus had been – there were anti-German outbreaks throughout Bohemia. Although Sigismund and Barbara were able to enter Prague long enough to hold an improvised, invalid coronation in 1420, they quickly fled to safety.

When Hussites confiscated their opponents' lands, the Teutonic Order was badly hurt. Soon afterwards Johannes Wallenrode died in Liége, the morning after a memorable feast. With him died the Order's best hope for a strong voice in European politics.

When the papal court returned to Rome, Wormditt tried to accompany it; but fell ill in Bologna. Despairing of recovery, he wrote to the grandmaster to send a replacement. He died soon after Johann Tiergart (1380–1456) took over his post. Wormditt left behind a miscellany of possessions that tells us much about him: one new cloak of Parma cloth, several old cloaks, a few old suits, a few old furs, a travel bag of cloth and another of leather, two old suits of underwear, an old rug, two boxes filled with correspondence, three horses, an old grey stallion, a mule, a wooden cup with silver and gold ornamentation, a silver jug and bowl, ten small silver bowls, nine silver spoons, twelve common small silver cups, one sword, one half-moon-shaped breast ornament with a jewel in it, a knife, an amber apple, two books containing the rules of the Teutonic Order in both German and Latin, a breviary and a missal, a book on law, and the history of *The*

Deeds of the Franks. It was not a long list of possessions for a man who had risen from lowly origins to become powerful and important, a lawyer-diplomat who had been acquainted with cardinals and princes, who had occasionally associated with popes and emperors, but it delineated his character well.

Wormditt was not bound to absolute poverty, but he apparently spent little on luxuries. He possessed ceremonial clothes, but when his white cloaks wore out, he had not thrown them away. While he must have given a seedy appearance much of the time, he had fought the order's battles with words as effectively as any knight with sword, spear and bow. He was able to experience the thrill of battle only vicariously in the pages of a popular history, but who had served the order better? A comparison of Wormditt's accomplishments to Küchmeister's or those of later procurators answers that.

For the short run Wormditt had frustrated all his opponents. The Polish delegates could argue for the benefits of toleration towards pagans, Russian Orthodox Christians and Jews, but they were out of step with a Church that was essentially medieval and intolerant. Moreover, they could hardly brag about the success of the missionary effort in Samogitia, not after the May 1418 uprising that resulted in churches being burned, the houses of boyars being sacked and priests fleeing the country. Vytautas had become as hated as he had once been loved.

Given these circumstances, Vytautas had difficulty elevating the bishop of Samogitia to the church at Vilnius and appointing a successor. This was probably because the grand duke had asked that the new bishop be spared the usual fees. Vytautas was not about to pay the fees himself because that would set a dangerous precedent, so papal approval came only after four years. By then everyone was ready to concede that conversion of the Samogitians would be slow and arduous, as indeed it was.

Paulus Vladimiri remained at the curia, concentrating on the now obscure ruling of 1339, by which Pomerellia and other territories had been awarded to Poland along with a huge indemnity. The papal legate at the time had been furious with the grandmaster for ignoring his authority. Now Paulus Vladimiri, too, appealed directly to the pope. When Pope Martin evaded hearing the complicated arguments by sending the matter to a legate, Antonius Zeno, nobody was pleased.

The Teutonic Knights protested, appealing to Sigismund that this infringed imperial rights. After Sigismund wrote to him, Martin V cancelled the legate's authority. Antonius Zeno, however, continued his work, summoning witnesses to Warsaw to testify. Meanwhile, Vytautas and Jagiełło played into the hands of the order's diplomats by negotiating with the Hussites in Bohemia.

This act infuriated Sigismund, for whom the Hussites were heretics and rebels. When Pope Martin heard of it, he wrote strongly worded letters to Vytautas and Jagiełło, summoned Antonius Zeno back to Rome, and supported Sigismund in his efforts to prevent Polish and Lithuanian aid from reaching Bohemia. This was all good for the Teutonic Knights. Sigismund, however, changed his attitude after meeting Jagiełło in May 1419. Already irked by the order's numerous delays, he ended a meeting with the grandmaster's representatives by shouting that he might well join the Poles in the next invasion of Prussia.

A Decision at Last

It came as a great surprise to everyone, including Jagiełło, that Sigismund's long-awaited ruling came down on the side of the Teutonic Order. The choice of place and time gave it special prominence: an assembly in Silesia in January 1420. The Poles left the meeting in a fury, addressing a letter to the pope without even consulting the king and grand duke, who were hunting in Lithuania, too far away to contact quickly. Długosz wrote that when Jagiełło heard the decision, he broke down in tears; then he quickly dispatched Zbigniew Oleśnicki with a long letter of complaint, listing all the times he had assisted Sigismund all the way back to helping pay the ransoms after Nicopolis. However, Pope Martin not only confirmed the imperial decision, but when Jagiełło attacked Prussia in 1422, in violation of the truce, the pope excommunicated him.

Antonius Zeno continued to hold hearings into 1423. He would work towards implementing the Peace of Melno that followed the 1422 campaign, but he was not able to see the process through to completion. Nor did his report persuade the pope to uphold the sentence of 1339 or the terms of the peace treaty. Pope Martin was simply unwilling to see a military order of the Church destroyed or seriously weakened.

Falkenberg was released from his Roman prison after the council dissolved, having abjured the contents of his book. He travelled to Prussia to ask the grandmaster for a reward, apparently unwitting of how this would look or not caring what propaganda advantage this might give to the Poles. Nor did he seem to understand that the assassination of Jean of Burgundy in 1419 at a meeting with his French enemies – a gross violation of the trust necessary for any kind of diplomacy – made it impossible for responsible rulers to associate themselves with his call for Jagiełło's assassination.

Küchmeister gave him only four marks to cover his expenses. Falkenberg was so disgusted that he threw the money on the ground and left – to write a *Satire* on the Teutonic Order. Right at the beginning of his journey to Basel to show the *Satire* to the council's representatives, he was detained on Prussia's southern border, and his book confiscated. He proceeded to the council, found no support for any of his ideas, and died in Silesia during his return journey.

The Teutonic Knights thus weathered the crisis, but their moral position was seriously undermined. Although the order's castles were stronger than ever before and the army more efficient (or so the procurator-general said), the pope concluded that the forces allied against it would inevitably prevail. Important to that conclusion was a map given to him by the Polish representative – it depicted the vast extent of the two great secular states overshadowing tiny Prussia – and the idea of crusading energies being wasted in Prussia disturbed him. Martin V, in spite of himself, began to favour the Polish crown in hope of bringing the conflict to a speedy end.

The churchmen at Constance had managed to turn history back onto its traditional course, but there would be no rest, no relief. Instead, there were days of exhausting labour ahead, followed by sleepless nights.

Chapter 7

New Crises

Business in Lithuania

Victory at Tannenberg had not completely reconciled Vytautas and Jagiełło, nor had it drawn the Polish and Lithuanian noble and knightly classes together. Instead, their relationships alternately attracted and repelled. This reflected the complex personalities of the cousins, and religious and political realities. These last included the challenges presented by the Ottoman Turks, the Hussite party in Bohemia, Sigismund – king of Hungary and claimant to be Holy Roman emperor – the Teutonic and Livonian Orders, and Basil I of Moscow.

Jagiełło was aware that Lithuanians were unhappy about not having got more out of *Žalgiris*, as they today call what Germans know as the great battle at *Tannenberg*; but nevertheless he continued to emphasise the role of the Poles at *Grunwald*. This alienated Lithuanians who believed that they deserved more credit. He had sent the captured battle flags to Cracow to be hung in St Stanislaus, the cathedral in Wawel Castle; but he did not hurry to Poland personally to glory in the public adulation. Instead, he went to Lithuania, then visited Samogitia, Polotsk, Smolensk and Kiev. He received delegations from the Tatars, from Novgorod, and other states in Ruś. This was perceived as an effort to restate his claim to supremacy in Lithuania, which he stood to inherit once Vytautas died because the grand duke had no son.

At this point, however, Jagiełło had no son either. Nor had Sigismund, for that matter. Nor Wenceslaus. Everyone was concerned about a succession crisis.

When Jagiełło arrived in Cracow in late 1411, he encountered grumbling that he had wasted everything he had gained at Tannenberg. He was accused of favouring Lithuanian interests at the cost of Polish claims on Pomerellia and Culm. Strengthened by his victory, though, Jagiełło could afford to ignore criticism, even to increase his authority over the powerful church. He replaced the bishop of Cracow, Piotr Wysz Radoliński (1354–1414), sending him to Poznań. Radoliński had been a dominant figure in both church and state, but he was now aged, by the standards of the time. In his place the king named Wojciech of Jastrzębiec (*c.* 1362–1436), who had been closely connected to the court since the days of Queen Jadwiga. For the archbishopric of Gniezno he selected Mikołaj Trąba (1358–1422), who had been bishop of Halych in Galicia-Volhynia and was one of the few men admitted into the personal conversations of the king and grand duke. He led the Polish delegation to Constance.

The royal court was an exotic mix of Lithuanians, Rusians, Tatars, Silesian princes of Piast descent, and Poles, with occasional delegations from Hungary, Germany, Denmark, Bohemia and Italy. Prelates and monks, warriors and diplomats, poets, jesters, musicians jostled one another for room in the crowded lodgings wherever the king's wanderings took him. Those who could, mounted a horse and followed him through the forests because that was the best way to come to his attention. Those who could not, fretted and complained to one another.

Vytautas, meanwhile, was giving extensive grants of lands and privileges to the most important Lithuanian boyars, making them the equivalent of Polish magnates. In doing this, he was breaking with the tradition of reserving important estates and offices for relatives of the ruling dynasty. His model was obviously Poland, with the Polish-born bishop of Vilnius serving as an adviser for both the theoretical and practical aspects of the process. The bishops had all been Polish, partly because the Polish church did not trust Jagiełło's countrymen, partly because there were no Lithuanians yet with sufficient Roman Catholic education and experience to fill the posts. The management of the church's lands in the diocese of Vilnius had followed Polish traditions; and now Vytautas, advised by these very Polish clergymen, began extending the same privileges, using the same forms, to the boyars whose favour he wished to curry.

The treaty of Horodło (October 1413) guaranteed the rights of the Lithuanian boyars and tied them closely to the leading Polish noble families. The assembled boyars also recognised Jagiełło's daughter, the five-year-old Jadwiga, as the rightful heiress to the two states. Clearly no one expected either cousin to produce a male heir at their advanced ages, especially not Vytautas, whose wife Anna was now beyond the age of sixty, and probably not Jagiełło, who was often away from his spouse, who had produced no children since giving birth to Jadwiga in 1408.

On this occasion, of course, Jagiełło had brought his wife and daughter, to display them to the boyars so that they might see for themselves that Jadwiga was neither stupid, nor ill-mannered, nor unmarriageable. Afterwards he took them to Samogitia, where his men destroyed sacred groves and burned idols. As he rode through one particularly dense and foreboding forest, he turned to a Polish knight and remarked: 'The gods once inhabited these woods.'

Vytautas established a bishopric in Samogitia in 1417, naming a German born in Vilnius, Matthias (1370–1453), to the post. One might be sceptical about the Samogitian enthusiasm for converting to Roman Catholicism, but it was more than the Teutonic Knights had ever dared attempt. One might say that Christianity triumphed less than that paganism slowly died. The ancient religion had lived by war, and it could not survive peace. Of course, aspects of paganism survived, such as the mythology, folk tales, superstitions and magic rituals carried out in secret, but as a living and breathing faith it was soon only a fading memory.

Equally important was Vytautas's policy of giving estates to favourite boyars. By providing livings for the most prominent Samogitians, the grand duke replaced the traditional means of enrichment and support (raids on Christian neighbours) with exploitation of the peasantry. Many farmers, naturally, were not pleased by this. They were now frozen in the lower ranks of the free society and made to contribute to the upkeep of the church and the new noble class.

One Marxist historian summarised this policy as class warfare: the peasants went with the lands 'as if they were the trees and stones', and when they revolted, they were treated as traitors to their owners and renegades to their faith. When the god Perkunas had been dethroned, the old unity between man and nature was severed. 'God was automatically on the side of power.'

Of course, one does not have to take the 'unity of man and nature' too seriously, though that is a fundamental belief of all those who assume with Rousseau that primitive man is at every time, in every way, morally superior to civilised man; and that the more civilisation human beings acquire, the more vices they have. Vytautas's models were not forest gods, but very real Rusian dukes and Mongol khans. Those men lived on horseback, in the taiga and on the steppe, in very real communion with nature; and they were very dangerous. One approached them only in the company of warriors.

Ruś

The political situation on the steppe changed when Jalal al-Din Khan, the green sultan, took control of the Horde in 1411. He moved quickly to reassert Tatar supremacy over Ruś, demanding that the dukes present themselves to him in person, bearing gifts and acknowledging his right to appoint or remove men from office as he chose.

Ruśian dukes hurried to Sarai, Basil I among them. Some travelled by horse, others by boat down the Volga, but all bore the richest presents they could afford. The khan, being too fully occupied with rebellions to discuss their situation, kept them nearby waiting. They were still waiting when he was shot by his brother, after which the Tatar empire dissolved into civil war. The dukes returned home as quickly as they could.

Novgorod, until then ruled by Lengvenis, sent him away because it did not need his protection any longer; they complained to Vytautas and Jagiełło that the Lithuanians had cursed them and called them infidels, whereas they were Christians who hated pagans.

Everyone worried what would happen when Vytautas passed away. Jagiełło could not govern Lithuania from Cracow or even Brest, perhaps not even from Vilnius. Many believed that power had to reside at Tver, Moscow or Kiev – on the spot. As if confirming that belief, as Vytautas spent less and less time in Ruś, his control there diminished. Perhaps the annual outbreaks of plague made it too risky to go from city to city, but more likely he was feeling his age. He was almost seventy, and travelling the immense distances must have been hard even on his small but hearty frame.

He preferred life in Trakai, his ancestral home on the lovely lake in the hilly country west of Vilnius. He rebuilt the two castles there on plans drawn by foreign engineers. The gothic fortress on the island bore a striking resemblance to the brick castles erected by the Teutonic Knights throughout Prussia. Some 130 feet wide by 170 feet long, slightly trapezoidal in form, with three 50-foot-high towers, it was an impressive building with a spacious outer court whose walls left little room for attackers to fasten foot on the island. No visitor to the restored castle today can fail to be struck by its graceful lines and beautiful location. Vytautas was well aware how comfortable and defensible a castle could be when a spacious central courtyard was flanked by two-storied arcades, with living quarters, supplies, meeting halls, and chapel all brought together under two roofs. The garrison lived in one large building which also contained the storerooms; Vytautas and his family lived in the six small rooms of the other building. The great hall, where the grand duke entertained, had star vaulting, ceramic tiles, frescoed walls, and central heating – warm air was brought up from the furnace in the half-cellar through ceramic pipes. The 80-foot-tall tower at the main gate provided quarters for the guards. The peninsula castle was even larger, but it was designed for war. Its ten stone towers, high walls and deep moats made it almost impregnable.

Next to the grand duke, the most important official in Lithuania was the palatine or *voewoda* of Vilnius. From 1419 to 1442 this office was held by Kristinas Astikas (1363–1442/4), the founder of the powerful Radziwiłł (Radvila) family, whose estates were in the westernmost parts of the grand duchy – hence, the most threatened in any war against the Teutonic Knights or Poland. Other *voewody* were based at Trakai, Kiev, Polotsk, Vitebsk and Smolensk. Samogitia was governed by a locally elected administrator. Vytautas's brother, Žygimantas, governed the south-eastern region from his base at Naugardukas (Novogrudok, Nowogródek). This also gave him responsibility for overseeing Volhynia (much of modern Belarus) as far south as Łuck (Lutsk); just to the south was Podolia, then turbulent Moldavia.

The limitations on the powers of the ducal officials were partly practical, partly traditional. The vast extent of their territories meant that they had to allow subordinates considerable autonomy. They had to rely on bishops and abbots, knights, gentry and burghers, and long-term minor officials for advice about local traditions and the impact that various options would have on the local power structure and the economy. They had to expect that local boyars and clerics would stubbornly defend their traditional rights and every new one they could think of. Lastly, they knew that the grand duke would mistrust any of his subjects who became too powerful. One man Vytautas seemed to trust was his jester, a wise and witty jokester he had acquired from the grandmaster in Prussia.

One of Vytautas's greatest concerns was the complaint by his Orthodox subjects that he favoured Roman Catholics. As a result, he never acted as swiftly or forcefully in religious matters as papal representatives demanded. This worked to the advantage of the Teutonic Order, which continued to argue that Vytautas was at best a half-hearted convert. Despite all papal misgivings, however, the popes and their cardinals were astute observers of every political scene; they saw that real power was in the hands of Vytautas and Jagiełło, not in those of their enemies and detractors.

Vytautas had two policies towards his Orthodox subjects. The first was to work towards creating a new metropolitan who could stand up to the church authorities in Moscow. Vytautas told the bishops they could elect whomever they wanted, but they had to elect *someone* to the long-vacant seat in Kiev. Defiantly, the bishops told him that the apostolic authority of a metropolitan was different from the secular power of a caesar and that because of the Tatars, who had recently tried to kidnap the metropolitan, he now chose to stay in Moscow; and even the Kremlin was none too safe a fortress when Mongols were concerned. In 1415 Vytautas resolved this in his usual manner. He told the bishops that unless they elected Gregory Tsamblak (1365–1420) as metropolitan of Kiev, he would execute them all. Tsamblak was a Bulgarian who had fled to Serbia when the Ottomans came, then fled to Kiev when they took Serbia. The churchmen cast the votes as directed, but Vytautas's blunt methods were not popular. Public opinion never accepted this metropolitan, and after his death in 1419 or 1420, Vytautas did not appoint a successor.

The second policy, even more unpopular, was to encourage a closer union of the eastern and western churches. Gregory Tsamblak even travelled to Constance in 1418 to present a plan for church union. Nothing came of this at the time since the council members were no more willing to make concessions to the Orthodox Church than they were ready to accommodate Hussites.

On the whole, after the Council of Constance Vytautas enjoyed a peaceful relationship with the Teutonic Knights. They had a common interest in protecting their Livonian possessions against Novgorod and their western ones against Jagiełło. That was merely his customary ability to recognise political realities and act on them. This did not preclude crises, however, or even war.

Švitrigaila Returns

The more Vytautas relied on Polish aid, the more his Orthodox followers fretted. As rivals rose up, he swatted them down, but his reluctance to kill members of his dynasty seemed to encourage new conspiracies. Imprisoning captured relatives was ineffective. For example, he had held Švitrigaila in chains in Kremenets as an example to the others. Dead, Švitrigaila was of no use to anyone. Alive, his claim to be Vytautas's successor precluded others from being taken seriously. Then, in 1418 several Ruśian nobles came to the commander at Kremenets, Konrad Frankenberg, to offer their service as mercenaries. Once they had secured his confidence, they let 500 friends in by night, slew the commander and other officials, liberated Švitrigaila, and then made their way west.

According to the Nikonian Chronicle, Švitrigaila rode to Hungary, then to Constance to see Sigismund, who sent him to Prussia, whence he slipped into Samogitia. More probable is the account by the Prussian chronicler Posilge, which had Švitrigaila going to Wallachia, then Austria, and after a while making his way back to Ruś via Hungary. Posilge would have known whether or not Švitrigaila had visited the

Teutonic Knights; Švitrigaila was a good friend of the order. While the news of his escape caused alarm in Lithuania and Poland, there was rejoicing in Ruś.

When the Samogitians rose in rebellion in 1418, causing Bishop Matthias and his priests to flee for their lives, they destroyed the homes of loyalist boyars, and finally raided the supposedly secure castle at Memel. Švitrigaila was clearly not in the country, nor was there any prominent leader among the rebels. That made it possible for Vytautas to march into Samogitia in October, reestablish order, and execute sixty of the peasant insurrectionaries.

Perhaps the rebels' attack on Teutonic Order territories persuaded the grandmaster that the peasants were unreliable allies, but more likely he recognised political reality. To intervene in Samogitia would be to risk a war that he was not ready to fight. What the incident demonstrated was, first of all, how difficult it was for anyone to govern the Samogitians; second, why the Teutonic Knights could still consider the natives pagans; and, lastly, how vigorously Vytautas could react when anyone challenged his will.

A Time to Wed

The death of Anna, Vytautas's influential wife, occurred in 1418. She had always been Vytautas's most trusted counsellor, and there are no suggestions that Vytautas was ever unfaithful to her. Nevertheless, he did not wait long after her burial to remarry. Both Posilge and Długosz believed that, lusting for Anna's niece, Juliana Halshany (Uliana Olshanska), he arranged for her husband's murder. (When the most important German and Polish sources agree on anything, we should take it seriously.) He then consummated the marriage against the wishes of the bishop of Vilnius, who was appalled that he would marry a relative of his late wife without a papal dispensation. (Martin V eventually provided one, long after it was moot.) More importantly, perhaps, Juliana's father was the head of a large and powerful clan in Ruś. Vytautas inherited his authority and thereby strengthened his position in the strategic borderlands that Jagiełło wanted.

Jagiełło and Elisabeth attended the wedding, then returned home slowly with about 500 men, hunting along the way. One day Jagiełło encountered a column of 3,000 horsemen sent by the grandmaster to offer his congratulations to the grand duke. Suspicious at being asked how many men he had with him, and knowing that his party would not be able to defend him against an attack on his camp, Jagiełło hurried back to Poland. His subjects were naturally outraged at the story of the cross-bearers' presumed treachery.

Vytautas was a devoted husband, who would leave his armies as soon as victory was won and fly home, changing horses in relays until he reached his wife again. Długosz, ever the chiding priest, condemned his addiction to the pleasures of the flesh and his habit of showering Juliana with presents. Despite every effort, however, the marriage produced no offspring. In contrast to the prolific families of all his relatives, he had only the one daughter, Sophia, who visited him in Smolensk in 1422 or 1423. Sophia may have come partly to escape the famine in central Ruś, a time when peasants wandered from the lands of Novgorod and Moscow to Lithuania in search of food; or she may have come to escape the ensuing plague; but more likely she hoped to restore the alliance between her husband and father, so that they could jointly repel the Tatar attacks that were once again so dangerous.

That paid off in 1424, when a Lithuanian army met the invading horsemen in pitched battle and inflicted a complete defeat on them, even slaying the khan's best general. Two wives of the khan were captured, one being sent to Vytautas, one to Basil I.

Jagiełło's marriages lacked such drama, perhaps because his personality made such passion impossible. But maybe it was because his wives, with one exception, were relatively colourless. Jadwiga had disliked him and disliked sex with him even more. Anne of Celje had produced a daughter, significantly named Jadwiga (1408–31), whom he reared as the heiress to the throne. Young Jadwiga was the apple of Jagiełło's eye, and for her sake he tolerated the mother.

Anne had avoided the notorious scandals later associated with her cousin, Barbara of Celje, but she was suspected of several affairs. The most damaging rumour concerned the archbishop of Gniezno, Mikolaj Kurowski, one of the heroes of Tannenberg. (Gossips attributed his death in 1411, in a riding accident, to his fear of having this sin exposed.) Anne was also believed to hate Sigismund for his treatment of her cousin, and, therefore, hated Sigismund's ally, the Teutonic Order.

After Anne's death in early 1416, the search was kept close to home, presumably to hurry matters, since Jagiełło was no longer young and one had to think about the succession not from the date a male heir was born, but when he would be mature enough to rule. In 1417 the king hurriedly and secretly married Elisabeth Pilecka (1372–1420), daughter of the *voewoda* of Sandomir. She was the wealthiest woman in Poland, but her past was at least as rich as her inheritance. Her first husband had kidnapped her in order to marry her. Her second husband had slain the first in order to possess her. Her third appears to have been a fortune-hunter. Długosz, who missed few opportunities to pass on gossip and fascinating titbits, was appalled at 'this kind of love, which would better be called infatuation'. He ridiculed the king's efforts to have her, his going from place to place, love-sick, asking confidential advice, until finally his sister Alexandra told him to ask Vytautas for help. There was some plausibility to this story because the lovers apparently sealed their engagement at Alexandra's court in Masovia when the king was on his way to Lithuania.

When the king finally revealed his plans, his nobles and boyars saw that his mind was made up and, therefore, resistance was futile. The wedding took place immediately after Walpurgis Night, the spring celebration when witches were believed to assemble for riotous dancing and drinking. By bad luck the weather was so bad that the streets flooded, forcing the queen to step out of her carriage and walk to the castle. The common people blamed the storms on God's displeasure with the marriage – first because of the disparity of their ranks, and second because it was commonly accepted that three marriages were all that were spiritually allowed. This was her fourth. Jagiełło quickly obtained a dispensation after the fact from the Council of Constance. When Elisabeth died in mid-1420, perhaps from tuberculosis, all the servants in the palace, clerics included, celebrated noisily.

Jagiełło next unsuccessfully sought a Bohemian bride, then for three years waited for his advisers to locate someone suitable. At last, he was persuaded by Vytautas to marry Sophia of Halshany (Holszany; 1405–1461), whose Orthodox belief could strengthen the king's ties to Ruś; the ceremony was held in Naugardukas, with Matthias, now Bishop of Vilnius, presiding. The public (at least the clergy) found the marriage between the increasingly decrepit king and the beautiful and spirited maiden inappropriate, but the animosity also reflected discomfort that Vytautas had strengthened his own position. This marriage also forfeited the opportunity to gain another claim to the Bohemian crown – Sigismund had proposed a marriage with Wenceslaus's widow – and the Polish nobles and Church were, of course, eager that their prince should take that kingdom from Sigismund. They blamed Vytautas for the failure to make the effort.

Intrigues at Court

Vytautas had far too much influence, as the Polish patriots saw it; and the churchmen, led by Zbigniew Oleśnicki, who became bishop of Cracow in 1423, were determined to curb it. Their chances were excellent because they were at court continually, and Vytautas could not recruit a party from the native Poles. Sophia, however, delivered what the king's three previous brides had not: sons. She bore Ladislas within a year of her wedding, two years later a son who died at the age of eighteen months, and Casimir in 1427. This made the Jagiellonian dynasty secure. Of course, Jagiełło was not an ideal husband, being not only seventy-three when his younger son was born, but also away much of the time, hunting or travelling. When courtiers began to whisper that the queen did not enjoy sleeping alone, this created some tension around the figure of young Jadwiga, who was at an age to consummate her long-arranged marriage to Friedrich II of Hohenzollern (the Iron-Toothed, 1413–1471), the second son of the powerful margrave of Brandenburg. Should Jagiełło die soon, she would make a better ruler or regent than the foreigner Sophia or her under-age sons.

Meanwhile, Vytautas was childless, except for Sophia, whose marriage to Basil I in 1391 made her more a Muscovite than a Lithuanian; and no one was suggesting that one of her surviving sons should inherit Lithuania. Concerns about Jadwiga's marriage were important because the Lithuanian boyars had already accepted Jadwiga as their future ruler, and her likely husband would become an elector of the Holy Roman Empire, a thorough-going German.

Jagiełło had succeeded in founding a dynasty, but his age was beginning to show. He was already sixty-nine when his first son was born and the daily press of business was wearing him down. He knew that he had to live until the infant Ladislas was at least a teenager. Therefore, he had to pass on some of his more onerous duties to subordinates. This must have been difficult since most of his reign he had fought with prominent nobles and prelates for the decisive voice in his own government. The nobles now insisted that they would not recognise any heir unless he conceded them great autonomy; the Church was even more difficult.

Zbigniew Oleśnicki's commanding personality and his unswerving loyalty to the Roman Catholic Church now made him the dominant figure in Polish affairs. Nothing happened without Oleśnicki's approval, nothing happened without his knowing about it – this would put increasing strain on his once close relationship with the king. In time he appointed family members to important posts (his brother was marshal of Poland 1431–40 and married his daughter to Ladislas of Płock, Jagiełło's nephew). Prominent among his programmes was giving Roman Catholics in Lithuania more and more privileges, hoping perhaps that Orthodox boyars would become converts out of self-interest. He advocated supporting the imperial war against the Hussites in Bohemia; and he supported sending crusading armies against the Turks in the Balkans.

The Hussites in Bohemia

The confusing developments in popular religious life had profound effects on the way conservative Roman Catholics followed the slow progress of Christianisation in Lithuania. Because the most vocal critics of the established Church were also perceived as anti-German, German clergymen found the Teutonic Knights' accusations against Vytautas, and Jagiełło as well, plausible and even likely. Heresy and apostasy seemed to be everywhere. Why not in distant lands where the country people were still believed to hold strongly to their ancient pagan beliefs?

Conservative churchmen were even more certain that the Hussites in Bohemia were heretics. Though disorganised as late as 1417, by 1420 the Hussites dominated most of Bohemia. Outraged that Jan Hus had been burned at the stake in Constance, they were determined to prevent Sigismund from ascending the Bohemian throne. When crusading armies crossed the frontier, they drove them back in disorder. That was no surprise – the Czechs were known as the best mercenary soldiers in Central Europe.

The Hussites could remain unified when faced by a common enemy, but they disagreed strongly over important points. The moderate Utraquists were strongest in Prague and among the Czech nobles; the more radical Taborites were mostly peasants, with their stronghold at Tabor in southern Bohemia. What held them together was the instinct for self-preservation in the face of the overwhelming odds, and the Four Articles of Prague.

The Hussite articles of faith will hardly shock any modern reader familiar with Protestantism, and informed individuals who heard of them in 1417 would have recognised a summary of the reform proposals of the previous century, especially the reforms inspired by John Wycliffe: first, that preachers be free to proclaim the Word of God; second, that the Holy Sacrament in both Body and Blood be given to all true Christians; third, that clergy should give up their earthly possessions and live in poverty and holiness like the apostles; and fourth, that secular authorities enforce the laws against the seven deadly sins and simony, punish mortal sins regardless of the sinner's status, and stop the spread of slanders about the nation. In addition, Latin was to be replaced in theological disputes and religious services with the language understood by the congregation.

What made these assertions so dangerous was they reflected the views of Bohemian nobles who hated Sigismund for violating his word of honour and his safe-conduct by allowing Hus to be burned by the churchmen. This anger was soon directed at Germans in Czech cities and the Church. This was spurred on by the demand of the Council of Constance and Pope Martin V in 1418 that the Czechs return all offices and properties confiscated during the unrest, then give up the rebels' properties to the Church, and require them all to report to Rome for trial. Thus, a movement on the verge of splintering into hostile factions was drawn back together for self-defence.

Ironically, Sigismund, perceived by Czechs as the personification of Germanisation, was viewed by Germans as having sacrificed their interests for his Hungarian and Bohemian kingdoms. But even Wenceslaus had done much the same, appointing German officials to govern his capital, Prague. That had led to the famous First Defenestration of Prague in 1419, when a mob, angry at rocks thrown at them, stormed the city hall and threw the imperial appointees from the tower onto the pavement of the main square. When Wenceslaus died a few weeks later, the Hussite nobles and burghers refused to accept Sigismund as his successor.

When Sigismund named Sophia (1376–28), Wenceslaus's widow, as governor, Germans immediately accused him of having been seduced (literally) by the ageing empress into violating his oath at Constance to crush the Hussite movement, and therefore of being unworthy to wear the crown. Apparently, efforts at compromise were neither going to appease the Hussites nor please Roman Catholic conservatives. Evidently nobody saw anything humorous in the idea that Sigismund would have to be seduced; sex was the one aspect of life in which Sigismund did not need encouragement to take the initiative.

Scandal had hovered around the queen since 1393, when Wenceslaus had tortured her confessor in an attempt to force him to reveal what she had said at confession. That priest, John of Nepomuk (Jan Nepomucký), became a major Czech saint – the location where he was thrown from Charles Bridge to drown is prominently marked today – but the immediate issue was clouded by the king supporting the Avignon pope and the archbishop of Prague. His accuser, his chancellor, backed the Roman pope. Sophia, though a Bavarian by birth, had supported Jan Hus until the papal excommunication in 1410; thereafter the Czechs did not trust her.

The Hussite doctrine, part religious reform, part class warfare, part Slavic nationalism, quickly spread throughout the Bohemian kingdom, even into Silesia, and from there to Cracow. In Breslau (Wrocław), conspirators seized the city hall in 1418 and beheaded the German councillors. Jagiełło watched unhappily as Sigismund exacted revenge in 1420, beheading twenty-three leaders after a two-month trial, then burning three religious radicals at the stake.

Consequently, Jagiełło was in a receptive mood when the moderate Hussites sent to him as chief of their delegation Wilhelm Kostka of Postupitz, a Bohemian mercenary who had served the Polish cause with distinction at Tannenberg and in 1414. Soon afterwards, in May 1421, Jagiełło was again approached by leaders of the moderate Hussites; this time being asked to become king of Bohemia. When Jagiełło heard the terms, namely, that he tolerate communion in both kinds (the laity would share in the wine as well as the bread) and promise to enforce the Four Articles, he neither declined nor accepted. The king hesitated to become involved in a war with Sigismund, whose vassals in Hungary, Moravia, Silesia and Brandenburg were capable of inflicting tremendous harm on his kingdom. On the other hand, who knew what might come of the offer? Though publicly rejecting any thought of negotiating with heretics, in private Jagiełło suggested that the delegates contact Vytautas.

Sigismund had hesitated, too, when the Czech Diet had offered him the crown in 1419. He had chosen not to attend the sessions, thereby allowing his supporters to be outvoted or persuaded to join the Hussite ranks. Moreover, he had denounced the terms in advance, making it clear that he would be a Roman Catholic monarch, and a strong one, a ruler who expected obedience and respect. The terms offered by the Czechs did not fit that definition; in fact, they required Sigismund to endorse the Hussite theology and its religious reforms. Sigismund, not wishing to sacrifice the German crown for a Czech one, rejected the offer. In retrospect, Sigismund might have wished to have back the six months he spent in Bosnia that year, because the Turkish threat had not been that serious. However, not all was lost. The Germans who demanded punishment of the heretics could be counted on for aid, and a good many Czech nobles indicated publicly or privately that they were ready to swear fealty to him. Anything was better than civil war.

Sigismund was also aware that the royal garrisons had remained loyal. Thus, he had control of the two castles in Prague – the Hradčany with the cathedral of St Vitus on the west bank, Vyšehrad on the east – and the powerfully fortified hunting lodge at Karlstejn, where the regalia were kept. Also, by and large the German-speaking burghers of the cities were ready to support him, partly out of fear of Czech nationalism, partly to keep the trade routes open to Germany, Austria and Hungary. His policy was tough talk, secret compromises.

Radical Hussites used the interval to sack monasteries and churches, then used the silver, cash, and other treasures to buy weapons, especially firearms. They also adapted agricultural tools, making the flail into a deadly weapon and wagons into movable fortresses. The combination of enthusiasm and repeated victories in local clashes made them bold, and all efforts by Germans and Czech moderates to contain their spread were frustrated by the geniuses who organised and led their armies.

The Hussite Wars

The most famous general of this era was the one-eyed Jan Žižka. An experienced mercenary who may have fought for the Polish king at Tannenberg, he now led the newest and most radical wing of the Hussites – the Taborites. His personal religious views were moderate, but Sigismund and his churchmen refused to negotiate with anyone associated with the heresy. Consequently, the radicals grew in influence and numbers, and the moderates did not dare risk a conflict in the Hussite ranks.

Sigismund believed that the German nobles, clerics and burghers were all that counted; and that he could frighten the Czechs into surrender. He might have read the Old Testament, or with half an ear heard it read to him; but he could not understand that men inspired by the thought they were fighting the Lord's battles did not fear more numerous enemies. Gideon had been outnumbered too.

He was similarly obtuse when it came to the tactical innovations that Žižka was introducing into warfare – fighting behind a wagon barrier (*Wagenburg*), using cannon and crossbows to cut down horsemen as they tried to force their way between the wagons. This was not a new idea, but nobody had yet perfected the use of a heavy and cumbersome moveable fortress. Vytautas had tried it in 1399, with disastrous results. It was vulnerable on the march, and could be blown apart by heavy artillery; but most importantly, it was only as good as the men defending it – and nobody had much respect for peasants in arms. Žižka's goose flag (in Czech *hus* = goose) seemed more laughable than serious. As a result, Sigismund expected that a combination of diplomatic skill and military threats would bring the Czechs to their senses.

Sigismund's slowness in dealing with the Czech radicals caused his German followers to grumble that he had sold them out to placate his Czech loyalists. This charge would haunt Sigismund, reappearing each time he tried to end the conflict by compromise. Only in March

1420, when Pope Martin V declared a crusade against the heretics, did Sigismund ask the electors to raise volunteers. When 100,000 men were assembled, Sigismund advanced into Bohemia with such incredible slowness that he could not find enough food for the men; and then he watched placidly when disease ran through the army. Some of the blame might be attributed to Filippo Buondelmonti degli Scolari (1369–1426), known as Pippo Spano, a Florentine nobleman who had served Sigismund through every campaign since Nicopolis. He was familiar with the tactics of the Italian *condottieri*, the mercenary leaders of free companies, who won their victories by manoeuvre and negotiation rather than pitched battles. This worked in Italy, where the peasantry had little at stake in the outcome of the wars, but not in Bohemia.

Sigismund was so confident of victory that he refused all offers to negotiate; after all, no one had ever seen an army as powerful as his. Also, believing that terror would paralyse his enemies, he allowed his forces to behave atrociously, killing loyal Catholics who did not know German, even burning some alive, on the assumption that all Czechs were Hussites. Soon there were more, after which the German crusaders learned how dangerous it was to stray too far from the main force.

Although Sigismund's men still held Hradčany castle, the city on the opposite bank of the river was a Hussite stronghold, so it was necessary to commence siege operations. Soon three great tent cities had sprung up opposite the city gates. His men broke the monotony by occasionally giving a chant similar to those still heard at sporting events and public celebrations in Germany today: 'Ha, Ha, *Hus, Hus, Ketzer, Ketzer*.' (*Ketzer* = heretic.)

However, before Sigismund was ready to storm the city walls, Jan Žižka arrived with a small but highly trained army of radical Hussites. He had marched from Tabor in three days, pushing aside Sigismund's blocking forces, and soon erected forts on all the hilltops around Prague. Sigismund sent men from Meissen and Thuringia to assault Žižka's wooden fort on the Vítkov, thinking that would both demoralise the defenders of Prague and cut off the last route for food and supplies into the city. However, the German knights fled in disorder from the well-timed counterattack by the small garrison, leaving hundreds of their number on the hill slope. Žižka then built an even larger fortification there.

Pressed by his mercenaries for their pay, Sigismund melted down the treasury in the cathedral and all the silver in the churches. But the mercenaries would not stay longer than to allow him to be crowned king of Bohemia in St Vitus's cathedral in the Hradčany castle. He dismissed the crusaders, then led 16,000 mercenaries to Kutná Hora, where the German miners refilled his coffers with silver.

Sigismund returned to Prague in September. If he had moved more swiftly, he would have found the defenders weak since the Taborites had left and their replacements, the Orebites, had not yet arrived from eastern Bohemia. But he had delayed so that the Moravian knights could join him. When the Orebites came out to fight, Sigismund was overjoyed, but the peasants won an overwhelming victory, slaying more crusaders than had fallen at Vítkov.

As the Hussite forces followed him out of the country, Sigismund sent his badly demoralised troops home. In March 1421 he rode to Hungary to conduct operations against Venice.

Later that year Sigismund ordered simultaneous advances on Prague from the east and the west. At first all went well: crusaders from Meissen crushed a Hussite force in northern Bohemia. Then in October, as the Saxons withdrew, 125,000 German crusaders advanced into western Bohemia, while a large Hungarian force entered Moravia. Sigismund joined the latter army somewhat late, then slowed the advance to fifty miles in twenty days so that he could negotiate with the Hussites.

Once again his troops committed terrible atrocities. When the imperial army approaching Prague from the west became frustrated at the siege of a minor stronghold, then dispirited by quarrels among the leaders, they fled at the first sound of the Czech war song. This unhinged the imperial strategy to make the Hussites divide their forces or to leave the city unprotected.

Sigismund's Hungarian army, under the command of Pippo Spano, still had an initial success at Kutná Hora, when the German miners lynched the Hussite officials and surrendered the city. He surrounded the Taborite forces, but Žižka, though now totally blind, employed his cannons effectively and broke out. Then Žižka called on reinforcements from the west, cut the city off from the Hungarian army, stormed the defences, and drove the soldiers and citizens in flight for their lives towards Hungary.

Sigismund found it necessary to hasten to Germany, where the electors were talking about deposing him for incompetence. For several years thereafter he was occupied with placating the electors, fighting Turks on the Hungarian border, and marrying his twelve-year-old daughter Elisabeth to Albrecht of Habsburg (1397–1439), who then took over much of the responsibility for the crusade. Albrecht accepted as her dowry Moravia, a region which was more German in those days than it was centuries later when it was still an important part of the

Sudetenland. Unfortunately, his enthusiasm for killing heretics extended to Jews and other outsiders.

Sigismund's reputation fell and fell, both in Germany and Hungary. The surrounded garrison in the Hradčany castle agreed to surrender if no relief force came; and soon afterwards other garrisons did as well. His supporters had no idea what to do other than raise more armies, but their armies were already larger than they could pay and feed, or even command effectively, and they had failed to prevail.

Hussite Dominance

At first Žižka's armies had been condemned to immobility, using their linked wagons to hinder cavalry charges and fortifying high hills; but as they gained experience and confidence, they learned how to move a wagon fort across open ground. And when the Hussites' nobles were present – most were Utraquists – Žižka could launch devastating counter-strokes. Moreover, their enemies' atrocities rallied recruits to their cause.

The composition of the Hussite movement was so complex that even contemporaries found it difficult to follow. The Utraquists and Taborites each had three distinct subgroups running from conservative to moderate to radical. The moderate Taborites led by Jan Žižka and Procop the Bald (1380–1434) were so appalled by the extremists of the Picart party (many of whom had come from France and the Low Countries) that they expelled them from Tabor and later almost wiped them out – a small number of 'Adamists' survived to live as nudists on an island near Tabor.

Sigismund's defeats were hard blows to the Teutonic Knights, who had contributed knights and their experience in recruiting crusaders. But the grandmaster was never personally involved. He had too much to do in Prussia. The harvest of 1419 had been almost non-existent. First, it was too cold for the crops to grow, then it was so warm that there was no rain. The bees perished, the herring vanished from their usual feeding grounds, and there were no hops for beer. The grandmaster had to demand a special tax, with no exceptions, to cover the order's expenses.

To make matters more complex, the Hussites were spreading their ideas into Poland. This was noticed particularly by the dean of the Cracow cathedral chapter, Oleśnicki's office at the time. The similarity of the Czech and Polish languages and the widespread antipathy towards Germans came together as an anti-clerical, anti-foreigner and anti-urban movement.

Oleśnicki feared that this sentiment would destroy Poland's multi-national character, harm prospects for increasing trade, frighten German-speaking burghers who were loyal citizens and paid taxes in hard cash, and ruin the Roman Catholic Church. Once rabid nationalists had dealt with the Germans, what would they do next? Turn against the Jews? The Lithuanians? How would he ever persuade Germans in Prussia to abandon the Teutonic Knights or Hungarians and Bohemians to accept Polish leadership, not to mention the vast multitudes in Ruś and the Balkans?

For Oleśnicki and Bishop Matthias, the matter was clear: Hussite beliefs were incompatible with the mission God had called Poland to. It was impossible to be both the shield of Christendom and at the same time a national state defined by language and a narrow definition of culture. Urged on by Pope Martin V, Oleśnicki called together a church council, then ruthlessly enforced the edict against the heresy.

Jagiełło, meanwhile, was in search of a wife. Widowed in 1420 and still without a male heir, he sent his officials to negotiate for a bride who could give him a plausible claim to the Bohemian crown, Sigismund's daughter Elisabeth. Sigismund's first reaction was anger. His second, to delay, to build his air-castle coalitions, to negotiate, and to exploit his friends and allies without scruple. What he seemed to be doing was to put off a response in hope of getting military assistance. If that failed, he wanted to prevent the Poles from sending assistance to the Hussites. To the extent he could use other issues to keep Jagiełło (and Vytautas) occupied, he would.

When Sigismund wed his daughter to Albrecht of Austria, this inducement was no longer available. In early 1422, when Jagiełło met Sigismund on the Polish–Hungarian border, Jagiełło offered to assist the emperor-elect against the Hussites if he would revise his verdict regarding Samogitia. Instead, Sigismund, knowing that the king was still interested in a Bohemian wife, offered the hand of Wenceslaus's widow, Sophia. Jagiełło, of course, had no interest in a scandalous woman past her childbearing years,

Meanwhile, the Hussite envoys that Jagiełło had sent on to Vytautas were encouraged by the grand duke's reception. Vytautas was not particularly interested in sending an army all the way to Bohemia, but he was furious about Sigismund's awarding Samogitia to the Teutonic Order – in fact, he had stormed about the castle, cursing at the Hungarian king's perfidy. This was probably more important in his response to the delegates' plea to save the peoples of Slav and Czech descent from extermination than taking a subtle and safe revenge on

Sigismund. In the end he sent Jagiełło's nephew, Sigismund Korybut (Kaributas, 1373–1435), to Bohemia, to investigate the situation. Korybut quickly won friends among both radical and moderate Hussites, a success that outraged Pope Martin V. The pope wrote Vytautas a strong letter, condemning his actions, and he was not pleased by Vytautas's response that he was simply trying to help restore unity to the church.

The pope excommunicated Korybut and threatened Vytautas, and even Sigismund began telling German princes about 'secret Hussites' in high places in the east. In accordance with later promises to Sigismund, Jagiełło ordered Korybut to come home from Bohemia. It was not his fault, he suggested to his critics, that the prince disobeyed.

Jagiełło may have occasionally dreamt of adventure late at night, when he was wandering sleeplessly about the palace or in the woods; but before dawn he was always a hard-headed realist again. Oleśnicki had built a party of nobles and clergy, and the king found it easy to let them think they ran the country, but he reserved every final decision for himself. Meanwhile, he enjoyed himself in the royal preserves, hunting in forests far wilder than even most contemporaries could imagine. As the years passed, the daily effort to influence politics wore him down; grand plans receded ever farther from his mind, and only occasionally could anger or memory of past slights move him to action.

Sigismund, in contrast, seemed to gain new strength and confidence from every crisis. He had weathered the most dangerous storms of his reign and no longer felt it necessary to deal with every emergency personally. He turned tasks over to trusted subordinates, and even to the kind of men who a generation before would have betrayed him at the first opportunity. Sigismund concentrated his mental and physical resources on the important tasks: diplomacy at the highest level, coordination of his subordinates' activities, and, of course, women.

The 1422 invasion of Bohemia, led by Friedrich of Hohenzollern, brought supplies to the garrison at Karlstejn, but further advance was frustrated by Czech forces led by Korybut. The Teutonic Knights had invested heavily in this venture, and its defeat was a hard blow to them. Their only consolation came in reports that the Hussite factions were fighting as viciously with one another as they were against foreigners. Žižka refused to make himself king and withdrew from the increasingly radical community at Tabor to the more moderate Orebites; two years later an illness ended his life.

The War of 1422 in Prussia

Küchmeister's repeated failures had cost the somewhat overweight grandmaster the respect of his knights. Moreover, he was suffering from bladder or kidney stones. At a formal meeting in March 1422 they held him to account, then demanded his resignation. He gave it.

His successor was a pious disciplinarian with a ready smile, Paul of Rusdorf (1385–1441), who had earned his office by loyal service. He had apparently not been in Prussia at the time of Tannenberg, since he is first mentioned in the voluminous records in 1412; nevertheless, within three years he was in the grandmaster's inner council, first as master of the robes, then as treasurer. He had been active in the negotiations with Jagiełło, and, therefore, was believed when he confidently promised that he could win concessions from him that had been refused to Küchmeister.

With Sigismund and the German master committed to the Hussite Wars, the summer of 1422 was perfectly suited for Jagiełło and Vytautas to test the mettle of the new grandmaster. They spread rumours that their war preparations and the gathering of armies were intended for the Bohemian war; nevertheless, the strengthening of the garrisons along the Hungarian, Prussian, Neumark and Livonian borders, and the northerly assembly point of the armies provided ample evidence of their intentions.

Paul of Rusdorf could not believe what was happening. He had come into office as a peacemaker. He had opposed Küchmeister's ruinous war policy, and had done what he could to reduce military expenditures. Naïve, one might call him, to believe Jagiełło, but no more naïve than to believe that Sigismund would back up his promises with deeds.

In any case, it was difficult to recruit more troops – partly because Friedrich of Hohenzollern had hired every experienced man for the Hussite war, partly because Friedrich, having arranging for his son to marry Jagiełło's daughter, had chosen sides against Rusdorf. The grandmaster's recruiters were still in the process of hiring second-class mercenaries when the royal array crossed the frontier.

The grandmaster was unable to persuade the Livonians to send assistance either, so all he could do was summon the local forces – the knights in the convents, the secular knights from the countryside and wealthy burghers from the towns, native Prussians operating both as light cavalry and militia, and burgher infantry units; in addition, there were a few mercenaries. While the grandmaster gathered his forces in the province of Culm, he ordered raids from West Prussia and the

Neumark. The most successful of these pillaging operations was by the commander of Schwetz, who reportedly burned down 117 Polish villages.

Jagiełło and Vytautas joined their forces along the Narew River at the end of July, then marched north to Osterode, apparently hoping that the grandmaster would meet them for a second battle at Tannenberg. Rusdorf declined the challenge, withdrawing ahead of the invaders. Jagiełło continued in the direction of Marienburg, pillaging farmsteads and villages.

By late August the king was in the Vistula River valley. Once again, the Lithuanian–Tatar forces made an enduring impression on their victims (churches burned, young women and matrons raped, and 'other terrible and loathsome deeds' committed). Meanwhile, Moldavian forces under Alexander demonstrated their superiority over any forces the Teutonic Knights could send out. In mid-September, as mercenaries slowly made their way east towards the grandmaster from the Neumark, King Jagiełło proposed a truce.

Each side named eight representatives, gave them full authority to negotiate a treaty, and brought them together in late September 1422. They met in the king's tent in the camp near Lake Melno, not far from Tannenberg. The grandmaster was represented by two important officers, the bishops of Ermland and Pomesania, the Livonian marshal, and three secular knights. Four days later, the diplomats had the 'eternal peace' of Lake Melno ready for signing.

The formal ceremony could not be held on the spot. The first difficulty lay in the delay necessary to bring the seals from their distant locations (as far away as Estonia). No one wanted to risk having his valuable seal fall into enemy hands; anyone so unfortunate might be deluged by forged but seemingly authentic documents. A second difficulty concerned the implication that some of the signatories were the grandmaster's subjects (the archbishop of Riga, the bishop of Dorpat, and even the estates in Prussia). Lastly, with Vytautas and Jagiełło having gone back to Lithuania to hunt, a formal signing had to be arranged at a date convenient to them.

This gave Rusdorf an opportunity to renegotiate critical passages of the treaty by exploiting the fear that the emperor-elect or the pope would declare the treaty null and void. The strategy was a carefully calculated combination of negotiation and delay, working particularly on Vytautas, who repeatedly contacted the officers in charge of the negotiations – he wrote to Rusdorf at least five times to ask if the order intended to honour its commitments on marking the border.

Rusdorf suggested only that they meet personally to discuss the matter. Meanwhile, he sent his marshal, the second most important officer in Prussia, to Breslau to press Sigismund for assistance. In January 1423, Sigismund and a group of Silesian nobles agreed to go to war the next summer, with the ultimate goal of dividing Poland among themselves.

Jagiełło, meanwhile, was working on the bishops who had been in the negotiating party. The bishop of Pomesania was a member of the Teutonic Order, but he was more cleric than friar-priest, and he wanted the prestige of being an independent sovereign prelate. The bishop of Ermland was preoccupied with protecting and increasing his sovereignty vis-à-vis the grandmaster.

When Jagiełło finally met Sigismund in person, he obtained every-thing he wanted – Sigismund turned his back on the grandmaster. In return, Jagiełło promised to end Lithuanian aid to the Hussites and to send 30,000 men to help suppress the heretical movement. Soon afterwards Jagiełło confiscated Korybut's Silesian estates and forbade his subjects to have any contact with him. In short, Sigismund sold out the Teutonic Order, and Jagiełło sold out Vytautas.

In the end, however, everybody got essentially what they wanted: Vytautas – Samogitia; Jagiełło – the final defeat of the Teutonic Knights; and the grandmaster – a peace treaty.

Rusdorf's officers were not happy with their grandmaster's strategic or tactical vision in either the making of war or the conclusion of peace. But it was hardly his fault that Sigismund had not lived up to his promises, nor could he get a better outcome of events. When Rusdorf wrote to the Livonian master that June about rumours concerning Moscow and the sultan, he confessed that, 'You know, by God's grace, as much as I myself do about how much is true. Also, so much is going on day after day that we would go crazy if we tried to describe it.' In the end he brought his order better through the crisis than many had expected.

Jagiełło's subjects were also unhappy, many seeing the king's actions as a betrayal of their interests. What seems to have occurred, though neither contemporaries nor modern historians have been able to sort out all the complications, is that a political revolution was occurring. With Sigismund's authority evaporating, Jagiełło was becoming the regional strongman.

A last footnote: in 1421 the Burgundian knight Ghillebert de Lannoy returned to Prussia in the company of French-speaking knights via Brabant, Westphalia, Bremen, Hamburg, Lübeck and Mecklenburg. However, finding that the grandmaster had concluded a truce and had no need of his services, he left one member of his group at Marienburg to learn German, and rode into Poland to deliver a letter from the king of England. He found Jagiełło far away, near Lwów (Lviv, Lemberg). Apparently the king found the contents of the letter pleasing because he plied the envoy with gifts, then sent him into the city where the citizens entertained him and his company with a feast and a dance. Afterwards he gave him a letter to the sultan that would facilitate his trip to Jerusalem.

Chapter 8

The Old Order Passeth

Vytautas in Power

In the aftermath of the Peace of Lake Melno a surprising friendship developed between Vytautas and the new grandmaster. This was not a personal whim, of course, but the grand duke's cold calculation of his interests. His boyars and magnates were pressing him to be more independent of Poland and the Polish church. Subsequently he supported the grandmaster in disputes over the marking of the new border with Poland, he invited him to his niece's marriage to Jagiełło, and he joined the Livonian Order in its war against Pskov. While each manoeuvre was tactically shrewd, Vytautas's less visible goal was to provide an alternative to Jagiełło's inheriting the grand duchy. The king was not as vigorous as he had been, and the nation needed a healthy ruler to protect its eastern frontiers.

The difficulty was that, technically, Jagiełło was the 'Supreme Prince of Lithuania'. Moreover, he had a better claim to rule than did Vytautas because his father, Algirdas, had been Supreme Prince. Furthermore, Vytautas had often given an oath of subservience and also often given way when their wishes conflicted. However, it was Vytautas who had the love of the Lithuanian people; and it was Vytautas who had the somewhat grudging loyalty of the Rusian boyars and clergy, most of whom saw Jagiełło first and foremost as a despised Roman Catholic and, for most practical purposes, a Polish one to boot!

Vytautas wore his Roman Catholicism lightly enough to avoid offending his Orthodox subjects. Also, though he hardly had more Lithuanians in his entourage than did Jagiełło, he was in the country continuously and the king was not. On those occasions that Jagiełło did visit Lithuania, he gave more time and attention to the hunt than to talking with local boyars. Lastly, Vytautas was the warrior, Jagiełło the diplomat, and right now Lithuania needed a warrior king.

Vytautas remained on good terms with the grandmaster, sending him falcons and hunting dogs, and promising to deliver six Tatar slaves. In return, the grandmaster sent him a silver necklace, a golden helmet, jewellery for Juliana, wine, and a warhorse. Vytautas had access to the trade route crossing the steppe from China, but he did not give Rusdorf exotic goods from the east; in this he correctly read the grandmaster's simple tastes.

Vytautas had profited from the renewed disintegration of the Tatar empire into several competing 'hordes'. Ultimately, that would result in the foundation of three distinct empires (Kazan, the Crimea and Sarai); but for the moment there was only chaos, as each khan tried to crush the others. Minor khans were coming to Ruś and to Lithuania for help and for refuge. This made it possible for Vytautas, in combination with his son-in-law, Basil I of Moscow, to expand his influence south and east as well as northward, not as spectacularly as he had done in the 1390s, but more securely. It also provided him with a steady supply of Tatar horsemen, refugees from the steppes.

As Basil I lay dying in 1425, he named Vytautas one of the regents for his ten-year-old heir. Within a year Sophia had fled to Smolensk with young Basil II to ask her father for protection. Vytautas, though already feeling his years, intervened in the war over the succession. His first siege, in August at Opochka, south of Pskov, was a disastrous failure: the citizens prepared a trap, leaving the city gates open and the drawbridge down. When Vytautas's Tatar horsemen rode onto the bridge, the citizens cut the ropes, throwing the Tatars into the moat onto sharpened stakes. Then, in plain sight on the walls, they tortured the captives, cutting off their penises and sticking them down their throats, then flaying the Poles, Bohemians and Wallachians alive. Vytautas had to watch, filled with anger and shame. He gave up that siege, but instead of retreating, moved on towards Pskov. There, after a fearful thunderstorm that frightened him into calling on the Lord for mercy, the citizens of Pskov appeared with a large ransom. On the advice of his grandson, he accepted only a portion of the money and made peace.

The next August, in 1427, following a terrible plague, Vytautas attacked Novgorod territory directly. One of his huge cannons, cast by a German specialist, was so large that it required forty horses to pull it until lunch, then another forty until midday, then another forty till evening. When fired at Ostrov the cannon exploded. It nevertheless blasted apart a tower with that single shot. The cannonball then flew through both walls of a church (not harming the priest at the altar) and outside the city walls exploded among Vytautas's own troops, killing the governor of Polotsk and frightening the horses. The gunmaster was blown apart so completely that nothing more could be found of him than half his coat. But Vytautas had made his point.

Novgorod sent a delegation to pay a huge ransom for the prisoners, and a larger tribute for having attempted to profit from Moscow's complicated civil conflicts. Vytautas was undoubtedly helped by the great city's dependence on Suzdal grain and imports from the Hanseatic League.

Lithuania's great nobles – the magnates – and the boyars alike wanted to expand eastward. The great obstacle was the hatred that the Orthodox lords and churchmen of Ruś felt towards the dogmatism of the Roman Catholics, who insisted on everyone recognising the pope as the head of the Church. That was why Vytautas supported a church union that validated other practices of the Orthodox Church, such as the use of traditional languages in the Mass and homilies. Such a compromise was the only way Vytautas saw to prevent a civil conflict inside Lithuania once he passed from the scene.

Poland and Lithuania Draw Apart

Many Lithuanians were similarly unhappy about the Polish decision in 1421 to betroth Jagiełło's daughter, Jadwiga, to an eight-year-old German prince, Friedrich II of Hohenzollern. That had come at the suggestion of Eric of Denmark and then been supported by Sigismund; the intent seems to have been to draw Poland back towards the west and to win Polish support in suppressing the Hussites. The young bridegroom was to be reared in Cracow, so that he would be completely Polish in language and culture when he reached maturity.

But what about his Lithuanian domains? How would Friedrich be able to speak with his subjects in Lithuania and Ruś? Moreover, Germans were losing their reputation for invincibility. In 1427 the imperial invasion of Bohemia had been repelled by the Taborites, with the Saxon (and even Danish) knights sent flying for their lives.

Jan Žižka was dead, but his last words reputedly advised using his skin for a drum whose beating would frighten all enemies into flight. The Orebite 'Orphans' (as his devoted followers from eastern Bohemia now called themselves) had learned his military lessons well. This meant that the Hussite revolt could be ended only by the Catholic Church making concessions similar to those proposed by Vytautas for the Orthodox Church.

However, Oleśnicki rejected that idea. He was committed to making Roman Catholicism stronger. In 1425 he gave the Lithuanian magnates new exemptions from taxes, laws and requirements to perform personal service. (In 1430 and 1432 he would extend those rights to the petty nobles and gentry.) Oleśnicki pursued the interests of the Polish state, but he also enjoyed the exercise of power.

This led to agitation in the mid-1420s to crown Vytautas as king of Lithuania. The proposal was not simply an old man's vanity, but a reflection of boyars' discontent with becoming Polish vassals. Vytautas put off these entreaties until it became obvious that church union would not happen soon, that Jagiełło just might outlive him, and that neither had more than a short time left.

Jagiełło had similar problems. He had obtained the Diet's consent to his succession plans in 1425, but when he submitted revised plans the next year, the assembled nobles seized the document and, drawing their swords in Jagiełło's presence, hacked it to pieces. As the king entered a bidding contest with Oleśnicki for support, the magnates and the petty nobles raised their prices.

Oleśnicki's dislike of Vytautas increased as the grand duke used Queen Sophia's influence to strengthen the Lithuanian party, but Jagiełło's response to the unpleasantness was to disappear into the primeval forest that lay athwart the Polish–Lithuanian border in Volhynia. He chased bison and elk, sought out the last of the vanishing aurochs, and left the details of administration to those who wished to concern themselves with it.

Adultery?

The next year, at age seventy-five, Jagiełło broke a leg on a bear hunt. He made a swift recovery and was soon hunting again, accompanied by a swarm of prelates and barons, university professors and magistrates from the towns, none of them accustomed to the cold and damp of the forest. The king showered them with presents, putting them in awe of his wealth, his liberality, his beneficence and his piety. However, he knew that no royal head was safe. Age may have been revered, but too much age was not good for rulers who wanted to keep the respect of their retainers. That was especially clear when rumours began to circulate that the queen had been unfaithful.

Sophia was, as anyone could see, 'by nature and upbringing designed for the arts of Venus'. Moreover, there was gossip, which, if true, threw suspicion on the parentage of the heir to the throne and his brother. Of course, for a long time nobody wanted to tell the king the stories, so the task eventually fell to Vytautas, who knew that any scandal would play into the hands of Oleśnicki. He informed Jagiełło of this when they met in Horodło at the end of August in 1427, then insisted on his having a secret investigation rather than an open hearing.

The queen swore a 'solemn oath' that she was innocent of all wrongdoing, which satisfied her husband. Nevertheless, Jagiełło left the four knights who were suspected of having been her lovers to rot in prison;

they were at the least guilty of having injured the dynasty's reputation. The Oleśnicki faction then declared that they had always believed the queen was innocent. Nevertheless, the Lithuanian party had suffered a heavy blow; and prominent Poles made certain that the stories were not forgotten.

In 1431 rumours surfaced after Jadwiga's sudden death, all claiming that Sophia had poisoned her to assure her own son's succession. At the funeral Jagiełło was not seen to shed a tear or give the slightest sign of emotion. That provoked a wide range of speculations: had he been complicit in the conspiracy, was he senile, or did he simply accept whatever fate gave him?

Jagiełło's increasing lack of interest in politics, or even awareness of it, made Vytautas furious. There were no obvious signs of mental debility. The king seemed to have his wits about him, but he had little interest in using them. When Vytautas needed Jagiełło to attend a meeting over the possession of a mill in the Prussian borderland, he could not persuade him to show up. When the king subsequently asked Rusdorf for permission to make a pilgrimage to St Brigitta's convent in Danzig, even the grandmaster responded that it would be best to settle the diplomatic business first.

Throughout the years 1428 and 1429 Jagiełło's signature appeared on letters supporting Sigismund in Bohemia. The hand holding the pen was Oleśnicki's. Jagiełło was now paying for his illiteracy. He could keep his most secret plans from the wily bishop only by sending a personal emissary to deliver an oral message.

The Teutonic Knights Enter the War against the Turks

For Sigismund the important events of the years 1426–8 were not the battles and conferences in Bohemia, but his war with the Turks. Bohemia he left to Friedrich of Hohenzollern, who was negotiating with the moderate Hussites. However, being overly optimistic about the prospects of victory, Friedrich had made unrealistic demands and obtained nothing. Sigismund, meanwhile, pushed for a relocation of the Teutonic Knights to Transylvania (where the order had brought German settlers before being expelled in 1225) and the Vojvodina, opposite Belgrade. In these areas he had castles, but no garrisons.

Jagiełło had sent 5,000 Poles and Moldavians to the Danube in 1426, but when Sigismund's army did not appear, they went home. Obviously, a more permanent force was needed – the Teutonic Knights.

The grandmaster sent knights to report on the situation, but did little until Sigismund led an army into Wallachia two years later. There the king almost lost his life in combat – his horse fell, spilling the no-longer youthful ruler into the Danube. Had Sigismund been killed or captured, Hungary would have been thrown into a constitutional crisis.

That prompted the grandmaster to send a force of 1,800 men the following year under Nicholas of Redwitz, a Franconian knight whose family had sent several sons to Prussia. This army included 178 men with crossbows, and 351 banners (a horseman with three men-at-arms) – to take up residence in Severin, in south-eastern Transylvania, to garrison sixteen castles along the Danube River. The expenses of 315,000 florins annually (!) were to be paid by a wide variety of taxes and monopolies. Nicholas lasted long enough to mint coins and, as *ban* of Severin, to be inducted into the Hungarian nobility. However, when the truce expired in 1432, several of the castles were lost to the Turks and many of his men slain. The order's venture ended after eight years, the grandmaster having concluded that he simply could not afford to support it.

However, this development had helped make Germans more aware of the Turkish threat to Hungary. Pope and emperor-elect called for a crusade to drive back the sultan, to liberate the Christians in the Balkans, and then to save Constantinople. Even the Poles, surely influenced by Oleśnicki, sent Sigismund aid.

This was a very chastened and changed Sigismund, who, if not yet chaste, was finally beginning to demonstrate maturity and statesman-ship. He had suffered one military and political débâcle after the other in recent years, personal embarrassments, and poor health. But at last there was more realism in his policies, even a little finesse. This at a moment when his ancient enemies/friends, Jagiełło and Vytautas, were ever less able to display those qualities.

The Great Conference of 1427

In January 1427 Vytautas was host to one of the most splendid gatherings of notables in east-central European history. (January was a good time for travel, the dirt roads being frozen.) Hoping to devise a common policy against the Muslims on the steppe and in the Balkans, with the ultimate goal being the rescue of Constantinople from the Turks, he brought together in Łuck Basil II, Sigismund and Barbara, Jagiełło, several Tatar khans, Alexander the Good (the *hospodar* of Moldavia, whose services were sought both by the Poles and Hungarians), Dan II of Wallachia, a papal legate, the Byzantine ambassador, dukes from Tver, Masovia, Pomerania and Silesia, representatives of Grandmaster Rusdorf, the Livonian master, Eric of Denmark, and some German electors; they were accompanied by every nobleman and prelate who was healthy enough to mount a horse or get into a litter. The number of servants, knights and clergy who came along was beyond counting. The guests ate daily 700 oxen, 1,400 sheep, 100 bison and boars; and they drank 700 barrels of mead, with additional quantities of beer and wine.

In the opening parade Jagiełło rode into Łuck in a carriage with Barbara, Sigismund's flirtatious empress. Vytautas rode at the head of 1,000 horsemen. The contrast in physical health was quietly noted by onlookers, but there was too much going on for anyone to reflect on the matter. There were disturbances in the camps, 'where man pressed against man, horse against horse', and everywhere one could see splendid clothes, extravagant decoration, exhibitions of lavish liberality and chivalrous gestures.

Sigismund was at his best. He joked about church unity, saying that the only difference between the Christian confessions was the priests' beards and the fact that Orthodox priests had one wife, while Roman Catholics had ten or more. Surely, he argued, church union should not be hindered by such minor matters, not when Constantinople was in danger. Sigismund's suggestion that the Teutonic Order be moved in its entirety to the Balkans, though long proposed by the Polish king to rid himself of the Teutonic Knights, now met with strenuous Polish objections. Jagiełło, probably at Oleśnicki's insistence, indicated that Poland was now ready to move south through Moldavia and Wallachia, and that he would not be pleased to find the Teutonic Knights blocking his route there as they still impeded his way to the Baltic Sea. The longer the discussions went, the more unhappy Vytautas became.

Sigismund, perhaps sensing the tension, suggested that Vytautas be crowned king of Lithuania. The guests, seeing Vytautas's interest in the idea, realised that this could have immediate and far-reaching consequences for politics throughout east-central Europe. That topic quickly became the dominant theme of the meeting.

Sigismund, whose support was essential to Vytautas's winning papal approval for making the grand duchy into a kingdom and the approbation of the other monarchs, slyly saw advantages for himself in establishing an independent state on Poland's eastern borders. Moreover, he might be able to eliminate completely the Lithuanian intervention in Bohemia that had helped sustain Hussite resistance. Sigismund observed that Vytautas was no longer willing to remain subordinate to Jagiełło, but was now determined to die the equal to his cousin, the ruler of an independent state that would not go to his life-long rival (who, by the time Vytautas died, might not even be able to realise that he had achieved his life-long goal, to rule both states).

Sigismund saw the emotions that burned in the old man's heart. This led him to believe that by crowning Vytautas he could divide Lithuania from Poland, then surround Jagiełło by an alliance of Lithuania, the Teutonic Order, Bohemia and Hungary. By so isolating Jagiełło, he might make him subordinate to the Holy Roman Empire.

Plans for War

Sigismund rode next to Moravia for talks with the Hussite leaders, but his demand that they disarm ruined all hopes that the truce would become a peace. He seemed to operate on the premise that if he repeated an offer often enough, eventually his opponents would accept it. That proposition may have worked on women, but not on Hussites. Instead, the Hussites went on the offensive.

When Rusdorf was informed of the plan to attack Poland, he agreed without enthusiasm. He had divided loyalties. There were his traditional ties to Sigismund, thanks for Vytautas's friendship, and concern about the increased prestige that a Lithuanian king would have over that of a grand duke. But most of all he feared that once Sigismund was occupied elsewhere, Jagiełło would declare war and make Prussia the scapegoat of his anger. Seeing that, in the short run at least, he might get some concessions from Poland in return for opposing the project, Rusdorf opened negotiations with Jagiełło about resolving the remaining disputes over marking of the border.

Word of this quickly got to Vytautas, who wrote to the grandmaster clearly and forcefully that he was not pleased. When Rusdorf subsequently struck a pose of absolute neutrality, Vytautas was once again all smiles and sweet talk. The grand duke, in return, assisted the Livonian Order in its dispute with the rebellious citizens of Riga and gave moral support to the grandmaster's plans for the Hussite Wars. Then, as the date for the coronation approached, he put pressure on the grandmaster to make a personal appearance.

Jagiełło was urged by Oleśnicki to oppose the Lithuanian plans. Personal and state ambitions should have coincided to spur the king to strong action, but Jagiełło was clearly not excited one way or another. Perhaps his revulsion for Oleśnicki equalled his supposed jealousy of Vytautas's achievements. Perhaps he simply lacked energy and alertness. More likely, he was surprised that the crisis had come up at all. Given the trivial origins of the quarrel, was this not a matter that some quiet personal diplomacy could resolve?

The king promised to visit Vilnius in the late summer, the very time that Vytautas was secretly planning to have the coronation. Meanwhile, he attempted to calm the grand duke, even rhetorically offering him his own crown. (Somewhat later Oleśnicki personally made a similar offer, knowing that Vytautas would soon die, leaving a united state to Jagiełło's elder son.) Vytautas responded that he would be crowned 'whether anyone liked it or not'.

Oleśnicki and the royal council were clearly worried by these developments. Sensing that Jagiełło could not be relied on to follow their instructions, Oleśnicki and his partisans now determined that the king should not be let out of sight or out of hearing. Meanwhile, Oleśnicki brought every pressure upon the pope to refuse his consent to the elevation of Lithuania to a monarchy; in this, certainly, the slow-working nature of tradition was on his side. New monarchies were not created every day (not even every century). He was partially successful. Although Martin V was more interested in church union and resisting the Hussites than in Polish dreams of national greatness, he attempted to discourage Sigismund and Vytautas from their plans.

The Coronation

The correspondence between the emperor-elect and the grand duke was supposed to be secret, but Oleśnicki managed to learn what the plans were. At Easter he visited Vytautas in an effort to persuade him to abandon his ambition, but Vytautas only became angrier and more determined.

In August 1430 Jagiełło sent a trusted representative who managed to quiet the grand duke's anger considerably. Offering to give him the crown of Poland and make his children Vytautas's wards was a nice flourish. Though both men realised that the Polish Diet would probably not have approved, the offer prompted the grand duke to send his own secretary to the king for secret talks. Soon Jagiełło's ambassadors went down on their knees to beg the grand duke to desist from his plans, but Vytautas replied that the matter had gone too far to turn back now. Jagiełło then announced that he would go to Vytautas personally, and without delay. Polish senators tried to persuade him to obtain a safe-conduct first. The king ignored them.

Vytautas's principal problem now was in obtaining a crown, sceptre and orb from the imperial workshop in Nuremberg. Without this regalia there could be no properly magnificent ceremony in St Stanislaus's Cathedral in Vilnius; Bishop Matthias had been looking forward to that. When Oleśnicki realised that the imperial messenger would probably travel to Vilnius via the Neumark and Prussia, he ordered an attack on the Neumark that made the area unsafe for any traveller. Then, when the imperial delegation headed by the archbishop of Magdeburg, Günther II of Schwarzenberg, attempted to bring the royal regalia directly through Poland, his agents confiscated the precious objects. The archbishop, seeing no point in continuing his mission, returned home.

That was still unknown to Vytautas when he welcomed Rusdorf and his most important officers to his court in Vilnius. They saw there Ruśian princes and Tatar khans. But when they heard that the regalia would not arrive as planned, they rode home again. Other guests began to disperse as well. Vytautas did what he could to keep enough guests in Vilnius to make the occasion respectable. He held the metropolitan practically a prisoner.

Vytautas's coronation plans were now too far advanced to abandon them. He told the grandmaster to write to Sigismund that there was no point in ordering another crown and sending it through Prussia. Instead, he hoped to work on Jagiełło, who had just arrived in Vilnius. Vytautas arranged a huge party in Trakai, his palatial island fortress west of Vilnius, hoping to keep some of his guests there long enough for the king to order the regalia sent to him.

Vytautas rode back and forth from Trakai to Vilnius that October, trying to negotiate with Jagiełło for the return of the regalia, trying to keep his guests entertained. But he might as well have tried to argue with the strong west wind – Jagiełło had personal, dynastic and national reasons to refuse, but most of all, he had Oleśnicki. The bishop would not cooperate. However, neither the king nor the bishop had reason to imagine that their policy would bear such satisfactory fruit as it did, nor so quickly. Vytautas, returning hurriedly to Vilnius, fell exhausted from his horse, fatally injuring himself. The grand duke was taken by carriage to Trakai, where he died two weeks later, surrounded by his weeping widow and her ladies. He was approximately eighty years of age.

Długosz eulogised the hero, praising his moderation in hunting and worldly diversions ('the bane of princes who fail to perform their duties to the state'). He commented on Vytautas's being conversant with international merchants whose gold and silver, gems, furs and other merchandise he collected for those occasions when he distributed them lavishly among his followers. He noted that the grand duke was 'in eating moderate, in drinking very moderate, and never once in his life did he drink wine'. He was less favourable towards the addiction to love-making that the grand duke indulged whenever it was convenient; but he ended his long passage by saying that, 'In our age nobody was to be compared to Prince Vytautas in taking an obscure, dark and ignoble fatherland and through the fame of his deeds making it shine brilliantly as no other duke was later able to do.'

The Succession in Lithuania

The passing of the grand duke left the succession unclear. His only child had been a daughter, Sophia, and her son, Basil II (1425–62), was still young. More importantly, the Poles objected even to considering anyone who would not convert to Roman Catholicism; they would have preferred a Polish prince, perhaps young Casimir. But the Lithuanians wanted a mature ruler, preferably a relative of Vytautas. As a result, several descendants of Gediminas put themselves forth as candidates. When Švitrigaila pressed Jagiełło at the funeral, reminding him of the times he had been held prisoner, the king only recommended that he keep his temper since the Poles would make the choice, not him. That only made Švitrigaila angrier, causing him to drink far too much, and noisier.

Rusdorf was pleased to hear all this, for there seemed to be good opportunities for him to win something out of the civil war that was likely to break out. There even seemed to be an excellent chance that he could achieve the separation of Lithuania from Poland. Such an achievement might be the salvation of the Teutonic Order. It would certainly please Sigismund, who wanted to distract Jagiełło as much as possible from the peace talks with the Bohemian heretics. Ungluing the long-planned union of Poland and Lithuania was the perfect distraction.

In the summer of 1431 Rusdorf made an alliance with Švitrigaila, who seemed the most likely of the candidates to make Lithuania independent of Poland. To distract the king from Švitrigaila's efforts to occupy Volhynia, the grandmaster declared war on Poland and called for help from the German and Livonian masters. His recruiting of mercenaries was hindered by a reluctance to guarantee the replacement of lost horses and equipment as had been the ancient practice, but he received a substantial reinforcement from Livonia.

Jagiełło's luck held. While he went to Lithuania himself, the forces he had left in Poland ambushed the proud army of the Livonian Knights at Nakel (Nakło nad Notecią) in West Prussia, then pursued the retreating force to the Netze River and cut it to pieces while the fugitives were trying to wend their way across the narrow bridges.

The grandmaster, dismayed by the swift destruction of such an experienced and well-ordered army, hurriedly signed a truce that left

Švitrigaila isolated. By so abasing himself in the eyes of the knights and the estates, Rusdorf undermined his prestige beyond recovery.

Švitrigaila had been elected grand duke unanimously by the Lithuanian nobles, but this was denounced violently by Bishop Oleśnicki as a violation of the Horodło agreement; subsequently, the conflict over Volhynia ended in a Polish victory, followed by a two-year truce that was broken by a Polish-inspired coup in 1432. Knowing that his followers inside Lithuania were too few to prevail in the civil war, Švitrigaila reached out to his Orthodox supporters – already he had granted them equality with Roman Catholics; now, it seemed, he had to go further.

Jagiełło then called on all Roman Catholics in the grand duchy to support Vytautas's aged brother Žygimantas. In June 1433, disgusted with the help that the grandmaster was sending to Švitrigaila via the Livonian Order, Jagiełło allowed a Hussite army to pass through his kingdom to Prussia and added forces of his own. For Jagiełło this had the additional advantage of irritating Oleśnicki, who hated Hussites even more than he did Teutonic Knights. Jagiełło, it seems, would have been willing to use the devil's own demons against Satan himself. The temptation to anger the powerful bishop and the grandmaster at the same time was irresistible.

Sigismund was furious. He knew that he had but few days left in which to accomplish his life-long goal of being universally recognised as king of Bohemia, and now the only goad he could use to distract the Poles had withered in his hand. Not that his grip was too strong in any case. Aged by the standards of the day, ill, and surrounded by sycophants, fools and fanatics, Sigismund had little to look forward to except the vanity of one last coronation

Sigismund's Coronation and Civil War in Lithuania

Sigismund had left Bohemia in defeat in August 1431 and gone straight to Italy to negotiate for safe conduct to Rome. He was crowned emperor, at last, in May 1433, but only after agreeing to abandon the Adriatic coastline to Venice. From there he went to the Council of Basel, which had already wasted two years in haggling with the pope over who had the authority to make reforms.

After half a year of negotiations, during which he helped arrange for concessions to the Hussites that could bring an end to their long rebellion, Sigismund went to Bohemia, hoping to persuade at least one of the feuding Hussite factions to accept the council's offer and to acknowledge him as king or, better yet, to kill one another off. Clearly,

Sigismund had neither time nor interest to deal with obscure matters in eastern Europe. Neither the Teutonic Knights nor Švitrigaila could count on imperial help; they were on their own.

Similarly, Švitrigaila could not rely on the Teutonic Order – he had to demonstrate to his Orthodox followers that he was their best hope to defeat Žygimantas, who was a Roman Catholic, and his own brother Jagiełło, who now represented everything Polish. In 1430 Švitrigaila had married a daughter of Ivan of Tver, a rival of Basil II for hegemony in Ruś. One could not know how many children he might beget. He was already sixty years of age, but he did not act old – and there was the precedent of Jagiełło, whose sons came at a similar age.

Švitrigaila had proposed a grand alliance with the Tatars that included the great khan, who had reconstituted the Golden Horde, his candidate to be grand duke of Moscow, and his Lithuanian supporters. However, the great khan's policy was to keep his enemies weak by supporting the weaker parties in any dispute. As a result, there was near chaos in Ruś for several years, with Basil II alternately victorious, then in flight, and finally taking refuge among the Tatars. His being blinded while in captivity should have disqualified him from ruling Moscow, but he nevertheless eventually prevailed over his ambitious relatives. Meanwhile, it appeared that Lithuania might suffer a similar fate.

The marriage did not help Švitrigaila much. Jagiełło sent an army under Mszczuj ze Skrzynna into Volhynia, rewarding him with an estate there after driving the rebels away. In 1431 Švitrigaila lost more support in Lithuania when Oleśnicki called a meeting of Polish nobles, who declared their support for Žygimantas. The year after that a carefully organised conspiracy took Švitrigaila's pregnant wife prisoner and almost captured him. The child, a son, died young and Švitrigaila would have no more children. While Švitrigaila fled to Polotsk, Žygimantas occupied the Lithuanian highlands and Samogitia.

In return for their help, the Poles extorted a promise from Žygimantas that Lithuania would return to Poland upon his death. This did not sit well with the Lithuanian boyars who favoured Žygimantas's son Michael (c. 1406–52), but they were too cautious to change sides openly. Švitrigaila was more fortunate with the grandmaster, who wanted to weaken anyone who held Samogitia or was allied to Jagiełło. He first sent secret aid to Švitrigaila, then rather more open assistance via Livonia to fight alongside his Orthodox supporters. This was offset by Žygimantas giving Orthodox boyars the same rights and privileges as Roman Catholics. (He was notorious for taking both sides on the religious issue, a fact that reflects why so few people who knew him trusted him.) This 1432 Act of Gardinas and the subsequent Privilege of 1434 also admitted the most prominent Ruśian boyars to the grand ducal council. Švitrigaila, for his part, became so paranoid about the intrigues and plots that he arrested his own metropolitan, Geresim (and in the summer of 1435 would burn him at the stake in Vitebsk).

This led to Švitrigaila becoming more and more dependent on aid from the Livonian Order, until at last German troops composed a substantial part of his army. Žygimantas, of course, received substantial help from Poland. Since Jagiełło was more powerful than Rusdorf or the Livonian master, the result was foreordained, unless fate stepped in. Finally, it seemed that fate had intervened. In May 1434 Jagiełło caught a cold from walking in the Moldavian woods at night to listen to a nightingale. He died a few days later. He was eighty.

Jagiełło's Death

The king's heir, Ladislas (1424–44), was still only ten years of age, a situation that usually leads to instability. But Oleśnicki browbeat the nobles and prelates into continuing the present political course. Memory of the late king made his task easier.

Długosz reflected this by dedicating a section of his chronicle to the 'life, customs and sins of Ladislas Jagiełło the king'. He described the small black eyes that never rested, the big ears, the deep, fast speech, the thin and graceful body. He criticised his prodigality, saying that he was 'more avid than was for the public good' in presenting his followers rare furs, horses, saddles and other expensive gifts. He criticised his love of the hunt for distracting him from public business; and he deplored the superstitions he had learned from his Orthodox mother. On the other hand, he praised Jagiełło's physical strength, his ability to endure cold and wet while travelling and hunting, his sobriety, his dependability in keeping promises, and his pious conversion of the Lithuanians and Samogitians. The chronicler did not spare the monarch's shortcomings: his passion for hunting, his failure as a husband, and – surprisingly – his strong inclination to sex, 'not only in permitted ways but also in forbidden ones'. Whatever that meant. He praised the king's heartfelt simplicity, his strong but selective intellect.

The chronicle established the standard narrative for Polish historians into the modern era.

The Second Tannenberg

Rusdorf had been secretly encouraging the Livonian master to support Švitrigaila, but his recruitment of German mercenaries in 1433 for

Livonian service had been frustrated by Jagiełło's timely assistance to the Hussites in their invasion of Prussia. With the king dead, Rusdorf could resume the aid, sending a number of knights and mercenaries to Livonia. More importantly, he was able to send Sigismund Korybut, one of the most accomplished generals of the era.

Korybut had been living in Silesia after Jagiełło had confiscated his properties, and the pope had excommunicated him, but both subsequently welcomed his help in negotiating with the Hussites. That, however, cost him the trust of the radical faction, and, it was clear that he had no future in Bohemia. When he tried to reach Lithuania through Prussia, he was arrested by the Teutonic Knights, who agreed to release him if he would fight for Švitrigaila.

Korybut, now a man without a country, agreed. At least that gave him some hope for a future. He knew that Oleśnicki would never allow him simply to go home. Korybut's heart was in the highlands, but he was ruled by his head. When he later observed the fine coats of mail worn by the Germans, then looked over at the semi-nude Lithuanians in the opposing army with the Poles, he wistfully said, 'I would rather be over there than in your splendid array.' But he honoured his promise.

The contribution from the Livonian Order was much less than it would have been earlier. When the prisoners taken at Nakel were finally released, they were in such poor physical condition that they could not perform any military service. Nevertheless, Master Cisse of Rutenberg, an experienced warrior, invaded Samogitia in 1434 and remained there ten weeks in hopes of capturing a castle that could serve as a base for Švitrigaila's operations, but the campaign failed, and he died of illness during the retreat.

Cisse was succeeded by Frank of Kersdorf – a minority candidate, selected by Rusdorf to enhance his authority in Livonia, and therefore not particularly popular. Kersdorf met Švitrigaila near Dünaburg to march into Lithuania, but they had barely started before it rained so heavily that they had to turn around. Kersdorf's diversionary attacks on Samogitia from Goldingen (Kuldīga) suffered an even worse fate – one army plundered the countryside, followed by a second that hoped to surprise the people as they emerged from their hideouts. The second army, however was surrounded and persuaded to surrender on honourable terms. As soon as the Livonians laid down their arms, the Samogitians closed in, slaughtering forty knights and 800 native warriors.

Rusdorf's subsequent correspondence encouraging the Livonian master to renew the offensive provides us a detailed and lively insight into the subsequent campaign. Kersdorf was able to recruit a sizeable force of German crusaders, some Livonian cities sent their militias (including a musical band from Reval), and some of the nobles appeared. He hoped that Korybut would attract Lithuanians who resented Polish domination, and that his knowledge of military tactics would offset the diversity of languages and military traditions in the coalition army. In September 1435 the combined army reached Ukmergė (Wiłkomierz), a strategic crossroads on the Swienta (Šventoji) River, from which it could strike either at Vilnius or Trakai – where Žygimantas had made his base. There the two armies collided. Kersdorf wanted to attack immediately, but when Švitrigaila ordered his men to stay back, he had to recall his units by a combination of flag signals and bugle calls.

The coalition army fell back to a favourable position near the village of Pabaiska and set up an intimidating wagon fort behind a stream and a swamp. There was apparently an intense discussion about tactics – the battle of Lipany (May 1434) had shown weaknesses in the employment of a wagon fort. For two days the two armies watched one another, the Polish–Lithuanian force declining to commit suicide by attacking wagons bristling with cannons. At length, after numerous skirmishes showed the superiority of Žygimantas's horsemen, Švitrigaila and Kersdorf decided to retreat slowly.

A Polish letter to the churchmen in Basel described what happened when the Livonian Knights began to move to the rear: Polish knights charged into the gap in the line. This led to a hotly contested fight. The Polish knights were numerous (estimates ran up to 12,000), perhaps outnumbering the Lithuanian contingent, and led by Mszczuj ze Skrzynna. Žygimantas had contributed his own followers, Tatars, his well-trained royal pikemen, and enthusiastic Samogitians led by his son Michael. Švitrigaila had the well-trained knights of the Livonian Order, a few Prussian knights, at least 500 Tatars, large numbers of Orthodox Ruśians, several Lithuanian dukes, and perhaps a small number of radical Czechs who had fled their homeland after the moderates' victory. It was an odd combination of forces for the German knights to join. Every enemy they had ever fought was on their side, but politics was politics.

The armies may have numbered as many as 30,000 men each, but were probably half that size or less. It was Czech experience, German artillery and knights, together with Ruśian, Lithuanian and Tatar horsemen, against the spear-bearing Lithuanian and Polish cavalry. Korybut should have been giving the orders, since only he had experience with a wagon fort, and he was known as a lucky general.

But Švitrigaila knew the Tatars and Rusians better; and, with reason, he mistrusted everyone.

Perhaps it made no difference. The Poles had brought the artillery needed to blow the stationary wagon fort apart, and it may have been somewhat disorganised by having been ordered to retreat, then recalled. When the Poles fired their massed guns, the noise was so great that men fell down semi-conscious. The defensive lines wavered, then when the Poles began singing the *Boga Rodzicza*, the sure sign of an imminent charge, the Tatars began to flee. Some took refuge in the wagon fort, looting and murdering, thoroughly disrupting the effort to fire on the advancing enemy; others fled to the river, where many drowned in a chaotic effort to swim to safety. The Livonian army hurried back, but was unable to form its lines in the confusion; soon the master and seven of his officers fell in the fighting. The Rusians, with Švitrigaila at their head, escaped into the forest. Those familiar with the taiga and the vast oak forests escaped easily.

Those familiar only with the steppe, such as the Tatars, or burdened by equipment, such as the Germans, or who did not know the region, such as the Czechs, were slaughtered, thousands being buried in mass graves. Many German knights, Rusian boyars and Lithuanian dukes were taken prisoner; but Švitrigaila escaped to Polotsk with thirty men. Korybut alone refused to flee or surrender. He fell, covered by wounds, and was taken to Žygimantas barely alive. He did not survive long, either dying of his wounds or being drowned by the Poles as a heretic.

Peace in Lithuania

Lithuania went to Žygimantas, who became a loyal subordinate to the Polish monarch, the young Ladislas III. Švitrigaila received Volhynia and Kiev, but he was so insecure there that when Polish forces withdrew in 1438, he thought it prudent to leave for Moldavia.

Rusdorf should have realised that Samogitia was lost for ever. Paganism was disappearing, Lithuanian influence in Novgorod was strong, and the grand duke was closely tied to Poland and to Roman Catholicism. In short, all hopes of reviving the military fortunes of the Teutonic Order in any form resembling the past were dead. The best Rusdorf might hope for was to hold on to what he had now, Ragnit and Memel, or anticipate that future tumult in Lithuania similar to what was now convulsing Ruś might present opportunities to those ready to profit from them.

Beyond that, neither Rusdorf nor anybody else seemed to know what the Teutonic Knights' role in Christendom was to be. Survival only as a home for unemployable younger sons of the nobility did not seem to be a very exalted calling. Still, with all parties tired of the war, all agreed to settle for less than their maximum demands. The peace treaty was negotiated, signed, and sealed with all the formality customary for that era; but with less delay than usual. Thus, 31 December 1435, marked the end of the Teutonic Order's crusade against Lithuania.

The emperor, catlike in his alternating fascination and boredom with events, was slow to learn of these events. When finally informed that his plans had failed, Sigismund said that it made no difference: nothing was valid without imperial and papal approval, and he was not about to give the deal his endorsement. He threatened to annul all the order's privileges unless the grandmaster repudiated his promise to uphold the peace.

Fearful of having his order's properties confiscated and immunities revoked, Rusdorf continued to make as much difficulty for the Polish crown as he dared; but he did so as secretly as possible, so that the Poles would have no proof of his intrigues. In 1438 the Livonian master arranged for the passage of a delegation of Muscovite churchmen through his territory en route to the Council of Ferrara, where church union was being discussed. The Poles attempted to block their passage, so that only Lithuanian churchmen of Polish descent could be present; but Rusdorf was able to arrange their travel safely to Italy. To no avail. Church union had become entangled in the quarrels between Pope Eugenius IV (1383–1447) and the councilmen at Basel over what reforms could be made in the Church and by whom, quarrels so fierce that when the pope had called for a new council to meet in Ferrara, the councilmen declared the pope deposed and elected a replacement – this anti-pope resigned after Eugenius's death, but for ten years his existence confused the political scene. In 1439, when plague broke out in Ferrara, the councilmen moved to Florence. There the participants reached agreement on the terms of church union, but when the Orthodox representatives returned home, they were unable to persuade their countrymen to accept the compromise solution of 'the accursed council'. They were joined in this by Bishop Matthias of Vilnius and the archbishop of Lwów who were outraged by the theological compromises.

Nor were traditional Catholics happier. Some considered the pope's calling a council at Florence only a poorly disguised effort to undermine the interminable council at Basel, while others denounced the subsequent transfer as inspired by Satan – the bishop of Vilnius and the archbishop of Lwów were especially blunt in rejecting the theological compromise. There were certainly no efforts to follow up the supposed agreement with the armies the Greeks needed to drive back the Turks.

The Polish queen mother, Sophia, continued Jagiełło's 'eastern' policy as best she could. Polish influence in Moldavia had been assured by her sister's marriage to Prince Elias (Iliaş, by whom she had two sons), but this was an alliance among Orthodox princes that did not advance Roman Catholic interests. In 1440, when Žygimantas was assassinated by two of Švitrigaila's supporters, Oleśnicki helped Sophia place her younger son, Casimir Jagiellon (1427–92), in Vilnius. This was the end of the long contest between the sons of Algirdas and Kęstutis. If Vytautas had kept the hearts of his countrymen, it was Jagiełło who, through his son, inherited the sceptre.

Oleśnicki's policy was not popular everywhere. Some Poles believed that their nation had suffered enough from the Lithuanian connection. They argued that Poland was abandoning its natural homeland (meaning Silesia) to pursue an unnatural expansion to the east and that the exchange of well-settled, prosperous lands filled with commerce and culture for a wild frontier was a fatal mistake. That debate was most intense at the Union of Lublin in 1569, but it lasted into the twentieth century.

Some Lithuanians were angered that clemency was shown to the assassins of Žygimantas. That smacked of a reward for treason. Others opposed the union on patriotic grounds, and were appalled at hearing that Casimir would be Ladislas's *viceroy*, a title which implied subjection to Polish superiors. Moreover, Casimir was only thirteen. However, the magnates were reluctant to resume the civil war. In time Casimir came to resemble his father physically and in his love for the hunt, but he would revel in banquets, have thirteen legitimate children, and learn to appreciate education.

Casimir's Reign

When the Polish prelates arrived in Vilnius with their ward, they learned that their victory was fleeting. As soon as they had crowned Casimir, they were ordered to leave the grand duchy. In their place came Lithuanian advisers and language teachers. Lithuania was henceforth ruled by the most powerful magnates, the *palatines*, and the regional governors, who jointly met in the Council of Lords. Peace with Švitrigaila was obtained by sending him to Łuck, to govern Volhynia as a separate, somewhat exotic eastern state, until his death in 1452. Alone and unadmired, he turned to alcohol for solace and companionship. In Trakai the *voewoda*, Jonas Gostautas (Goštautas; *c.* 1383–1458), used his office to make himself a secular counterpart of Oleśnicki.

Casimir's advisers moved quickly to deal with Samogitia, where support for Žygimantas's son, Michael, remained strong. First a Lithuanian–Polish army overawed the rebels, then they offered the Privilege of 1441 that guaranteed the Samogitians some autonomy as long as they recognised Casimir as their ruler. The advisers then suppressed revolts in Smolensk and Kiev, after which they once more made concessions to local feelings. This undercut Michael Žygimantaitis, who fled to Masovia, then went to the Tatars and made joint war on Poland. Eventually he died a prisoner in Moscow, perhaps poisoned.

Casimir, perhaps acting on advice from Oleśnicki and partisans of the union with Poland, abrogated some older Lithuanian traditions, so that when he accepted the call to the throne of Poland in 1447, it was relatively easy to unite the Polish and Lithuanian states in his person. Everything else remained as before – separate, relatively equal, and mistrustful. As it happened, the new arrangements would contribute to a wider spread of serfdom. That institution, which was dying out in western Europe, became more common in Ruś, Livonia, Lithuania and Poland as landlords sought to prevent their workers from moving away.

To summarise, the ethnic rivalry of Poles and Lithuanians slowly gave way to more interaction: Polish culture, in fact, proved so attractive to the best minds in Lithuania that many boyars, gentry and artisans chose to speak and write in Polish rather than Lithuanian or Russian. Awkwardly, Polish acceptance of Lithuania's most talented poets, scholars and politicians into Poland's pantheon of national heroes won no thanks from Lithuanians (and Belarusians and Ukrainians), who came to resent the Poles' airs of cultural superiority as much as Poles resented those same sentiments in Germans.

Meanwhile, the regional balance of power was shifting. Hungary, long stable under Sigismund, began sliding into chaos after his death in 1437. The nobles, determined to resume their ancient rights and feuds, refused to recognise Sigismund's heir, Albrecht of Austria, who was too concerned with the Bohemian throne to resist their demands effectively.

The Succession in Poland

Ladislas Jagiellon faced a new political constellation in east-central Europe when he became king of Poland in 1434, then king of Hungary in 1440. All the familiar actors had died within a short time of one another – Basil I, Vytautas, Jagiełło, Korybut and Sigismund. The options available to him were many, and the consequences of his choices profound. Should he send a brother to Prague to become king of Bohemia? No. The terms proposed would legitimise the Hussite innovations in church and state, and Oleśnicki was opposed. Should he become king of Hungary? Yes. Accepting the proffered crown on the grounds of his distant descent from Louis the Great and the potential help his Polish subjects could give against the Turks, was not popular anywhere, but Oleśnicki urged him to take it.

Oleśnicki had rivals for power, but none had his combination of personality and position. As the bishop of Cracow, he was a determined enemy of heresy, Orthodoxy and Islam. Those were not imaginary threats, either. The Hussites, angered by his efforts to acquire the Bohemian throne for Ladislas and make their country Roman Catholic once again, encouraged a rising of radically inclined peasants in Poland. In Lithuania Orthodox hatred of the dictatorial regime of Žygimantas resulted in his brutal assassination, followed by insults to the corpse. Queen Sophia was not beyond suspicion of being involved in both events. She more than anyone would have profited from Žygimantas's death. A Ruśian princess to the end, she was not popular in Poland.

Oleśnicki was especially enthusiastic about the opportunity to acquire Hungary, which was being invaded annually by Turkish armies and which could not now expect any aid from Germany. The price was sixteen-year-old Ladislas Jagiellon being willing to marry Albrecht of Habsburg's pregnant widow Elisabeth. There were Poles who saw the irony of having as their queen the daughter of Sigismund, but they wisely confined their comments to themselves and those they trusted to share gossip discreetly.

As it happened, Queen Elisabeth was not willing to be bought and sold so easily. Rallying her adherents, she fought for the rights of her son, Ladislas Posthumous (1440–57) to be both king of Hungary and king of Bohemia, Elisabeth placed on the head of her infant son the crown smuggled out to Austria. Oleśnicki then sent Polish forces into Hungary and drove her away. Even after Elisabeth died in exile in 1442, the Hungarians accepted their Polish king with poor grace. In order to persuade Polish diets to levy war taxes, Ladislas Jagiellon sold offices and gave away lands. In effect, he followed Jagiełło's policy in his last years of buying friends: he sold Poland to the great magnates.

The Crusade to Varna

By 1443 Ladislas Jagiellon had sufficiently pacified Hungary that he could deal with the Turkish threat. Guided by Oleśnicki's friend, Cardinal Cesarini, and led by the capable general John Hunyady (1406–56) – a master at employing the wagon fort – a Polish–Wallachian–Hungarian army captured Sofia in Bulgaria, thereby forcing the sultan to sign a ten-year peace treaty favourable to the Christians. Soon thereafter, however, the sultan's position weakened so greatly that Ladislas became persuaded that he could drive the Turks completely out of Europe. Unsure how to justify the truce as an irrelevant piece of parchment, he was persuaded to remember a previous oath drawn up by Cesarini to continue the war even if he made peace with the sultan. (Cesarini knew how to word an oath. It was not for nothing that Italians had a reputation for underhanded politics a half-century before Machiavelli). The hope of rescuing Constantinople and achieving church union was balanced against a prince's word of honour. When the pope and other churchmen said that his promise was not valid, the youthful king bowed to the pressure. Ladislas gave the orders to return to the Balkans.

In November 1444 Turks and Christians faced one another in Wallachia, on the shore of the Black Sea. Hunyady seemingly had the situation well in hand in spite of facing a larger army than expected – the Genoese had transported Ottoman warriors from Anatolia, thus repaying the sultan for the monopoly of trade in his realm. Hunyady had set up a wagon-fort in the Hussite fashion, planning to use the barrier to offset the Turks' superior numbers and élan. All he had to do was remain on the defensive and prevent a breakthrough until the attacking forces were demoralised by the thundering artillery. Then, when the Turkish forces were reeling back, trying desperately to retreat, to charge out onto their exposed backs. An attack at the right psychological moment would almost certainly provoke a panic from which the Ottoman army could not recover.

However, Ladislas chose to station his horsemen in front of the wagons, then led a charge at the main janissary position where the sultan was praying, perhaps hoping that killing him would demoralise the Ottoman host. The impetuous charge failed. While the sultan survived, Ladislas was surrounded and cut down. When the Poles saw the royal head waving atop a spear, they panicked. The result was a disaster equal to Nicopolis a half-century earlier. Almost no one from the Christian host at Varna escaped and the king's head was preserved in honey for public display. Cesarini died in the flight, probably murdered by a boatman for his money, though many preferred to believe that he had been painfully martyred by the Turks, skinned alive. A handful of the most physically impressive prisoners were led in their armour, bound hand and foot, as far as Egypt as a demonstration of the sultan's power to defeat even the most stalwart of warriors.

Hungary immediately fell into anarchy. Hunyady struggled to restore order, but without success. Only in 1452 could the quarrelling factions agree upon recognising Ladislas Posthumous, a minor who had spent most of his childhood as a hostage in Austria, as king. Hunyady's efforts to drive back the Turks, Austrians and domestic enemies were universally unsuccessful, but he was widely admired for having achieved anything against the overwhelming odds.

The disaster at Varna was immediately fatal to the fading hopes of church union. Orthodox priests in Moscow had already rejected the compromise proposals of the Council of Florence, even arresting the metropolitan, Isidore. Such popular resistance might have faded away if the crusaders had saved Constantinople because the Second Rome still had tremendous prestige. However, God now seemed to have spoken. The Byzantine Empire and church union were both doomed.

Liviu Pilat and Ovidiu Cristea show in *The Ottoman Threat and Crusading on the Eastern Border of Christendom during the 15th century* that for all the bold talk about a great crusade, after Varna there were only scattered wars for control of Moldavia.

It appeared for a while that Moscow would collapse too; but Basil II emerged victorious from a complicated struggle for the throne to introduce a better strategy for limiting Tatars raids – he built forts along the long steppe frontier, especially at fords and passes. These became bases for scouts and raiders, trading posts which could supply rebel Tatars and Cossacks, and assembly points for armies. In time Moscow saw itself as the Third Rome, and the title of *tsar* ('caesar') as appropriate for its ruler.

The Poles and Lithuanians, too, took steps to curb the Crimean Tatars, who were still carrying away large numbers of youths and maidens, horses and cattle. This struggle gave Poles an enduring self-image of being defenders of Christendom's eastern frontier (the famous *antemurale christianitatis*).

A New Generation of Royalty

Immediately after the news from Varna arrived, Oleśnicki urged Casimir to hurry to Cracow for his coronation. However, Casimir and his advisers chose to delay, hoping they could bargain for more favourable conditions. Only after three years, in 1447, when it appeared likely that the frustrated Poles would turn to Bolesław IV of Masovia (1421–54), an attractive Piast candidate for the crown with close ties to Oleśnicki, did Casimir leave Lithuania.

Casimir IV was fortunate that Oleśnicki moved out of the kingdom and onto the international scene when both the pope in Rome and the antipope elected by the Council of Basel offered to name him

cardinal, making him the first Pole to wear the red robes, and the first
to be a plausible candidate for the Papacy. Casimir initially opposed the
nomination so strenuously that the bishop had to smuggle his cardinal's
hat into the country.

Oleśnicki saw participation in the council on the distant upper
Rhine as an opportunity to work against the spread of Hussite
influence. To his horror, he had discovered that even in the university
in Cracow, practically under his nose, professors had been discussing
the dangerous ideas of Wycliffe. This tied into recent demands to end
the ancient practice of paying Peter's Pence, the special tax that went to
the distant Papacy. Oleśnicki had thought that crushing Polish radicals
in battle in 1439 had ended the matter. He now made certain that he
had rooted out the remaining heretics before going to Germany, but the
king's advisers had noted how the lower nobility could be employed to
lessen the power of the Church.

Once Oleśnicki was gone, Casimir became king in more than name.
He was not a well-travelled man in the usual sense of that phrase (he
had covered many miles of steppe and forest, but he had not visited
great cities or seen ancient ruins, and he knew almost no contemporary
ruler personally); nor was he a linguist or a scholar. Steady, temperate
and considerate, but unyielding, he presided over an era when Poland's
economy and culture developed rapidly. As the reputation of his
kingdom grew, Casimir inherited without effort what Jagiełło had
worked so hard to earn: trust and respect.

Lithuania experienced a similar change in power once Casimir was
gone. Gostautas moved to make himself supreme in the Council of
Lords. Already in 1443, he had become palatine of Vilnius; after 1447
he was the dominant figure in the country. When Casimir challenged
his authority in 1453, under great pressure from Polish patriots, whose
gangs were beating any Lithuanians who dared attend meetings of the
Polish Diet, two of the palatine's agents attempted to assassinate the
king, leaving him severely injured. Afterwards the authority of the
Council of Lords, led by Gostautas until his death in 1458, was seldom
contested effectively.

A similar situation developed in Hungary. Because Casimir delayed
his coronation, the magnates established a regency, then in 1452 crowned
young Ladislas Posthumus king, with Hunyady as regent. While
Hunyady was fighting the Turks, Ulrich II of Celje (1406–56) seized
power, thereby dividing the Hungarian and Bohemian kingdoms along
party lines. Hunyady and his co-worker, the Franciscan friar, Giovanni
Capistrano, did manage to revitalise the crusading spirit and to slow

the Turkish advance until Hunyady's death from plague in 1456 while successfully defending Belgrade. With Ladislas Posthumus dying soon afterwards and Hunyady's son, Matthias Corvinus (1443–90), being a minor, there was another regency, one which reflected the deep split between the great lords and the lesser nobility.

Matthias would eventually become a great Renaissance prince, but meanwhile there was a complicated struggle in which the papal legate, Aeneas Silvius Piccolomini (1405–64), the future Pope Pius II, sought to bring the central European monarchs together against the Turks and the Hussites.

Throughout this time Casimir was the logical leader of the wars against the Turks. He had married Elisabeth of Hungary (1436–1505), Sigismund's granddaughter, but the Hungarian magnates rejected his multiple claims upon the throne. Nevertheless, Elisabeth was an outstanding choice as helpmate, and would also produce thirteen children, four of whom later reigned over Poland. Though a Habsburg, she was a Polish patriot, who never left the country except to visit Lithuania.

Vytautas and Jagiełło entered the realm of folk memory and myth, to loom almost as large there as they had upon the political scene earlier. Their descendants (Vytautas – Basil II; Jagiełło – Casimir) might as well have well been sired by completely different men. Neither Vytautas nor Jagiełło would have been ashamed of their descendants, but they left them a heavy legacy in the form of expectations. Basil II, being Orthodox and Muscovite, was freed from the comparisons; but in his early teens he had lived with his grandfather long enough to learn much from him. Casimir had been only seven when Jagiełło died; yet, when he grew up, many looked to see in him the spiritual heir of both Jagiełło and Vytautas. Casimir was a talented and successful ruler, but no man could have lived up to these expectations.

Chapter 9

Hussite Invasions and Internal Dissent

Every effort to put stories into a larger context risks the greater picture obscuring the smaller ones. In this case, Prussian concerns were overshadowed by events elsewhere. Thus, to understand the fate of the Teutonic Order after the Council of Constance, it is necessary first to follow events in Bohemia.

The Hussite Wars

As far as the grandmaster was concerned, the war in Bohemia was no substitute for fighting Samogitian pagans; but the crusade against Czech heretics was nevertheless important for the German branch of the order. No member of the order could imagine not supporting Sigismund, the Council of Constance, and Pope Martin V; and so they committed their order's increasingly scarce resources in Germany to the invasions of Bohemia.

By 1423 the Hussites were rooting out the last of the royalist supporters in Bohemia. Sometimes it only took the Taborites beginning to sing their war hymn, *'Ktož jsú boží bojovníci'* ('You who are warriors of God'), to send their panicked enemies into flight. But not all was well in their ranks. Jan Žižka died without a charismatic successor, and Sigismund Korybut was so determined to be accepted as Bohemia's legitimate monarch that he refused to be led any farther from orthodox Roman Catholicism than the moderate reforms advocated by the Utraquist nobles in the Four Articles of Prague.

Those were not issues likely to inflame anybody except bishops, abbots, university professors and members of military orders. The Teutonic Order was furious to see its position in Bohemia undermined, first, by a Lithuanian prince; second, by demands that it give up its power and property; and third, that all disputes be debated in Czech, which for German knights was a very foreign tongue (the very name for a German in Czech, *němec*, means 'one who can't speak our language'). As a result of the increasing commitments to the crusade in Bohemia, the officers and priests of the order found it ever more difficult to persuade German secular knights, burghers and peasants that their order's problems in Prussia were truly as serious as those of Sigismund in Bohemia. Whatever justifications the Teutonic Knights might find for maintaining themselves in Prussia were slowly eroded by the Hussite Crusade.

Korybut had hoped to bring the moderate Hussites together, to make them the dominant faction, and then to find a formula for compromise with the pope. However, he took the wrong men into his confidence; they informed the authorities, who then arrested him. He was saved by his friends and by the arguments of the imperial representatives, who feared that no one would dare negotiate with King Sigismund if even a prince could be executed. His only punishment was to go into exile in Silesia.

Korybut had remained in Silesia quietly until 1430, watching events in Bohemia. He was arrested briefly by Jagiełło, who then gave him command of a body of Polish knights to fight alongside the Hussites against a force of 130,000 crusaders led by Cardinal Cesarini. The Germans lacked enthusiasm for this fight; after slaughtering countless innocent peasants, they panicked at the first clash of arms with disciplined troops and fled home as quickly as their horses would carry them. Under Procop the Bald the Hussites went on the offensive. This made it clear that the crusade had failed. In 1432, the churchmen at Basel – the successor assembly to Constance – recognised the new political reality. They invited the Hussites to send representatives to discuss reconciliation.

The Hussite Crusade had become a parody of earlier heroic actions in the Holy Land. Neither Sigismund, nor the Teutonic Order, nor the Germans and Hungarians came away with anything approaching honour. This, however, was not the only aspect of the order's affairs which burlesqued past ideals: there was the way diplomacy was conducted after the Council of Constance. The competence and advice of Peter of Wormditt was sorely missed.

Diplomatic Efforts in Prussia

The centre of diplomatic activity was, as before, at the curia in Rome. In 1420 Martin V had sent a legate, Antonius Zeno of Milan, to negotiate between the emperor, the king of Poland and Grandmaster Küchmeister. Zeno was suspected of being partial to the Polish king because he did not go to Sigismund as he was directed to do, but went straight away to Poland. Therefore, when Zeno came to Marienburg, the reception was frosty; and he was unable to talk to the margrave of Brandenburg because he was in Bohemia. Subsequent activities were equally fruitless.

Bohemia and the Hussites

Although the order sent its representatives to Thorn as the legate ordered, when they insisted that Sigismund, as emperor-elect, had to approve any actions they took, the Poles walked out of the conference. The grandmaster reported this to his subordinates everywhere – in Livonia, Germany and Italy – and urged them to recruit volunteers and novices for the impending war; but no mercenaries, he wrote, for he had no money.

There was no support from the pope or the officials at the curia. The new procurator-general, Johannes Tiergart, wrote plaintively that nobody would pay attention to him because he didn't have the funds to buy favour. He brought out copies of all the old documents granting the disputed lands to the order – the privilege of Friedrich II, the confirmations by Pope Gregory IX and Alexander IV, and then document after document from Polish princes, Brandenburg margraves, Holy Roman emperors, Lithuanian grand dukes, and Polish kings – but the Polish representatives provided documents countering or annulling those of the crusaders.

The main Polish argument was not based on bulls, but on the contention that Prussia had once belonged to the Polish kingdom, especially the regions of West Prussia (Pomerellia and Culm), and that Memel belonged to Lithuania. The title to West Prussia, of course, had been discussed often at the curia, but Memel was a relatively new issue, one that had only come up now that the Samogitians claimed to be converts.

The procurator-general and his assistants took pains to tell listeners that the Teutonic Knights had never been as strong militarily as they were at this moment, and that surrendering Memel would be a disaster because Livonia would be left absolutely isolated. These arguments were irrelevant to the legal question, but they were useful in persuading the pontiff that if the military order was to be saved, he should give the matter further attention.

At the next meeting the pope called for a map so as to get a clearer idea of the territories being discussed. Nobody had a map, but when documents described the boundaries in 1337 and 1349, Martin V declared that Prussia did not lie within the boundaries of the kingdom of Poland. It was a notable triumph, even if it only nullified one of many Polish claims.

Nevertheless, the pope advised privately that the grandmaster give up some territory in return for peace. The procurator-general related this to the grandmaster and concluded his report, saying: 'God knows in what state of mind I came home, after I heard that the justness of our order's cause was so little appreciated.'

The diplomatic manoeuvring continued. The Polish representatives displayed considerable skill in the use of 'the silent lawyer', the florin, employed so effectively by the Teutonic Order in the past. A knight wrote to Küchmeister that he saw little danger of losing Culm, but he saw great difficulties in retaining Pomerellia and Samogitia. He advised the grandmaster to send money for bribes immediately if he wished to avoid losing the cases by default. At last the pope appointed a legate to travel to Prussia for a personal inspection. This was considered so dangerous to the order's interests that Tiergart travelled to Prussia personally to confer with the grandmaster and explain to him how the matter had to be handled.

When Tiergart was named bishop of Kurland, it was an appointment he had been angling for all along, and one the grandmaster supported, since he needed trusted men in the bishoprics. As a result, however, the formerly excellent diplomatic service fell into the hands of a brash young man of Prussian origin, Kaspar of Wandofen.

Kaspar of Wandofen at the Curia

Related to the powerful Stange family, Wandofen had begun his career in the Church in the Pomesanian diocese and then had gone to Italy to study; there he impressed Tiergart, who was eager to find a replacement so that he could hurry off to his new see in Kurland. Appointed to office in 1428, Wandofen quickly proceeded to destroy the moral reputation and friendships so carefully cultivated by his predecessors.

Like many incompetent men who rise to high rank, Wandofen had talents which persuaded his superiors that he was a good choice for his office. He was handsome, charming when he wished to be, and an eloquent speaker. Unfortunately, he was also careless, hot-tempered, amoral and foolish. Worst of all, he was a womaniser – and unlike many clerical contemporaries who were guilty of the same fault – he was not discreet about it. First, he moved a Rhenish prostitute into his convent, made her pregnant, and allowed her to remain until the child was born. Then, for some unknown reason, he arrested her mother, which caused the girl to take her newborn daughter and rush to the Lateran Palace, calling out to all the important papal officials that the procurator-general had given her a child and taken away her mother! Incensed, Wandofen locked away all the women's possessions until he was summoned before the curia and summarily reprimanded.

Subsequently, Pope Martin V forbade Wandofen to enter his presence, which was a severe restriction on his diplomatic activities. When imperial representatives visited Rome in 1430, Wandofen was shut out of those hearings too. He then took up with a Bavarian prostitute, and, after she was ordered out of Rome, he made a new arrangement with a local lady of the evening. Also, he gave refuge to runaway knights. Among these was Goswin of Ascheberg, an officer of the Livonian master, who was sought for the notorious abduction and assassination of several Rigan diplomats. Wandofen later gave him a horse so that he could return to Germany. Other guests included a knight named Stibur, who stole Wandofen's silver and had to be arrested, and the notorious Odil Stockmann, the reputed mistress of the late Livonian master, who moved into Wandofen's residence with Stibur.

The procurator-general had one opportunity to make up for his past – when Martin V died in February 1431, Wandofen was appointed to command the fortress of Castel Sant' Angelo, where the papal treasury was kept. However, he conducted himself there in such a lackadaisical manner that, on the first inspection by the new pope, Eugenius IV, the pontiff found the walls almost unguarded, and, when a second visit disclosed that the situation had not improved, Pope Eugenius summarily dismissed him. Wandofen took this rebuff with dignity: he called together his small retinue, ordered the trumpets blown, and rode out amid the derision of the courtiers.

Shortly afterwards, a capable Polish diplomat, Nicholas Lasocke, arrived in Rome with gifts of armour, horses and money for the most prominent prelates and lawyers. He quickly learned his way around the curia and hired the most capable and powerful of the courtiers as his cardinal-protector, to lobby on Poland's behalf. Then he began attacking the Teutonic Order for violating the truce with the Polish king.

The matter was presented to the pope in early 1432, but after a long and vigorous debate, Pope Eugenius said only that he had heard such loud and contradictory presentations that he would have to confer with his cardinals and respond at a later time. This was equivalent to awarding the decision to Poland. Lasocke settled down permanently in Rome, ready to take on any new challenge from the discredited procurator-general.

In 1433 Rusdorf investigated various charges of immorality against Wandofen and summoned him to Prussia. In the next year he apparently had him quietly murdered.

The Hussite Invasion of Prussia

When the Hussites tired of fighting a purely defensive war, a tactic that had sacrificed wide areas to their enemies, they went on the offensive: into Silesia in 1428, 1429, 1430 and 1431, Saxony in 1429, the Upper Palatinate in 1430, Austria in 1428 and 1429, and Hungary in 1430 and 1431. These raids were so successful that the Czechs called them 'beautiful rides'. It was only natural, then, that they wanted to strike hardest of all at Sigismund's most loyal subjects, the military–religious order which had given unstintingly of its manpower and wealth – the Teutonic Knights.

Somehow, probably as the result of discreet inquiries through inter-mediaries, the Hussites received word that the king of Poland would not object if the well-disciplined army of 'the Orphans' crossed peacefully through his kingdom during 1433 to attack the Teutonic Order's strong-holds in West Prussia. The king could not have endorsed this openly – the pope would have been shocked at his traffic with heretics, and Archbishop Oleśnicki would have objected furiously – but that did not stop him from offering the Hussites 10,000 *Schock Grosschen* to cover their expenses.

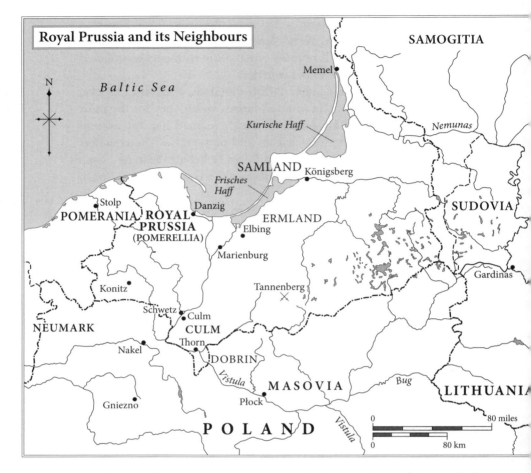

The grandmaster was not surprised when he learned that Polish forces were gathering on both sides of the Vistula – he must have expected some pay-back from his treaty-breaking invasion of 1431. It was something else when he heard that the invincible heretic army was on its way to the Neumark. With such little warning, how could he organise a defence for that region?

The governor in charge there gathered mercenaries promptly, but when he was unable to pay them, they mutinied. That would have made his situation difficult enough, but when the Pomeranian duke of Stolp invaded from the north, his position became hopeless. Rusdorf's efforts to send reinforcements failed because the scattered garrisons in East Prussia could not be brought together. Meanwhile, Polish volunteers had joined in the attack on West Prussia, and the grandmaster fell gravely ill. The most that the incapacitated Rusdorf could do was write to the pope, the Council of Basel, Emperor Sigismund, the Hanseatic League and various German princes asking for help. His prayers probably helped more, though not by much. Although the marshal gathered forces together with the intention of attacking the Poles before they could join the main Hussite army, in the end he thought it wiser to use his men to strengthen the garrisons of the most threatened towns and castles.

The Hussites thought they had found a base for their raids in Konitz, a strong fortress with a weak garrison. Surely their reputation would frighten the surrounded troops, and the swift professional start to the siege provided sobering confirmation that their reputation was deserved. They first drained the lake that served as a moat, then wheeled up four giant cannons. The first shot, a cannonball the size of a bucket, bounced down one street without causing any harm; a second struck a church filled with terrified worshippers praying to the crucified Christ and the Holy Mother. After a powerful bombardment, the armoured wagons drew up under the walls, disgorging ladders while other men threw ropes over the walls and climbed upwards. There they encountered women with buckets of boiling soup. Three times the Hussites stormed the walls; three times the defenders hurled them back. The commander's chaplain proved to be an extraordinary marksman, shooting down man after man among the enemy ranks. The Hussites' next effort was to tunnel under the walls, but their approach was heard by the defenders, who dug a countermine and put a cannon into their tunnel to welcome them when they broke through the last inches of dirt.

In August the Hussites gave up. They had no desire to attempt another direct assault. The German commander had been more imaginative and capable than expected, and the garrison more courageous. In addition, the supplies in the surrounding region were insufficient to feed the invaders and their horses. The Hussites moved to Schwetz, then north along the Vistula towards Danzig.

The Hussites remained the masters of any battlefield and could be challenged only if the grandmaster stripped every castle and town of its garrison and wagered the fate of the country on one engagement, a gamble that Rusdorf was unwilling to make. He would not put his demoralised forces up against the best army in all of Europe.

The Hussites met no significant opposition as they bypassed Danzig to burn the cloisters at Pelplin and Oliva (Oliwa), two of the oldest monasteries in the Baltic, then collected sea water from the Baltic as souvenirs. After ravaging the area, they made their way south-west, pillaging the countryside until they reached the Polish border again.

There was hardly a district in West Prussia which had not been burned by the Bohemians or their Polish allies.

Jagiełło's tacit support of the heretics had precipitated another dispute with Oleśnicki, who was already publicly denouncing the king for sabotaging efforts to defend the kingdom. Oleśnicki, however much he disliked the Teutonic Order, hated Hussites more. But Jagiełło's instincts were correct – his subjects had given the heretics an enthusiastic welcome. Some Polish knights in Prussia had taken Czech mercenaries prisoner, then given them to the Hussites to be burned at the stake as turncoats; this prompted another Polish knight to set fire to a building where imprisoned pirates were being held.

This raid was, as it turned out, the Hussites' last great adventure, the last and most impressive of their 'beautiful rides'. Talks were already under way to end the crusade. Martin V had resisted negotiations with the heretics as long as he could, but when he died, the way was open for negotiations. This was, however, complicated by the quarrel between Pope Eugenius IV and the churchmen at Basel over the reform movement, a quarrel that became focused on a seemingly minor point of theology.

The Hussites made a mistake in assuming that the council had made itself superior to the Papacy. The Utraquist faction had come to an agreement with the churchmen on many topics, and the pope had gone along until they reached the matter of the communion service. Hussites believed that all communicants should be allowed to partake of both bread and wine, while the pope insisted that only a priest could drink the wine. The belief in transubstantiation (the conversion of the bread into the actual body of Christ and the wine into His blood) was fundamental to the mystery of the Mass, but historically the matter of who could drink the wine was interpreted differently by the Orthodox and Catholic churches. The churchmen were open to a compromise. The pope was not.

Formal negotiations between council representatives and the Hussites continued into June 1433 at the Czech Diet in Prague. The Hussites did not do well in discussions of theology. Fine points of scripture and church tradition eluded them as much as their militant piety, deep sincerity and tales of cruel persecution escaped the council's members. The radicals wanted a social revolution, with the goal of establishing society on the basis of the Gospels; there should be democracy in religion, class structure and government. This frightened the moderates, largely nobles and Prague burghers belonging to the Utraquist faction, as much as it did the council's spokesmen.

The primary obstacle was the obstinacy of Germans who saw any concession to the Czechs as an affront to national honour. That was countered by the council spokesman, Juan de Palomer, who persuaded some members that the real problem had been the Czechs' unilateral adoption of the practice; the churchmen in Basel had just approved a similar formula for the Union church, thus reconciling those who clung to Orthodox practices. He compared the Czechs to a highly bred horse, which had to be handled gently, calmly and kindly, until the bridle was put on; afterwards, like even an untamed stallion, the Germans could lead them into the stable and tie them up. Cardinal Nicholas of Cusa was even less subtle in his private arguments. He pointed out that the Basel Council, by having approved the use of the chalice by those who accepted all the other rites of the Church, had provided the grounds for a destructive civil war among the Hussites.

The cardinal was correct. Civil war became inevitable when the churchmen offered the Utraquists autonomy similar to that proposed for Orthodox worshippers in Ruś and later granted to the Greek Church at the Council of Florence, namely that they could keep their use of the Czech language in worship and communion in both kinds, if they would recognise the authority of the council and pope. When the radicals realised they had been sold out, they made war on the moderate Hussites, only to be wiped out at the Battle of Lipany, just east of Prague, in May 1434.

This was followed by negotiations with Sigismund over the shape of the emperor's future administration. The churchmen at Basel, seeing their future role in Church government dependent on ending the heretical revolt, hurried to make whatever additional minor concessions would serve to bring the crisis to an end. If they wanted representative government in the Church, they could not allow the pope to bring an end to the rebellion without them. Sigismund, now too old for more waiting, also made concessions readily.

In July 1436 Sigismund entered Prague in state and presided at a formal meeting of the Czech Diet. It is highly likely that the Czechs had heard reports of his comments to German supporters that whatever he promised now, he could reverse later. He remained a schemer and liar to the end.

Sigismund's End

The emperor's health was declining so obviously that everyone began to speculate about the future. Not all the speculation was benign. Sigismund was furious to learn that his wife Barbara had been talking with prominent Hussites, talks that had gone so far as to propose a marriage between the 45-year-old empress and the thirteen-year-old Ladislas of Poland. He arrested Barbara and as many of her co-conspirators as he could locate. Then, in late 1437, he left Prague. Surrounded by loyal troops, he was borne on a litter and followed at a short distance by a large band of jesters and prostitutes. Too weak to reach Hungary, he stopped at one of his estates in southern Moravia. One last time he had himself seated on his throne, wearing the crown and holding the regalia while he heard Mass, then he took to his bed and died.

As the Czechs put it, 'the heretical king, betrayer of the Lord God and His Scriptures, violator of unmarried and married women, murderer, arsonist, and wreaker of destruction on the Czech language,' was dead. In 1755, when his grave was opened for inspection, onlookers saw Sigismund's corpse clad in gold brocade, holding the orb and wearing a silver crown.

His officials did not allow Barbara to attend the funeral, but held her in prison until authority could be passed to Elisabeth and her husband, Albrecht of Habsburg. Nevertheless, Barbara's spirit was hardly broken. When a priest suggested that during the period of mourning for her husband, she should live for a little while in chastity, she replied that the turtle dove was a stupid bird, that she much preferred the gay, singing sparrow. She escaped to Poland in 1438.

The death of Sigismund almost completed that passing of a generation which had begun with Basil I (1425), Vytautas (1430), Jagiełło (1434) and Korybut (1435); only Žygimantas (1440) and Švitrigaila (1452) remained, and neither of them had the opportunity to affect so many lives in so many ways as did the others. Contemporaries found much to admire in Sigismund, despite his many shortcomings. At the beginning of his reign the Hungarian kingdom was in chaos, the Holy Roman Empire and Church in schism, and Bohemia was experiencing ethnic difficulties that later evolved into a religious war. He had left them all relatively peaceful and stable. In his last years he had begun to implement real reforms, such as calling on the cities to participate in important assemblies more than had been done before. Those were not daring proposals. Sigismund was not a man of imagination, but there was eventually more to him than a skirt-chaser.

In his last days he was planning another crusade to rescue the Balkans and further Church union. He toyed with ideas for more basic reforms. Even so, Sigismund never advocated the radical ideas attributed to him within a short time of his death, when his name was linked with a strange document, *The Reformation of the Emperor Sigismund*. Half common-sense proposals for reform, half a mystical vision, it made suggestions for remoulding the practices of every major religious order. It linked the Teutonic Knights and the Hospitallers together in accusing the officers, great and small, of carrying the cross on their cloaks but doing nothing else Christian, neither singing nor praying, and of treating their priests as nothing more than servants. The anonymous author recommended that the churchmen summon their leaders to Basel and straighten them out!

Weak states would have welcomed rule by the mythical Sigismund, but the real emperor would help only if bribed at a level they could ill afford. The degradation of morality in politics – which had never been very high – was certainly fatal for the Teutonic Order. Contrary to the knights' vow of poverty, they began to write testaments disposing of clothing, weapons, horses and even money, proving that those items were now considered personal possessions, not order property used by individuals during their lifetimes. The concern with wealth was shown in falsified accounts, worldly display and more frequent nepotism.

The Decline of Discipline

Not only had the losses at Tannenberg been heavy; they had struck at that part of the membership which best represented the traditions of the military order. The membership was now composed of older knights who had been left to guard the castles and very young ones sent from Germany who did not yet know the country or its customs, that is, men either past the age of effective leadership or not ready for it. After 1410 younger men advanced quickly into positions of command, making changes in convent life and practice and later defending the semi-autonomous authority they had inherited in the period of crisis. That development was unavoidable and not always bad, but it made reform from the top more difficult.

The knights had already begun to realise that they were less important in modern warfare than were mercenaries, but that had never been demonstrated so brutally as in the years after Tannenberg. The knights understood that officers and administrators were needed more than warriors; nevertheless, not all of them were capable of exercising those functions and even fewer liked their new roles. The convents in Germany were not attracting recruits for Prussia in the numbers needed to keep up even a reduced membership.

Few men of quality wanted to join a military order in decline. More-over, the officers were not certain that they needed common knights, because the incomes needed to support them might be better spent on mercenaries; the officers were desperate to save money against the time when new armies would be wanted. The result was dissatisfaction among the knights who did join the order, unhappiness with the present state of affairs, and bruised class pride. Victories would have resolved this problem, but victories were seldom won.

Paul of Rusdorf sought to bring in more revenue. He emphasised replacing free peasants with renters, a practice that ultimately increased the percentage of serfs. He sought to increase the taxes that came directly to his office, eliminating lower offices that would soak up the income, and reducing the number of knights that he had to support.

In his own mind Rusdorf was reversing the tendency to concentrate on money, just as he fought the spread of excessive drinking and gambling, vices which seemed to occupy the time of common knights and many of the discouraged officers. In fact, his efforts to stamp out 'abuses' may have led contemporaries and modern historians alike to conclude that the problem was greater than it was. Rusdorf became a paranoid personality who saw conspiracies and immorality everywhere and who considered any deviation from his own puritanical lifestyle as treason. No wonder officers may have bribed his inspectors to give a good report about their garrisons, and bribing a man to tell the truth is not a large step from bribing a man to lie.

When Rusdorf called a general chapter meeting in Prussia to discuss reforms proposed by a Carthusian friar, Heinrich Beringe, he met strong opposition from the German master. The proposed reforms were purely spiritual in nature and lacked a means of enforcing them, but they caused a great uproar.

Schism

The dispute with the German master, Eberhard of Saunsheim (1385–1443), hinged upon the newly discovered Orselnian Statutes, an agreement supposedly reached in 1329 between the Livonian master and the German master in Marienburg which gave the latter a predominant role in the election of the grandmaster and in supervising his conduct in office. As Saunsheim witnessed Rusdorf's ineptitude and increasing arrogance, he concluded that the grandmaster was mentally ill; the Orselnian Statutes provided a means to remove him. Rusdorf's logical response was to ask: why had no one mentioned this agreement at the elections held immediately after it had supposedly gone into effect? Obviously, it was a forgery.

The German convents, steeped in resentment from the Egloffstein dispute decades before, declared the document valid, after which Saunsheim went to Sigismund and to the Council of Basel to ask for a confirmation of the order's statutes, including the Orselnian document. The grandmaster wrote to Pope Eugenius IV, who was feuding with the Council at Basel. When Saunsheim refused three times to attend a general chapter in the Neumark, Rusdorf suspended him from office. The German convents then denounced the grandmaster and refused obedience. The order was divided.

The Livonian Order was next. It had been divided into two ethnic blocks, 'Westphalians' who spoke Low German and 'Rhinelanders' who spoke High German. Of course, those designations did not accurately reflect the origins of all the knights, but they were convenient. Historically Saxons and Westphalians had dominated the ranks and the high offices alike. However, Rusdorf had been sending ever larger numbers of Rhinelanders north so that he would have more influence in the order's policies regarding Ruś and Lithuania. After an initial election, the Livonian Order usually submitted two names to the grandmaster, who usually chose the knight who had received the most votes. Rusdorf, however, chose the minority candidate.

In 1433 Rusdorf's efforts to increase the Rhinelanders' influence had provoked discontent that swelled greater after the disastrous 1435 Battle on the Swienta. When Rusdorf selected yet another minority Rhinelander in 1438, the Westphalians revolted. They would not have acted had the German convents not already declared that the Orselnian rule required the grandmaster to abdicate. However, neither side wanted a civil war now, especially not after the Livonian Order had made vital concessions in 1435 at the regional assembly in Walk (Valga/Valka), creating what became the Livonian Confederation. The nobles, prelates and burghers could thenceforth legislate on behalf of the entire country, and they were unlikely to support a war with Prussia. So the Livonian Order's defiance was purely oral or written.

The 'language dispute' in Livonia ended with the Westphalians in possession of the most important offices and castles and Rusdorf bereft of vital support in his dispute with Saunsheim.

The grandmaster next faced a revolt by three of his most important officers – the commanders of Königsberg, Brandenburg and Balga – in protest against his manner of acting without consulting them or the membership. Efforts to resolve the disagreement left matters worse than ever. In fact, while Rusdorf was away from Marienburg, another group of disaffected high officers seized the fortress and refused to let him back in. They demanded a redistribution of the offices so as to remove the grandmaster's last remaining friends. They then chose Konrad of Erlichshausen (*c.* 1390–1449) as marshal. This made him the leading candidate to replace Rusdorf, so that they would not have to elect the unappetising Saunsheim.

Meanwhile, the Prussian estates (the burghers, secular nobles and the bishops) had reached the limits of their endurance. In February 1440 they met in Elbing to discuss local problems, but by March had decided on forming a 'Prussian League' (*Preussischer Bund*) to resist more taxes and tariffs and to oppose any new war.

The crises continued to deepen, with Rusdorf vainly seeking to escape his predicament. At last, in January 1441, he gave up his office, and before the meeting of the general chapter to elect Konrad of Erlichshausen his successor, Rusdorf was dead.

Erlichshausen faced a formidable task. Piety and good intentions had proven insufficient to restore Prussia's fading fortunes. The new grandmaster could cure the schisms, but he could do little about the inner rot that now sapped the strength of the military order. The decline in discipline had not yet reached the point of public ridicule, which a later proverb summarised as 'Get dressed, undress, drink, and sleep; those are the skills of the Teutonic Knights.' Nevertheless, discipline was hard to enforce, especially on mercenaries who had good reason to doubt that their wages would be paid. Nor was drinking as excessive as Sebastian Munster later described it:

> They drink beer immoderately, encouraging and forcing one another to such excesses as would be too much for an ox. And they are not satisfied with drinking to satiety but drink until they are sober again. So they pass the entire day and often the entire night, and whoever overcomes the others in drinking, he is praised and honoured . . .

Behaviour

Beer was an important part of convent life, as it was everywhere in an era when water was both unsafe and unsavoury. The inventories listed the finer Wismar brew, the Danzig variety (also very good, and widely consumed in Prussia), and common table beer. Bromberg beer was the best, brewed by the order itself. The brewing industry was encouraged because the order received important revenues from the taxes paid on the beer, from the licensing of taverns, and from the sale of barley. Because beer and other homemade beverages were cheap, the knights and their men could afford to drink heavily. The knight-friars were not given a salary or (in theory) permitted to own private possessions, but everything they needed was supplied free, including their beer, wine and mead. The vow of poverty no longer implied a reduced standard of living, while the vow of obedience meant an unlimited toleration of stupidity.

Efforts were made to control undesirable behaviour, and, thanks to the better record keeping of the fifteenth-century bureaucrats, we know more about the problems of discipline. In Schwetz, for example, there was a quarrel between the commanding officer and a knight. First the officer impolitely asked the knight what he meant by seeking him out in the kitchen, and in the ensuing cursing and shouting the knight rather outdid his commander (but not by much). Later they fought in the dormitory, the officer going down with a stab wound. The world at that time was not different from today. It was the knight who was punished, not the officer. In 1434, after he had spent at least six years in an unheated tower, a petition was submitted for his release. (We do not know if the petition was granted.)

Unfortunately, specific incidents appear all too rarely in the surviving records, so that we cannot determine if offences became more common or less so. We can observe the failure of morale and discipline only in its grand sweep, as decade by decade the order sank lower in its general reputation and in its own esteem.

What Had Happened?

Rusdorf had destroyed morale by his frequent political mistakes and his refusal to admit that he had ever been wrong. He had signed the Peace of Lake Melno over the strong protests of many knights, and he had needed all his authority to obtain the seals of the German and Livonian masters for the treaty.

He had followed a peace policy, believing that the Polish royal army was too strong, and that the Prussian cities would rebel; but his policies were neither popular nor consistent. Many just thought he was incompetent. Whether he made war or peace, that decision seemed to be wrong at the moment. He seemed preoccupied with the spiritual life of the membership, while missing opportunities to reestablish the military power of the state. Knights who wanted to fight to the bitter end despaired over his avoiding battle; they considered his accepting unfavourable truces as cowardly, foolish and even treasonable.

Rusdorf's piety was never questioned, but the grandmaster's orders to attend religious services and to pray privately were out of step with the reform movements of the times. Certainly, many noble patrons of the order saw it less as a religious organisation than a place to put their unemployed younger sons, a provider of comfortable jobs that still had some prestige and occasional purpose. However, to conclude the story with the lesson that the Teutonic Order was out of step with the times would miss an important aspect of the era: the conservative reaction to the violent revolutionary heritage of the Hussites and the conciliar movement. The restoration of ancient traditions could only be achieved, reasoned conservatives such as Martin V, Eugenius IV and Paul of Rusdorf, by concentrating power in the hands of popes, emperors, kings and grandmasters, and by crushing those democratic elements that were bringing disorder and chaos to every branch of society.

Rusdorf believed that every order had to be *re*formed from time to time, but the *re*forms were always *re*turns to the founders' intentions, not innovations. Obedience, poverty and chastity were the virtues that gave his military order meaning in an era of secularism and mercenary soldiers, the duty to serve as examples to knights throughout Christendom.

Chapter 10

The Thirteen Years War, 1450–1463

Defeat and Disorder for the Teutonic Knights

By the 1440s one grandmaster after another had failed in almost every endeavour. Their once prosperous state was destitute. Morale among the knights was low; and the pope and emperor had given up on their survival.

In addition, the burghers and knights of Prussia were alienated by heavy taxes and the rejection of their wish to share in political power. Moreover, the Teutonic Order was recruiting increasingly from southern Germany, bringing in knights and officers whose High German was very different from their subjects' Low German. This accentuated their assumption that their subjects were socially and militarily inferior.

Had the military order established a centralised state immediately after entering Prussia, matters might have been different. But that had not been possible in the thirteenth century, and perhaps not even they themselves had imagined how much success they would have after Poland had fallen into civil conflict and royal impotence. They had made bishoprics into independent states (or semi-independent), given rights and tax-exemptions to cities, brought in secular knights who resented any and all restraints, and even allowed native warriors to move into the class of land-owning gentry, then assimilate. Efforts to tame these forces were not working.

But those matters soon seemed less important than one to the north.

Schism in the Livonian Order

Paul of Rusdorf had sought to preserve the remaining strength of his order by taking more personal control over daily operations. He was successful in this only in the Neumark, where he signed a new treaty with the secular vassals to make them subject to him alone, not to his officers. He did not attempt this in the remainder of Prussia. He concentrated instead on restoring religious discipline in the semi-autonomous convents.

Religious discipline had declined everywhere in Europe, but there was more reason to worry about it now as disagreements over every policy seemed to be leading towards a schism. What gave everyone pause was the example of Livonia, where the northern branch of the order had been so weakened by internal disputes that it had to permit the cities, bishops, abbots and secular nobles to form a 'Livonian Confederation'. Henceforth, commoners traditionally treated as inferiors were the master's equals.

At a time when discerning men could see that the future lay with princes who could organise their states properly, the Livonian Knights had lost their chance. Instead, they could only offer advice to an unwieldy confederation that had no power to tax, no authority to summon up armies, and no means of persuading anyone to put the interests of the community above those of family and class.

Rusdorf briefly contemplated a 'crusade' against the Livonian Order, but it was as impractical to invade a land so strongly fortified as Livonia as it was for the German master to invade Prussia. It was a totally absurd idea, one that would have made him and his order the scandal of Christendom.

In the end, the Livonian master and the German master became practically autonomous. Rusdorf's successors retained the right to choose between candidates proposed by the regional chapter assemblies, but each election provoked a constitutional crisis that boded ill for the future. From this time on the German master looked to the emperor for leadership, not to the grandmaster. For several years he sent neither money nor men to Prussia.

The personalities of individual figures are often more important than we realise. They might not have changed the stream of history, but they affected the ebbs and flows within the general flood. They made decisions that either aided or impeded the ways that human capital develops and flourishes. Paul of Rusdorf was a case in point. From the standpoint of *Realpolitik*, the decisions he made were perhaps the right ones; but in practice he dissipated his energies, failed to support his allies, and refused to take risks.

Rusdorf's economic policies were conventional wisdom for the time; that is, they were statist and exploitative. To the extent that his resources and imagination permitted, he tried to direct agriculture, industry and commerce; and he encouraged a greater use of unfree labour. There were no champions of economic freedom in those days. Everyone supported their own class interests, except heretics such as the Taborites, who had little use for trade and commerce.

His enemies were not much more enlightened. The Prussian cities wanted monopolies that would guarantee them good profits, and they argued for tax relief to an extent that would have rendered the grandmaster bankrupt.

As the friendly manner of Rusdorf's early years failed to achieve the results he desired, he became arrogant. He never possessed that aura of leadership that inspires loyalty. His virtues were those of a crabbed monk – chastity, prayer, silence and obstinacy. His diplomacy was convoluted and secretive, easily misunderstood and never explained. Since his efforts to reform the military order were all based on the false proposition that it still held absolute power in Prussia, he had no interest in building a party among the secular knights and burghers.

He gave a free hand to officers who agreed with him and overlooked all complaints about their conduct. To questioning or resistance he had but one answer: a haughty demand for obedience. After the officers finally rebelled, his insistence on unconditional submission became a monomania. The fate of his recent predecessors weighed heavily upon him, but he did no better than they had done. A tragic, symbolic figure, it is no wonder that he failed.

Rise of the Prussian League

The secular nobles and cities represented in the estates – social classes that met together periodically to talk with their rulers – wanted a stronger voice in taxation and declarations of war. At first, these were relatively humble requests, but this changed when they heard the dismissive responses of the order's officials, who acted as though they were the law itself. In 1440, while Rusdorf was stalemated by the schism in the ranks of his knights, he was confronted by the Prussian League. Fifty-three nobles, the seven Hanseatic cities, and twelve other towns swore to assist one another in defence of their rights and privileges. Soon they were joined by others. The complaints were minor, but numerous: the devaluation of the currency, heavy taxes, illegal exactions, repeated military levies, corrupt officials, arrogant knights and unjust judicial rulings. The grandmaster refused to recognise the legitimacy of the League, but was too ill to act against it.

His successor, Konrad of Erlichshausen, avoided a confrontation, just as he hoped to coexist peacefully with the powerful Polish–Lithuanian state. This gave his order a final opportunity to put its house in order and prepare for the future. As one historian put it, it was the last breathing space before the storm of war broke over the Teutonic Order's head and swept away all hope of recovery.

Konrad of Erlichshausen was just over fifty years of age when he took office in 1441. Handsome, golden-haired, with his beard trimmed stylishly short, he had the look and bearing of an important personage. His preparation for office was thorough. However, in all his experience

with the last of the pagan Samogitians, Christian Poles, heretic
Bohemians and rebellious convents in Germany and Livonia, he had
known neither victory nor success. Conditioned to expect failure, he
was careful to avoid problems. A thoroughly likeable man, one suited to
reconciling disputes, he believed that all decisions were to be arrived at
through consultations ratified by formal assemblies.

He began his reign with a four-month-long procession through
Prussia, visiting even the most remote districts. His subjects – German,
Polish and Prussian – turned out to give the oath of fealty and size up
their new ruler. He met with Eric, the exiled king of Denmark, and later
with a Pomeranian duke. All seemed to be well. But the reality was
different.

In theory, the Prussian branch of the Teutonic Order was strongly
organised, with leadership given by the grandmaster and his officers
and obedience required of those below. In practice the grandmasters
had abused their powers, so the members had sought to guarantee
that Konrad and all future grandmasters would govern according to
regulations and customs (in other words following both written and
unwritten practices). But the problem was not confined to the top ranks
of the order. When knights took their vows as friars, they brought with
them habits they had acquired in their youth; and the traditions and
customs of the convents were better designed to make them into pious
warriors than to mould them into understanding administrators of a
changing secular society.

Konrad did his best to pacify the factions. By recognising the
validity of the Orselnian Statutes, he persuaded the German master to
meet him at a grand chapter in the autumn of 1442; shortly thereafter
the Livonian master was reconciled as well. Both recognised him as
the legitimately elected grandmaster, an acknowledgment that opened
the way for future reorganisation. But these were tactical retreats on
his part, not surrenders. When the right moment came, after the death
of the German master in 1447, he asked Pope Eugenius IV to annul
the Orselnian statutes. Then he warded off efforts by the next German
master to reinstate them by reminding the pope that his enemies at
the Council of Basel had confirmed the statutes, as had the new Holy
Roman emperor, Friedrich III (1415–93); in contrast, he had supported
the pope.

In 1449 Pope Nicholas V asked the bishops of Ermland and Pomesania
to look into the dispute. When they reported that the document was a
forgery, the pope was satisfied that the issue was resolved. He was right.
Once all the parties involved had died, the dispute faded away

Konrad did not achieve much, for all the talk his ideas generated. When he spoke of reform, he meant a return to the practices of 1198 or 1230 (the last codifications of the rules), not to mould the Teutonic Knights into a new creation. This appeal to the medieval past rather than looking towards the future doomed his plans to failure.

Breaking the vow of chastity, for example, was not the order's fundamental problem. No matter how many warnings the grandmaster issued about the year-long suspension from membership with no food every other day, or punishing homosexuality with life-long imprisonment, unless he made examples of some notorious knights, no one was going to take his preaching seriously.

Nor was doubling the penalty for vocal opposition to a grandmaster's orders likely to be effective if no official attention was paid to failing silently to carry orders out. Providing livings for aged knights probably did improve the quality of leadership, in that men too old to carry out their responsibilities could pass them on to younger men; a number of knights apparently did subsequently retire to Germany, often to enter convents belonging to other orders.

Younger knights were leaving to serve as administrators and mercenaries for secular lords. Not all men were suited to the clerical state, especially not in years when the demands of poverty, chastity and obedience could not be balanced by pride in one's organisation and its achievements – and reasons for pride had been hard to find in recent years. Unable to deal with these fundamental issues, Erlichshausen worked on superficialities. Neither forbidding the ownership of individual clothing, dice games and hunting, nor setting higher standards for the noble birth of members, for attendance at worship services, and observing fast days were likely to make much difference in the order's success in managing a state. If the Teutonic Knights were going to make themselves into a purely religious order, yes, certainly. But to be a successful state in competition with larger and more powerful neighbours, those reforms were irrelevant.

Nothing demonstrated the challenge of the modern to the past better than the rise of the Prussian League to demand a share in making laws and enforcing them. The breakdown of law and order was already serious – there were pirates, highwaymen, rebellious peasants and contentious nobles in the diocese of Ermland. The order's knights asked how making concessions to upstart townsmen, however capable and wealthy, would help to resolve those problems – the grandmaster's freedom of action would become as restricted as the king of Poland's. Konrad of Erlichshausen, however, was not yet in a mood for confrontation; at least, he saw no point in it.

Consequently, he readily made concessions to the League on minor points such as amending inheritance laws, swiftly confirming the charters and privileges of the towns, and promising to make no innovations in the administration. At great assemblies in 1441–2 in Elbing he won the hearts of his hearers by promising to correct abusive behaviour by local officials and administrators, by his friendly attitude and his constant respect for the Prussian League's representatives and their requests.

What he said was important, but the manner in which he said it was even more significant. Erlichshausen's very bearing conveyed sincerity and a desire for compromise, without any loss of the manly virtues by which the upper classes maintained the respect of their social inferiors. Frank presentations of the order's financial needs, the problems of keeping trade routes open, and foreign policy initiatives won their trust. Also, by allowing debate on taxes, he divided the opposition into feuding parties, while he himself enjoyed the role of mediator.

He had to choose among three paths towards the future. One was to recognise the Prussian League as a legitimate parliament similar to the ones coming into being in nearby Poland, in France, in England, in Scandinavia and in the Holy Roman Empire. These were all different states, with different means of representing the cities and nobility, but all had some form of representative government. The second was to crush the estates by force, which was the way the pope had chosen to deal with the churchmen at the Council of Basel. The third was to supplant feudal practices by legally gathering authority into his own hands, then deciding what changes had to be made. The choices seemed clear: representative government, force or administrative reforms.

Konrad chose none of the three possibilities. He put off the decision by making minor changes, exhorting his officers to avoid provocations, and assuring peace with Poland. In short, he always looked back – towards traditions of honour, pride and service. Those traditions were still valued by most contemporaries, but by confirming the *status quo*, as in Poland, they impeded the reforms necessary to create a successful Renaissance state. Konrad kept the peace while he lived, but the basic issues of the day needed a more permanent resolution. The Teutonic Knights had to decide on the order's future; but that debate never took place.

Foreign Affairs on the Cheap

Foreign affairs were less difficult for Konrad of Erlichshausen than for Paul of Rusdorf, but the quiet of his little pond was nevertheless periodically disturbed by waves made by his neighbours. With Poland agitated by the disputes between King Casimir and Bishop Oleśnicki, the archbishop of Gniezno, Vincent Kot (1395–1448), was eager to use the grandmaster to counterbalance the regional influence of the Hohenzollerns in Brandenburg.

The grandmaster reciprocated the friendship, knowing well how eager the Hohenzollerns were to exercise the 'right to repurchase' the Neumark, a point in Sigismund's original grant that had been ignored until now. At lengthy meetings in Frankfurt an der Oder in 1443, with Margrave Friedrich occasionally attending, the grandmaster agreed to pay him handsomely (30,000 *Gulden*) for abandoning this right and signing a treaty of mutual neutrality in one another's foreign policy disputes. Erlichshausen then had to obtain imperial and electorial approval of the treaty.

Hanseatic politics claimed the grandmaster's attention because Prussian fleets were now sailing as far as Portugal in search of markets. Queen Margaret's heir, Eric, had provoked revolts which led to the establishment of a true Swedish parliament in 1435; the unrest then spread to Norway and Denmark. By 1442 all three national bodies had deposed Eric and replaced him with his nephew, Christopher of Bavaria (1416–48), a grandson of Ruprecht of the Rhine.

Christopher made a good start in his reign, overcoming peasant rebellions and regional efforts to secede from the Kalmar Union that linked the three countries. But he was unlucky later, finding the many challenges too great for his resources. He could not even prevent his predecessor, Eric, from leading pirate attacks on ships of the Hanseatic League. Laughing at his hopeless predicament, he pawned his last assets to live as a wanderer from court to court; and when he died in 1448, he left his heir, Christian of Oldenburg (1426–81), limited means for rebuilding royal authority. Marrying his predecessor's widow strengthened Christian's lack of local connections, and inheriting lands in Germany offset the loss of Sweden.

In these contests the grandmaster's influence had been very small. Nevertheless, he had a ceremonial role to play in the negotiations. He was repeatedly offered Gotland, but there was no way he could pay the sum requested. Moreover, he knew that he could not subdue the pirates. When the Swedes seized the island in 1448, the grandmaster hesitated to take one side or the other because he was worried that the Swedes would take control of the mouth of the Neva River, thereby cutting the Hanseatic League out of the trade with Novgorod. By the time the grandmaster died in 1449, the order had entirely lost its once powerful influence on Baltic politics.

Konrad of Erlichshausen had done about as much as personal charm, honesty and piety allowed. He had tried traditional means to eliminate crime, wastefulness, idleness, poverty and superstition in society, to instil in his subordinates humility, orderliness and responsibility, to ensure that poverty and chastity were practised in the convents and to make his contribution to international stability and peace. He understood that in the future education would be more important than good intentions, and therefore he sent young men off to study law (not theology, which was not the order's concern) to prepare them for administrative careers in Prussia. Nevertheless, his patience slowly unravelled at the lack of progress, at the obstacles which arose, at the obstinacy of his men and his subjects. Clearly, God did not reward his servants in any manner that made sense by human standards. Goodness may have been its own reward, but it was no way to achieve worldly success.

The Will to Power

After Grandmaster Konrad's death in 1449, the representatives to the grand chapter elected as his successor a nephew, Louis (Ludwig) of Erlichshausen (1410–67). Eager to force issues to a decision, Louis believed that the order's problem was not a paucity of means, but a lack of will. Correctly sensing that the Prussian League was his principal challenge, the new grandmaster followed the example of contemporary German princes in attempting to curb, then crush, its most influential members. In this he was not only supported, but pressured by important officers to act even more decisively. He was offended not only by the protesters' tone and the demand that he end the emergency taxes on commerce, but by their insistence that he send his Italian-trained lawyers out of the assembly, so that he could not turn to them for advice.

Louis of Erlichshausen saw that the League's weak point was its lack of legal standing. Therefore he sent a young lawyer, Laurentius Blumenau (1415–84), a Danzig-born patrician who had studied in Italy, to speak to Pope Nicholas V. Blumenau was greatly assisted by the bishop of Ermland, who had strongly recommended striking down the League at its birth, but had been ignored. Now, in late 1450, Blumenau persuaded the cardinals to send a legate to investigate whether any such league could be legitimate. Awkwardly, he could not arrange for a prominent churchman to carry out the task – the cardinals showed their lack of interest in Prussian affairs by naming an obscure Portuguese bishop, Louis de Silves. That prepared the way for a clash of two of the most powerful movements of the future – autocracy and representative government.

A more important figure soon became involved, Cardinal Nicholas of Cusa (1401–64), bishop of Brixen, whose reputation as diplomat and scholar guaranteed having his opinion heard throughout Germany and at the court of Friedrich III. His extensive correspondence with the grandmaster contained advice that the officers of the military order took seriously. Meanwhile, the order's procurator-general at the curia, Jodocus of Hohenstein (*c.* 1415–71), argued that the League was an illegal 'conspiracy'. The grandmaster employed that argument when he moved against the Prussian League.

He was encouraged in this by the new Livonian master, Johann of Mengede, a Westphalian. Traditionally his party had been willing to work with the Livonian Confederation, but less so the independent-minded citizens of Riga; when he found himself facing a hostile archbishop of Riga too, he warned that the Prussian League was dangerous and had to be crushed.

Thus encouraged, Erlichshausen and Blumenau moved to limit the authority of the Prussian League. This frightened the secular nobles and burghers who had been most opposed to the grandmaster's claims of absolute sovereignty. Soon the Prussian League was discussing armed resistance. Nevertheless, still hoping that his opponents would accept a papal or imperial ruling in his favour, Erlichshausen sent Blumenau to ask whether the Prussian League was even a legal corporation. Of course, when papal and imperial lawyers looked at the order's charters, they found no provision for such a representative assembly. This warned the cities and nobles to be wary of lawyers, especially clever ones like Blumenau, who had demonstrated that the League's expensively forged documents were not genuine.

The League's high-powered lawyer, Martin Mair (best known for his plans for imperial reform), was overmatched by the grandmaster's experts, Gregor Heimburg and Peter Knorr. Blumenau could dig into the order's extensive archive and come up with whatever document the experts needed, and the League's lawyers could not.

It was not long before this dispute came to the attention of Aeneas Silvius Piccolomini, the papal legate to the imperial court. Piccolomini remembered an evening years before at the Council of Basel, when he had listened entranced to a missionary's stories about life in Lithuania and the problems caused by the Teutonic Knights. He had more recently been working closely with the legate Louis de Silves. This moved him to become more involved.

Piccolomini was a spectacularly gifted scholar. One of eighteen children, he had attended the universities of Siena and Florence, where he mastered rhetoric, law and conversation, then advanced swiftly in the Church at the Council of Basel. His elevated style of composition transformed the way that Latin was spoken and written, so that those who continued to use old-fashioned Latin were soon sniggered at – this quickly led practical men and women to abandon Latin in favour of the languages spoken in their homeland.

As the 'Apostle of Humanism to the Germans', Piccolomini's efforts to impress the 'barbarians' made as many enemies as friends. Either he was unaware that his mail would be opened or he did not care. Perhaps he was just as happy to have his pen-portraits of his enemies distributed by his enemies. His ability to change his mind outraged the 'simple, honest' Germans, who quickly concluded that he was a shifty Italian, not to be trusted in any way.

Piccolomini's priority was to prevent churchmen from calling for another church council, thus repeating the challenge to papal authority that the Council of Basel had represented. Christendom needed leadership, not feuds. Reform was necessary, of course, but only such as would free churches and monasteries from secular control. As for financial reforms, no pope could be an effective force in the world if he lacked money.

At the same time Piccolomini had to protect those princes who were undermining the pope and emperor – without them there would be no effective government. This caused Piccolomini to oppose all leagues of cities and knights because they threatened to make the Holy Roman Empire totally impotent. If that happened, who could stop the advance of the Turks?

He worked diligently to persuade the emperor, the kings of Hungary and Poland, and the princes to support a new crusade in the Balkans. Since this meant stopping all wars in east-central Europe, Piccolomini gave the Prussian matter highest priority – a fortunate event for historians because his extensive narratives were full of details, insights and humour.

The fall of Constantinople in 1453 sent shock waves through Christendom, but the impact was felt especially among humanists, who reacted to stories of the destruction of ancient manuscripts with a fury that surpassed their horror at the fate of the citizens. No wonder that the foremost of the humanists, Aeneas Silvius Piccolomini, became a crusader. When he became Pope Pius II in 1458, he waxed eloquent over the fate of princes and virgins, but everyone understood that princes and virgins appear every generation, whereas a lost book of Greek literature would not.

Piccolomini's efforts to negotiate a just peace in Prussia were set back when someone ambushed the League's representatives and stole their papers. Then the Polish ambassador warned the imperial court that his master would not join any crusade if 'outsiders' interfered. This provoked such shouts from the Germans present, that Piccolomini had to postpone a decision.

Piccolomini's letter to Cardinal Oleśnicki in October 1453 illustrates well how he attempted to cajole, persuade and intimidate his listeners and readers. It was a masterpiece of eloquence, classical citations, wisdom and flattery:

> I am fully aware of the many ecclesiastical responsibilities of your office which involve not only yourself but the king, and that after him you by virtue of your rank as cardinal are the second most important man in Poland. I am also aware that decrees are not passed without your approval, that higher courts seek your opinion, and that plans for war and peace are not made without consulting you.

There was also bragging, irony and criticism of Polish efforts to seize the thrones of Hungary and Bohemia. By the time he concluded, his letter had, as Piccolomini put it, become a book; but the power of his style made it certain that the letter would be read by a far larger audience than the cardinal would have liked.

Piccolomini's speech to the *Reichstag* (the Imperial Diet) was among his greatest orations. As reported in his history, *De Pruthenorum origine*, he had said: 'This quarrel, most high Caesar, seems to me neither small nor contemptible ... It is not the fields of Arpinas or Tusculanus that are contested, but great provinces which are desired by a powerful king.' The speech persuaded the emperor to rule against the Prussian League.

The imperial edict left Louis of Erlichshausen with a dilemma – how to enforce the decision without agreeing that the Teutonic Order's Prussian possessions were henceforth in the Holy Roman Empire. In contrast, the German convents were willing to make any concession, if the emperor would give the German master more independence. Louis of Erlichshausen was not willing to allow that. Nor was Friedrich III going to become involved in a distant war. He was notoriously lazy and cautious, and he saw the safest path to success lay in producing heirs

('*Bella gerant alii, tu felix Austria nube*' – 'Let others wage war, you happy Austria marry'), and he was only recently married.

As for Piccolomini's crusade to recover Constantinople, that died with Pope Nicholas V in 1455. Nothing could be done before the next pope was elected, and then only if he believed the crusade was important. As it happened, the new pope, Calixtus III, believed strongly that the Turks had to be driven out of the Balkans, so much so that he made Piccolomini cardinal to lead the mobilisation. But a critical year had been lost.

The Thirteen Years War

The Prussian League acted before Louis of Erlichshausen could raise a mercenary army. Not having a large army of their own, the delegates turned to the king of Poland. Naturally, King Casimir welcomed their eagerness to become his subjects, though he was not ready to go to war at that moment.

Polish help was not necessary at first – the rebels easily captured Elbing, Danzig and Thorn, destroying fully or partially the order's castles. In Thorn they left only the mighty *Danzker*, a toilet facility, as a reminder that the Teutonic Knights once ruled there. Soon only Marienburg, Stuhm and Konitz were held by the grandmaster. The grandmaster's troubles provoked little rejoicing in Poland, where the nobles and clergy worried that once the king was master of Prussia, he would be so powerful that he could overawe them, too.

To Casimir's delight, the rebels' victories made it seem likely that the destruction of the Teutonic Order would be cheap, quick and total. Casimir rode through Prussia in a triumphal procession, cheered by the inhabitants of city and countryside, welcomed by mayors and nobles. As the Prussian League laid siege to Marienburg, the end of the Teutonic Knights as a territorial power seemed assured, a matter of days rather than months.

This did not happen because the German master had recruited 15,000 mercenaries from Saxony, Meissen, Austria, Bohemia and Silesia led by Duke Rudolf of Sagan (1414–54) and Bernard Szumborski (of Zinnenberg), a Moravian knight. The Bohemians were the finest troops in Europe, still enjoying the prestige won in the Hussite wars. Casimir sent a feudal levy from Great Poland to intercept them as they crossed into Prussia, but he had not reckoned on Heinrich Reuss of Plauen (c. 1400–70). When Plauen saw the two armies engaged in battle below his fortress at Konitz, with the Polish knights' assault on the wagon fort stymied, he sallied out and struck the royal army in the rear. The battle became a rout, hundreds drowning in a marsh, perhaps 3,000 left on the battlefield; about a hundred of the order's troops died, along with Rudolf of Sagan. The king wanted to fight on, a bravery that would have cost him the war and an enormous ransom, but his knights wisely led him away. Szumborski was captured in the initial cavalry battle, but was released by Plauen's men to take part in the pursuit; afterwards, he considered himself still a prisoner because he had given his parole. For the rest of the war he served as one of the grandmaster's most trusted officers.

Piccolomini's version was simpler: Casimir had wisely waited for the German attack to slow, then led a counter-charge that seemed to win the day until the king was unhorsed. At that the Poles panicked and fled.

In the months to follow, the grandmaster recaptured several towns that had gone over to the king. He was handicapped by the border with Lithuania being sealed so that neither messengers nor reinforcements from Livonia could cross.

On the other hand, Casimir could not afford to hire mercenaries because the Polish Diet refused to appropriate money; and his knights refused to extend their time of service long enough to accomplish anything – one raiding party spent more time collecting fodder than fighting, then retreated after some of the knights had frozen to death. The Prussian League, led by Danzig, taxed itself far more heavily than the grandmaster would have, but alone it could not force the grandmaster to yield.

As a result, the war became a complex mixture of local contests, with nobody able to prevent raids by the other side. The peasants were plundered by everyone, and trade suffered. The League's navy consisted of three vessels, but it defeated a larger Livonian–Danish fleet in August 1457 near the island of Bornholm in a night-time engagement, causing Denmark to pull out of the war. Otherwise, nothing changed.

Both sides levied heavy taxes and seized crops, but neither could pay its mercenaries. In desperation Erlichshausen pawned his cities and fortresses to his mercenaries, even Marienburg. When his efforts to extort more money from his remaining subjects failed, the best he could do was to make a partial payment on the enormous debt of 500,000 Hungarian ducats. This was sufficient to win a few minor military successes, but the mercenaries grew ever more worried that they would never see their back wages. When the grandmaster pointed to the League's difficulties – especially uprisings by the poor, bloodily repressed with royal assistance – they only became bolder in their demands. (Victory by either side meant unemployment.) In February 1457 Louis of Erlichshausen made one more partial payment, then promised, if he could not make more, he would allow them to sell the fortresses. Of course, the sum he now owed was beyond what could ever be paid.

At that moment the Danzig merchants demonstrated what resources a great city had; not even Denmark declaring war had hurt Danzig's trade – quite the contrary, Danzig had prospered. In contrast, though Casimir had got a subsidy from his Diet to purchase the castles, he had first needed to pay his own mercenaries, which took all that money.

The mercenaries sold Marienburg to Danzig for 190,000 ducats – part in cloth, beer and other commodities. Danzig transferred the fortress to Casimir when he granted privileges that improved the city's trade and political dominance. Meanwhile, the city council took Louis of Erlichshausen prisoner, transferred him to Konitz, and told him that he would be turned over to the king. Blumenau, who had eloquently told the mercenaries that their actions were 'against God, against justice, and against Holy Scripture', was beaten and thrown out the gate.

Then, just as it appeared the war had ended in a Polish victory, the grandmaster made a dramatic escape to Königsberg. That fortress was too far away for the League's army to reach, and the Polish king lacked the resources for a siege. Thereafter, Königsberg was the grandmaster's residence.

Cardinal Piccolomini then intervened, to deal with speculation about the impending demise of the bishop of Ermland. The Prussian League was hoping to elect a friendly successor, thereby tipping the balance of power. Three canons were in Danzig, six in exile in Silesia, and seven were prisoners of the grandmaster (an offence that had brought a papal excommunication). When Erlichshausen heard that the Silesian canons were proposing that the bishop retire on a pension so that they could elect a Polish under-chancellor, he sent the Ermland cantor, Bartholmaus Liebenwald, to Rome to speak with Piccolomini. Liebenwald was on his return journey when he learned that the bishop had died.

Liebenwald shared Piccolomini's advice to choose a person known both to the pope and the emperor, not the minor figures so far proposed, and then suggested that Piccolomini be elected. The six canons present agreed, sending Liebenwald back to Rome to announce their choice to Pope Calixtus III (Alfonso Borgia, 1378–1458). This was a pope who could not speak proper Latin, but who understood politics.

Calixtus confirmed Piccolomini's election and gave him full authority to arrange matters in Ermland and throughout Prussia as he wished. Of course, Piccolomini had too much to do in Rome to leave, and the pope was not in good health; so he gave Liebenwald detailed instructions and named him episcopal vicar with full authority to negotiate, to raise armies and to collect taxes. He wrote encouraging letters to the Polish king, urging Casimir to send a representative to Rome to negotiate a peace treaty. When the king remained unresponsive, the cardinal increased the pressure.

When the bishop of Culm died, the opposing sides sent their candidates to Rome. Piccolomini spoke on behalf of the Polish contender, only to have the pope refer the matter to a jurist, who then told Piccolomini to resolve the matter. Everyone believed that Piccolomini was behind the pope's action, but could not see what he was up to. The confusion was doubled when he refused a sizeable bribe. What was the world coming to when an Italian (and a churchman, to boot) wouldn't take a bribe?

One of the issues in doubt was whether he would require East Prussia to pay the tax known as Peter's Pence. Those lands had previously been exempt, even though the pope had always been in dire need of money. The tax had long been collected in West Prussia, a fact that Poles claimed was proof that it was part of their historic kingdom. However, since that tax had not been paid since 1450, West Prussia was under an interdict, with church services suspended.

This issue died in August 1458 when Piccolomini became Pope Pius II. He had no time for Prussian matters after that, but he kept the title of bishop of Ermland and sent an administrator to manage the diocese on his behalf. That administrator was first the grandmaster's ally, then neutral and finally a supporter of the League. His most important action was to make Ermland an independent territory from both the grandmaster and the king.

Piccolomini's career had been unusual for a man of letters, beginning as a reformer, then becoming a diplomat and author, and ending as a crusader. However, his long-planned expedition against the Turks proved a total disappointment. His small force was too ill-disciplined even to be put aboard the vessels that were to transport it from southern Italy to the Balkans. Nor could he persuade the mercenaries to obey orders. Unable to walk and ill, he died before he could send that motley army to its destruction. Thus, the proud Papacy of Pius II, the epitome of Renaissance Humanism, had begun its slow descent into its pre-Reformation squalor. Papal interest in Prussia was confined to demanding that all taxes be paid.

Meanwhile, nobody could pay the mercenaries in Prussia, not even Danzig. But letting the soldiers go simply turned them loose on the peasantry. Sometimes the unpaid soldiers claimed to be in the service of one side or the other, but sides did not matter; they were joined by bands of impoverished peasants who took what they needed from other villages through threats or force.

Making things worse, Danzig's fleet of privateers interrupted the grandmaster's trade with Denmark and harassed the coastlines of his remaining territories. This could not be endured for ever. Therefore, at the end of 1461 the grandmaster raised a small body of mercenaries and marched west. He was so successful against his exhausted enemy that he seemed likely to sweep its armies from the field. In response, the League gathered its forces at Danzig, paying its 2,000 mercenaries with new local taxes and a special tax that Casimir obtained from his knights by releasing them from the obligation to perform military service. This led to the only major battle of the war. Neither army was impressive – civic militias, dispossessed farmers, unruly mercenaries, and a handful of knights – but the Prussian League stood behind a wagon-fort and routed the army of the Teutonic Knights. Then, in the autumn of 1463 the League's navy destroyed the grandmaster's entire fleet.

Neither side rested, but each only became more exhausted. At last, in 1466, a papal legate, Rudolf of Rüdesheim (*c.* 1402–82), arranged a settlement that the grandmaster was too weak to reject.

The Second Peace of Thorn

The peace treaty 'returned' Pomerellia and Culm to the king of Poland and declared Ermland independent. The most important castles – Marienburg, Elbing and Christburg – went to Poland. In addition, Louis of Erlichshausen agreed to terms that he knew the emperor would cancel – to cut the military order's ties to the Holy Roman Empire, become a fief of the Polish crown, and accept up to half of its members from Polish subjects. Erlichshausen had established his residence in the marshal's quarters in the Königsberg castle, taking advantage of the marshal being a prisoner for a time in Poland. This fortress was not as impressive as Marienburg, but he improved its appearance as best he could. Real power, though, was soon held by the marshal, Heinrich Reuss of Plauen.

No one was happy with the treaty, but none felt strong enough to resume the war. Poland was the greatest victor: having got title to long-disputed territories, it had rendered the Teutonic Knights impotent. Danzig, the king's most loyal ally, had won its naval contest with the Hanseatic League; in the years ahead it would become richer and more powerful.

Erlichshausen's death the next year created an electorial crisis because it was difficult to bring representatives together. His nephew, Heinrich Reuss of Plauen, took charge. In 1469 he went to Casimir and swore to uphold the peace, but he refused to offer homage, arguing that this was incompatible with the historic commitments to pope and emperor. He suffered a stroke on the way home and died the next year. Nevertheless, he declared the treaty void, a violation of papal charters and harmful to the interests of the Church. Nor were Polish knights interested in joining the Teutonic Order. That provision of the treaty was a dead letter from the beginning.

Nevertheless, the next grandmaster, Heinrich Reffle of Richtenberg (1415–77), went to the Polish king right after his election to render homage. His successor, Martin Truchseß of Wetzhausen (c. 1435–89) swore that he would rather drown in blood than do so the same, but the year after his election, 1479, he offered personal homage – after managing to have his oath so carefully worded so as to apply only to himself, not to the Teutonic Order or its lands. Still, once Casimir had obtained the repeated submissions, the precedent would not be forgotten.

We know that Heinrich Reffle was no more successful than his predecessors in ending internal quarrels and curbing his officers. However, since the tradition of writing chronicles had deteriorated with the decline of the order, we are poorly informed about these years, except through the collected correspondence and foreign chroniclers.

The Thirteen Years War had resolved little. The cities were richer, the labourers poorer and a new land-owning class had come into being – mercenaries paid with confiscated fiefs replaced many native warriors and secular knights of German and Polish ancestry – but there was still dissatisfaction up and down the social scale. The Teutonic Knights were marking time, without an idea of what to do if an opportunity presented itself.

Poland had achieved its long-held dream of retaking lands lost in the thirteenth century – Culm, Pomerellia and Danzig – and now claimed Stolp and western Pomerania. Casimir had the opportunity to lay a new foundation for royal authority, basing it on the cities and gentry; but he did not extend this formula into Poland. This was as great a mistake as the one he made earlier by not taking Oleśnicki's advice to accept the concessions the grandmaster was offering.

Chapter 11

Lithuania, Poland and the Teutonic Order in the Late 1400s

A Changing World

Change sometimes rushes upon us, but more often it happens almost unnoticed. In east-central Europe it happened during a period when most historians have concentrated on events in France, England and Italy. Even Germany was beyond their vision until Luther appeared, hammer in hand, demanding reforms in the Church.

We are unfamiliar with many of the conventions that governed the lives of people then. The *estates*, for example, were always vividly conscious of their rights. Whether composed of nobles, ecclesiastics, burghers or peasants, each estate defended its traditional rights and privileges fiercely. At no time did they submit to abuses without complaint; and they hedged as many protections around traditionally acknowledged rights as they could. That characteristic can be seen in the widely recognised medieval practice of *Geleit*, the *salvus conductus* that we have seen violated in the case of Jan Hus. It is one example among many that illustrates the differences between those days and ours.

Geleit was an old and necessarily respected means of assuring that heralds and messengers could travel safely. Safe-conduct was so universally recognised that moral force alone was generally sufficient to guarantee compliance by every lawful authority. *Geleit* was given to those accused of crimes, allowing them to appear at hearings and to depart safely. But it could also apply to armies, travellers, merchants, pilgrims, clergy and Jews. In effect, it involved a wide range of customs and understandings, most unwritten but nevertheless internationally recognised.

A legal *Geleit* was impossible outside a highly structured format: the letter of invitation, listing the conditions, the time of validity, the roads to be travelled; the officials issuing the letter sometimes provided escorts; and occasionally diplomatically agreed-upon letters were the equivalents of treaties. All rested on a near-universal willingness to assist one another in the kinds of matters that every ruler had to deal with regularly, if not daily, and that every citizen could imagine being involved in at some future time. People there, in their time, determined to make life as safe and comfortable and convenient as possible, were constantly working out ways to overcome the obstacles that time, circumstance and personality present.

Tradition, as the song from *Fiddler on the Roof* indicates, is not immutable; but in east-central Europe, it is always important to remember that *change occurred in traditional ways.*

Poland

The reign of Casimir IV Jagiellon (king of Poland 1447–92) was a happy one for his kingdom, at least in the short run. Long-term royal authority decayed, bargained away year by year in return for immediate help from the nobility. The younger son of Jagiełło and Sophia, he had been reared from childhood to govern, but his inheriting the throne so young gave his advisers great power. He was a gentle man, one who disliked injustice or even impoliteness; but he was also duty-bound to do the best for his people, and he could persist in arguing for necessary policies longer than most people could resist. The outcome was usually a compromise of some kind. The Thirteen Years War was a long and expensive ordeal, and once it was over, Casimir found himself having to provide livings for six adult sons and five daughters.

In 1471 he managed to place Ladislas on the throne of Bohemia and he almost did the same for Casimir (1458–84) in Hungary, thanks to a claim through his mother, Anne of Austria. That having failed, the king waited for his son to attain his majority, then began to assign him ever-more demanding tasks. The son was not only able, but he lived a remarkably ascetic existence. Encouraged by Długosz, who was a canon in Oleśnicki's church, he even wore a hair shirt underneath his robes. As a result, immediately after his untimely death, he was proposed for canonisation. In 1520, St Casimir entered the calendar of saints. He became the patron saint of Poland and Lithuania.

Casimir IV married all his daughters to German princes, and Jan Olbrecht (1459–1501), Alexander Jagiellon (1461–1506), and Sigismund the Old (1467–1548) were to succeed him, and Fryderyk (Friedrich, 1468–1503) entered the church. His eldest son, Ladislas (Vladislaus, 1456–1516) became king of Hungary and Bohemia. As time passed, Casimir spent more and more time in Lithuania, seeking to defend its eastern lands against Basil II and Ivan III (the Great, 1440–1505). He was utterly unable to persuade the Polish Diet of the seriousness of the situation.

Royal authority eroded slowly. The basic problem was geographic. First of all, the plains in Poland and Lithuania were made for horses, for grazing animals and for grain production; but they lacked sufficient variety to stimulate internal trade. With the population too thinly spread to sustain a market, and overland transport expensive, whatever was produced locally was more costly and of lower quality than goods produced abroad.

The nobles happily rusticated on their estates; they could earn a modest profit selling grain for export if they could prevent their peasants from moving away. But since peasants persisted in wanting to better their lot, the nobles exploited every opportunity to make them serfs. Wealthy farmers, tradesmen, artisans and village managers, recognising the trend towards social degradation, took advantage of the still fluid class system to have themselves classified as gentry. Minor gentry, to be sure. Moneyless gentry, perhaps. Later, to maintain their pretensions to noble status, their descendants took care not to involve themselves in any occupation other than war and government service; and except for the offices at the top, those occupations often paid poorly.

Boasting that they lived by the motto, *nothing new*, Poland's nobles looked back with pride on several pasts: one that never existed, of a golden age of peace and contentment, when a special race of nobles, the semi-mythical Sarmatians, ran the nation without clergy and foreign monarchs; a past which consisted of military victories (most prominently, Tannenberg); and a past based on the glories of the Piast and Angevin dynasties, when the court in Cracow was aglitter with chivalry, poetry and music.

Attitudes that today would be considered racist were based on class rather than skin colour. Birth was destiny. It was the way life was. Religious thought concentrated more on the attainable hereafter than on the elusive justice of the here and now.

The Polish Church's contribution to national interests was mixed. Of course, the Church paid no taxes. The Church collected the tithe, 10 per cent of every income (with the exception of exempted nobles), and it determined how this was spent. Equally true, the archbishop of Gniezno and his subordinates, especially the bishop of Cracow, could raise large forces of men for the royal service when they chose to do so and when the Diet required it. These men spoke in the royal council with powerful voices. Not only were they heavily endowed with men and money, but also the process of advancement in the Church was more rigorous than in the secular nobility, so that only men of talent with strong personalities reached the highest offices.

The king, whose principal advantage was that he was raised as royalty and therefore developed early and instinctively the habit of command, was limited by age and experience in his knowledge of the real world, spoiled by nursemaids and courtiers, seduced by fawning flatterers and flunkies, misled by scheming advisers, and distracted by women who wished to be known for having made the conquest of a monarch. The limitations of natural talent were circumscribed further by insufficient income, most of which was spent in maintaining the court, the castles and palaces, and the army. About the only tax that the king could count on receiving directly was that paid by the Jews, who were protected as a royal resource (and were, therefore, unpopular). The king's so-called regalian rights (land, mines, market rights and tolls) could be collected only by sharing the income with the nobles who acted as tax-farmers. Occasionally, extraordinary taxes could be raised for war, a dowry or a wedding. Service obligations, such as military duty, building fortifications, repairing roads, and so forth, helped reduce the need to spend money on important projects, but they brought in little income. Even though the king and his councillors never had the funds to carry out properly all the policies they thought important, those who paid the taxes always said that the exactions were too great (and most likely they were); and when hard times made paying the royal contribution hard, the term 'tax revolt' came to have more than its modern symbolic meaning.

The foregoing notwithstanding, this was a golden age for Poland in many ways. The frontiers were secure. Internal peace was maintained. Humanism took root in Poland, never to die out.

The four fountainheads of Polish humanism were Italy, the Jagiellonian University, the Church, and the royal court. Students were flocking like crows to Cracow, their black gowns flapping, to study at the small but proud new university, after which the best (or best-connected) went to Italy for master's degrees and doctorates in law and theology, then took up careers in the ecclesiastical and secular bureaucracies. Every bishop, every royal official, was on the lookout for talented young men who could make their ramshackle administrative systems function.

Latin made the administration of a multi-ethnic commonwealth possible. Though this posed a problem for parts of the grand duchy, where Church Slavonic had long served as the language of record, everywhere else it meant that an individual's origin was of less significance than the ability to write correctly in Latin. (Hence, the importance of studying in Italy, where the rough and tumble Latin of the episcopal school or the parish priest's instruction could be refined into polished, elegant language.) In addition, one was expected now to know mythology, art, music and the new sciences – especially astrology.

The most important chronicler of the era, Jan Długosz, had a prag-
matic pre-Renaissance attitude that history should serve the kingdom.
An educated man or woman had to know history, but unlike in Italy,
where the vernacular was supplanting Latin, in multi-national Poland
the elite read his Latin chronicle to learn the stories of their national
struggles against Germans, Tatars and other foreigners, including
Lithuanians This infuriated some Lithuanian nobles, but fewer every
generation, as they were steadily Polonised.

It was not even necessary to know Polish well. Every educated
person has heard of a nephew of the bishop of Ermland who learned
Polish well enough to converse in it, just as he probably learned some
Italian while studying mathematics in Italy; but he wrote in Latin and
followed the humanist tradition of latinising his name – Kopernik to
Copernicus. More importantly, to conduct business as an Ermland
canon, he had to know Low and High German. He always thought of
himself as a Prussian. Nevertheless, he is celebrated as one of Poland's
greatest contributions to European culture.

The upper classes of Poland and Lithuania sensed that Renaissance
humanism was something considerably more important than a means
of following the Mass or participating in the occasional meeting of
international notables. They had their sons and daughters instructed
in Latin and the liberal arts by first-class tutors because the vision of
the Ancient Roman Republic led by patrician patriots appealed to the
innermost reaches of their souls.

Lithuania

There was a remarkable amount of westernisation occurring, but
not always in the same way or at the same time. Christianisation (in
1386) had made this possible, but it became important only a century
later. That delay was largely because the vast majority of the duchy's
population was Ruśian and Orthodox, mistrustful of a Roman Catholic
Church dominated by Poles.

The Church naturally strove to convert nobles by offering legal
privileges and swifter advancement at court; in addition, kings later
discriminated against Orthodox nobles as a means of gathering
authority in their own hands. The Lithuanian noble class began to
resemble the magnates and knights associated with Cracow: in 1432
and 1434 they received charters giving Orthodox boyars equal rights
with Roman Catholics; in 1447 all nobles received immunity from
taxes and duties; and they began to meet in a General Diet designed
on the Polish model.

The establishment of a Uniate Church in 1458 was the foundation stone of the new Lithuanian state. By combining Orthodox rituals and the use of the traditional church language with a recognition of the supremacy of the pope and actions of western church councils, the prelates sought to avoid offending parishioners, priests and bishops while persuading western clergymen that the compromises were no greater than those allowed the moderate Hussites.

They hoped that these concessions would dampen religious controversy at a time when all Christians needed to stand together against the Turkish sultan and his Tatar allies. Even as Orthodoxy experienced a mighty revival in Moscow, that did not greatly affect the bishoprics in the Polish–Lithuanian state. The spread of the Uniate Church remained slow – even into the sixteenth century the majority of churches in Lithuania were Orthodox. That was true even in strongholds of Roman Catholicism such as Vilnius. Moreover, the speed by which sixteenth-century Lithuanian magnates took to religious innovations such as Calvinism suggests that all was not well in the Lithuanian Church.

Westernisation confined to the nobility and the Church would have been of little importance if it had not been accompanied by economic changes in the countryside and the towns. Large towns existed already, but we tend to mark their acquisition of 'German law' as a sign that a western mercantile presence had become important.

Vilnius received Magdeburg law in 1387, Brest in 1390. Within a short time there were forty towns and 400 smaller towns in the territory of modern Belarus alone. Vilnius became a more important centre of commercial and administrative activity, with weekly markets and two annual fairs. The royal residence and the cathedral in the upper and lower castles were strongly fortified, but the rest of the city had no wall. Nevertheless, there was constant construction under way: a city hall, new churches, *Kontors* (a combination storehouse and dwelling) for the Ruśian and German merchants, brick residences, mercantile houses and guildhalls. Weavers, brewers, and a wide range of artisans prospered.

The first wall around Vilnius was begun in 1503, when Tatar raiders in Moscow's service were coming too close to ignore. To a great extent the urban citizenry had little in common with the rural population: they were immigrants, to a great extent German and Jewish, some Poles and Russians (as we can call them now that Moscow was the dominant state), a handful of Tatars. By Lithuanian tradition and now Magdeburg law as well, they were self-governing.

The nobles, meanwhile, were undergoing Polonisation. That implied not just speaking Polish and wearing western dress (though westerners found it remarkably exotic – to their eyes it was a mixture of Russian and Turkish), but also adopting the attitudes of the Polish landowners: resisting royal authority wherever possible and exalting a life based on the chase, expensive entertainment and the chivalric gesture; and, as often happens in the case of massive inferiority complexes, demanding equality with their Polish models. The Lithuanian and Russian peasantry were expected to pay for it all.

Samogitians, meanwhile, were emigrating to Prussia, beginning that long process which settled the coastal lands once inhabited by Kurs, then depopulated by war.

In the meantime, sweeping changes were taking place in Moscow. The passing of Basil II brought to power his son Ivan III. A ruler of great ability and even greater good fortune, he was able to marry a niece of the last Byzantine emperor and thereby solidify the loyalty of the Orthodox Church. He defeated the Tatars, occupied Novgorod, and established traditions which later characterised the grand dukes' administration – extensive rights for the boyars, limited authority of the *Duma* (parliament), and encouragement of trade and commerce.

As Lithuanian boyars realised that the balance of power was shifting, some calculated that they could retain their estates only by making a timely change of loyalties. Since many of them were Orthodox Christians uneasy with Roman Catholicism, their defections seemed doubly justified.

The dilemma for Poland–Lithuania was basic: if the state was to be unified, there was a pressing need for religious unity. But every effort at creating this unity was denounced by both western and eastern churchmen and by their publics. While Poland was widely considered the most tolerant state in Christendom, efforts to convert the Jewish congregations persisted. In addition, there were extremes of wealth and poverty, ethnic rivalries and family ambitions. In short, there was no shortage of contradictions that made it difficult to achieve national unity.

When Ivan III began to chip away at the edges of the Lithuanian grand duchy, Casimir was required to spend more time there; after 1479, in fact, he was in Lithuania more than in Poland. Realising that he could not persuade the Diet to vote funds for war, and finding his personal revenues insufficient to pay an army, he started to look for ways to bypass the constitutional obstacles. He began to consolidate administrative districts along the eastern frontier, taking advantage of the demise of office-holders to replace magnates with his own officials.

The success he was having led to an assassination attempt in 1481. This warned the king that little loyalty could be found among some of his most important vassals. In the years to come, the defection of key officials to Moscow would unravel the eastern portion of the Lithuanian state. The causes of these 'betrayals' were various. They were often personal, but more often a result of having seriously analysed the declining fortunes of Lithuania compared to the rising ones of Moscow. Personal reasons ranged from dissatisfaction with a wife to religious zeal, from hatred of a brother to ambition for wealth and fame, from escaping punishment for crime to a lack of fear of being captured. All contributed to the authority of the state slipping away. Casimir maintained the peace, but at great cost; ultimately, that cost had to be paid.

When the Golden Horde collapsed, it was replaced by new confederations in the Crimea and north of the Caspian Sea. But as far as Lithuania and Poland were concerned, little changed – the new khans continued to gather human merchandise from their lands and sell the captives to the Turks. Casimir's reaction was to negotiate, but he was no more successful with the khans than he had been with the nobility of Lithuania and Poland.

The decisive blow against the Crimean Tatars had actually been struck earlier, in 1475, by the Moldavian prince Stephen the Great (1433/40–1504), who was loosely associated with the ruler of Wallachia, Vlad the Impaler (*c.* 1395–1476) – better known as Dracula (and whose inflated reputation was explained by Matei Cazacu as an imperial effort to blame him for the failure of a crusade, while the Hungarian king pocketed the money the pope had sent). It was a tough corner of the Balkans, as more Polish kings would learn.

The sultan had reacted by sending Turkish forces to supervise the khan and to protect Muslim interests in the region. Henceforth, Polish–Lithuanian armies had to contend more with Turks than with Tatars. Christian and Muslim rulers alike faced awful choices in protecting their subjects: financing the war machine required either the regular collection of tribute, or booty or taxes, and services from the peasantry. That made these frontier societies 'predatory', draining the lifeblood of farmers and herders to support military elites. Whether these elites were professionals or aristocrats, they expected that they would be properly remunerated in money and honours for the risks they took and the efforts they made.

However deplorable that was, no state facing the steppe or the Balkans could do without a military elite. Rulers had to support warriors in some way, and the invasion of enemy lands brought in cattle, slaves and nobles for ransom, while deaths in battle culled the number of men who expected payment for their services. Once having created an effective warrior class, the rulers then had to find ways to assure loyalty and enthusiasm. Ideological purity was as good a test for loyalty as could be found, but that had the further result of intensifying the warfare along the frontier.

The Priests' War

The minor conflict that in 1471 grew into a war originated in a disputed election in Ermland. The very name, *Pfaffenkrieg* (War of the Priests) implies a pseudo-serious quarrel among somewhat disreputable clerics. That indeed was the origin of this serio-comic war: the Ermland canons rejected Bishop Vincenz Kielbasa of Culm – his name prompting humorists to call this the 'sausage war' – and elected Nicholas of Tungen (Thüngen) as bishop. Kielbasa persuaded King Casimir to support him, while Grandmaster Richtenberg backed his rival.

Tungen employed an army of Hungarian mercenaries to drive Kielbasa from the diocese, while the order's marshal raised knights and peasants who were quickly routed by unruly mercenaries brought in for a separate feud. By the time Casimir intervened, the diocese had been ravaged.

Grandmaster Richtenberg next found himself in a prolonged dispute with the bishop of Samland,undermanned Dietrich de Cuba, over who was sovereign in his lands. Since the bishop was a priest of the Teutonic Order, Richtenberg felt justified in imprisoning him, and he showed no remorse when the bishop starved to death. As a result of these two conflicts, Casimir came to believe that the grandmaster was plotting against him. He resolved to keep an eye on him.

The next crisis originated in a failed political intrigue. In early 1477 the grandmaster had signed a treaty of friendship with Matthias Corvinus of Hungary, sending Martin Truchseß of Wetzhausen to discuss the implementation of the treaty's terms. Some of Truchseß's correspondence was intercepted by Polish officials, who informed the king that the Teutonic Order had committed itself to tying down Polish forces if he went to war with Hungary over possession of Bohemia; the king then made a personal inspection trip to Marienburg to see that it was in defensible condition.

Grandmaster Richtenberg died in early 1477. His piety, strict discipline and parsimony were doubted by none. His efforts to balance expenditures with incomes and to encourage commerce were conceded to be well-intentioned; but no one credited him with having turned the fortunes of the order around. The grand chapter met in August to select Martin Truchseß as his successor. Truchseß was a Franconian noble who had distinguished himself in diplomacy and administration, which meant that if he had not done as well as hoped, he had at least done better than anyone else. He now hoped to exploit West Prussian dissatisfaction with Casimir to reunify the country.

True to his promise to the assembled knights and priests at the time of his election, Wetzhausen refused to give the oath of personal homage to Casimir. He gave as grounds the papal legate's excommunication of Casimir and his son Ladislas of Bohemia, for interfering with the crusade against the Turks. However, once Casimir had made peace with Matthias Corvinus and the Emperor Friedrich III, he summoned the grandmaster to attend court and perform the act of homage. Wetzhausen's response was to ride out of Königsberg and hide on the frontier so that the Polish heralds could not deliver the summons. Of course, the king was not to be put off so easily. Wetzhausen had to comply.

As for the pope, Casimir did more than ignore the excommunication. Having determined that Sixtus IV (1414–84, pope from 1471) was an immoral thug and bully, he threatened to break with the Papacy and establish a national church. Sixtus IV backed down.

Royal Prussia

By tradition, the Polish kingdom allowed great autonomy to its various regions. That won the king the loyalty of the citizens and secular knights in Royal Prussia, but they still remained as fearful of a strong king as the Polish Diet. Only after the grandmaster had openly joined the king's enemies in 1478 did Casimir ask the Prussian estates for aid in crushing the military order once more.

Once an army was raised, it did not take Casimir long to capture the grandmaster's undermanned castles in Pomesania and Ermland. The conflict came quickly to an end, and in the summer and autumn of 1479 Bishop Nicholas of Tungen and Grandmaster Wetzhausen respectively prostrated themselves at the king's feet. It was the most humiliating moment in the history of Teutonic Order.

Restructuring Trade and Politics

King Casimir still did not know how to make East Prussia a part of his kingdom. The Teutonic Order, as a religious organisation responsible to the Holy Roman Empire and the Holy Father, could not submit to a secular monarchy.

More pressing was the restoration of the economy in the regions devastated by the Thirteen Years War. In 1464, for example, an epidemic had swept through the land, reputedly killing 20,000 people in Danzig alone. Although we must be sceptical about any numbers cited in this era, there is little doubt that many died.

The response to this was exactly that which had been done in past epidemics: prayers for the dead, penance for the living, food for the hungry, homes for the orphans, provision for 'fallen women' who had taken to prostitution to escape starvation, laws to protect the purity of the food and water, and more prayers. Cajoled, inspired and bullied by the local bishops who led the way by personal action, communities cared for the many unfortunates – the blind, the ill, the physically and mentally handicapped. Every town was to have a hostel for *Béguines* (for women) and another for *Beghards* (men), and the guilds accepted responsibilities for one essential service or another, until each category of needy persons had somebody responsible for seeing to its welfare.

Fortunately, the grain trade was stimulated by the new connection with Poland. Each year over a hundred ships left Danzig laden with grain. So much wool was exported that Poland suffered shortages, and shipments of lumber, wax and honey (all traditional Baltic products) grew in importance. This stimulated local commerce. The annual autumn fairs expanded to include spring and summer fairs, offering year-around opportunities to entirely new groups of entrepreneurs – entertainers, prostitutes and thieves – as well as merchants.

There was a fundamental restructuring of trade in the Baltic, with English competitors becoming first tolerated, then important in Danzig's ever more ambitious trade network. Many-sided trade wars continued, with frequent embargoes and unofficial acts of war, as merchant communities and monarchs sought to retain, extend and restrict commercial advantages.

Order Prussia

The Thirteen Years War had ended what little hope the Teutonic Knights had of recovery; even the memory of past greatness was fading. There was little money to hire mercenaries, not even enough for the grandmaster's regular expenses. In desperation each grandmaster sold offices (under the usual subterfuges); and one needs only to glance at the debased coins of this era to see that the financial situation was not good. Many secular knights and gentry were bankrupted as well, or dispossessed; their lands were taken by mercenary officers in lieu of back wages. Many free farmers had to seek new homes or take up work under new labour conditions, practically as serfs.

Many villages that had been laid waste were resettled by immigrants brought from Poland and Germany. Dispersed native Prussians found it difficult to maintain their ancestral tongue amid the German- and Polish-speaking majorities; within a few generations Old Prussian was practically a lost language.

The agrarian crisis drove this assimilation. As farm workers fled the countryside, the managers of estates demanded that steps be taken to keep the labourers in the fields. With serfdom not encouraged, the best alternative was to forbid anyone who did not speak German from moving into the towns, migrating to other villages, or taking up employment as artisans, tavern-keepers or servants. Such was the law by 1474; as the years passed, new rules were applied to unemployed Germans as well as native Prussians.

Just as in Poland, Latin flourished among the educated elite. Students from Prussia went to Italy, then returned to work for the grandmaster, the bishops and the city councils. The prince-bishop of Ermland was important in cultural and educational life, but also in politics as a royal adviser. Lucas of Watzenrode (1447–1512), perhaps the most prominent figure ever to hold the Ermland see, saw to it that his nephew, Nicolaus Copernicus (1473–1543), received a good education in Cracow and Italy, then found employment in his bureaucracy.

The common people lost faith in progress. Local chroniclers, who had always been so proud of the order's achievements, even its defeats, were now reduced to recording homilies such as that concerning two peasants who had gone out to work on St Lawrence's Day. When the time to go home for a rest came, one began greedily to eat a piece of cheese. The other chided him, saying that it was a fast day. The first responded, 'Lawrence here, Lawrence there; I can't go hungry, I have to work, and therefore I must eat.' Immediately, he fell down, choking on the cheese, and died. That anecdote received almost as much space in the chronicle as did the Polish invasion of 1478.

The knights of the order did little better. When Count Heinrich of Tübingen fell severely ill in 1472, he left Prussia to return home; when he recovered he became what was called a *Rentenjäger*, going from job to job, wherever his skills were in demand. Other knights left their posts to seek employment that paid regularly and offered a modicum of orderliness and pride in what they were doing.

Imperial pressure increased: Friedrich III referred routinely but unofficially to Prussia as a part of the Holy Roman Empire; in 1488 he persuaded the German master to place his region under imperial jurisdiction. Nevertheless, the grandmasters stubbornly refused. They continued to press the curia in Rome and the court in Wiener-Neustadt for moral support, their friends in Germany for money and soldiers, and their members to pray fervently for divine intervention against their enemies, but they insisted on remaining independent.

When Jan Olbrecht became king of Poland in 1492, the question of succession was complicated. His elder brother Ladislas was already king of Hungary and Bohemia, and there was little enthusiasm beyond personal ambition to create a gigantic central European monarchy. Even union with Lithuania was too ambitious – that great land went to his younger brother Alexander Jagiellon. As grand duke, Alexander thought the best way he could preserve his lands intact was to marry the daughter of Ivan III, Elena, but this was ineffective in eliminating defections. His wife even demanded a new Orthodox church to worship in – a request he refused – and his father-in-law wanted to be called the *sovereign of all Russia*. It was a difficult balancing act.

The Moldavian War

The Polish kings had long proposed resettling the Teutonic Knights on the Danube frontier, to protect Poland and Hungary from the Turks. But the Teutonic Order had become a landlord organisation, and the knights were not willing to exchange their possessions for a risky venture in the Balkans, even if the king had made a truly generous proposal.

The situation along the Black Sea shore had deteriorated badly. In 1484 the Ottomans had taken Akkerman, a strongly fortified port, and deported all of its 20,000 surviving citizens; soon the entire coastline was in the sultan's hands. Stephen the Great had called for Hungarian help, only to be told that the king had signed a truce with the sultan that did not cover Moldavia. Stephen turned to Casimir in 1485, rendering homage, then paying tribute to the sultan. Marrying a daughter to Ivan III's eldest son was further evidence of his growing political importance.

The sudden and unexpected death of King Matthias Hunyady in 1490 brought even more sweeping changes to the region. The Hungarian magnates rejected every candidate who threatened their ambition to dominate the government. They finally selected Ladislas of Bohemia, who was known as Ladislas the Good for saying '*dobze*' ('good') every time he was presented a document to sign without reading it. The magnificent Black Army of mercenaries was allowed to deteriorate, the Renaissance art collection was sold, and border fortifications were neglected. This created a political vacuum that drew Casimir IV farther into Moldavia, then Jan Olbrecht, as Pilat and Cristea illustrate in *The Ottoman Threat*. Until then the principal Polish interest had been to fight the Tatars.

In late 1496 Jan Olbrecht summoned Grandmaster Johann of Tiefen to participate in a campaign against Islam. Tiefen was of such obscure birth that no one today can even guess where he was from beyond the general area of Switzerland. He knew that his knights did not have their hearts in this project, and he shrank from the cost of taking a properly equipped army such a long distance. Moreover, the summer heat would be hard for men and beasts used to breathing Baltic Sea air. Nevertheless, the aged grandmaster set out with his small force for Galicia where the royal army was assembling.

We know from studies of medieval burials how a lifetime spent in the saddle while wearing armour wore down the bones and muscles. Every aged knight of the Teutonic Order must have suffered arthritis, especially the more painful osteoarthritis affecting joints in the limbs and the back. Their diet did not help, leading as it did to corpulence, stomach pains and gout. Past popes had relaxed the rules from time to time, allowing some officers to eat eggs during the long fasts that were part of Christian observance at the time. But it was a hard life, and war was for young men.

When Tiefen set out, he did not even know which enemy he would face. Military secrecy was strictly enforced by the Polish leaders (especially in the presence of vassals who could not be trusted, foremost of whom would have been the grandmaster). Still, no one could be prevented from making educated guesses.

Probably they expected to attack the Tatars, who had been more active in recent years and because Alexander might have planned a Christian coalition of Poland, Lithuania and Moscow. Lastly, if the king could advance into the Crimea, he would deliver a devastating blow that would be of more significance than ever so many skirmishes on the steppe. In attacking cities and fortifications the Christians would have as significant an advantage as the Tatars had on the rolling prairie.

As it happened, the Lithuanians were reluctant to cross the steppe to the Tatar homeland. Better to capture a port on the Black Sea, a feasible objective that would benefit every Christian state by making trade easier and less expensive; but better yet, to protect the flanks of the Polish army, but not contribute forces to the royal array. The ruler most affected by the campaign, Stephen the Great of Moldavia, was not eager to find himself in the middle of a Polish and Ottoman war.

Moreover, Ladislas Jagiellon – Jan Olbrecht's elder brother – opposed the plan. The Hungarian nobles were, for the moment, violently anti-Polish, fearing that the Polish king would resume the southward advance abandoned after Varna. Religious feelings were also divisive since most Moldavians were Orthodox Christians, and the Poles expected them to respond to papal directives.

Jan Olbrecht gave no indication of what he intended. He kept his own counsel, both as to his goals and his motives until the army was assembled. Then he directed his forces against Stephen of Moldavia. It may be that he intended to make his brother Sigismund king there; in any case, when Stephen heard that rumour, he called for Hungarian assistance.

Grandmaster Tiefen fell deathly ill in Halych, angry at being treated like a mercenary of little value, ignored by the king and his inner circle, but he was unwilling to return home alone and entrust his men to royal command. In the end, he allowed himself to be taken back to Lwów. With his dying breath he sent a message to the king, begging him to send his knights home so that they could hasten to the aid of the Livonian Order. In vain. The king said that he needed every man.

The royal host, perhaps 40,000 warriors, besieged the Moldavian capital briefly and without success, until it was surrounded by Moldavian and Ottoman forces. Rescue came in the form of an ambassador Ladislas had sent from Prague – he negotiated a truce that allowed the Poles a safe exit from the country. However, Jan Olbrecht decided to take a different route home than the one agreed on to seek pastures that had not been burned over. The king passed through the woods without trouble, but his rearguard was ambushed by Hungarians and Wallachians. The king turned back to rescue his men but found that heavily armed knights were poorly equipped for that kind of fight.

The degree to which the Polish army suffered may have been exaggerated by the king's critics, but it was severe. When the Polish cavalry reached the steppe, it found that the grass there, too, had been burned ahead of them. Rumours of dreadful losses during the march became folklore, and years later passers-by reportedly saw high mounds where the dead had been buried. Those who made it home alive owed their salvation to the Lithuanians sent by Alexander who held the crossing of the Prut River for them.

The Teutonic Knights lost several of their 400 horsemen in the rout; those who escaped lost all their equipment, tents and supplies, and returned home in scattered small bodies, never having managed to regroup into a fighting unit. That was the greatest effort made to involve the military order in the Polish campaigns against the Turks. Thereafter, Prussian participation was practically nonexistent.

Jan Olbrecht's defeat was followed by others. Tatars fell on the unprotected frontier; Turks crossed into Poland for the first time; the Holy Roman Emperor Maximilian (1459–1519), seized parts of Silesia; and the grand duke of Moscow advanced into Lithuania. The new grandmaster took advantage of the confusion to refuse to perform homage. A few years later, the king's brother, Fryderyk, who had been bishop of Cracow, then in 1489 a candidate for the bishopric of Ermland, became archbishop of Gniezno and a cardinal. He died during a virulent epidemic of syphilis. Jan Olbrecht suffered from it too.

The king died in 1501 without children; if he had lived or sired an heir, the connection with Lithuania might have been dissolved for ever. Instead, Alexander succeeded him, reuniting the two states in his own person. Alexander had already made such concessions to the Lithuanian magnates that he was happy to hurry to Cracow, where some semblance of authority still remained. His loss of authority in Lithuania was such that he could barely raise an army when war with Moscow came in 1500. After suffering a seemingly decisive defeat, he was then overwhelmed by a Tatar invasion. Subsequently, there were more defections among his principal vassals.

Alexander was saved by an alliance with the Livonian master, Wolter of Plettenberg (1450–1535). At the time the alliance had seemed almost irrelevant because the Livonian Knights had long been unable to govern either themselves or their country, and almost nobody expected them to win a battle against the grand duke of Moscow, Ivan the Great. Nevertheless, in 1501 Wolter of Plettenberg employed a modern army of *Landsknechts* (infantry with long spears fighting in a phalanx) supported by heavy cavalry and cannon fire to bleed the Russian army, then in 1502 defeated it again at Pskov. That allowed Alexander to concentrate on driving back the Tatars in the south.

The alliance of the Livonian Order and the Lithuanians made the former enemies almost friends; in common they had their Roman Catholic faith and Orthodox enemies. At home Alexander did less well. Even after becoming king of Poland in 1501, he never succeeded in persuading his Polish magnates to commit themselves to long and expensive campaigns in the east, nor could he interest them in forging closer ties with the Uniate Church. They considered their wars with the Turks quite a sufficient undertaking for one kingdom.

Friedrich of Saxony

The Teutonic Knights sought to counter Polish claims to sovereignty over their lands by seeking a connection with a nearby German state. They reasoned that if they chose a younger son of a powerful elector as grandmaster, especially one with a strong personality, his independent wealth would allow him to overawe the dissidents in the order and the unruly subjects in Prussia, after which he could talk with the king as an equal.

Already before Tiefen's death his officers had decided to elect Friedrich of Saxony (1473–1510) as his successor. His father, Duke Albrecht (1443–1500, founder of the Albertine line of Saxon dukes), was high in the counsels of the emperor. His mother was the daughter of King George of Podiebrady of Bohemia (Jiří z Poděbrad, 1420–71). Friedrich was thus related to everyone of importance; and his brother George had married Barbara Jagiellon, a sister of the Polish king. Friedrich was not obtained cheaply, however – provision had to be made for an income suitable to his station. When that was assured, the 25-year-old prince went to the emperor in Ulm, where he was dubbed a knight and accepted into the order by the German master. Subsequently, Maximilian said that the ceremony had confirmed that Prussia was in the Holy Roman Empire, a claim that Friedrich quietly declined to acknowledge. In late 1498 the Saxon prince went to Prussia to be installed in office.

He was lucky in his timing. Jan Olbrecht could not act immediately to punish Friedrich for his declaration of independence, and when in 1501 the king finally raised an army and put it into motion northward, he was struck by a paralytic stroke during a ceremony in Thorn and died soon afterwards. His heir, Alexander, abandoned his campaign against Moscow and hastened to Poland, there to accept such restrictions on his authority that his reign is generally considered to be a royal disaster. Unable to persuade the new grandmaster to come to Poland and render the oath of homage, he appealed to the pope. Julius II (Giuliano della Rovere, 1443–1513) surprisingly sent an order to Grandmaster Friedrich to hasten to the king and perform homage. However, Rome was far away and the king of Poland temporarily weak. The new grandmaster ignored both of them.

Friedrich had grand ideas which he set into effect in the next years. Everything was reorganised on the Saxon pattern: defence, justice, taxes. Fewer knights were inducted into the order now because their duties were being performed by secular bureaucrats. In reorganising his state, Friedrich was remaking Prussia along contemporary German lines. Old practices, such as making ad hoc decisions or relying on local traditions that varied from place to place, were slowly abandoned.

The grandmaster oversaw the creation of a truly representative *Ständetag* (diet, parliament). The Ordinance of 1506 created a supreme council (*Hofgericht*) consisting of the prelates and four representatives each from the Teutonic Order, the secular nobles and the burghers. Other similar but lesser councils and courts made the citizens co-responsible for all decisions and for carrying them out. Of such responsibilities comes a willingness to share sacrifices and to moderate self-interest for the greater good of the whole. In short, patriotism.

That programme envisioned an essentially secular state, retaining the form of a religious order. It would remain an honourable place for surplus sons, one that offered a comfortable life – good meals, hunting and drinking. At its centre was a single set of administrative procedures and regulations that eliminated much of the unpredictability and unfairness from the old system – simple enough for subjects to understand and predictable enough to know that one was being treated fairly. Its foreign policy ignored traditional obligations when they were suicidal and paid nothing more than lip service to national and religious goals. Within a few years, while Poland was fighting the Turks in Wallachia, desperately attempting to reverse the progress of the crescent banner northward, the Teutonic Order was allying itself with Moscow!

That surprising development had been strongly encouraged by Emperor Friedrich III, whose complex reasoning had led to an alliance with Ivan III to keep Poland occupied while he made war against France. The grandmaster's advisers were slow to realise that imperial policy had changed, as well they might, because the emperor was not one to explain what his true goals were. As late as 1501 Moscow had still been the principal enemy of the Livonian Order, with Prussian knights fighting alongside Roman Catholic Lithuania against the Orthodox foe. A few years later, when Friedrich of Saxony understood better what was expected of him, he accepted financial subsidies from Moscow that would allow him to defy the wishes of the king of Poland. The grandmaster now legitimately claimed to be too ill to travel to Cracow to offer homage. In 1507 he returned to Saxony, where he died three years later.

Brandenburg

In recent decades the Hohenzollern dynasty had begun to make something of the sparsely populated region that Friedrich I had purchased in 1415. They had subdued the towns, established control over the bishoprics and installed a more efficient administrative system; they had gained an elector's vote in the Holy Roman Empire, though that title was becoming ever less important.

Friedrich II of Hohenzollern, once the intended spouse of Jadwiga of Poland, had expected to rule all Poland. After her sudden death, he never recovered emotionally. He returned to Brandenburg and concentrated on raising that land from its traditional poverty. In time he purchased small territories in the Lausitz and in 1455 bought the Neumark from the Teutonic Order, paying 40,000 marks partly to give the grandmaster funds for his war against the Prussian League, partly to keep it out of Polish hands.

He fought in the indecisive Bohemian war of 1460–1, but his only significant failure had been in the Pomeranian inheritance wars of 1464–72. He earned fame by establishing the Order of the Swan to honour the Virgin Mary, basing it on a legend that was eventually used by Richard Wagner in his opera *Lohengrin*. In 1470 Friedrich II moved south to Ansbach, leaving Brandenburg to his brother, Albrecht Achilles (1414–86).

In 1478 Albrecht Achilles became involved in a dispute over the Bohemian inheritance, surprising everyone by joining the Polish alliance. For this he was rewarded by Casimir giving his daughter Sophia to Albrecht's son Friedrich. The allies of the Hungarian claimant – the Teutonic Knights in Prussia, the duke of Pomerania and Silesian dukes – fell on Brandenburg.

Polish forces came to his aid, knocking the Teutonic Knights out of the war. Henceforth, Albrecht Achilles's ability to raise mercenaries quickly and to pay them promptly made him a figure to reckon with. When Johann (1455–99) inherited Brandenburg, his younger brother, Friedrich (1460–1536), continued to reside in Ansbach. Friedrich and his royal Polish wife were to have a houseful of sons, most of whom were sent into clerical careers. The ninth of their eighteen children, Albrecht (1490–1568), would become grandmaster of the Teutonic Order in 1512.

Chapter 12

The Reformation

The Reformation came suddenly to Prussia, Lithuania and Poland, one after the other. In Prussia it was in part a response to the impossible situation of the Teutonic Order, trapped between pressure from the emperor, the pope and the Polish king; and dissatisfaction among the citizenry. In Poland–Lithuania (now essentially one state) it reflected demands for reforms by German burghers and Polish knights, Lithuanian resentment of Polish domination, Uniate desires for more autonomy, and Orthodox hatred for Catholicism, and uncertainty as to how to ward off attacks by, Tatars, Turks and the grand duke of Moscow. Nevertheless, Stephen Rowell finds evidence that Roman Catholicism was vibrant and confident.

The Renaissance popes had very little interest in the region; for them east-central Europe was a distant and unimportant distraction from more pressing business – the prospect of armies from Spain, France and Germany moving into Italy. While the Protestant movement in Germany was troubling, it was less important than Ottoman attacks in the Balkans and across the Mediterranean Sea. Consequently, the Polish king received very little advice on what to do about the religious chaos in his kingdom until the Jesuits arrived in 1564. Until then Poland–Lithuania observed a broad, if tumultuous, toleration of dissenting religious beliefs.

Poland and Lithuania in the Pre-Reformation Years

King Alexander Jagiellon returned to Lithuania as quickly as he could after his coronation in 1502 because Ivan III of Moscow and the Tatars were pressing on his frontiers. Alas, Alexander was not the man to cope with his nation's problems; in fact, some historians have speculated that he might have been feeble-minded. In any case, he stumbled from one crisis to another. The peace treaty of 1503 with Moscow cost him a quarter of Lithuania; then in 1505 the Radom Diet made the motto *Nihil Novi* ('Nothing New') into constitutional law. The king was henceforth prohibited from any action not approved in advance by both houses of the Diet, and the laws were published so that the king would know what was permitted. That summer Alexander suffered the stroke from which he died the following year (with complications from syphilis).

He was buried in Vilnius, a choice that perhaps reflected his love of Lithuania.

This brought Sigismund ('the Old') to the throne. As the fourth son of Casimir Jagiellon, he was already forty and unmarried – neighbouring royal families, never expecting he would become king, had refused to consider him as a spouse for their daughters. Even upon becoming king, it took six years to arrange his wedding to Barbara Zápolya and, after her death, two more to arrange the famous alliance with Bona Sforza, who brought Italian Renaissance culture to Poland in all its characteristics, both good and evil.

Bona Sforza was very unpopular among her husband's Orthodox subjects, who believed that paintings of human figures were forbidden, that the pope was the anti-Christ and that women should live in seclusion. In their mind, Sigismund could not have chosen a worse wife.

Sigismund had been named for his mother's grandfather, the Holy Roman emperor; it may be that she had hoped this would help win him the Bohemian crown. He was not promiscuous enough to attract attention, but he had three children by a respectable mistress before he became king. Sigismund named the son, Jan (1499–1538) bishop of Vilnius even though he was neither of legal age nor a priest. This was protested by Lithuanian patriots, one of whom even physically assaulted the young bishop. This did not intimidate Jan, who strongly opposed the rise of Protestant ideas, but he was less able to resist Bona Sforza, who insisted on his being transferred to the less important see at Poznań.

In 1526, when the Ottomans annihilated the Hungarian army at Mohács, King Louis Jagiellon was among those slain. When he became king at age ten, he had refused to pay the tribute. He then beheaded the Ottoman envoy and sent his head to the sultan. His army, being too small and somewhat old-fashioned, was cut to pieces by Ottomans employing muskets. When the fleeing monarch's horse fell in a stream, he drowned, held down by the weight of his armour. The Hungarian kingdom fell apart in the ensuing years, most of it into the hands of the sultan. A remnant of the nobility elected John Zápolya, who soon had to take refuge in Poland. Bohemia went to the Habsburg emperor, Maximilian, who had been fighting the Turks in Croatia all his life. This left Poland and Austria as the first line of defence against the advance of Islam. How, given the constitutional limitations of his office, was Sigismund to perform his duty to protect the country?

The constitutional deadlock explains much about the Reformation in Poland. With the nobles obstinately behind the motto *Nothing New*, Sigismund could not govern at all without the support of the Church.

He avoided appointing Germans to official capacities on the premise that every German was a potential Lutheran. He authorised searches for heretical books and he changed the language of the homilies in the churches in Cracow from German to Polish; but the printing press had made it harder to combat Protestants than it had been to deal with Hussites. Also, there were many more Germans in Poland than there had been radical Czechs, and their demands were familiar to well-informed individuals and were relatively unthreatening.

In any case, the king's heart was not in the task. Sigismund was no religious fanatic. He is said to have commented that he was the king of the people, not of their consciences. As he grew older, he lost interest in governing, letting his wife fill the vacuum. As Bona Sforza became more important, the clergy and nobles were outraged; they disliked her as a foreigner, an Italian, a personification of secular ideas, a spendthrift – and as a woman. Polonism was in the saddle, and it was riding into the forests to escape its problems, angry that the world would not leave it alone.

Bona Sforza's influence in Lithuania became even more important. After a fall from a horse in 1527 that caused her to give birth prematurely, she compensated for her subsequent sterility by becoming more involved in the Grand Duchy's affairs. To increase royal revenues, she introduced the three-field system to the extensive royal estates, thereby reducing many farmers to serfs. This was soon copied by most of the great landowners. She also opposed the spread of Lutheranism, but after 1539 backed away from a policy of repression after seeing a convert to Judaism burned alive. She already had great influence in important church dioceses, thanks to grants by Pope Leo X in 1519 that allowed her to appoint priests to the cathedral chapters. Her deep knowledge of politics, the handling of money, and her fiery temper made her a formidable person. Eventually, she came to dominate the Lithuanian state, leaving her husband to oversee Poland.

Opposition to her interference added fuel to an irrational anti-foreigner sentiment. With the Turks besieging Vienna in 1529, the Habsburgs were not likely to be a danger; the Jews lacked any power whatsoever. Logical or not, Polish patriotism resulted in extremes of glory and humiliation, with too little in between. Among the few unifying memories was the battle of Grunwald (Tannenberg). The battle flags hanging in Cracow may have been showing their age, but everyone still heard the '*Hejnał Mariacki*', that haunting melody King Louis the Great had ordered blown by a trumpeter from the church tower at dawn and dusk to mark the opening and closing of the city gates. A more modern story connects this to the 1241 Mongol conquest of Cracow, the trumpeter being shot dead in mid-note by a Tatar archer.

In short, while the rest of Europe wrestled with reforms, Poland insisted on retaining the *status quo*. Not that reform was not needed, but in that many-sided struggle between monarch, church, magnates, petty nobles and burghers that every nation in western Europe was experiencing, the result was a deadlock in Poland. The nobles had won, and their sole concern was to maintain their social and economic position.

The Reformation in Prussia

Among German states it was Saxony that best applied Renaissance ideas to government reform. Scholars trained in the humanities despised the do-nothing noble-born officeholders and proposed to end inefficiency and waste by centralising authority and raising greater revenues through the encouragement of trade and commerce. So successful were the Saxon princes that the Teutonic Order had elected the physical weakling Friedrich of Saxony as grandmaster, hoping that his advisers could work the same magic on the economy and government of Prussia. At the least the power of the nearby Saxon state would offset the ability of the Polish king to dominate Prussia.

Grandmaster Friedrich did what he could. While unsuccessful in reversing the downward trend of military power, he did prepare the way for the reforms that in a few years would be proposed by a professor at the university at Wittenberg, Martin Luther.

Friedrich did this by encouraging the bishops to introduce more humanists into their cathedral chapters and give them a free rein to improve economic and moral life in their dioceses. He also hired humanists to create a more efficient and more just government. Today we would call these scholars bureaucrats, but order and predictability were what every medieval state needed to escape the lethargy of tradition and the restraints of inherited authority.

Friedrich had gathered around him a solid core of well-educated and hard-working humanists – Paul Watt, his former tutor, a professor at Leipzig, then Dietrich of Werthern, a lawyer. They removed ageing knights from administrative posts, consolidated convents, appropriated incomes for the grandmaster's use, curbed the ability of the estates to veto legislation, redefined court procedure and etiquette, and through ruthless bureaucratic warfare drove their conservative enemies from the country.

When the German master died, Friedrich's brother, Georg the Bearded (1471–1539), came up with a plan for dealing with potentially obstructionist successors by abolishing the office. However, the idea found little support in Germany, and the new master there organised opposition to any changes in traditional practices. Friedrich's visits to Germany in 1504 and 1507 led only to a clarification of issues, not their resolution.

Relations with Poland were relatively quiet because neither the king nor grandmaster could afford to raise an army; the king could not persuade the Diet to levy war taxes to fight any enemy, not even one as insignificant as Prussia.

The death of Grandmaster Friedrich in late 1510 presented another opportunity to consider new ideas at the 'national' level. One suggestion, made principally by Polish nobles and clerics, was to elect the Polish king as grandmaster, with Sigismund taking a vow of chastity. They would have welcomed a celibate monarchy because that would have guaranteed the elective nature of their kings. Sigismund, in fact, was willing to consider this proposal for his descendants, provided he could get a papal exemption for himself to marry! The Teutonic Knights, however, had their own candidate already selected: Albrecht of Ansbach (1490–1568). The family was one of the most important in Germany, but it was hardly wealthy enough to endow eight sons with a suitable living. The military order's interests and the Hohenzollerns' coincided perfectly.

Approval of the order's choice was not easily obtained, but the outcome was foreordained. The young man, only twenty years of age, was related to the king of Poland and the king of Bohemia and Hungary, and he had excellent connections to the Empire and Church. The convents in Germany and Livonia approved – there was no proper election – and the matter was settled. Albrecht was made a member of the order and installed as grandmaster on the same day. He was welcomed into the highest levels of imperial policy-making by the emperor himself, who urged him to attend the *Reichstag* and then reminded him to pay attention to imperial wishes.

In Nuremberg in early 1512, Albrecht explained to Maximilian that before he could give his oath, he had to be freed from his obligation to the king of Poland to render homage. (The emperor was delighted to do this.) While Albrecht carried on the internal and foreign policies of his predecessor, he developed a very different personal lifestyle. The new grandmaster was forthright about his distaste for poverty and chastity, after which his officers hastily explained that while ordinary knights and priests had to follow the rules, a man of his birth would naturally be exempt from such petty requirements. All that he had to avoid was marriage. Surely, if popes could live openly with their women, and cardinals and archbishops could flaunt their mistresses in public, a great German prince could be excused for not playing the role of a lowly friar.

Albrecht saw that the future belonged to princes who acted decisively, suppressed nobles and uncooperative assemblies, encouraged trade and industry, taxed the increased prosperity of their subjects, and created a modern army. Only such princes could take advantage of opportunities when they appeared. This made him among the first of the absolutist rulers, with the advantage of knowing that discipline and order were state traditions. Although those ideals had fallen low in recent years, his predecessor had reduced internal strife and reasserted control over the officers. While the knights' impressive parades and public ceremonies with elaborate costumes, the bishops and their canons, the abbots with their friars and monks, the burghers with their guilds, and the mounted knights were first-class spectacles, Albrecht's predecessors had not appreciated fully the difference between spectacle and power. He learned how to discern the difference. The young prince's plans involved great patience, first to make the necessary reforms so as to increase his power, second to await opportunities to exercise that power.

At first he relied on Hiob, the 'Iron Bishop' of Pomesania from 1501 to 1521. Hiob was one of the great humanists of the era, whose respect for tradition and moderation was not lost on the Polish monarch and his prelates. In 1515, however, Albrecht came under the influence of Dietrich of Schönberg (1484–1525), a charismatic young charlatan who specialised in mathematics, astronomy and astrology. The young grandmaster, always alert to the latest cultural trends, became an enthusiastic listener to his favourite's astrological predictions. He also became Schönberg's companion on nocturnal adventures in local houses of pleasure. Freed from the company of priests and elderly pious knights, Albrecht proved himself an accomplished student of libertine life, at least such as Königsberg offered. Schönberg also persuaded him that the time had arrived to interject himself into foreign affairs, to use Prussia's strategic position in the rear of Lithuania now that Sigismund was about to go to war with Ivan III.

Schönberg travelled to Moscow, returning with a treaty promising financial support for an army sufficient to tie down Polish troops or even inflict devastating defeats on them. Schönberg then used his considerable rhetorical skills to confuse the Prussian assembly and whip up a war fever among the representatives. He outlined in graphic detail Polish plans (mostly fictitious, at the least exaggerated, but with just enough truth in them to be plausible) to require that half the knights in the order be Poles and to introduce a tyrannical government on the Polish model, with the inevitable result of seeing poverty and serfdom spread into the yet prosperous provinces of Prussia. The townspeople and knights of Prussia were not complete fools, but their lack of knowledge about what Polish nobles and prelates were really doing to their country made them susceptible to the grossest propaganda and ethnic prejudice.

Such activities could not be kept secret from Sigismund, nor did Albrecht want them to be. Only when universally recognised as the man who could tip the balance between the great powers could Albrecht make the kind of demands that would restore the lands and authority his order had possessed eleven decades earlier. That obviously required a different kind of ruler than those whose piety and loyalty had led them from one disaster into another.

Albrecht was probably no more intelligent than his predecessors. He may not even have been more devious; certainly he did not work harder, at least not when he was young. What he had was a kind of presence, an understanding that he stood above tradition and customary rules. His knights were awed by his birth and breeding. This was not unusual. Most nobles had a finely developed air of authority, assumed that they had the right to make judgments and give orders, and possessed a posture and tone of voice that made inferiors aware that they were in the presence of their betters. It was very intimidating. Certainly no previous grandmaster would have considered holding a tournament, much less participated in it personally; but Albrecht staged one in Königsberg in 1518 and not only jousted, but, like his contemporary, Henry VIII of England, joined in the mêlée.

While Albrecht's adventurous policies made him important in the considerations of high diplomacy, his programme was fundamentally unsound. As long as there was no war, he could strut about as a great figure, impressing the German master with his plans and plans for plans; but when it actually came to war between Poland–Lithuania and Moscow in 1519, he learned that the promised Russian subsidies would not come; and therefore he could not pay his mercenaries. Imperial help was likewise absent; Maximilian was rather more interested in Polish help for his own ventures than in rescuing the grandmaster.

Königsberg's stout defences repelled the Polish assaults, and much of the ground lost in the opening months of the war was recovered;

but all Albrecht's hopes rested on the arrival of an army raised by the German master – 1,800 horsemen and 8,000 foot soldiers passed through Brandenburg to Danzig. There, however, the mercenaries waited in vain for the grandmaster and his money. Albrecht was unable to appear because Polish garrisons blocked the crossings of the Vistula, and Danzig warships patrolled the seas. Moreover, he had too little money to pay the army. In the end, the mercenaries went home, undoubtedly spreading the word about the grandmaster's unreliability as a paymaster.

If Sigismund had not been occupied in the south, that would have been the end of Albrecht, but in fact, he had only a small force in Prussia. These were insufficient to hold the order's troops in check for long. The grandmaster's small army ravaged Royal Prussia, reconquered the Neumark, and worried about the intervention of Polish knights. When the Poles came at last, they brought with them Tatars, Bohemian mercenaries and good artillery; but their numbers were still insufficient to capture Albrecht's fortresses. Nevertheless, the grandmaster, knowing that all would be lost if a larger royal force came north, and seeing that he now possessed but few subjects who had not been robbed of the means to provide food for his troops and pay taxes, willingly signed a truce at the end of 1520. Schönberg left for Germany, to die in the battle of Pavia (1525), fighting for Emperor Charles V (1500–58). He was unable to spin a magic web over the emperor as he had Albrecht because Charles V had too many problems already with the Turks, the French and the Protestants to seek a confrontation with the Polish monarch over the distant and unimportant province of Prussia.

Albrecht meanwhile was becoming desperate for peace. His mercenaries had tired of waiting for their wages and begun to wander about the countryside like bandits. And what would happen when Poles returned? He even proposed to move the entire order to the Hungarian border, an old idea that met with little enthusiasm (perhaps because everyone recognised it as a desperate diversionary tactic). In 1523, Albrecht sold to the Livonian and German masters complete autonomy. This gave him some cash, but at the cost of ending the unity of the Teutonic Order, as it turned out, for ever.

The end of the military order in Prussia was foreseen by many now. During Albrecht's 1522 visit to Nuremberg to plead (in vain) for money from the princes of the Holy Roman Empire, it was clear that he had been visibly affected by Lutheran teachings. In early 1523 Martin Luther directed one of his major statements 'to the lords of the Teutonic Knights, that they lay aside false chastity'.

It was not hard for Protestant ideas to make inroads among the membership. The knights, and there were fewer now, had been reared in a Germany seething with unrest over Church corruption. They understood the issues involved in Luther's protests, and they were unhappy with the lack of morality at the papal curia. Albrecht, perhaps aware of the public mood and certainly personally concerned about ecclesiastical corruption, took steps to prepare the members of his order for reform proposals: during the Christmas holiday of 1523, while he was still in Germany, he allowed Lutheran preachers to deliver sermons at his court in Königsberg.

This was not hypocrisy. The once-brash young prince had learned piety through harsh experience. His youthful sins had led not only him to disaster, but also his innocent subjects. Albrecht apparently decided to devote the rest of his life to atoning for his early foolishness and indiscretions. Unlike repentant men of an earlier generation, however, he never contemplated withdrawing into a cloister for prayer and penitence. This Renaissance-era prince instead reflected on the choices available to him, and he selected a hard one: the correction of the basic flaw in his order's status that had condemned Prussia to a century of foreign invasion and civil conflict – its awkward mixture of secular and clerical duties that made it something more than a religious order and less than a sovereign state.

The grandmaster quietly sought to discover what response neighbouring princes would make if he followed Luther's advice, as many northern German princes and bishops were doing, and became a Protestant. Already during his absence clergymen had carried through the essentials of the Protestant reforms: they had introduced the German language into the worship services, had begun the singing of hymns, and had abolished pilgrimages and the veneration of saints. These were very practical reforms, ones based on outrage at current church conditions, but they still lacked methodological or theological justifications. Those came later. As monks, nuns and priests renounced their vows of celibacy, rumours inevitably began to circulate that the grandmaster, too, was planning to set aside his vows, marry, and make himself the head of a secular state. The most serious charge was that the grandmaster might contract a marriage.

Surprisingly, there was little outrage at secularising the Prussian state. The pope and the emperor, of course, warned Albrecht not to do it, and his Brandenburg relatives did not approve; but the knights in Prussia and the cities and nobles favoured the proposal decisively. The king of Poland allowed himself to approve. Secularisation resolved two pressing problems at once: confiscation of the remaining ecclesiastical properties made money available to pay the grandmaster's debts, and the way was open to incorporate all of Prussia into the Polish Commonwealth, thereby establishing a peaceful and mutually unthreatening relationship with the Polish king. On 10 April 1525, Albrecht gave the oath of allegiance in Cracow, a scene immortalised on one of the greatest Polish canvases by the patriotic nineteenth-century painter, Jan Matejko.

The formal, legal subordination aside, East Prussia was not absorbed into the Polish state even to the minimal extent that Royal Prussia had been. The new duke maintained his own army, currency, assembly and a more or less independent foreign policy. The administrative system changed hardly at all, and existing laws remained in force. A few titles were revised. But the introduction of Lutheran reforms led to profound changes.

The establishment of Albrecht University in Königsberg was important in this. It was also the primary vehicle to bring Protestantism to the Lithuanians, an effort that then seemed likely to succeed. Ironically, Luther's defence of Jan Hus as an early reformer protesting papal abuses put the Teutonic Knights in the position of defending ideas they had strongly denounced a century earlier.

In 1526 Albrecht entered 'true chastity of marriage' with Dorothea, the eldest daughter of Frederik of Denmark (1471–1533). The Danes specialised in providing spouses to the German rulers along the Baltic; Prussia completed the collection of regional alliances. This provided Albrecht with a powerful protector and a number of well-placed brothers- and sisters-in-law, and his father-in-law was also the most important Lutheran ruler of the time.

The uproar in Catholic Germany was as loud and denunciatory as was the applause in Protestant Germany. In Prussia all was quiet – knights who disagreed were too intimidated to speak up. There were a few knights who were too old to change or unprepared to assume the demands of secular knighthood; seven who wanted to remain Roman Catholics went to southern Germany, where they were accepted into convents and hospitals. The remaining forty-eight knights who remained in Prussia were given fiefs or offices. A few married and founded families, becoming a part of that *Junker* class for which Brandenburg-Prussia was later famous. However, on the whole, the noble class changed little in its composition.

One important change was that the nobles' authority over their serfs increased considerably. The Great Peasant Revolt of 1525 – a reaction to rumours that free labourers would be reduced to serfdom by their new lords – aided this. The panic among the ruling classes led to harsh repression.

The new duke of Prussia abandoned his early efforts to be named a prince of the empire and thus under the protection of the Holy Roman Empire. Charles V had been too far away, in Spain, or too busy with Luther and the Turks, to give careful consideration to such a minor matter while there was still time. In 1526, however, having seen what happened in Prussia, the emperor granted that status to the Livonian master and his possessions. In 1530 Charles named the German master to be the new grandmaster. Henceforth, the Teutonic Order was expected to serve the Habsburg dynasty's political programmes.

These actions limited Albrecht's ambitions to include Livonia in his new state or to assist his nephew there – Wilhelm of Brandenburg (1498–1563) was archbishop between 1539 and 1561, during which time he had schemed to secularise his diocese along the model of North German prelates. In the contest of wills Wilhelm was no match for the stubborn and capable Livonian master, Wolter of Plettenberg, who had cleverly obtained recognition as a prince of the empire and was thus no longer bound by previous oaths or obligations.

Royal Prussia was not affected by the secularisation of Albrecht's state, except, of course, in that Protestant ideas circulated from town to town more easily. Potentially, the population of Royal Prussia already considered their province an autonomous German-speaking part of the Polish kingdom with the right to make independent decisions on religion. The people in the towns welcomed both the prospect of peace and the spread of the Lutheran reforms. The way to a spiritual and cultural reunification of Prussia seemed to have opened, and the change also gave more authority to the commercial classes and gentry over the ecclesiastical figures who were the nominal rulers of many cities and much of the countryside.

Many who might have objected to the reforms found themselves muted by the even more appalling prospect of a peasant revolt. The rising of peasants here and there in Prussia during 1525 in imitation of the Great Peasant Revolt in Germany was a sobering warning that there were worse changes possible than those associated with cleaning up long-festering problems in local churches and monasteries. The 1526 uprising in Danzig further demonstrated that unrest had spread to the lower classes in the towns. This was not a time for the upper classes to quarrel over religion. Live and let live was the only practical policy.

Albrecht did not consider himself a rebel or disrupter of church unity. Years later he was still continuing his correspondence with Rome and honouring the pope as the head of the Church. The formal separation came later, as one inevitable step of many. The nature of the transformation of Prussia would be easy to exaggerate; in 1525 Protestantism was a reform advocated and welcomed by many devout Roman Catholics. Within a year Sigismund the Old could congratulate himself on his foresight. Louis Jagiellon fell in the battle of Mohács, leaving the remnants of Hungary and his claims to other kingdoms to the Habsburg Ferdinand of Bohemia (1503–64). With Poland now besieged by strong enemies on the east (Moscow), the south (the Turks), and the west (the Habsburgs), it was fortunate that Sigismund had at least relieved himself of worries about the north.

Duke Albrecht took immediate steps towards bringing 'Old Prussia' back together. The cooperation of the two parliamentary bodies led to the adoption of a common currency in 1528, a codification of the laws in 1529, and an effort at a common tariff policy. The duke, though extending the hand of friendship to his somewhat suspicious colleagues in Royal Prussia, was not willing to sacrifice one whit of his own sovereignty in order to unify the two provinces. He did not allow his vassals to see the Polish Diet as anything but foreign foes. He was loyal to his new sovereign, but he would not have his Protestant state absorbed more deeply into Roman Catholic Poland.

He worried more about the efforts by the surviving members of the Teutonic Order to approach the Polish monarch. Already they were urging Charles V to remove Albrecht from his office and return the land to the Catholic Church. This made Albrecht conclude that he was safer as a Protestant than as a lapsed Catholic, but it complicated his relationship with Sigismund the Old. On the one hand, Albrecht wanted a weak king in Cracow who would be no danger; on the other hand, he wanted a strong king who could maintain order and defend the frontiers. This dilemma was not unlike what the bishops and cities in Royal Prussia confronted in trying to work with Albrecht in bringing about a certain reunification of Prussia, so that everyone would benefit without anyone feeling endangered.

Prussia had been prepared for the change by twenty-seven years of rule by grandmasters who had been reared as German dukes. They had not been grandmasters in the old style but rather like prince-abbots in the Holy Roman Empire. Now Albrecht was merely another minor prince. The lords of the order, long on the way from a monkish life to a secular one, had at last passed the final milestone.

It had not gone quickly. From the loss of purpose after the Christianisation of Lithuania, to the loss of control over the cities and nobles had taken a half a century; a further half-century had persuaded the knights stationed in Prussia that their traditional role as crusaders was past, that something new had to take its place, and that was the formation of a secular state which retained as much of the old chivalric, knightly, landlord virtues as possible. Prussia had always been an exception among territorial states; it was to remain so in the future as well.

The Reformation in Lithuania

The crusade to convert the pagan Samogitians now took on a new aspect: Lutheran Prussians seeking to convert Roman Catholic Samogitians. In effect, they hoped once again to bring the former pagans from a *false* faith to another *true* one. Protestant ministers circulated the new gospel in the Samogitian dialect, hoping to save the souls of that people from damnation and also to bring the Samogitians away from the domination of the Polish kingdom.

The failure of the Roman Catholic rulers to provide sufficient priests and churches there had been a scandal even to devout Roman Catholics; now it was a call to action for radical reformers. There were only thirty-seven churches in Samogitia, and only twice as many in the much larger highlands of central Lithuania. Moreover, the conditions in some of the churches were abominable.

Official visitors wrote devastating descriptions of the deplorable filth of churches which had obviously not been used for religious services for time out of mind. The priests' evasions of queries about their parishioners' religious practices left little doubt that, while church attendance was slowly increasing, underground paganism was alive and well.

In time the Samogitians came to adopt Roman Catholicism with the same fervour they had once held to their ancient gods, but only after Poland and Lithuania went through a period of experimentation with a variety of Protestant models and even relapses into paganism. In time paganism became folklore, and its stronghold in the Lowlands became known as 'Holy Samogitia'. Lutheranism faded away for lack of state support, replaced by a Calvinism that promised to increase the authority of the great magnates. Both contributed to the salvation of the Lithuanian language, partly by emphasizing its use in worship, partly by the printing of books. However, Calvinism declined after Sigismund Augustus reasserted royal authority. Bona Sforza withdrew to Masovia, then to her birthplace in the kingdom of Naples, where she was poisoned, presumably by King Philip II of Spain – then experiencing the first of his state bankruptcies – to avoid paying her the debts he owed.

The Poles had relied on the Jagiellonian University in Cracow to educate their brightest young men, but indoctrination there was ineffective until the disputes between Lutherans, Calvinists and Arians discredited all Protestant reformers. In any case the debates had been almost completely confined to the upper classes. Lithuanians were long familiar with the principle of *cuius regio, ejus religio* before the Diet of Augsburg issued its decree in 1555 allowing rulers to decide what religion their subjects must follow. They had understood that religious toleration was for national groups, not individuals, and that no one could change his religion without his lord's consent.

As a result, when the Radziwiłł and Chodkiewicz (Katkus) families returned to Roman Catholicism, the reform movement suffered a fatal blow; and the language barrier (including widespread illiteracy) prevented outsiders from reaching past them to address the population directly. By the time the Jesuits arrived in 1570 Lithuania was committed again to the Roman Catholic Church. Through the University of Vilnius the Jesuits guaranteed that nobles and future priests could be given a first-class education dedicated to the principles of religious orthodoxy and Polonisation.

Lithuania, long hovering between east and west, Russia and Poland, Russian Orthodoxy and Roman Catholicism, chose the west. Without that history, the magnificent scene in Rome in July 1987 (the 600th anniversary of the Christianisation) could never have taken place. Lithuanian bishops celebrated Mass in Santa Maria Maggiore before thousands of Lithuanian worshippers in national costumes – many from America – while Radio Moscow fumed, arguing angrily to anyone who would listen that Lithuanians were perfectly happy in their Soviet homeland. Communists suggested that only a Polish Pope (John Paul II) could think that Lithuanians would not choose to be ruled by Russians.

But that is a different story. This era concludes with two endings: first, the dissolution of the proud Teutonic Order in Prussia and the creation of a new relationship in 1525 between the former grandmaster (now duke of Prussia) and the Polish king, vassal and lord; second, the Diet of Lublin (1569) merged Poland and Lithuania into a *Commonwealth* – one nation, one Diet, one ruler, but dual administrations, with minor provisions incorporating Royal Prussia more closely into the Polish kingdom. Poland was now truly a Baltic nation, and its future would be shaped by the new responsibilities and the new rivalries it was to acquire by having finally vanquished and partially absorbed the lands of its ancient enemy, the Teutonic Order.

Four great multi-national states now existed east of the traditional heartlands of Europe: the sometimes united Scandinavian kingdom, Poland–Lithuania, Moscow, and the Ottoman Empire. Each represented an important religious viewpoint that enabled it to exercise influence and power for many years to come. In the middle position, confronting the three others was Poland–Lithuania. To the west was the fractured Holy Roman Empire, with Catholic states in the south, Protestant ones in the north.

Dusk had come to the day when tiny principalities mattered in politics; after a night of chaos and reorganisation, the dawn would rise on the great empires of the future. Poland–Lithuania would be among them.

Chapter 13

What Did It All Mean?

Much had changed in the last years of the Teutonic Knights. The fragile states inherited by Jagiełło and Vytautas had become stable, robust, united, and prosperous; the quarrelling states of Ruś, typified by the weak Moscow of Basil I, had been united; Sigismund's unruly Hungary was about to fall to the Ottoman Turks; Western Christendom, once divided between two popes (three for a few years), was soon to be divided into Roman Catholic, Lutheran, Evangelical, Zwinglian, Calvinist, Anabaptist, and Anglican regions. Prussia had fallen from the colourful heights of chivalric pride and pomp to black-clad Lutheran piety.

There had been progress. The Tatar raids into Russia, Lithuania and Poland were being resisted. There was more consistency in local governance, less banditry and local warfare, more material wealth, greater literacy, less paganism, better table manners, more bathing and improved beers.

There is no changing the past, but we can change what we understood happened then and what it meant.

To Poland

The central question in Polish historiography concerns the kingdom's move to the east. Beginning in the fourteenth century under Casimir the Great, it was accelerated by the policies of the Jagiellonian dynasty. This gave Poland two great missions: first, to spread the Roman Catholic Church to Lithuania, Belarus and Ukraine; second, to protect east-central Europe from steppe raiders and the sultan. Poland prided itself on being the *antemurale christianitatis* ('bulwark of Christendom'). However, in doing that Poland had to turn away from the west, with its more vibrant economy, culture and religious life. It had to abandon provinces to the slow-moving, unplanned German *Drang nach Osten* ('drive to the east').

What motivated the Poles to make this sacrifice? First, they believed that saving a soul was the most worthwhile act that any person can do; and that saving the souls of an entire nation would be the greatest achievement any state could aspire to. Second, that bringing barbarians to civilisation was a noble achievement. It offered effective justice to replace individual revenge and clan warfare; a moral code with roots in Judaism, Greek and Roman philosophy, and the teachings of Christ; a sophisticated mythology; fine literature, impressive architecture and well-developed decorative and musical arts; an evolving technology; organised means of passing on the knowledge of the past and the inventions of the present. It was also a way to earn riches and honour.

The challenges they faced were immense: distance, tradition and language. It was a heroic effort, and eventually they were exhausted by that effort. The nobles retired to their estates, to enjoy the pleasures of the hunt, the family and gallantry. It is no accident that chivalric gestures have survived in Poland more than elsewhere. Whether in the kiss-the-hand gentility or the impulsive disregard of life and property in pursuit of justice and honour, there is something instinctively chivalric in Polish culture. That old-fashioned, aristocratic courtesy cannot be separated from the history of the nation.

An era of peace and prosperity seemed within reach. The Polish–Lithuanian state was a multi-cultural marvel, with toleration for Protestants, Orthodox Christians, and Jews. There was growth in trade and commerce, scholars and nobles were known for their knowledge and sophistication, clergymen for their taste in education and architecture. The Polish Renaissance was a marvel in every way.

Then came the Protestant Reformation and the Counter-Reformation, after which Ivan the Terrible appeared on one frontier, while Turks approached from another. As civil unrest and foreign invasion demonstrated the backwardness of the economy, a fear and suspicion of all things German arose.

This comes as almost a surprise. The Polish culture of those years had been so attractive that Germans, Lithuanians and Russians learned the language, hummed the music, and donned whatever dress was being worn in Cracow. Yet, the very dominance of this *Sarmatian* culture, freely adopted by so many various nationalities, was the cause of jealousy, envy and fear. Lithuanian boyars hated being thought uncultured, Orthodox burghers worried about their very salvation, and Jews ... Well, anti-Semitism was already a problem. Jews were foreigners with a foreign religion, they tended to live in the cities, and they were protected by the monarchs who were being blamed for all the nation's ills. The Church, challenged by Lutherans and Orthodoxy, saw greater uniformity as essential to its survival, indeed, the survival of the Polish people. The stage was set, again, for debates about the east/west orientation of the Polish state.

To Lithuania

The Communist government that dominated the nation from 1945 to 1989 summarised its history thus: 'The Polish feudal lords attempted to liquidate the Grand Duchy of Lithuania.' But Lithuanian patriots became too busy overthrowing Soviet rule to pay much attention to this view. After independence was attained, there were numerous ways that Lithuanians identified their nation with its glorious past: almost everyone refused to speak the Russian they had been forced to learn in school; radical patriots denounced the Roman Catholic Church for having attempted to Polonise the nation and for having stolen its most talented individuals; and parents named their children for pagan heroes as often as for saints.

At the same time, the Roman Catholic Church was respected for having saved the Lithuanian people from being absorbed into Russia during those 200 years when tsars and secretaries-generals ruled their land. As a result, churches were repaired and repainted in spite of the economic challenges of the new era.

There was resentment at the loss of territory, but satisfaction that the Communists had taken from Poland the area around Vilnius, now largely emptied of its vibrant Polish and Jewish culture. There was also a memory of sixteenth-century Lithuania in what is now Belarus, a nation with its own language and culture.

Paganism survived the Reformation as folklore, but it died out as a public religion. The descendants of pagans became devout believers who carved wooden crosses, saints and Madonnas, raising them high on poles to decorate cemeteries, crossroads and homes. Folklore survived in herbal cures, healing practices, spells for finding lost items, harming enemies, and changing the weather. Roman Catholic priests denounced these practices from time to time, but without much effect because they were part of pan-European folk practices that Germans and Poles could not suppress even at home. Mythology survived, part of the fairy-tale tradition that was found everywhere.

Samogitia remained a distinct region inside the Lithuanian state. Long isolated, it was now allowed more local autonomy. There were more free peasants and more private estates than elsewhere; farmers migrated down the Nemunas to take up lands that had been depopulated by war. Serfs existed, as did royal estates, but not to the same extent as in the Lithuanian highlands. It was no accident that Poles and Lithuanians looked with pride on the Samogitian boyars and peasantry.

To Royal Prussia

The tradition of Prussians working together for common goals, whenever possible having a common law and a single set of taxes and tariffs, had not diminished significantly after West Prussia was incorporated into the kingdom of Poland in 1466. The unity represented in Janusz Małłek's phrase, the Two Parts of Prussia, was undermined when local patriotism grew in the two regions.

Royal Prussia's nobles and burghers had objected to the Union of Lublin, but as they watched with apprehension as Hohenzollern absolutism grew first in Brandenburg, then in Brandenburg-Prussia, they saw their interests best served by a closer association with the Commonwealth of Poland–Lithuania.

This did not mean assimilation into Poland. German-speaking citizens objected to anything that smacked of Polonisation. What burghers and nobles wanted was freedom from interference from above. Whenever Poles made statements criticising Germans and Protestantism, some West Prussians wondered if they should draw nearer to East Prussians. But not too near. For Polish-speaking citizens, of course, a closer connection to the kingdom was desirable, and the more distance between them and Königsberg, the better.

To the Teutonic Knights

The crusades had evolved from an effort to recover the Holy Land from Seljuk Turks to a means of defending Christendom against Ottoman Turks, an ideal many nationalities could understand and share; that was a religious ideal perfectly suited to the medieval mind. The crusade was also a means of enlarging the state of the Teutonic Knights, who represented the Papacy and the Holy Roman Empire as well as themselves. They justified holy war as the only way to pacify and Christianise pagans whose religion exhalted warfare.

They had done that successfully in Prussia and Livonia, it was being done with Muslims in Spain and Portugal. The kings of Poland and Hungary used the same reasoning for warring against Tatars and Turks: what was good for them was good for Christendom; these co-joined reasons justified the cost in blood and treasure.

What most late medieval crusades had in common was that they were popular struggles of western Europeans against dangerous enemies on the borders of Christendom. There was an aura of romanticism connected with them that the nineteenth-century public was able to grasp, but which eludes the modern mind. This was also bound up in a concept of chivalry that Hollywood has attempted with varying success to exploit. This concept was made real for a half-century in Prussia, but declined after 1410. The future lay with the courtier, not the knight. As for that impact on the crusades, as Maurice Keen said, there was no decline in holy zeal, but they had rather too much of it at home; and some of the energy that had once gone into crusading was diverted into travel and adventure.

Nevertheless, for a very long time medieval men and women were upset by the mere existence of pagans on their frontier, even the existence of pagans who were peaceful and tolerant. They feared the magic and superstition of the pagan priests, believed that their charms and incantations were effective, and looked upon war against such manifestations of devil-worship as a holy project; nor were Eastern Christians pleased at having dangerous neighbours like the Tatars.

Lithuanians were not children of nature. The Gediminid dukes and their boyars lived in a political and social environment far too sophisticated and complex for them to qualify as examples of Rousseau's noble savage. When the rulers became Roman Catholic, their warriors were only newly baptised, and their armies contained numbers of Muslims, Orthodox Christians and pagans. For a long time it was not clear whether they would end up as Roman Catholics or Orthodox.

The crusade against paganism bound many characteristics of western religion and secular life together – as crusade, as pilgrimage, as sport, as chivalric display and as recognition of worthy achievement. That was an age of accomplishment. For nobles who wanted to prove themselves by doing noble deeds, the Samogitian Crusade provided an almost universally approved means to demonstrate their valour, daring and knightly worth. By the middle of the fourteenth century this aspect of the crusade became more prominent than the religious obligations. Slowly the expeditions became more secular, more chivalric, until the crusade suffered the fate of idealistic knighthood everywhere – becoming an arthritic anachronism.

For ten years the Teutonic Order had ruled in Samogitia, or at least in the immediate neighbourhood of its fortresses along the Nemunas River. Its policies had not been unusually oppressive except in the opinion of those they had conquered. However, it frightened the pagan priests and their followers who knew that it was only a matter of time before missionaries would appear among them, and it appalled the pacifist wing of the Church that had long supported the plans of neighbouring rulers to take the crusaders' lands for themselves. The advocates and officers responsible for maintaining order had never been secure in the countryside. They had not even been able to introduce the Dominican missionaries who were responsible for instructing the pagans in the essentials of Christianity. Whether that was a policy of toleration, or a wise restraint to avoid offending the more fanatic adherents of the old beliefs, or an application of ancient church doctrine forbidding forced conversion, or a mere preoccupation with taxes and a desire for land, with no concern for the souls of the natives (as was later charged), it was at least the opposite of the policy of driving men, women, and children to baptism at sword's point, as modern critics occasionally claim was done.

The order had never exercised authority in Samogitia long enough to make substantial changes, much less to bring in priests to evangelise the population. Knowing that any effort to make innovations in native life would provoke a revolt, the grandmasters and marshals did little beyond forbid their erstwhile subjects to go to war. The officers and advocates sat in strong castles on the margins of Samogitia, holding tightly to their riverine lines of communication with Prussia, but they had little influence in the interior.

By that time the order found it difficult to admit that the crusade had run its course, that it had achieved its purpose. Whenever that subject was broached, they pointed out the rebellions of the unrepentant pagans, the untrustworthiness of Jagiełło and Vytautas, and the need to defend the earlier converts in Prussia and Livonia. Always there was an excuse; often it had some valid aspects. But *the heart of the matter was the difficulty that all organisations face when their former duties vanish, when it comes time to dissolve themselves or find another reason for continuing to exist.*

That was especially difficult for the Teutonic Knights because they did not know whether or not Prussia and Livonia would be safe if they sent their warriors elsewhere. The Samogitian uprisings which culminated in the revolt of 1409 seemed to confirm their mistrust, a proof that the order had to keep its warriors in the Baltic to guard against apostasy.

Perhaps the crusade would have revived if Ulrich of Jungingen had not led his army into one of the greatest defeats in medieval history. Among those who fell at Tannenberg were the order's most experienced and capable officers and knights. The First Peace of Thorn was less a peace than an armed truce that undermined the order's financial resources to the point that future grandmasters could neither hire mercenaries in sufficient numbers to fight or support knights of their own. The grandmasters were temporarily successful in their efforts to hold Culm and West Prussia against Polish onslaughts, but their ambition to retain a legal claim on Samogitia was not. The Peace of Melno ended the international crusading era in the Baltic altogether in 1422.

Eventual defeat was almost foreordained for small states in that era. Certainly there was more to the decline than being worn down by overwhelming forces: more than the personal failure of leading personalities; and more than the simple operation of the law of inertia. But most of the immediate problems can be traced directly to the military disaster at Tannenberg.

At a critical and chaotic moment many local officers who might never have earned promotion had been thrust into positions of responsibility; in the course of time they became used to acting independently, then resented orders that limited their autonomy. Factions arose, often organised around regional origins – south Germans were suspicious of Rhinelanders, and vice versa. The authority of the grandmasters was undermined by successful resistance, a tradition was established of opposing even the most minor reforms.

Religious reform became an obsession. In an era that believed that God judged organisations and states for moral shortcomings, it was logical for the Teutonic Knights to conclude that the defeats were divine punishments for failing to live up to the vows of poverty, chastity and obedience. There is no indication that this was true before 1410.

Visitors considered Prussia a model state. Pride was the deadly sin of the pre-Tannenberg knights, eclipsing the other venal sins. Later, complaints about misgovernment began to heap up as hard-pressed officers and advocates collected emergency taxes year after year, squeezed the citizenry for extraordinary services, and haughtily rejected cries for justice and mercy.

Insecurity may well have contributed to this injustice. The officers had seen how quickly their subjects had gone over to the Polish king, and they surely knew what was said behind their backs (partly because it was occasionally said to their faces). Cruelty grows out of fear as much as out of the exercise of power without restraints or from cowardice and laziness.

A state in decline rarely governs well. The Teutonic Order was no exception, and monastic reform was essentially irrelevant to that collection of problems. Perhaps more prayer and a greater emphasis on chastity could have resulted in treating the order's subjects better, but the connection is not easily demonstrated. The grandmasters were, without exception until Albrecht, true to their monastic oaths, even pious, devout and puritanical. Of course, their example alone was insufficient to keep the officers and men within the narrow bounds prescribed by the rules, but there must have been a substantial majority of the membership who agreed with their efforts to enforce the rules. After all, the knights, priests and sergeants at the general chapters elected one reforming grandmaster after another.

The real problem was that the grandmasters issued edicts they could not enforce or which were irrelevant to the problems the officers and advocates had to deal with. It was not that the convents were overrun with women and other secular creatures, but that the discipline that had once been the pride of the military order was gone. When defeats followed hard on one another's heels, the officers had a difficult time keeping men and mercenaries in order. As drink and minor luxuries became commonplace, morale sank under public ridicule and criticism. The religious community was on the defensive, unable to prevail by force of arms or by exhortation. The answer to the problem of discipline was peace, a restoration of the financial health of the country, and finding a new military task which would keep the knights busy and spiritually satisfied.

The number of knights was declining, but the prestige of the order was too low to attract good recruits. That was not the disaster it would have been a century earlier, thanks to changes in military tactics which made knights less useful than mercenaries, but it still affected morale. The most successful fifteenth-century armies were composed of men in the prime of life, trained in arms and hired for short periods, then dismissed. *Landsknecht* armies had proved their ability to defeat levies of horsemen, mobs of peasant infantry and ageing knights who had once been formidable warriors. Moreover, the soldiers (in German *Sold* means pay) were willing to campaign as long as necessary, as long as the pay lasted. Mercenaries had already become common in Prussia; now they were indispensable.

The handful of friar-knights now served only as officers, supervising the hired troops, the levies and the military specialists such as the cannoneers, engineers and quartermasters. Since money was in short supply, the grandmasters spent it on mercenaries and equipment. The knights sensed that their role was changing, and not all of them were pleased. Few of them fitted easily either into the form prescribed by practices common 250 years earlier or those necessary for the future.

As taxes were raised to hire mercenaries, the merchant oligarchy in the cities and the secular knights in the countryside became resentful As long as their mercantile interests were defended against competitors and pirates, the cities did not complain too loudly; but after Tannenberg they were giving out more and more money for less and less protection.

At the least they wanted a voice in foreign affairs. The nobles felt the same way. One by one the grandmasters had to yield to those protests until finally there was the choice of giving the Prussian League full participation in the government through some type of assembly or of attempting to suppress it

Those causes of the decline still do not explain fully the reasons why the Teutonic Order fell so low. For that it is necessary to look beyond the narrow horizons of the Baltic, to the greater problems besetting all Europe at that time.

First of all, the grandmasters' loss of authority was not a uniquely local problem. The inability of the head of state to exercise power was seen in the Holy Roman Empire, the Roman Catholic Church, the kingdom of Poland, the grand duchy of Lithuania, and the United Kingdoms in Scandinavia. Everywhere the lower orders challenged the right of the nobility to give orders, while the nobles challenged the king; everywhere, at every level, individuals and groups attempted to strip power from those above them and gather it into their own hands. Pictorial expressions of the Wheel of Fortune illustrate the problem: the ruler sits atop a loosely fastened wheel, hands holding orb and sceptre, wearing a tall crown and draped in expensive robes; but the balance is delicate, and the slightest wisp of air disturbs the equilibrium. How easily and swiftly one can he be thrown from the heights to utter despair and humiliation!

Second, crusading goals had changed. As long as the Lithuanians, even the Samogitians, had remained pagan, there was still a religious justification for the crusade. However, once Jogaila had become King Władysław Jagiełło and Vytautas had been baptised as Duke Alexander and had sent his delegates to Constance to proclaim all Samogitia to be Christian, it became increasingly difficult for the grandmasters' representatives to persuade European knights that the operations in Lithuania were crusades, that war against Poland was justified, and that they should volunteer their services and contribute their wealth to those ventures. The procurators-general found it ever more difficult to persuade the popes with the traditional arguments.

The principal danger to Christendom was now clearly to the southeast. The Ottoman Turks were on the move, or seemed to be. They might have been more interested in rounding up slaves and cattle than in acquiring new provinces, but that was hardly a comfort for those who fell into their hands. The Islamic advance into the Balkans in the late fourteenth century frightened traditional supporters of the crusading movement because they were unable to prevent their possessions in

Greece from being overwhelmed and they foresaw the fall of Christian kingdoms in the Balkans. The great crusade of 1396, which was supposed to reverse that momentum, ended in disaster at Nicopolis.

How much the Nicopolis crusaders' fatal contempt for their adversaries was a result of their experiences in Samogitia can only be guessed. The Lithuanians were tall and muscular men, renowned as good warriors; in their forests and swamps they were the equal to any in Europe, and on the steppe they were very nearly a match for the Mongols. Yet the crusaders had repeatedly bested them. Surely that was proof that French and Hungarian crusaders could whip the Turks and their local Slavic allies? No, they couldn't. After Nicopolis, the French sent no further major expeditions to Prussia. They left the northern crusades to Germans who were now led by the defeated organiser of the Nicopolis venture, Sigismund, king of Hungary and later Holy Roman emperor, whose sole interest in crusading was to guard against the Turkish menace and to crush the Hussites. He had little sympathy for the border wars of the Teutonic Order except as a means of applying pressure on Jagiełło over possession of Silesia and Bohemia.

A third danger was heresy. The Hussites in Bohemia not only defended themselves, but they went on the offensive. The Teutonic Knights suffered damage to their properties in Germany and Prussia, reaping all the problems of defeat without any of the rewards expected for their efforts. Between the Turks and the Hussites, the crusading energies of central Europe were exhausted. There were none left to be used against Christian peoples in Lithuania and Poland.

Fourth, there was an attitude of depression among the general population, a feeling that one's endeavours would lead only to failure, that even the best success was transitory and vain. Johan Huizinga called that era *The Waning of the Middle Ages* and compared it to the senility of old age. Certainly there were fewer nobles who were willing to abandon their comfortable lives for a religious avocation, fewer who were willing to travel far to 'journey' into the cold Samogitian wilderness. Talk replaced action, show superseded performance. What was the use in any case? Was there really much hope of accomplishing anything? The world was doubtful, suspicious and cynical. If anything should be done, it should be done against the Turks. But even there, God seemed to be on the other side.

Chivalry was not dead, of course, but what remained was an expensive form of display that only the greatest lords could afford. It had priced itself beyond the reach of the minor nobles who had formerly accompanied the territorial princes to Prussia. After Tannenberg the

Teutonic Knights lacked the money to entertain on the new scale of lavishness. What had been wealth in the fourteenth century was poverty in the fifteenth, and the grandmasters could not maintain even the old scale. No one wanted to travel on a tourist-class crusade, and few could afford to go first class.

In short, crusading was no longer fun. The extravagance of activity, the delight in adventure and the search for fame that were the hallmarks of fourteenth-century chivalry were gone. The Samogitian crusade had combined the excitement of the hunt, the danger of warfare and the adventure of travel with a brilliance of display and entertainment that no one else could match. Now the crusaders did not raid Lithuania to chase down villagers, nor did they offer open battle. They could not even provide the chivalric spectacle that was the vogue from Burgundy to Italy. Nor could any other crusade provide a substitute. Consequently, potential crusaders stayed at home and talked wistfully of olden days.

The crusade from Prussia was over. The Teutonic Knights had outlived their usefulness there. There was still a future for the Teutonic Order. Several futures, in fact, because the military order broke into three distinct parts in 1525. Its fate was not preordained; it merely came about.

The future of Prussia was as an independent state, one often confused with Brandenburg, whose rulers took the title King in Prussia while working towards a better one – German emperor.

The fate of the reputation of the Teutonic Knights afterward is well told by Jürgen Sarnowsky in an article in *Preußenland* (2018); it suffered during the years of Protestant domination and the Enlightenment, then recovered in the Romantic era and especially after the national uprising against Napoleon. The order's symbolic importance was exaggerated by the nationalist historian Heinrich von Treitschke (1834–96) and from the First World War onward by Germany's political enemies, but is almost forgotten by today's popular press.

The Livonian Knights survived longer because they had the mission of protecting Livonia from the Russians. That was an undoubted crusade, though an unconventional one. At a critical moment in their history they had the leadership of Wolter of Plettenberg, one of the greatest men to serve as Livonian master. When they finally dissolved in 1562, they had at least fought to the last, succumbing to superior numbers. The problem was that a Roman Catholic military order found it impossible to recruit knights and men-at-arms from North Germany, which had become Protestant.

Into the vacuum came Poland–Lithuania, Sweden and Russia. None was particularly interested in acquiring the Baltic coastline, but all were determined that the others would not get it either. Therefore, though each new mega-state had more important problems – Sweden with Denmark, Poland–Lithuania with the Turks, Russia with Tatars – all would be drawn into war over the pitiful remains of Livonia.

The German master became the new grandmaster. This reduced Teutonic Order loyally served the Holy Roman Empire for almost another three centuries, fighting Turkish sultans, French kings and Protestant princes. Most members were Roman Catholics, but in accordance with the Augsburg Treaty of 1555, they had to share the faith of the rulers in the Lutheran and Reformed parts of Germany. Hence some members of the order were Protestants.

It had a distinguished and varied career. It was a baroque order, appropriate to its new setting in south Germany and Austria – much different than the gothic of Prussia. Its time eventually expired too, and Napoleon abolished it along with other relics of bygone times. The Teutonic Order was revived after Napoleon's fall as a private order for the Habsburg family. The personal tie to the dynasty ended in 1923. In 1929 it was reconstituted as a preaching order. When Hitler occupied Austria in 1938 he had the order dissolved and banned, but it was reestablished after the end of World War II.

Today the Teutonic Order provides priests for German-speaking Catholic communities in non-German-speaking countries, particularly in Italy and Slovenia. In this it has returned to another major aspect of its original mission, the spiritual care of Germans who are being neglected by other orders.

This mission harkens back to the order's foundation at Acre in 1190 – the care for the sick, the aged and the troubled. That was an aspect of the order that has not been emphasised in this book, but hardly a middle-sized town in Germany was without a hospital, church or convent, which street names commemorate today. By serving local needs, the order kept alive the memories and traditions of the past. Today its lay members do the same in colourful Catholic celebrations, especially in Vienna, and its church near Stephanplatz has become a tourist attraction, as has Bouzov castle in the Czech Republic.

A Last Reflection

For the principal enemies of the Teutonic Knights – the Lithuanians – accepting Christianity became the means of beating the crusaders, Tatars and, ultimately, the tsars and commissars who came to rule over them. It established a national identity separate from German Lutherans and Russian Orthodox Christians.

The most the Teutonic Knights could claim to have achieved here was to have humbled the warrior pride that was so important in Lithuanian paganism. But they left the people suspicious of those strange men who came from Germany without wives or family to make fierce war on them. The very nature of the crusading order's organisation made it impossible for the knights to eliminate the warrior ethos that permeated their own Christian society, nor could they seek closer ties with their neighbours. If the Teutonic Knights had been secular nobles with sons and daughters to marry off, they would probably have made swifter progress in converting the pagans than by making war on them. Albrecht of Hohenzollern overcame those two impediments by dissolving the Teutonic Order in Prussia and marrying.

When Poland and Lithuania disappeared as states in the eighteenth century, while Germany became an eastern power which could associate its traditions and aspirations with medieval Prussia, that caused subsequent generations to view the medieval crusades in eastern Europe as the first stage of a German imperialism that culminated in Nazism. Historians must share more than a small burden of the guilt for spreading this overly simplified misreading of history, more even than that borne by the history-makers themselves.

History is more than triumphs and victimisation. More, alas, than any historian can write. But one must do what one can. Above all, we should remember that *historians who simplify the complexity of the past for political or ideological purposes do a disservice to future generations who must live with the impressions their work makes on readers.*

Recommended Reading

Titles marked * are particularly highly recommended.

Backus, Oswald, *Motives of West Russian Nobles in Deserting Lithuania for Moscow, 1377–1514,* Lawrence, KS: University of Kansas Press, 1957

Burleigh, Michael, *Prussian Society and the German Order: An Aristocratic Corporation in Crisis c. 1410–1460,* Cambridge: Cambridge University Press, 1984

Cazacu, Matei, ed. Stephen W. Reinert; trans. Nicole Mordarski *et al., Dracula,* Leiden: Brill, 2017

Christiansen, Eric, *The Northern Crusades: The Baltic and the Catholic Frontier 1100–1525,* Minneapolis: University of Minnesota, 1980*

Dabrowski, Patrice. M., *Poland, the First Thousand Years,* DeKalb: Northern Illinois Press, 2014*

Davies, Norman, *God's Playground: A History of Poland,* I: *The Origins to 1795,* Oxford: Oxford University Press, rev. edn., 2005

de Hartog, Leo, *Russia and the Mongol Yoke: The History of the Russian Principalities and the Golden Horde, 1221–1502,* London & New York: British Academic Press, 1996

Długosz, Jan, eds. Jane Allen, Maurice Michael (trans.) & Paul Smith, *The Annals of Jan Długosz: A History of Eastern Europe from A.D. 965 to A.D. 1480,* I. M. Publications, abridged edn., 1997

Frost, Robert, *The Oxford History of Poland–Lithuania,* I: *The Making of the Polish–Lithuanian Union 1385–1569,* Oxford: Oxford University Press, 2015*

Fudge, Thomas, *Jan Hus: Religious Reform and Social Revolution in Bohemia,* London & New York: I. B. Tauris, 2010

——, *The Trial of Jan Hus: Medieval Heresy and Criminal Procedure,* Oxford: Oxford University Press, 2013

Goffman, Daniel, *The Ottoman Empire and Early Modern Europe,* Cambridge University Press, 2002

Haberkern, Phillip, *Jan Hus in the Bohemian and German Reformations,* Oxford: Oxford University Press, 2016

Halecki, Oscar, *Borderlands of Western Civilization: A History of East Central Europe,* New York: Ronald, 1952

——, *From Florence to Brest (1439–1596),* Hamden, CT: Archon, 2nd edn., 1968

—— (ed. Thaddeus Gromada), *Jadwiga of Anjou and the Rise of East Central Europe,* Boulder, CO: Social Science Monographs, 1991

Halperin, Charles, *Russia and the Golden Horde: The Mongol Impact on Medieval Russian History,* Bloomington: Indiana University Press, 1985

Jasienica, Pawel, trans. Alexander Jordan, *Jagiellonian Poland,* Miami, FL: American Institute of Polish Culture, 1978

———, *Piast Poland,* Miami, FL: American Institute of Polish Culture, 1992
Kassen, John, *The Nobility and the Making of the Hussite Revolution*, Boulder: East European Quarterly, 1978
Kirby, David, *Northern Europe in the Early Modern Period: The Baltic World 1492–1772,* London & New York: Longman, 1990
Knoll, Paul, 'A *Pearl of Powerful Learning': The University of Cracow in the Fifteenth Century,* Leiden: Brill, 2016
———, *Rise of the Polish Monarchy: Piast Poland in East Central Europe, 1320–70,* Chicago: University of Chicago Press, 1972
Koncius, Joseph, *Vytautas the Great, Grand Duke of Lithuania*, Miami, FL: Franklin, 1964
Kuczyński, Stefan, *The Great War with the Teutonic Knights in the Years 1409–11,* Warsaw: Ministry of National Defence, c. 1960
Martin, Janet, *Medieval Russia, 980–1584,* Cambridge, Cambridge University Press, 1995
Mickūnaitė, Giedrė, *Making a Great Ruler: Grand Duke Vytautas of Lithuania,* Budapest: Central European University, 2006
Murray, Alan V. (ed.), *The North-Eastern Frontier of Medieval Europe: The Expansion of Latin Christendom in the Baltic Lands,* Ashgate Variorum, 2014
Nicolle, David, *Teutonic Knight: 1190–1561,* London: Osprey, 2007
The Nikonian Chronicle, Vol. IV (*From the Year 1382 to the Year 1425*) and Vol. V (*From the Year 1425 to the Year 1520*), Princeton, NJ: Darwin, 1988, 1989
Piccolomini, Aeneas Silvius, trans. Robert Brown, intro. etc. Nancy Bisaha, *Europe (c. 1400–1458),* Washington, DC: Catholic University of America, 2013
Rowell, Stephen, *Lithuania Ascending: A Pagan Empire within East-Central Europe, 1295–1345.* Cambridge, Cambridge University Press, 1994
Raffensperger, Christian, *Reimagining Europe: Kievan Rus' in the Medieval World,* Cambridge, MA: Harvard University Press, 2012
Stone, Daniel, *The Polish–Lithuanian state, 1386–1795,* Seattle: University of Washington Press, 2001
Thomas, Alfred, *Anne's Bohemia: Czech Literature and Society, 1310–1420,* Minneapolis: University of Minnesota Press, 1998
Turnbull, Stephen, *Crusader Castles of the Teutonic Knights: The Red-Brick Castles of Prussia, 1230–1466,* London: Osprey, 2003*
———, *The Hussite Wars 1419–36,* London: Osprey, 2004
———, *Tannenberg 1410: Disaster for the Teutonic Knights,* London: Osprey, 2003
Urban, William, *The Livonian Crusade,* Chicago: Lithuania Research and Studies Center, 2nd edn., 2004
———, *The Samogitian Crusade,* 2nd edn., Chicago: Lithuanian Research and Study Center, 2nd edn., 2006
———, *The Teutonic Knights: A Military History,* London: Greenhill, 2003
Vernadsky, George, *The Mongols and Russia,* New Haven & London: Yale, 1953 (Vol. III of *A History of Russia*)

Index

13586323R10088

Made in the USA
Middletown, DE
23 November 2018

SO WHO IS  SALZMAN?

In 2008, Jill Salzman launched **The Founding Moms**, the world's first and only collective of offline meetups and online resources for mom entrepreneurs. A graduate of Brown University and law school, she started a music management firm and then launched and later sold a baby jewelry company before building this community. She's the author of *Found It: A Field Guide for Mom Entrepreneurs* and the co-host of *Inc. Magazine*'s top-rated entertaining business podcast, Breaking Down Your Business.

She gave her own TED talk on 11/11/11, CNNMoney has called her a "mommy mogul," and MSN Live thinks she's a "Cool Mom Entrepreneur We Love." She was named one of the Top 50 Women to Watch In Tech, a Top 100 Champion Small Business Influencer, and Forbes even said this website is one of their Top 10 Websites For Entrepreneurs. She's shared the speaker stage with Richard Branson, Sheryl Sandberg, Daymond John, Marilu Henner, and Desmond Tutu. In her spare time, Jill enjoys kloofing, baking, and preventing her daughters from lighting the house on fire.

Have you joined The Founding Moms yet?
Do it at FoundingMoms.com.